THE ROOTS OF AMERICAN FEMINIST THOUGHT

edited and
with introductions
by

James L. Cooper
and
Sheila McIsaac Cooper

ALLYN AND BACON, INC. BOSTON

Library of Congress Catalog Number: 72–92094

Printed in the United States of America.

Contents

Preface

Today's feminist movement has a centuries-old tradition that brings a rich history to the struggle for feminine equality. Well before the post–World War II formation of the National Organization for Women and other women's liberation groups, thousands of women and men had already thought, written, and organized against various aspects of sexual discrimination. Theirs was a social struggle worthy of study and analysis in its own right, let alone as a prelude to the contemporary feminist movement. Although the student of social movements would be interested in the Old Feminism even if there had been no New, the contemporary woman's movement does give an added poignancy to these venerable documents. For whatever reason, many current readers may wish to examine some of the most significant, though frequently neglected, early works of the modern feminist movement.

This collection conveniently gathers seven of these major works under one cover. Making the selection for any anthology has a certain arbitrary quality about it, one that is further complicated when the editorial design limits the number to a handful. We can hope only that many readers will find our criteria and judgments close enough to their own for this volume to be serviceable.

We have chosen works written by feminists of the last two centuries who drew on different intellectual traditions and who conceived of the woman question in novel ways. We did not include those American activists who, despite invaluable work for feminism, never contributed much to its ideology or whose writing was limited to brief articles focused primarily upon immediate and circumscribed objectives. We also omitted certain important contributions to Western feminist thought, such as those by Friedrich Engels and August Bebel, because they had little direct influence upon American feminism; we did, however, include two British selections which were more widely read in the United States than many feminist treatises penned by Americans. We shortened the list of potential selections further by choosing between feminist works which arose from similar currents of Western thought. We selected, for example, a book by the well-known American, Margaret Sanger, which wove European analysis into the fabric of American argument, over the essays of the sometime immigrant-resident, Emma Goldman, whose Continental arguments remained essentially unalloyed and were less widely circulated in the United States.

Originally book-length essays, all of the selections have been edited and abridged. We eliminated footnotes and appendices and modernized spelling, punctuation, and capitalization (with the exception of material under copyright) as an aid to the contemporary reader. When abridging the selections, we tried to remove redundancies, nonfeminist materials, arguments against male sexist rhetoric or action that has generally disappeared, and cursory literary or other allusions not commonly known to the current reading public. We have tried to expose the structure of each author's feminist analysis while keeping the intellectual skeleton covered with the flesh of essential argument and illustration. We hope that the substantial length of our selections guards against misrepresenting each feminist's thought more effectively than the snippet printed in usual anthologies. At the same time, we believe that many of these earlier documents require substantial editing in order to make them readily accessible to most contemporary readers. Despite our best efforts to avoid both printing labyrinthine obscurities and distorting the author's analyses through careless cutting, we recognize that the process of abridgment remains somewhat arbitrary.

The essay preceding each selection attempts to provide a modest amount of biographical information concerning the writer, to furnish an intellectual, social, and historical context within which to read his or her treatise, and to identify textual references to particular persons, works, and movements. The essays complement the texts; they do not summarize them. The notes accompanying each introduction contain bibliographic suggestions for those interested in pursuing further study.

The editors are deeply grateful to the many people who helped them to prepare this volume—to Robert Calvert, F. Walker Gilmer, Peggy Platt Gilmer, Robert Kern, Fred Silander, Howard Simon, and Sara Jane Williams, all of DePauw University, and to James F. Findlay, Jr., of the University of Rhode Island, R. Kenneth Johnson of Suffolk University, and William J. Petrek of Hofstra University.

J. L. C.

S. M. C.

Introduction

Although the conditions of subjection and the feminine response to it have varied, men have dominated women in the Western world since ancient times. There have been important legal, educational, occupational, medical, and technological advances for women, especially since the eighteenth century. Yet nearly all still face sexual discrimination, and the greatest number follow the traditional domestic route from cradle, to altar, to housework and motherhood, and finally to grave. A woman's world, though it has improved, remains more intellectually limited, culturally derivative, socially atomized, geographically restricted, and economically dependent than a man's of the same socioeconomic class. Although improvement in woman's lot has not ended her subjection, modernization has shaken confidence in traditional beliefs concerning the biological and psychological differences between the sexes and called into question the appropriateness of the conventional social roles of females. Modernity has consequently aroused interest in "the woman question," given rise to arguments for sexual equality, and spawned a feminist movement dedicated to eradicating sexism.

In the preindustrial, traditional society, men's and women's functions overlapped more than they do now. Life centered in the village where both sexes often performed relatively undifferentiated tasks. Agriculture was as unspecialized as domestic routines, crafts operated on a household basis, women frequently worked in the fields and shops alongside their husbands and sons, and most goods and services were valued for their use rather than their exchange potential. While women were by no means equal to men, their situations were more alike than they would become in modern, industrial society, and the ideological superstructure of traditional society rationalized the position of both men and women much better than it has done since.[1]

In contrast to their modern counterparts, traditional man and woman accepted a high degree of geographic, social, and psychic immobility, embracing the local not the national, resignation not ambition, constancy not change. Few men and fewer women travelled far beyond the bounds of the home village or thought much about the larger world. Outside the family most human contacts, even with other villagers, occurred only at church services, on market days, and at fairs. Widespread illiteracy further restricted the average person's sources of knowledge and reinforced the role of custom in prescribing thought and conduct. Within the home, as within the village and the society at large, most people accepted their designated places in a hierarchy believed to be God ordained. Drawing an analogy between society and the human body, traditionalists compared individuals or groups to physical organs whose assigned functions, properly performed, guaranteed a healthy body. Thus any person who longed to change his or her place in the chain-of-being threatened the body politic. The traditional society placed a high priority on order, continuity, obedience, and subordination. Patriarchy—the supremacy of the father in the family or clan—fit the overall social pattern quite well.

Under the pressures of modernization the foundations of the traditional order crumbled slowly in Europe from the sixteenth century onward. The growth of commerce, the development of market economies and commercial classes, the rise of nation-states with centralized administration, the advance of technology, and the spread of education heralded the coming of the modern industrial order. The merchant-industrial economy revolutionized the life of man, specializing his trade, removing his work to an office, store, or factory, turning his labor into a commodity purchased by employers for money wages, and reorganizing social institutions. Modernization greatly increased man's geographic and social mobility, often forcing him to move from the village with its stable primary-group relationships to the city with its ever changing heterogeneous masses and impersonal political and social relations. Many villagers were compelled to exchange the security of customary patterns of thought and action for the insecurity of opportunity and change where one's status might be based more on personal skill than on birthright.

As the foundations of traditional society eroded, the ideological rationale supporting it also came under attack and was gradually destroyed. Enlightenment slowly replaced illiteracy, reason supplanted authority, activity superseded passivity, individualism challenged an organic or corporate conception of society, and the idea of progress displaced the view that the existing order was eternal. The mercantile-industrial society promised freedom from a specific piece of earth, a given class, or a particular social position and opened the way for the emergence of the self-made bourgeois male.

From the increased mobility developed a new and strong middle class of merchants, professionals, industrialists, and civil servants who served as the vanguard for reform of the institutions of traditional society. Most of their victories were gained peacefully and piecemeal. But where the old order yielded too slowly or rejected change altogether, the self-assured middle class sometimes resorted to violence and even to revolution. Through argument and political action the emergent classes of the eighteenth century replaced feudal remnants and monarchical institutions with the market economy and a complementary republican political system; nineteenth-century reformers struggled to adjust merchant capitalism to industrialism; and late nineteenth- and twentieth-century reformers have been seeking to control the corporate aspects of maturing industrial capitalism.

The flood of institutional and ideological changes associated with modern mercantile-industrial society swept the social mainstream but left significant pockets of the traditional order intact. Except for certain by-products that trickled down from a man to his wife and daughters, women did not gain the liberation which men achieved.[2] Even today most Western women still perform essentially undifferentiated and unspecialized tasks, produce goods and services for use and not exchange, work for maintenance and not for pay, and labor primarily in the home. Necessary advances in education spilled over to women, medicine healed both sexes, technology supplied better birth-control devices and labor-saving appliances, and machinery increasingly made man's innate physical superiority industrially obsolete. Woman's life has consequently improved in absolute and relative terms. She is better educated, healthier, faced with less drudgery, and ever more present in man's work world. These improvements in her situation have mitigated but not eliminated her basically premodern condition. The primary responsibility of even the working woman—who is still in the minority of her sex and paid scarcely half as much as man—remains the care of her children and her home. She may "work"—that is, become a wage earner—but the second sex usually provides only a second income. Contemporary woman's personal and social roles are still typically defined in traditional terms.

The great social changes which modernized man's activity and thought did not leave woman untouched. The modification of man's life affected women by at least marginally improving their physical condition and by providing an alternate social model. As the victory of commerce and industry over agriculture lengthened the distance between male and female social roles, it supplied the necessary ideological ammunition for feminist assaults upon the growing inequality. Middle-class women, more than their sisters from other classes, profited from their men's victories and felt most keenly the deprivations associated with the sexually fractured social system. With greater access and exposure to education, medicine, and technological development and with sensitivity to the newer systems of thought, they could best wield for feminist objectives the ideologies with which their men had gained their own liberation from traditional society. Modernization offered the occasion for the rise of feminism. It also provided the ideological weaponry and the class of women who would fashion and wield the instruments of the movement for sexual equality.

Despite current proclamations announcing the advent of the post-industrial age, most feminists from Mary Wollstonecraft to the present have struggled for woman's equality within the mercantile-industrial order. The example of masculine middle-class social reform provided the major impetus for Western feminism and defined the boundaries of the movement in America. Feminists have traditionally sought an individual liberation for modern woman equivalent to that of modern man, a freedom for the self-made woman to find the limits of her own development without social interference. None of the feminists presented in this volume—and certainly only a few of those not included herein—have wanted to coerce women into liberation. Their emphasis has been upon giving those who wanted a different role the opportunity to pursue it, not upon forcing all women into alternative patterns.

The theme of individualism—the belief that personal initiative, action, and interest should be independent of governmental or social control—has coursed through feminist thinking from the eighteenth century to the twentieth. Mary Wollstonecraft became the Tom Paine of the feminist movement, arguing for liberation from the eternally servile status assigned to women in traditional society. Sarah Grimké used powerful arguments from the left wing of the Protestant Reformation to seek woman's release from corporate religious and social control. Margaret Fuller marshalled forceful nineteenth-century transcendentalist themes to do battle for full freedom for the spiritual and intellectual development of each woman. John Stuart Mill fit feminism into the liberal arguments which he and his friends had so successfully employed to further democratize English society. Infusing Lester F. Ward's sociology with the spirit of Edward Bellamy's liberal socialism, Charlotte Perkins Gilman tried to reform the home in order to allow those women who wished it an equal place in the market-oriented, transactional society.

Her feminism followed the peculiarities of Ward's sociocracy and Bellamy's Nationalism to their markedly liberal objective of securing opportunity for private endeavor by a plurality of individuals and groups. Thus she extended their emphasis upon personal responsibility and private destiny to women. Margaret Sanger turned the thrust of the ideas of Friedrich Nietzsche, Georges Sorel, H. G. Wells, and Havelock Ellis into a powerful plea for woman's control of her body and thus for unimpeded feminine emotional self-expression. And Suzanne LaFollette carried the logic of Albert J. Nock's radical individualism (or anarchistic libertarianism) to feminist conclusions. From the eighteenth century to the present, feminist argument has owed a great debt to the reform impulse of individualist thought.

The concentration of so much feminist thought upon securing the opportunity for individual development and self-expression further illustrates the reliance of feminists upon the strategies of masculine middle-class reform. Calls for more equal education, intellectual development, the suffrage, or birth control were tailored to the needs of middle- or upper-class women. From these classes have come most of those women who especially resent their sexual subordination and who also have the requisite social experience and self-assurance to capitalize on such reforms. They are the ones who see education as a crucial prerequisite for social mobility, who have the economic security and leisure to find relevance in the demand for intellectual development, who perceive the ballot as a meaningful weapon for change and know how to manipulate political instruments, and who have the motivation to seek out birth-control information and the requisite socialization for using contraceptive devices most effectively. The struggles of lower-class women for food, clothing, and housing have often been close to all-consuming. Many have found experiences with racial or ethnic discrimination nearly devastating. Life in the subculture of poverty has dampened the hope or expectation which nourishes reform rather than revolution or resignation. Regardless of sex, the economically downtrodden seek bread more than ballots, houses more than schools, and income more than self-expression.

I.

Not only have feminists generally relied on reworked modern masculine reform ideologies to win an equal place for women in the mercantile-industrial society, they have also joined an important debate which has divided and enriched Western social thought—whether the human being is essentially rational or emotional, whether mankind obtains knowledge primarily through reason and experience or by imagination and intuition.

This polarity stretches at least as far back as the ancient Greek commitment to ordered knowledge, the disciplined mind, and sagacious judgment as opposed to the Hebraic search for righteousness, moral perfection, and divine rules for human conduct.

When modern feminism was born in the late seventeenth and early eighteenth centuries, Enlightenment rationalism was pre-eminent. Enlightenment thinkers modified the classical rationalist belief that the world has a logical order, the principles of which the reasoning mind can grasp independently of the senses. By the late eighteenth century, at least, traditional rationalism had become increasingly empirical, guided primarily by experience or experiment. Among the popularizers of modern science, Enlightenment empiricists believed in the existence of a rational objective order, knowable partly through the human mind and partly through the senses. They not only believed that science would reveal the physical order but also had technocratic faith in the application of natural knowledge to human life. Christians traditionally promised paradise only after death. But the empirical rationalists proposed that, once human affairs had been precisely observed and analyzed, scientific law would replace confusion, complexity, and superstition and thereby remove the source of much human misery. They believed deeply in the idea of progress and a secular paradise, in part because they equated human knowledge with power.

Enlightenment emphasis upon the authority of the human mind, the call for reform, and egalitarian rhetoric provided a useful structure for feminist thought. Did not women have minds? Did they not have the same inalienable rights as men? Rationalist feminists stressed woman's ability to reason and argued that this talent is not inconsistent with her maternal role. Rationalists also tended to be environmentalists, sensitive to the ability of science to discern, control, and alter both nurture and nature. In consequence they generally affirmed the essential equality or identity of the sexes or argued that whatever was not the same might be made so. Rationalist feminists assumed that obtaining an equality of rights would lead the sexes to as equal a condition as possible, and they rarely doubted that the resulting sexual equality would be nearly complete.

Enlightenment rationalism flowed directly through the feminist treatise of Mary Wollstonecraft, a supporter of bourgeois revolution. The Enlightenment's particular marriage of rationalism and empiricism reverberated in Anglo-American thought through the succeeding centuries, as a triumphant mercantile order merged into industrial capitalism and rural life gave way to urbanization. It ran through the utilitarian liberalism of John Stuart Mill in the mid-nineteenth century. It passed into the evolutionary socialism of Charlotte Perkins Gilman and was extended in Suzanne LaFollette's radical libertarianism.

Enlightenment thought did not go unchallenged for long. Romantics, philosophical idealists, and irrationalists revived and secularized the nonrationalist tradition. Nineteenth-century Romantics emphasized the primacy of feeling over thinking, of intuition over reason, of the metaphysical over the physical, and of the subjective over the objective. They felt Enlightenment thinkers undervalued the diversity and complexity of life by abstracting Man from individual men. Enlightenment preoccupation with equality, Romantics pointed out, negated the profound differences between individuals. In short, the emphasis on equality seemed to obliterate genuine individuality and thus restrict the individual liberty that Enlightenment leaders claimed to honor. Idealists extended the attack on empirical rationalism by challenging the basis for and the value of scientific knowledge. Observation and reason, they argued, expose only the most superficial aspects of the phenomenal world. The human being can best approach wisdom, truth, and the fundamentals of reality through intuition and most adequately express his discovery through poetry and metaphor. Late nineteenth-century irrationalists also explored and emphasized the place of will, instinct, the subconscious, and emotion as the main currents and creative sources of human life.

Some feminists recognized the potential uses of the various nonrationalist dimensions of Western thought, especially the revival of certain aspects of the premodern emphasis on functional differences. Nonrationalist feminists extolled those characteristics which male sexists assigned women. If woman was more emotional, imaginative, pacific, and intuitive than man, then the weaker sex abounded in the more substantial human qualities. Concerned with the cultivation of the emotions, nonrationalists often spoke approvingly of sex as passion, whereas empirical rationalists thought of it primarily as a function of reproduction. Homage to Nature also inclined nonrationalists to pay more attention to the demands of biology, whatever they might be in the case of woman.

While rejecting the male sexist's denigration of the feminine character, the nonrationalist feminists rarely embraced identity of the sexes. When they spoke of sexual equality, they generally meant equivalence or equality of worth rather than sameness. They emphasized the development of each individual according to his particular inner means, sex among them, and allowed for the possibility of certain patterns related to sex. The modern nonrationalist's allowance of sexual differences did not connote feminine inferiority any more than the premodern thinker's organic social analogy denied intrinsic worth to the various social functions. An individual woman's status ought to depend more upon the development of her innate capabilities than upon her relationships with other persons of whatever sex or station. But rationalists found these allowances anathema and asserted that sexual distinctions invariably led to continuing masculine rule camouflaged with praise of feminine virtue and deference to feminine morality. The nonrationalists duly ignored such alleged dangers, developing and handing down a feminist tradition to our own day through the radical sectarian analysis of Sarah Grimké, the Romantic idealism of Margaret Fuller, and the Romantic irrationalism of Margaret Sanger.

II.

Few feminist theorists contributed substantially to the development of their borrowed ideologies beyond giving them a feminist dimension; and none, understandably, created a system of thought especially for feminist purposes. Women, who have naturally supplied most of the feminists, have been poorly equipped in Western society to overcome male-dominated language, thought, and culture. Lack of formal and equal education, geographic immobility, limited experience with the process of generalizing or abstracting, and the absence of a supporting feminist subculture sealed the woman feminist's dependence on male-oriented theory. Thus existing schemes have gained a feminist perspective without altering their fundamental thrust.

Generally Europeans manufactured the theoretical systems upon which American feminists built. The historic unwillingness or inability of Americans in general to develop social or political theory has led them to borrow heavily when they realized a theoretical need. Most American thought and culture—whether establishment, moderate reformist, or radical—has been derivative. Although largely from British sources, the borrowing has on occasion extended to French, German, and Italian thought as well. Besides taking theoretical systems within which they elaborated feminist themes, Americans have also imported fully developed feminist arguments. Mary Wollstonecraft, John Stuart Mill, and Simone de Beauvoir are examples from each of the last three centuries of significant European feminists whose place in American thought rivals or surpasses that of native thinkers and gives an Atlantic quality to American feminist argument.

The extent to which borrowed theoretical systems were more specifically male than generally human remains an open question, although their preoccupation with masculine needs is evident. Indeed, the masculine creators of many such systems left little doubt that they thought their ideas justified feminine subordination. For example, the great American rationalist, Thomas Jefferson, excluded women from the inalienable rights of man to life, liberty, and the pursuit of happiness which he proclaimed. And major nonrationalists from Jean Jacques Rousseau to Sigmund Freud insisted vigorously on feminine dependence. The feminist theorists, then, have worked with philosophical materials that were not of their own making and which were often used by their originators directly against feminist interests.

The reliance of feminist theorists on adaptations of masculine ideologies has had certain advantages as well as weaknesses. These borrowed systems met women's crucial need to justify the demand for social change, and the extension to women's rights of the familiar masculine claims inherently appealed to men. Men, after all, have granted whatever equality or freedom women have so far achieved. But feminist appeals have been jerry-built: Not one of the analogies was altogether appropriate to the woman question nor adequate for her emancipation. Granting an Enlightenment appeal for equal rights, for example, gives the self-assured bourgeois man opportunities he is capable of exploiting but offers considerably less to a home-bound woman. Socializing a capitalist economy might advance the interests of male proletarians without directly affecting woman's precapitalist estate. Conceding to woman an equal opportunity for sexual or emotional fulfillment may be used as a substitute for granting her other forms of feminine equality or freedom, forms the male Romantic or irrationalist already possesses.

The peculiar elements of sexism, moreover, complicate feminist use of conventional class analysis. As customarily defined, the socioeconomic class structure of modern Western societies is implicitly masculine. The elaborate categorization of people according to their relationship to the means of production and their resulting social station has been designed primarily for men. Women fit into the conventional description of classes by proxy; in general they assume the rank of their fathers or husbands and respond accordingly. Traditional class analysis can help to explain certain divisions that tend to prevent women from uniting against male dominance, but it is of little use to the feminist who wants to explain the cause and find a cure for sexual discrimination which crosses class lines. Extensions of class analysis that treat women as a separate class in society can be quite incisive, yet they are complicated by the fact that women by their association with men also relate to the conventional classes. The application of the concept of caste to feminist argument is likewise flawed. Caste analysis emphasizes the disabilities which women share in common and therefore has little to say about crucial divisions or differences among females. Women live in a much closer, and often more loving, association with men than members of most castes have traditionally done with their masters, suggesting that a caste analysis of woman's role is not likely to be altogether successful.[3]

A critique of the status of women by analogy to that of modern racial or minority groups has been especially popular. Few feminists have failed to draw a parallel between the situation of blacks and women; most have compared black slavery to woman's estate. White racists have imposed the weight of their doctrine and social control upon the blacks; male sexists, it is said, have enforced the subordination of women. Both racist and sexist ideologies lie deep in American society and have flowed through the acts and policies of the public sector—in law, corporate regulation, educational practice. And such ideology has found significant expression in private activity—in social mores, family structure, and social life. The formal bars and the informal pressures have added up to an effective prohibition of certain kinds of equality.[4]

But the racial or minority analogy, like the others, is far from exact. Although American women, particularly before the twentieth century, were in a state akin to legal slavery, very few white women ever suffered from the severe deprivations typically imposed upon the average black slave. In America racism has led to more consistent and harsher treatment than sexism. Unlike blacks, women are neither a small minority of the total population nor as able to marshall their numbers for social and political purposes. They are not concentrated in particular regions, neighborhoods, or ghettoes but usually live in greater intimacy with men than with other women. While the subjected black's or immigrant's attack is generally directed at the oppressor outside his community, the woman feminist must often challenge those closest to her—father, husband, and sons.

Sex roles, furthermore, are learned and reinforced much earlier and more often than racial, religious, or ethnic identification. In our society there is so little formal training or education for marriage and parenthood that the traditional roles taught in the family from childhood generally go unchallenged in youth and therefore unmodified in adult life. If a majority, with its position rationalized through the existing social institutions and reinforced by the dominant ideology, oppresses a minority, the minority can usually find solace and material for counterattack in the institutions, mores, and ideology of the ghetto subculture.

When the contemporary civil rights movement began, most natural and social scientists had already reached a consensus on the significance of racial differences. There neither was nor is any such consensus on the importance of gender. Differences between men and women are obviously more than skin deep. The reproductive function is divided between the sexes and performed by specialized organs in each sex that complement rather than duplicate one another. As nearly all feminists admit, most women are also of slighter build and possess less physical strength than most men. The physical differences between blacks and whites are therefore generally considered minor compared to the differences between the sexes. The white man has more in common physiologically with the black man than either does with the woman of his particular race. Yet no one knows the exact extent of physical differences between the sexes or if they differentiate the emotional and intellectual capacities of men and women.

The job of the feminist theorist or activist has been further complicated by the fact that not all the disabilities which a woman faces originate because of her sex. Some arise from social dimensions that women share with men, thus creating the problem—sometimes the agony—for the feminist of establishing priorities. The black, poor, or immigrant woman with feminist sympathies, for example, is torn between loyalty to her sex and/or her race, ethnic group, or male-associated class. Which set of disabilities is of more consequence? Which would be rectified more easily? Can she afford an intramural challenge to her husband when the family is struggling to escape economic or political domination? Consequently, feminism has rarely reached beyond the middle-class white women who gave the movement its impetus. No ideology, no strategy, no organization for female liberation has ever mobilized more than a handful of black or poor women in America.

Even white middle-class feminists have suffered from conflicting loyalties. Many feminist theoretical and organizational leaders joined the woman movement after being affiliated with other protest efforts. Mary Wollstonecraft was first committed to the revolutionary movements of the Enlightenment, Sarah Grimké emerged from the abolitionist movement, Charlotte Gilman first advocated Bellamy's special brand of American socialism, Margaret Sanger had been immersed in New York City radical causes, Suzanne LaFollette had inherited a commitment to progressivism, and many contemporary feminists have been coming to women's liberation from the civil rights, peace, and student movements. In some cases sexual discrimination hampered the feminist's work for her original cause, so she turned to feminism in self-defense. In most cases the feminist's reform activities gave her the tools, experience, and confidence necessary to analyze and confront an early but often undefined resistance to feminine subjection. Time spent in other reform groups helped many emerging feminists to articulate their discontent with sexual discrimination and to learn the organizational tactics necessary to launch an autonomous women's movement. But her associates from the first movement inevitably demanded that the new feminist drop her pursuit of feminine equality and concentrate solely on her earlier and allegedly more important commitment. In consequence, the deep anxiety which leaders of male-oriented reform groups often caused feminists usually overbalanced their occasional and minimal support of the feminist movement.

Those satisfied with piecemeal reform in woman's condition usually do not confront many of the large and numerous obstacles that have regularly inhibited the development of a wide-ranging feminist ideology and an inclusive feminist movement. Middle-class reform feminists can continue to work effectively within the prevailing bourgeois ideology, justifying and securing limited objectives with conventional argumentation. But they should be aware of the pitfalls which ensnared woman suffragists, for the liberal tradition of middle-class reform in America trapped them into overvaluing the feminist consequences of a modest structural change. Without any specifically feminist ideology the woman suffrage movement became so "pragmatic" that it finally sold whatever was left of its feminist soul to secure the franchise. Without an agreed upon, overall feminist framework within which to place any specific reform, means get easily confused with ends, and the particular object is likely to prove as useless once achieved as the vote did for woman's liberation. Some of the feminist theorists included in this volume warned the suffragists of the danger, offering advice which contemporaries who glory in their movement's ideological casualness ought to weigh carefully.

The need to face the ideological task is especially strong for that small but growing minority of feminists who seek feminine equality in a new social order, not merely the extension of bourgeois privilege to women. Revolutionary feminism must, as William L. O'Neill advised, "have its Marx before it can expect a Lenin."[5] It will take a powerful radical analysis both to harness conventional thought where it can generate insight into woman's subjection and to develop original theory for the unique elements of sexism. Such theory must reach beyond male-associated class and racial barriers to apply and appeal to women generally, and it should point invariably toward equality for women in a fundamentally different social order. This is a major assignment under any condition; it is a monumental one in a society so remarkably resistant to ideological innovation and radical change.

NOTES

1. For a general definition of traditional society, see Daniel Lerner, *The Passing of Traditional Society: Modernizing the Middle East* (New York: The Free Press, 1958), 1–107. For a description of traditional society in sixteenth- and seventeenth-century England—social patterns which were carried in somewhat revised form to colonial America—see Peter Lazlett, *The World We Have Lost* (New York: Charles Scribner's Sons, 1965).

2. This critique of woman's socioeconomic position owes much to Margaret Benston, "The Political Economy of Women's Liberation," conveniently reprinted in Leslie B. Tanner (ed.), *Voices from Women's Liberation* (New York: New American Library, Inc., 1970), 279–292.

3. Margaret Benston's article (cited in the preceding note) has offered the most useful and least flawed class analysis of woman's situation. For an interesting critique built around caste, see Roxanne Dunbar, "Female Liberation as the Basis for Social Revolution," in Mary Lou Thompson (ed.), *Voices of the New Feminism* (Boston: The Beacon Press, 1970), 44–58.

4. For a more detailed discussion of the analogy between the positions of minority groups and women, see Alice S. Rossi, "Sex Equality: The Beginnings of Ideology," in Thompson, *New Feminism,* 61–66.

5. William L. O'Neill, "Feminism as a Radical Ideology," in Alfred F. Young (ed.), *Dissent: Explorations in the History of American Radicalism* (DeKalb: Northern Illinois University Press, 1968), 298.

PART I

Mary Wollstonecraft: *Enlightenment Rebel*

Mary Wollstonecraft (1759–1797) shocked genteel Englishmen and Americans "with the most indecent rhapsody . . . ever penned by man or woman." *A Vindication of the Rights of Woman* (1792) was nonetheless "so run after" that on occasion there was "no keeping it long enough to read it leisurely."[1] It attracted immediate public notice that ensured its author's fame and notoriety as a champion of women's equality through a "revolution in female education and manners."[2]

Shaken by the republican thought and revolutionary action of the emerging middle classes, British and American conservatives of the late eighteenth century had "had enough of new systems" proposed by "philosophizing serpents," such as Mary Wollstonecraft and Thomas Paine. Conservatives felt that attacks on tradition had promoted disruption of the British Empire in the American Revolution and demolition of established European institutions in the French Revolution. Reckless assaults on the political order threatened society by altering the particular tasks which nature and tradition seemingly had assigned to each group. Thus careless or premeditated levelling of functional differences pierced the veneer of civilization and led immediately to either an absolute equality or anarchy. Attacks upon social institutions were numerous, intense, and serious before Mary Wollstonecraft, a "hyena in petticoats," proposed an equality between the sexes. Few things seemed more obvious to conservatives than that differences between the sexes were deeply rooted in physical nature and broadly reinforced by tradition. All evidence—from physiology to the Bible—supported the subordination of woman to man as a rightful and necessary condition for pursuit of the general welfare.[3]

Republicans and rationalists were about as interested in feminine equality as conservatives. Few carried their espousal of reason, questioning of tradition, and support of reform or revolution to feminist conclusions. Concerned primarily, if not explicitly, with the problems of white, bourgeois men, they rarely extended their social analyses to consider and challenge the traditional subordination of blacks or women. To the degree that they explored existing racial and sexual distinctions, they tended to find subordination essentially reasonable and consistent with the natural order. Republicans and rationalists did not always approve inequality with assurance and without qualification. But despite possible guilt, equivocation, or reservation, they generally found the principle of feminine equality uncongenial.[4]

Mary Wollstonecraft was not the first to raise the woman question in eighteenth-century England or America. Indeed, as the century passed, the number of newspaper articles, pamphlets, books, and sermons about woman's role gradually increased. The longer the discussion continued, the more the arguments for improving woman's condition gained cautious acceptance. Some writers advocated basic changes in woman's position, but the greater number and the better known recommended limited improvements. Wollstonecraft took issue with the most widely read commentators among the latter group. She paid special attention to the writings of Jean Jacques Rousseau, the famous French *philosophe,* and Dr. John Gregory, a medical professor closely associated with the leaders of the Scottish Enlightenment.[5]

Whether conservative or rationalist, these authors considered women physically inferior, domestic beings necessarily subordinate to their male protectors. Only in their hopes for heaven did women stand an even chance. Almost no one argued for civil or economic equality between the sexes. All sought improved education for women, but none believed in intellectual equality. The range of ideas on feminine education extended from training in advanced domestic arts to extensive reading (excluding such disciplines as classical language, philosophy, and science). Whatever the differences in program, however, most reformers sought to make women better companions for men and better teachers of children.

Mary Wollstonecraft constructed her argument for feminine equality upon commonplace principles of contemporary rationalist and republican thought. Associated after 1786 with such radical Enlightenment thinkers as William Godwin, Thomas Paine, Dr. Richard Price, and Joseph Priestley, she absorbed their protests against an authority based on revelation, precedent, or power. Extending from the physical to the social realm Isaac Newton's idea of a universe governed by natural law, she believed that human beings could discern through reason the absolute and unchanging law of nature and bring their conduct into harmony with it. Through science and education they could perfect society by assuring that each individual and group filled its appointed role in the natural order. But artificial authorities and hierarchies in church and state only obstructed human potential. Received doctrine and traditional institutions required testing, therefore, and deserved acceptance only if found in accord with the great rational design of the universe.

In the crowning events of the eighteenth century—the American and French Revolutions—lay both rationalist hopes for social institutions founded on natural law and conservative fears of the abyss of anarchy. Revolutionary statesmen and soldiers spoke eloquently of natural rights and republican liberties as opposed to the traditional prerogatives of monarchs, oligarchs, and aristocrats. In the flush of republican triumph, one of Mary Wollstonecraft's friends, Dr. Richard Price, enthusiastically endorsed the expected fruits of revolution. But his comments triggered the most devastating conservative attack on rationalist assumptions and revolutionary activity ever penned—Edmund Burke's *Reflections on the Revolution in France* (1790). Burke challenged the quick scrapping of a political system and the abstractions of the *philosophes*. Preferring historic privilege, he rejected the doctrine of natural rights as advanced by the revolutionary thinkers and admired the average Briton's continuing fear of God, awe of kings, affection for parliaments, duty to magistrates, reverence for priests, and respect for nobility.

Angered by Burke's assault on a good friend and an enlightened cause, Mary Wollstonecraft responded with the hastily written *Vindication of the Rights of Men* (1790), which established her reputation as a successful rationalist polemicist. This frequently emotional and vituperative reply attacked Burke's preference for tradition over theoretical or right reason. She thought that Burkean reverence for historic antecedents inevitably led to worship of the "savages, thieves, curates, or practitioners in the law" who founded states. Surely the admired British constitution had been "settled in the dark days of ignorance, when minds of men were shackled by the grossest prejudices and most immoral superstitions." "Somewhere," Wollstonecraft insisted, "implicit submission to authority . . . must stop, or we return to barbarism; and the capacity of improvement, which gives us a natural sceptre on earth, is a cheat." Only when human beings learn "to respect the sovereignty of reason" will they "discern good from evil" and "break the ignoble chain" of the past.[6]

Neither in her response to Burke nor in her *Vindication of the Rights of Woman* did Wollstonecraft endorse all the major positions of her radical rationalist friends. She allowed that Dr. Price's zeal carried him beyond "sound reason" to "utopian reveries." Unlike many of the radicals, she did not press beyond republicanism into open support of democracy or anarchy. Nor did she give up Christianity for deism, agnosticism, or atheism, although she was opposed to clerical establishments. Some of the radicals who considered human reason powerful enough to shape as well as discern nature looked forward to a state of social perfection in which absolute equality would be engineered. But Mary Wollstonecraft never expected "a heaven on earth." "I know that the human understanding is deluded with vain shadows, and that when we eagerly pursue any study, we only reach the boundary set to human enquiries."[7]

Thus she never asserted that the establishment of the natural order through reason would create an absolute equality between man and man or between man and woman. She accepted the existence of a "common law of gravity" which assigned to each individual or group an appropriate position in society. She admitted that women have less physical strength than men, a condition that no environmental effort could eradicate. And she acknowledged that greater physical strength made men better able to practice certain virtues. She also argued that women have a certain sphere of activity, particular duties, and a "maternal character" naturally different from men's. Furthermore, she conceded that historically women had always been subordinate to men.

Insisting that "it is justice, not charity, that is wanting in the world," Wollstonecraft demanded an equality of rights or opportunities for all human beings, even if such functional equality resulted in some groups or individuals being subordinate to others. Full access to the Creator through reason would free woman from the artificial stations arbitrarily assigned by man and allow her to find her God-ordained place in the natural order. Society could never achieve perfection until all groups or individuals functioned in harmony with the law of nature. But man assured woman's physical dependence and lowered her level of mental activity by denying her adequate physical exercise, providing inappropriate education, and permitting only a cramped sphere of activity. Denial of civil existence and work outside the home only extended woman's deficiencies, finally leaving her destitute of virtue. Man thereby created unnatural physical, intellectual, and moral inequalities between the sexes and sealed woman in an artificial inferiority.

Mary Wollstonecraft's belief in the essential rationality of mankind led her to place special emphasis upon the ability of correct education to overcome man-made degradation. She had initially ventured into print with *Thoughts on the Education of Daughters: with Reflections on Female Conduct, in the more important Duties of Life* (1787). Although *Thoughts* did not contain the greater feminist thrust of her later work, it indicated an early concern not only about women's education but also about their interest in "frippery" and their maternal negligence, points she later expanded in *Rights of Woman*. She also considered and bemoaned their limited career opportunities as well as the confining nature of the marriage relationship.

Wollstonecraft's thoughts about education of women were greatly influenced by Catherine Macaulay, author of a notable history of England, whose *Letters on Education* (1790) attributed much of woman's inferiority directly to faulty education.[8] Wollstonecraft thus supported an educational system with reduced sexual distinctions. She proposed the establishment of a national system of public and coeducational schools encouraging maximum student participation and self-regulation. By dedicating the *Rights of Woman* to Charles Talleyrand-Perigord, Mary Wollstonecraft publicly asked this French revolutionary leader to build more feminine equality into his country's most important social institution—its schools. Not until the demands of reason were more fully satisfied through education, Wollstonecraft argued, could women know what their natural function in society was.

Rationalist thought and republicanism effectively served the male bourgeois struggle to win freedom from aristocratic and feudal authorities. Mary Wollstonecraft hoped to extend similar freedom to bourgeois women as well. Few of the rationalists and republicans who preached "the rights of man" recognized the extent to which they were talking primarily about the privileges of the middle class. But Wollstonecraft openly acknowledged her "particular attention to those in the middle class." Indeed, her assertion that "the majority of mothers . . . leave their children entirely to the care of servants" offers one illustration of this class bias.

Equality of right or of opportunity would lift certain conventional restraints from all women. Yet functional equality was not of equal use to every woman, for all the disadvantages of poverty would prevent the lower classes from capitalizing effectively on the new freedoms. Since Wollstonecraft laid most stress upon education to eradicate the worst sexual distinctions, the class implications of her educational reform have special importance. Critical of Talleyrand for advocating an identical education for boys and girls to age eight and ending formal feminine education then, she proposed to extend this absolute educational equality another year and allow women additional schooling. But her program for education beyond age nine allowed for rapidly increasing class and sexual differences. Although the benefits of the general attack on patriarchy and the proposed egalitarianism in early schooling spilled over to all classes, the *Rights of Woman* remained a feminine Declaration of Independence particularly for middle-class women.

Born into a middle-class home, Mary witnessed the desire for upward mobility and experienced the bitter taste of poverty which made rationalism and republicanism congenial. And having learned the meaning of social and economic displacement at the hands of man, she was likely to read a middle-class feminism into a middle-class rationalism. Surely her early experiences with men were too devastating and the roles thrust upon her as a youth too unconventional for her to equate the traditional position of women with the natural order.[9] Her father, a master weaver who squandered a sizeable inheritance attempting to become a gentleman farmer, failed miserably as protector and provider. His alcoholic bouts and abusive disposition rendered his timid wife cowering and ineffectual. Mary, the eldest daughter, provided financial and psychological support for her parents and most of her siblings for years.

An eighteenth-century adolescent girl with great drive but only a few years of day-school education had very limited resources for maintaining her own independence, let alone for supporting other people. At nineteen, Mary temporarily escaped from the oppressive family atmosphere to become a companion to an elderly woman. She returned home to nurse her ailing mother. Upon Elizabeth Wollstonecraft's death, Mary went to live with the family of her good friend Fanny Blood and sewed with the Blood women well into the night to supplement the meager income of another inadequate man. Mary, her sister Eliza, and Fanny opened a school which survived for three years. Then Mary served briefly as governess to the children of an Irish peer whose profligate wife neglected maternal duties, thereby accounting for much of Wollstonecraft's scorn for "ladies of fashion."

Mary Wollstonecraft determined in 1788 to make her living by the pen. But in spite of her extensive programs of self-education, she never overcame all the deficiencies which she attributed to inadequate schooling. Among the many causes which helped "to enslave women by cramping their understanding and shaping their senses," Mary thought "the disregard of order" did "more mischief than all the rest." An inadequate or misdirected education left women unable to generalize from observation and incapable of giving sufficient "vigor to the faculties and clearness to the judgment." She squeezed a modest living from translating and from writing essays, fiction, and review articles. But her treatises continued to lack that disciplined argument and logical organization characteristic of authors with an extended formal education or of radicals with an instinct for and commitment to theoretical consistency. She could not resist the temptation to dart off on tangents, to substitute polemic for argument, or to intrude parenthetical comments. Indeed after she became famous as a writer, Godwin appointed himself her grammar instructor.

While Mary tried in turn the occupations available to intelligent girls of her background and breeding, she did not consider that most popular alternative to autonomy—marriage. Too many of the marriages of relatives and close friends were disastrous. Her parents' example encouraged her to foreswear marriage at fifteen, and little that she saw thereafter shook her resolve. The ineffectual Mr. Blood depended first on his wife and later on Mary to support his family. And her dear friend Fanny died in childbirth in Lisbon, summoned there by the suitor who had originally rejected her. Mary had also spirited her distraught sister, Eliza, away from her husband and what Mary viewed as an emotionally disastrous union. Thus she despaired both for the single woman without support and the married woman who paid dearly for what support she received.

For all the apparent nonconformity of her life-style, Mary Wollstonecraft sought the substance of conventional relationships with men. A year after the publication of the *Rights of Woman,* she formed a liaison with Gilbert Imlay, an American painter then resident in France, where Mary was observing the Revolution. Becoming his mistress, she gave birth to a daughter. But Imlay tired of the relationship and took a new mistress in England. Distraught by this seeming betrayal, Mary attempted suicide. Within a year, however, she drifted into an affair with the noted radical, William Godwin.[10] He had argued in *Political Justice* for an end to matrimony as an institution, but he forsook this position in taking Mary as his legal wife. Neither in her life nor in her writing did she seek complete independence of woman from man. Unlike Godwin, she never renounced the institution of marriage, although she wanted to strip it of forms which had entrapped so many of her female friends and relatives. Recognizing certain essential functional differences between man and woman, she accepted the legitimacy of woman's domestic and maternal roles as long as they were not made enslaving. She and Godwin experimented with the appropriate degree of independence within the marriage bond by continuing to live and work in separate lodgings. But it was to the maternal that she finally succumbed: Mary Wollstonecraft Godwin died in 1797 from the complications of childbirth. She left an autobiographical novel, *The Wrongs of Woman; or, Maria,* a sequel to the *Rights of Woman,* unfinished.

More sensitive to form than substance, the public noted those conventions which Mary Wollstonecraft flouted, not those she affirmed. She did not espouse many of the fundamental political, religious, or absolute-egalitarian tenets of her radical rationalist friends. Yet she did not escape judgment by association, especially after her anarchist husband, Godwin, eulogized her in a widely read memoir which publicized her honest but unconventional arrangements with Imlay. Association with radicalism was not altogether unfashionable at the height of the revolutionary era, but Burke's stunning assault on revolutionary republicanism and rationalism and the continuing radicalization of the French Revolution turned the tide of opinion in Britain and America. Public openness to feminist and other proposals for social reconstruction decreased noticeably as the fortunes of republicanism, rationalism, and revolution waned.

Wollstonecraft's feminist attack on convention was nevertheless too telling to be completely ignored in the United States. Although the shift from seventeenth-century religious argument to eighteenth-century rationalism had not drastically affected many Americans' conception of woman's place, the popularity of Gregory, Rousseau, and others reflected a gradual improvement in social convention. However, not until Wollstonecraft's treatise appeared did Americans in any significant number face arguments for sexual equality directly. Even though the implications of her call for such equality immediately repelled most people, the issue had been effectively raised and a debate started that could not be dismissed easily.[11]

Charles Brockden Brown, the American novelist, discussed woman's rights in *Alcuin: A Dialogue,* published in 1798. Brown borrowed his ideas of sexual differences, education, and, to a lesser extent, marriage from Wollstonecraft. *Rights of Woman* also received serious attention from "Constantia" or Judith Sargent Murray, daughter of a prosperous and prominent Gloucester, Massachusetts, merchant. She published a three-volume collection of essays in 1798 dealing with several of Mary Wollstonecraft's themes. Brown and Mrs. Murray were not typical of their age, yet a few others shared their sentiments, including Aaron Burr, who considered the *Rights of Woman* a work of genius.[12]

A number of other Americans cited some of Mary Wollstonecraft's premises in the early nineteenth century. In *Observations on the Real Rights of Women* (1818), Hannah Mather Crocker found the "*Rights of Woman* . . . replete with fine sentiments, though we do not coincide with her opinion respecting the total independence of the female sex." While not a radical, Cotton Mather's granddaughter desired freedom for her daughters to study "every branch of science, even jurisprudence." Mary's ideas also circulated among the more important British and American communitarian reformers of this period. Frances Wright, radical feminist and leader of the interracial Nashoba experiment, and Robert Owen and his son, Robert Dale Owen, of the New Lanark, Scotland, and New Harmony, Indiana, model communities, endorsed the *Rights of Woman.* Calling for a strike of mill girls in 1834, a still more militant young woman from Lowell, Massachusetts, delivered "a flaming Mary Wollstonecraft speech on the rights of women and the inequities of the 'monied aristocracy' " from atop the town pump.[13]

New editions of the *Rights of Woman* became available after 1833, and it was probably one of these that Lucretia Mott and Elizabeth Cady Stanton read. Shut out, along with other female delegates, from the 1840 World Anti-Slavery Convention, Mrs. Mott wandered the London streets with Mrs. Stanton discussing "Mary Wollstonecraft, her social theories, and her demands of equality for women." At this time they agreed to hold a woman's rights convention in America. If "the movement for woman's suffrage, both in England and America, may be dated from this World's Anti-Slavery Convention," then surely the spirit of Mary Wollstonecraft was present at its birth.[14]

NOTES

1. The most accessible, complete edition of Mary Wollstonecraft, *A Vindication of the Rights of Woman with Strictures on Political and Moral Subjects,* is edited by Charles W. Hagelman, Jr. (New York: W. W. Norton & Co., Inc., 1967).

2. Contemporary English commentary on the *Rights of Woman* is quoted and summarized in Ralph M. Wardle, *Mary Wollstonecraft: A Critical Biography* (Lawrence: University of Kansas Press, 1951), 157–162. Emma Rauschenbusch-Clough, *A Study of Mary Wollstonecraft and the Rights of Woman* (London: Longmans, Green, and Co., 1898), 39–45, provides an extended formal analysis of Wollstonecraft's feminist ideas. See also Margaret George, *One Woman's "Situation": A Study of Mary Wollstonecraft* (Urbana: University of Illinois Press, 1970) and Eleanor Flexner, *Mary Wollstonecraft* (New York: Coward, McCann & Geoghegan, Inc., 1972) for fine contemporary examinations of Wollstonecraft's life and work.

3. Rauschenbusch-Clough, *Study of Wollstonecraft,* 43–45.

4. Excellent analyses of rationalist ambivalence toward blacks are developed in David Brion Davis, *Problems of Slavery in Western Culture* (Ithaca: Cornell University Press, 1966), 391–421, and Winthrop D. Jordan, *White over Black: American Attitudes toward the Negro, 1550–1812* (Chapel Hill: University of North Carolina Press, 1968), 349–356, 429–481. For rationalism and women, see Mary S. Benson, *Women in Eighteenth Century America: A Study of Opinion and Social Usage* (Port Washington, New York: Kennikat Press, Inc., 1966 reissue of 1935 edition), 65–78, 127–171.

5. The best survey of eighteenth-century English and American thought about the position of women can be found in Benson, *Women in America,* 34–78.

6. Mary Wollstonecraft, *A Vindication of the Rights of Men, in a Letter to the Right Honourable Edmund Burke; Occasioned by His Reflections on the Revolution in France* (Gainesville, Florida: Scholars' Facsimiles & Reprints, 1960 reissue of 1790 edition), 19, 22–23, 61, 97. For analysis of this

treatise, see Rauschenbusch-Clough, *Study of Wollstonecraft,* 71–86; Wardle, *Wollstonecraft,* 111–123; George, *Situation,* 87–89.

7. Wollstonecraft, *Rights of Men,* 33–35, 76–77.

8. For Wollstonecraft's debt to Macaulay, see Wardle, *Wollstonecraft,* 110, 144–145, 150–151.

9. For the details of Wollstonecraft's early life, see especially Wardle, *Wollstonecraft,* 3–110.

10. On Godwin and Wollstonecraft, see Rauschenbusch-Clough, *Study of Wollstonecraft,* 13–16, 176–185; Wardle, *Wollstonecraft,* 258–316; George, *Situation,* 149–168.

11. Benson, *Women in America,* 100–171.

12. Benson, *Women in America,* 172–187; Wardle, *Wollstonecraft,* 158, 357. Charles Brockden Brown's *Alcuin: A Dialogue* has been carefully edited by Lee R. Edwards and conveniently reprinted by Grossman Publishers (New York, 1970).

13. Aileen S. Kraditor, (ed.), *Up from the Pedestal: Selected Writings in the History of American Feminism* (Chicago: Quadrangle Books, Inc., 1968), 43; Wardle, *Wollstonecraft,* 334, 340; Rauschenbusch-Clough, *Study of Wollstonecraft,* 188; Eleanor Flexner, *Century of Struggle: The Woman's Rights Movement in the United States* (New York: Atheneum, 1968 reissue of 1959 edition), 55.

14. Wardle, *Wollstonecraft,* 340; Elizabeth Cady Stanton, Susan B. Anthony, Matilda J. Gage, and Ida H. Harper (eds.), *History of Woman Suffrage* (6 volumes, Rochester, New York, and New York, 1881–1922), I, 62.

A VINDICATION OF THE RIGHTS OF WOMAN WITH STRICTURES ON POLITICAL AND MORAL SUBJECTS (1792)

TO M. TALLEYRAND-PERIGORD,
LATE BISHOP OF AUTUN.

Having read with great pleasure a pamphlet which you have lately published, I dedicate this volume to you to induce you to reconsider the subject and maturely weigh what I have advanced. . . .

Contending for the rights of woman, my main argument is built on this simple principle, that if she be not prepared by education to become the companion of man, she will stop the progress of knowledge and virtue; for truth must be common to all, or it will be inefficacious with respect to its influence on general practice. And how can woman be expected to co-operate unless she know why she ought to be virtuous, unless freedom strengthen her reason till she comprehend her duty and see in what manner it is connected with her real good? If children are to be educated to understand the true principle of patriotism, their mother must be a patriot; and the love of mankind, from which an orderly train of virtues springs, can only be produced by considering the moral and civil interest of mankind; but the education and situation of woman, at present, shuts her out from such investigations.

In this work I have produced many arguments . . . to prove that the prevailing notion respecting a sexual character was subversive of morality, and I have contended that to render the human body and mind more perfect, chastity must more universally prevail and that chastity will never be respected in the male world till the person of a woman is not, as it were, idolized. . . .

Consider, sir, dispassionately these observations—for a glimpse of this truth seemed to open before you when you observed "that to see one half of the human race excluded by the other from all participation of government was a political phenomenon that, according to abstract principles, it was impossible to explain." If so, on what does your constitution rest? If the abstract rights of man will bear discussion and explanation, those of woman, by a parity of reasoning, will not shrink from the same test, though a different opinion prevails in this country, built on the very arguments which you use to justify the oppression of woman—prescription.

Consider—I address you as a legislator—whether, when men contend for their freedom and [struggle] to be allowed to judge for themselves respecting their own happiness, it be not inconsistent and unjust to subjugate women, even though you firmly believe that you are acting in the manner best calculated to promote their happiness? Who made man the exclusive judge, if woman partake with him the gift of reason?

In this style argue tyrants of every denomination, from the weak king to the weak father of a family; they are all eager to crush reason yet always assert that they usurp its throne only to be useful. Do you not act a similar part when you *force* all women, by denying them civil and political rights, to remain immured in their families groping in the dark? For surely, sir, you will not assert that a duty can be binding which is not founded on reason? . . . The more understanding women acquire, the more they will be attached to their duty—comprehending it—for unless they comprehend it, unless their morals be fixed on the same immutable principle as those of man, no authority can make them discharge it in a virtuous manner. They may be convenient slaves, but slavery will have its constant effect, degrading the master and the abject dependent.

But if women are to be excluded . . . from a participation of the natural rights of mankind, prove first, to ward off the charge of injustice and inconsistency, that they want reason—else this flaw in your NEW CONSTITUTION will ever show that man must in some shape act like a tyrant; and tyranny, in whatever part of society it rears its brazen front, will ever undermine morality.

I have repeatedly asserted, and produced what appeared to me irrefragable arguments drawn from matters of fact to prove my assertion, that women cannot by force be confined to domestic concerns; for they will, however ignorant, intermeddle with more weighty affairs, neglecting private duties only to disturb by cunning tricks the orderly plans of reason which rise above their comprehension.

Besides, whilst they are only made to acquire personal accomplishments, men will seek for pleasure in variety, and faithless husbands will make faithless wives; such ignorant beings, indeed, will be very excusable when, not taught to respect public good nor allowed any civil rights, they attempt to do themselves justice by retaliation.

The box of mischief thus opened in society, what is to preserve private virtue, the only security of public freedom and universal happiness?

Let there be then no coercion *established* in society, and the common law of gravity prevailing, the sexes will fall into their proper places. And now that more equitable laws are forming your citizens, marriage may become more sacred: Your young men may choose wives from motives of affection, and your maidens allow love to root out vanity.

The father of a family will not then weaken his constitution and debase his sentiments by visiting the harlot nor forget, in obeying the call of appetite, the purpose for which it was implanted. And the mother will not neglect her children to practise the arts of coquetry when sense and modesty secure her the friendship of her husband.

But till men become attentive to the duty of a father, it is vain to expect women to spend that time in their nursery which they, "wise in their generation," choose to spend at their [looking] glass; for this exertion of cunning is only an instinct of nature to enable them to obtain indirectly a little of that power of which they are unjustly denied a share; for if women are not permitted to enjoy legitimate rights, they will render both men and themselves vicious to obtain illicit privileges.

I wish, sir, to set some investigations of this kind afloat in France; and should they lead to a confirmation of my principles, when your constitution is revised, the Rights of Woman may be respected, if it be fully proved that reason calls for this respect and loudly demands JUSTICE for one half of the human race. . . .

INTRODUCTION

After considering the historic page and viewing the living world with anxious solicitude, the most melancholy emotions of sorrowful indignation have depressed my spirits, and I have sighed when obliged to confess that either nature has made a great difference between man and man or that the civilization which has hitherto taken place in the world has been very partial. I have turned over various books written on the subject of education and patiently observed the conduct of parents and the management of schools; but what has been the result?—a profound conviction that the neglected education of my fellow-creatures is the grand source of the misery I deplore and that women, in particular, are rendered weak and wretched by a variety of concurring causes originating from one hasty conclusion. . . . One cause of this . . . I attribute to a false system of education, gathered from the books written on this subject by men who, considering females rather as women than human creatures, have been more anxious to make them alluring mistresses than affectionate wives and rational mothers; and the understanding of the sex has been so bubbled by this specious homage that the civilized women of the present century, with a few exceptions, are only anxious to inspire love when they ought to cherish a nobler ambition and by their abilities and virtues exact respect. . . .

. . . In the government of the physical world it is observable that the female in point of strength is in general inferior to the male. This is the law of nature, and it does not appear to be suspended or abrogated in favor of woman. A degree of physical superiority cannot, therefore, be denied—and it is a noble prerogative! But not content with this natural pre-eminence, men endeavor to sink us still lower, merely to render us alluring objects for a moment; and women, intoxicated by the adoration which men, under the influence of their senses, pay them, do not seek to obtain a durable interest in their hearts or to become the friends of the fellow-creatures who find amusement in their society.

. . . The instruction which has hitherto been addressed to women has rather been applicable to *ladies* . . . ; but addressing my sex in a firmer tone, I pay particular attention to those in the middle class because they appear to be in the most natural state. Perhaps the seeds of false refinement, immorality, and vanity have ever been shed by the great. Weak, artificial beings raised above the common wants and affections of their race in a premature [and] unnatural manner undermine the very foundation of virtue and spread corruption through the whole mass of society! As a class of mankind they have the strongest claim to pity; the education of the rich tends to render them vain and helpless, and the unfolding mind is not strengthened by the practice of those duties which dignify the human character. . . .

My own sex, I hope, will excuse me if I treat them like rational creatures, instead of flattering their *fascinating* graces and viewing them as if they were in a state of perpetual childhood, unable to stand alone. I earnestly wish to point out in what true dignity and human happiness consist—I wish to persuade women to endeavor to acquire strength, both of mind and body, and to convince them that the soft phrases, susceptibility of heart, delicacy of sentiment, and refinement of taste are almost synonymous with epithets of weakness and that those beings who are only the objects of pity and that kind of love . . . will soon become objects of contempt.

Dismissing, then, those pretty feminine phrases which the men condescendingly use to soften our slavish dependence and despising that weak elegancy of mind, exquisite sensibility, and sweet docility of manners supposed to be the sexual characteristics of the weaker vessel, I wish to show that elegance is inferior to virtue, that the first object of laudable ambition is to obtain a character as a human being regardless of the distinction of sex, and that secondary views should be brought to this simple touchstone. . . .

The education of women has of late been more attended to than formerly; yet they are still reckoned a frivolous sex and ridiculed or pitied by the writers who endeavor by satire or instruction to improve them. It is acknowledged that they spend many of the first years of their lives in acquiring a smattering of accomplishments; meanwhile, strength of body and mind are sacrificed to libertine notions of beauty, to the desire of establishing themselves—the only way women can rise in the world—by marriage. And this desire making mere animals of them, when they marry, they act as such children may be expected to act: They dress, they paint, and nickname God's creatures. . . .

If then it can be fairly deduced from the present conduct of the sex . . . that the instruction which women have hitherto received has only tended, with the constitution of civil society, to render them insignificant objects of desire—mere propagators of fools!—if it can be proved that in aiming to accomplish them without cultivating their understandings they are taken out of their sphere of duties and made ridiculous and useless when the short-lived bloom of beauty is over, I presume that *rational* men will excuse me for endeavoring to persuade them to become more masculine and respectable.

Indeed the word masculine is only a bugbear: There is little reason to fear that women will acquire too much courage or fortitude, for their apparent inferiority with respect to bodily strength must render them in some degree dependent on men in the various relations of life; but why should it be increased by prejudices that give a sex to virtue and confound simple truths with sensual reveries?

Women are in fact so much degraded by mistaken notions of female excellence that I do not mean to add a paradox when I assert that this artificial weakness produces a propensity to tyrannize and gives birth to cunning, the natural opponent of strength, which leads them to play off those contemptible infantine airs that undermine esteem even whilst they excite desire. Let men become more chaste and modest, and if women do not grow wiser in the same ratio, it will be clear that they have weaker understandings. . . .

I. THE RIGHTS AND INVOLVED DUTIES OF MANKIND CONSIDERED.

In the present state of society it appears necessary to go back to first principles in search of the most simple truths and to dispute with some prevailing prejudice every inch of ground. . . .

In what does man's pre-eminence over the brute creation consist? The answer is as clear as that a half is less than the whole: in Reason.

What acquirement exalts one being above another? Virtue, we spontaneously reply.

For what purpose were the passions implanted? That man by struggling with them might attain a degree of knowledge denied to the brutes, whispers Experience.

Consequently, the perfection of our nature and capability of happiness must be estimated by the degree of reason, virtue, and knowledge that distinguishes the individual and directs the laws which bind society: and that from the exercise of reason knowledge and virtue naturally flow is equally undeniable if mankind be viewed collectively. . . . That the society is formed in the wisest manner whose constitution is founded on the nature of man strikes, in the abstract, every thinking being so forcibly that it looks like presumption to endeavor to bring forward proofs, though proof must be brought or the strong hold of prescription will never be forced by reason. . . .

The civilization of the bulk of the people of Europe is very partial; nay, it may be made a question whether they have acquired any virtues in exchange for innocence equivalent to the misery produced by the vices that have been plastered over unsightly ignorance and the freedom which has been bartered for splendid slavery. The desire of dazzling by riches, the most certain pre-eminence that man can obtain, the pleasure of commanding flattering sycophants, and many other complicated low calculations of doting self-love have all contributed to overwhelm the mass of mankind and make liberty a convenient handle for mock patriotism. . . .

Impressed by this view of the misery and disorder which pervaded society and fatigued with jostling against artificial fools, Rousseau became enamoured of solitude, and, being at the same time an optimist, he labors with uncommon eloquence to prove that man was naturally a solitary animal. Misled by his respect for the goodness of God, who certainly . . . gave life only to communicate happiness, he considers evil as positive and the work of man—not aware that he was exalting one attribute at the expense of another equally necessary to divine perfection.

Reared on a false hypothesis, his arguments in favor of a state of nature are plausible but unsound. I say unsound, for to assert that a state of nature is preferable to civilization in all its possible perfection is in other words to arraign supreme wisdom; and the paradoxical exclamation that God has made all things right and that error has been introduced by the creature whom he formed, knowing what he formed, is as unphilosophical as impious.

When that wise Being, who created us and placed us here, saw the fair idea, he willed, by allowing it to be so, that the passions should unfold our reason because he could see that present evil would produce future good. Could the helpless creature whom he called from nothing break loose from his providence and boldly learn to know good by practising evil without his permission? No. How could that energetic advocate for immortality argue so inconsistently? Had mankind remained forever in the brutal state of nature, which even his magic pen cannot paint as a state in which a single virtue took root, it would have been clear . . . that man was born to run the circle of life and death and adorn God's garden for some purpose which could not easily be reconciled with his attributes.

But if to crown the whole, there were to be rational creatures produced [and] allowed to rise in excellence by the exercise of powers implanted for that purpose [and] if benignity itself thought fit to call into existence a creature above the brutes who could think and improve himself, why should that inestimable gift . . . be called, in direct terms, a curse? A curse it might be reckoned if the whole of our existence were bounded by our continuance in this world; for why should the gracious fountain of life give us passions and the power of reflecting only to imbitter our days and inspire us with mistaken notions of dignity? Why should he lead us from love of ourselves to the sublime emotions which the discovery of his wisdom and goodness excites if these feelings were not set in motion to improve our nature, of which they make a part, and render us capable of enjoying a more godlike portion of happiness? Firmly persuaded that no evil exists in the world that God did not design to take place, I build my belief on the perfection of God.

Rousseau exerts himself to prove that all *was* right originally, a crowd of authors that all *is* now right, and I that all *will be* right. . . .

Disgusted with artificial manners and virtues, the citizen of Geneva, instead of properly sifting the subject, threw away the wheat with the chaff without waiting to inquire whether the evils which his ardent soul turned from indignantly were the consequence of civilization or the vestiges of barbarism. He saw vice trampling on virtue and the semblance of goodness taking place of the reality; he saw talents bent by power to sinister purposes and never thought of tracing the gigantic mischief up to arbitrary power, up to the hereditary distinctions that clash with the mental superiority that naturally raises a man above his fellows. He did not perceive that regal power in a few generations introduces idiotism into the noble stem and holds out baits to render thousands idle and vicious. . . .

It is impossible for any man, when the most favorable circumstances concur, to acquire sufficient knowledge and strength of mind to discharge the duties of a king entrusted with uncontrolled power; how then must they be violated when his very elevation is an insuperable bar to the attainment of either wisdom or virtue, when all the feelings of a man are stifled by flattery and reflection shut out by pleasure? Surely it is madness to make the fate of thousands depend on the caprice of a weak fellow-creature whose very station sinks him *necessarily* below the meanest of his subjects! But one power should not be thrown down to exalt another—for all power inebriates weak man; and its abuse proves that the more equality there is established among men, the more virtue and happiness will reign in society. . . .

In the infancy of society, when men were just emerging out of barbarism, chiefs and priests, touching the most powerful springs of savage conduct, hope and fear, must have had unbounded sway. An aristocracy, of course, is naturally the first form of government. But clashing interests soon losing their equipoise, a monarchy and hierarchy break out of the confusion of ambitious struggles, and the foundation of both is secured by feudal tenures. This appears to be the origin of monarchical and priestly power and the dawn of civilization. But such combustible materials cannot long be pent up; and getting vent in foreign wars and intestine insurrections, the people acquire some power in the tumult, which obliges their rulers to gloss over their oppression with a show of right. Thus as wars, agriculture, commerce, and literature expand the mind, despots are compelled to make covert corruption hold fast the power which was formerly snatched by open force. . . .

It is the pestiferous purple [of royalty] which renders the progress of civilization a curse and warps the understanding till men of sensibility doubt whether the expansion of intellect produces a greater portion of happiness or misery. But the nature of the poison points out the antidote; and had Rousseau mounted one step higher in his investigation, . . . his active mind would have darted forward to contemplate the perfection of man in the establishment of true civilization, instead of taking his ferocious flight back to the night of sensual ignorance.

II. THE PREVAILING OPINION OF A SEXUAL CHARACTER DISCUSSED.

To account for and excuse the tyranny of man, many ingenious arguments have been brought forward to prove that the two sexes in the acquirement of virtue ought to aim at attaining a very different character; or to speak explicitly, women are not allowed to have sufficient strength of mind to acquire what really deserves the name of virtue. . . . Men complain, and with reason, of the follies and caprices of our sex, when they do not keenly satirize our headstrong passions and grovelling vices. . . . The mind will ever be unstable that has only prejudices to rest on, and the current will run with destructive fury when there are no barriers to break its force. Women are told from their infancy and taught by the example of their mothers that a little knowledge of human weakness, justly termed cunning, softness of temper, *outward* obedience, and a scrupulous attention to a puerile kind of propriety will obtain for them the protection of man; and should they be beautiful, everything else is needless, for at least twenty years of their lives. . . .

How grossly do they insult us who thus advise us only to render ourselves gentle, domestic brutes! For instance, the winning softness, so warmly and frequently recommended, that governs by obeying. What childish expressions, and how insignificant is the being . . . who will condescend to govern by such sinister methods! . . . Men, indeed, appear to me to act in a very unphilosophical manner when they try to secure the good conduct of women by attempting to keep them always in a state of childhood. . . . Still the regal homage which they receive is so intoxicating that till the manners of the times are changed and formed on more reasonable principles, it may be impossible to convince them that the illegitimate power which they obtain by degrading themselves is a curse and that they must return to nature and equality if they wish to secure the placid satisfaction that unsophisticated affections impart. But for this epoch we must wait—wait, perhaps, till kings and nobles, enlightened by reason and preferring the real dignity of man to childish state, throw off their gaudy hereditary trappings; and if then women do not resign the arbitrary power of beauty, they will prove that they have *less* mind than man. . . .

Many are the causes that in the present corrupt state of society contribute to enslave women by cramping their understandings and sharpening their senses. One, perhaps, that silently does more mischief than all the rest is their disregard of order.

To do everything in an orderly manner is a most important precept, which women, who, generally speaking, receive only a disorderly kind of education, seldom attend to with that degree of exactness that men, who from their infancy are broken into method, observe. This negligent kind of guess-work . . . prevents their generalizing matters of fact—so they do today what they did yesterday merely because they did it yesterday.

This contempt of the understanding in early life has more baneful consequences than is commonly supposed; for the little knowledge which women of strong minds attain is, from various circumstances, of a more desultory kind than the knowledge of men, and it is acquired more by sheer observations on real life than from comparing what has been individually observed with the results of experience generalized by speculation. Led by their dependent situation and domestic employments more into society, what they learn is rather by snatches; and as learning is with them in general only a secondary thing, they do not pursue any one branch with that persevering ardor necessary to give vigor to the faculties and clearness to the judgment. In the present state of society a little learning is required to support the character of a gentleman, and boys are obliged to submit to a few years of discipline. But in the education of women, the cultivation of the understanding is always subordinate to the acquirement of some corporeal accomplishment; even while enervated by confinement and false notions of modesty, the body is prevented from attaining that grace and beauty which relaxed half-formed limbs never exhibit. Besides, in youth their faculties are not brought forward by emulation; and having no serious scientific study, if they have natural sagacity, it is turned too soon on life and manners. They dwell on effects and modifications without tracing them back to causes; and complicated rules to adjust behavior are a weak substitute for simple principles. . . .

. . . Rousseau declares that a woman should never for a moment feel herself independent, that she should be governed by fear to exercise her *natural* cunning and made a coquettish slave in order to render her a more alluring object of desire, a *sweeter* companion to man whenever he chooses to relax himself. He carries the arguments, which he pretends to draw from the indications of nature, still further and insinuates that truth and fortitude, the cornerstones of all human virtue, should be cultivated with certain restrictions because with respect to the female character obedience is the grand lesson which ought to be impressed with unrelenting rigor.

What nonsense! When will a great man arise with sufficient strength of mind to puff away the fumes which pride and sensuality have thus spread over the subject! If women are by nature inferior to men, their virtues must be the same in quality, if not in degree, or virtue is a relative idea; consequently, their conduct should be founded on the same principles and have the same aim.

Connected with man as daughters, wives, and mothers, their moral character may be estimated by their manner of fulfilling those simple duties; but the end, the grand end of their exertions, should be to unfold their own faculties and acquire the dignity of conscious virtue. They may try to render their road pleasant but ought never to forget, in common with man, that life yields not the felicity which can satisfy an immortal soul. . . .

Probably the prevailing opinion that woman was created for man may have taken its rise from Moses' poetical story; yet as very few, it is presumed, who have bestowed any serious thought on the subject ever supposed that Eve was literally speaking one of Adam's ribs, the deduction must be allowed to fall to the ground—or only be so far admitted as it proves that man from the remotest antiquity found it convenient to exert his strength to subjugate his companion, and his invention to show that she ought to have her neck bent under the yoke, because the whole creation was only created for his convenience or pleasure.

Let it not be concluded that I wish to invert the order of things; I have already granted that from the constitution of their bodies, men seem to be designed by Providence to attain a greater degree of virtue. I speak collectively of the whole sex; but I see not the shadow of a reason to conclude that their virtues should differ in respect to their nature. In fact, how can they, if virtue has only one eternal standard? I must therefore, if I reason consequentially, as strenuously maintain that they have the same simple direction as that there is a God. It follows then that cunning should not be opposed to wisdom, little cares to great exertions, or insipid softness, varnished over with the names of gentleness, to that fortitude which grand views alone can inspire. . . .

To speak disrespectfully of love is, I know, high treason against sentiment and fine feelings. . . . To endeavor to reason love out of the world would be to out-Quixote Cervantes and equally offend against common sense; but an endeavor to restrain this tumultuous passion and to prove that it should not be allowed to dethrone superior powers or to usurp the scepter which the understanding should ever coolly wield appears less wild. Youth is the season for love in both sexes, but in those days of thoughtless enjoyment provision should be made for the more important years of life when reflection takes place of sensation. But Rousseau, and most of the male writers who have followed his steps, have warmly inculcated that the whole tendency of female education ought to be directed to one point—to render them pleasing. . . .

. . . The woman who has only been taught to please will soon find that her charms are oblique sunbeams and that they cannot have much effect on her husband's heart when they are seen every day, when the summer is passed and gone. Will she then have sufficient native energy to look into herself for comfort and cultivate her dormant faculties? Or is it not more rational to expect that she will try to please other men and, in the emotions raised by the expectation of new conquests, endeavor to forget the mortification her love or pride has received? When the husband ceases to be a lover—and the time will inevitably come—her desire of pleasing will then grow languid or become a spring of bitterness; and love, perhaps the most evanescent of all passions, gives place to jealousy or vanity. . . .

. . . How then can the great art of pleasing be such a necessary study? It is only useful to a mistress; the chaste wife and serious mother should only consider her power to please as the polish of her virtues and the affection of her husband as one of the comforts that render her talk less difficult and her life happier. But whether she be loved or neglected, her first wish should be to make herself respectable and not to rely for all her happiness on a being subject to like infirmities with herself.

The worthy Dr. Gregory fell into a similar error. I respect his heart but entirely disapprove of his celebrated Legacy to his Daughters. He . . . recommends dissimulation and advises an innocent girl to give the lie to her feelings and not dance with spirit when gaiety of heart would make her feet eloquent without making her gestures immodest. In the name of truth and common sense, why should not one woman acknowledge that she can take more exercise than another or, in other words, that she has a sound constitution? And why, to damp innocent vivacity, is she darkly to be told that men will draw conclusions which she little thinks of? Let the libertine draw what inference he pleases; but I hope that no sensible mother will restrain the natural frankness of youth by instilling such indecent cautions. . . .

In a seraglio I grant that all these arts are necessary; the epicure must have his palate tickled, or he will sink into apathy; but have women so little ambition as to be satisfied with such a condition? Can they supinely dream life away in the lap of pleasure or the languor of weariness rather than assert their claim to pursue reasonable pleasures and render themselves conspicuous by practising the virtues which dignify mankind? Surely she has not an immortal soul who can loiter life away merely employed to adorn her person that she may amuse the languid hours and soften the cares of a fellow-creature who is willing to be enlivened by her smiles and tricks when the serious business of life is over.

Besides, the woman who strengthens her body and exercises her mind will, by managing her family and practising various virtues, become the friend and not the humble dependent of her husband; and if she, by possessing such substantial qualities, merits his regard, she will not find it necessary to conceal her affection nor to pretend to an unnatural coldness of constitution to excite her husband's passions. In fact, if we revert to history, we shall find that the women who have distinguished themselves have neither been the most beautiful nor the most gentle of their sex.

Nature, or, to speak with strict propriety, God, has made all things right; but man has sought . . . out many inventions to mar the work. I now allude to that part of Dr. Gregory's treatise where he advises a wife never to let her husband know the extent of her sensibility or affection. Voluptuous precaution, and as ineffectual as absurd. Love from its very nature must be transitory. To seek for a secret that would render it constant would be as wild a search as for the philosopher's stone or the grand panacea; and the discovery would be equally useless, or rather pernicious, to mankind. The most holy band of society is friendship. . . .

Love, the common passion in which chance and sensation take place of choice and reason, is in some degree felt by the mass of mankind; for it is not necessary to speak at present of the emotions that rise above or sink below love. This passion, naturally increased by suspense and difficulties, draws the mind out of its accustomed state and exalts the affections; but the security of marriage allowing the fever of love to subside, a healthy temperature is thought insipid only by those who have not sufficient intellect to substitute the calm tenderness of friendship, the confidence of respect instead of blind admiration and the sensual emotions of fondness.

This is, must be, the course of nature—friendship or indifference inevitably succeeds love. And this constitution seems perfectly to harmonize with the system of government which prevails in the moral world. Passions are spurs to action and open the mind; but they sink into mere appetites, become a personal and momentary gratification, when the object is gained and the satisfied mind rests in enjoyment. The man who had some virtue whilst he was struggling for a crown often becomes a voluptuous tyrant when it graces his brow; and when the lover is not lost in the husband, the dotard, a prey to childish caprices and fond jealousies, neglects the serious duties of life, and the caresses which should excite confidence in his children are lavished on the overgrown child, his wife.

In order to fulfill the duties of life and to be able to pursue with vigor the various employments which form the moral character, a master and mistress of a family ought not to continue to love each other with passion. I mean to say that they ought not to indulge those emotions which disturb the order of society and engross the thoughts that should be otherwise employed. The mind that has never been engrossed by one object wants vigor—if it can long be so, it is weak. . . .

. . . If all the faculties of woman's mind are only to be cultivated as they respect her dependence on man [and] if, when a husband be obtained, she have arrived at her goal and, meanly proud, rests satisfied with such a paltry crown, let her grovel contentedly, scarcely raised by her employments above the animal kingdom; but if struggling for the prize of her high calling, she look beyond the present scene, let her cultivate her understanding without stopping to consider what character the husband may have whom she is destined to marry. Let her only determine, without being too anxious about present happiness, to acquire the qualities that ennoble a rational being, and a rough, inelegant husband may shock her taste without destroying her peace of mind. She will not model her soul to suit the frailties of her companion but to bear with them: His character may be a trial, but not an impediment to virtue. . . .

I own it frequently happens that women who have fostered a romantic, unnatural delicacy of feeling waste their lives in *imagining* how happy they should have been with a husband who could love them with a fervid, increasing affection every day and all day. But they might as well pine married as single—and would not be a jot more unhappy with a bad husband than longing for a good one. That a proper education or, to speak with more precision, a well-stored mind would enable a woman to support a single life with dignity I grant; but that she should avoid cultivating her taste lest her husband should occasionally shock it is quitting a substance for a shadow. To say the truth, I do not know of what use is an improved taste if the individual be not rendered more independent of the casualties of life, if new sources of enjoyment only dependent on the solitary operations of the mind are not opened. . . .

Gentleness of manners, forbearance, and long-suffering are such amiable, God-like qualities that in sublime, poetic strains the Deity has been invested with them; and perhaps no representation of his goodness so strongly fastens on the human affections as those that represent him abundant in mercy and willing to pardon. Gentleness, considered in this point of view, bears on its front all the characteristics of grandeur combined with the winning graces of condescension; but what a different aspect it assumes when it is the submissive demeanor of dependence, the support of weakness that loves because it wants protection and is forbearing because it must silently endure injuries, smiling under the lash at which it dare not snarl. Abject as this picture appears, it is the portrait of an accomplished woman according to the received opinion of female excellence, separated by specious reasoners from human excellence. Or they kindly restore the rib and make one moral being of a man and woman, not forgetting to give her all the "submissive charms."

How women are to exist in that state where there is to be neither marrying or giving in marriage we are not told. For though moralists have agreed that the tenor of life seems to prove that *man* is prepared by various circumstances for a future state, they constantly concur in advising *woman* only to provide for the present. Gentleness, docility, and a spaniel-like affection are on this ground consistently recommended as the cardinal virtues of the sex; and disregarding the arbitrary economy of nature, one writer has declared that it is masculine for a woman to be melancholy. She was created to be the toy of man, his rattle, and it must jingle in his ears whenever, dismissing reason, he chooses to be amused.

To recommend gentleness indeed on a broad basis is strictly philosophical. A frail being should labor to be gentle. But when forbearance confounds right and wrong, it ceases to be a virtue; and, however convenient it may be found in a companion, that companion will ever be considered as an inferior and only inspire a vapid tenderness which easily degenerates into contempt. . . .

It is difficult for us purblind mortals to say to what height human discoveries and improvements may arrive when the gloom of despotism subsides which makes us stumble at every step; but when morality shall be settled on a more solid basis, then, without being gifted with a prophetic spirit, I will venture to predict that woman will be either the friend or slave of man. We shall not, as at present, doubt whether she is a moral agent or the link which unites man with brutes. But should it then appear that like the brutes they were principally created for the use of man, he will let them patiently bite the bridle and not mock them with empty praise; or, should their rationality be proved, he will not impede their improvement merely to gratify his sensual appetites. He will not, with all the graces of rhetoric, advise them to submit implicitly their understanding to the guidance of man. He will not, when he treats of the education of women, assert that they ought never to have the free use of reason, nor would he recommend cunning and dissimulation to beings who are acquiring, in like manner as himself, the virtues of humanity.

. . . If they be really capable of acting like rational creatures, let them not be treated like slaves or like the brutes who are dependent on the reason of man when they associate with him; but cultivate their minds, give them the salutary, sublime curb of principle, and let them attain conscious dignity by feeling themselves only dependent on God. Teach them in common with man to submit to necessity instead of giving, to render them more pleasing, a sex to morals.

Further, should experience prove that they cannot attain the same degree of strength of mind, perseverance, and fortitude, let their virtues be the same in kind, though they may vainly struggle for the same degree; and the superiority of man will be equally clear, if not clearer; and truth, as it is a simple principle which admits of no modification, would be common to both. Nay, the order of society as it is at present regulated would not be inverted, for woman would then only have the rank that reason assigned her, and arts could not be practised to bring the balance even, much less to turn it.

These may be termed Utopian dreams. Thanks to that Being who impressed them on my soul and gave me sufficient strength of mind to dare to exert my own reason till, becoming dependent only on Him for the support of my virtue, I view with indignation the mistaken notions that enslave my sex.

I love man as my fellow; but his scepter, real or usurped, extends not to me unless the reason of an individual demands my homage, and even then, the submission is to reason and not to man.

In fact, the conduct of an accountable being must be regulated by the operations of its own reason, or on what foundation rests the throne of God?

It appears to me necessary to dwell on these obvious truths because females have been insulated, as it were; and, while they have been stripped of the virtues that should clothe humanity, they have been decked with artificial graces that enable them to exercise a short-lived tyranny. Love in their bosoms taking place of every nobler passion, their sole ambition is . . . to raise emotion instead of inspiring respect; and this ignoble desire, like the servility in absolute monarchies, destroys all strength of character. Liberty is the mother of virtue, and if women be by their very constitution slaves and not allowed to breathe the sharp, invigorating air of freedom, they must ever languish like exotics and be reckoned beautiful flaws in nature.

As to the argument respecting the subjection in which the sex has ever been held, it retorts on man. The many have always been enthralled by the few; and monsters, who scarcely have shown any discernment of human excellence, have tyrannized over thousands of their fellow-creatures. Why have men of superior endowments submitted to such degradation? . . . *Men* have submitted to superior strength to enjoy with impunity the pleasure of the moment—*women* have only done the same, and therefore till it is proved that the courtier, who servilely resigns the birthright of a man, is not a moral agent, it cannot be demonstrated that woman is essentially inferior to man because she has always been subjugated.

Brutal force has hitherto governed the world, and that the science of politics is in its infancy is evident from philosophers scrupling to give the knowledge most useful to man that determinate distinction.

I shall not pursue this argument any further than to establish an obvious inference, that as sound politics diffuse liberty, mankind, including woman, will become more wise and virtuous.

III. THE SAME SUBJECT CONTINUED.

. . . Women, as well as despots, have now perhaps more power than they would have if the world, divided and subdivided into kingdoms and families, were governed by laws deduced from the exercise of reason; but in obtaining it, . . . their character is degraded and licentiousness spread through the whole aggregate of society. The many become pedestal to the few. I therefore will venture to assert that till women are more rationally educated, the progress of human virtue and improvement in knowledge must receive continual checks. And if it be granted that woman was not created merely to gratify the appetite of man or to be the upper servant who provides his meals and takes care of his linen, it must follow that the first care of those mothers or fathers who really attend to the education of females should be, if not to strengthen the body, at least not to destroy the constitution by mistaken notions of beauty and female excellence; nor should girls ever be allowed to imbibe the pernicious notion that a defect can, by any chemical process of reasoning, become an excellence. . . .

. . . Should it be proved that woman is naturally weaker than man, whence does it follow that it is natural for her to labor to become still weaker than nature intended her to be? Arguments of this cast are an insult to common sense and savor of passion. The *divine right* of husbands, like the divine right of kings, may, it is to be hoped, in this enlightened age be contested without danger, and though conviction may not silence many boisterous disputants, yet when any prevailing prejudice is attacked, the wife will consider and leave the narrow-minded to rail with thoughtless vehemence at innovation. . . .

Throughout the whole animal kingdom every young creature requires almost continual exercise, and the infancy of children, conformable to this intimation, should be passed in harmless gambols that exercise the feet and hands without requiring very minute direction from the head or the constant attention of a nurse. In fact, the care necessary for self-preservation is the first natural exercise of the understanding, as little inventions to amuse the present moment unfold the imagination. But these wise designs of nature are counteracted by mistaken fondness or blind zeal. The child is not left a moment to its own direction, particularly a girl, and thus rendered dependent—dependence is called natural.

To preserve personal beauty—woman's glory!—the limbs and faculties are cramped with worse than Chinese bands, and the sedentary life which they are condemned to live whilst boys frolic in the open air weakens the muscles and relaxes the nerves. As for Rousseau's remarks, which have since been echoed by several writers, that they [girls] have naturally, that is from their birth [and] independent of education, a fondness for dolls, dressing, and talking—they are so puerile as not to merit a serious refutation. That a girl, condemned to sit for hours together listening to the idle chat of weak nurses or to attend at her mother's toilet, will endeavor to join the conversation is indeed very natural; and that she will imitate her mother or aunts and amuse herself by adorning her lifeless doll as they do in dressing her . . . is undoubtedly a most natural consequence. For men of the greatest abilities have seldom had sufficient strength to rise above the surrounding atmosphere; and if the pages of genius have always been blurred by the prejudices of the age, some allowance should be made for a sex who, like kings, always see things through a false medium.

Pursuing these reflections, the fondness for dress conspicuous in women may be easily accounted for without supposing it the result of a desire to please the sex on which they are dependent. The absurdity, in short, of supposing that a girl is naturally a coquette and that a desire connected with the impulse of nature to propagate the species should appear even before an improper education has, by heating the imagination, called it forth prematurely is so unphilosophical that such a sagacious observer as Rousseau would not have adopted it if he had not been accustomed to make reason give way to his desire of singularity and truth to a favorite paradox.

Yet thus to give a sex to mind was not very consistent with the principles of a man who argued so warmly, and so well, for the immortality of the soul. But what a weak barrier is truth when it stands in the way of an hypothesis! Rousseau respected—almost adored—virtue and yet he allowed himself to love with sensual fondness. His imagination constantly prepared inflammable fuel for his inflammable senses; but in order to reconcile his respect for self-denial, fortitude, and those heroic virtues which a mind like his could not coolly admire, he labors to invert the law of nature and broaches a doctrine pregnant with mischief and derogatory to the character of supreme wisdom. His ridiculous stories, which tend to prove that girls are *naturally* attentive to their persons without laying any stress on daily example, are below contempt. . . .

I have probably had an opportunity of observing more girls in their infancy than J. J. Rousseau. I can recollect my own feelings, and I have looked steadily around me; yet so far from coinciding with him in opinion respecting the first dawn of the female character, I will venture to affirm that a girl whose spirits have not been damped by inactivity or innocence tainted by false shame will always be a romp, and the doll will never excite attention unless confinement allows her no alternative. Girls and boys, in short, would play harmlessly together if the distinction of sex was not inculcated long before nature makes any difference. I will go further and affirm as an indisputable fact that most of the women in the circle of my observation who have acted like rational creatures or shown any vigor of intellect have accidentally been allowed to run wild—as some of the elegant formers of the fair sex would insinuate.

The baneful consequences which flow from inattention to health during infancy and youth extend further than is supposed—dependence of body naturally produces dependence of mind; and how can she be a good wife or mother, the greater part of whose time is employed to guard against or endure sickness? Nor can it be expected that a woman will resolutely endeavor to strengthen her constitution and abstain from enervating indulgences if artificial notions of beauty and false descriptions of sensibility have been early entangled with her motives of action. Most men are sometimes obliged to bear with bodily inconveniences and to endure occasionally the inclemency of the elements, but genteel women are, literally speaking, slaves to their bodies and glory in their subjection.

I once knew a weak woman of fashion who was more than commonly proud of her delicacy and sensibility. She thought a distinguishing taste and puny appetite the height of all human perfection and acted accordingly. I have seen this weak sophisticated being neglect all the duties of life, yet recline with self-complacency on a sofa and boast of her want of appetite as a proof of delicacy that extended to, or perhaps arose from, her exquisite sensibility; for it is difficult to render intelligible such ridiculous jargon. Yet at the moment I have seen her insult a worthy old gentlewoman, whom unexpected misfortunes had made dependent on her ostentatious bounty and who, in better days, had claims on her gratitude. . . .

Such a woman is not a more irrational monster than some of the Roman emperors who were depraved by lawless power. Yet since kings have been more under the restraint of law and the curb, however weak, of honor, the records of history are not filled with such unnatural instances of folly and cruelty, nor does the despotism that kills virtue and genius in the bud hover over Europe with that destructive blast which desolates Turkey and renders the men, as well as the soil, unfruitful.

Women are everywhere in this deplorable state; for in order to preserve their innocence, as ignorance is courteously termed, truth is hidden from them, and they are made to assume an artificial character before their faculties have acquired any strength. Taught from their infancy that beauty is woman's scepter, the mind shapes itself to the body and, roaming round its gilt cage, only seeks to adore its prison. Men have various employments and pursuits which engage their attention and give a character to the opening mind; but women, confined to one and having their thoughts constantly directed to the most insignificant part of themselves, seldom extend their views beyond the triumph of the hour. But were their understanding once emancipated from the slavery to which the pride and sensuality of man and their short-sighted desire . . . has subjected them, we should probably read of their weaknesses with surprise. . . .

IX. OF THE PERNICIOUS EFFECTS WHICH ARISE FROM THE UNNATURAL DISTINCTIONS ESTABLISHED IN SOCIETY.

From the respect paid to property flow, as from a poisoned fountain, most of the evils and vices which render this world such a dreary scene to the contemplative mind. . . .

One class presses on another, for all are aiming to procure respect on account of their property; and property, once gained, will procure the respect due only to talents and virtue. Men neglect the duties incumbent on man, yet are treated like demi-gods; religion is also separated from morality by a ceremonial veil, yet men wonder that the world is almost, literally speaking, a den of sharpers or oppressors.

There is a homely proverb which speaks a shrewd truth, that whoever the devil finds idle he will employ. And what but habitual idleness can hereditary wealth and titles produce? For man is so constituted that he can only attain a proper use of his faculties by exercising them and will not exercise them unless necessity of some kind first set the wheels in motion. Virtue likewise can only be acquired by the discharge of relative duties; but the importance of these sacred duties will scarcely be felt by the being who is cajoled out of his humanity by the flattery of sycophants. There must be more equality established in society, or morality will never gain ground, and this virtuous equality will not rest firmly, even when founded on a rock, if one half of mankind be chained to its bottom by fate, for they will be continually undermining it through ignorance or pride.

It is vain to expect virtue from women till they are in some degree independent of men; nay, it is vain to expect that strength of natural affection which would make them good wives and mothers. . . . The society is not properly organized which does not compel men and women to discharge their respective duties by making it the only way to acquire that countenance from their fellow-creatures which every human being wishes some way to attain. The respect, consequently, which is paid to wealth and mere personal charms is a true north-east blast that blights the tender blossoms of affection and virtue. Nature has wisely attached affections to duties to sweeten toil and to give that vigor to the exertions of reason which only the heart can give. . . .

. . . I have then viewed with pleasure a woman nursing her children and discharging the duties of her station with perhaps merely a servant maid to take off her hands the servile part of the household business. I have seen her prepare herself and children, with only the luxury of cleanliness, to receive her husband, who returning weary home in the evening found smiling babes and a clean hearth. My heart has loitered in the midst of the group and has even throbbed with sympathetic emotion when the scraping of the well-known foot has raised a pleasing tumult.

Whilst my benevolence has been gratified by contemplating this artless picture, I have thought that a couple of this description, equally necessary and independent of each other because each fulfilled the respective duties of their station, possessed all that life could give. Raised sufficiently above abject poverty not to be obliged to weigh the consequence of every farthing they spend . . . [they have] sufficient to prevent their attending to a frigid system of economy which narrows both heart and mind. I declare, so vulgar are my conceptions that I know not what is wanted to render this the happiest as well as the most respectable situation in the world but a taste for literature to throw a little variety and interest into social converse and some superfluous money to give to the needy and to buy books. . . .

The being who discharges the duties of its station is independent; and speaking of women at large, their first duty is to themselves as rational creatures and the next in point of importance as citizens is that, which includes so many, of a mother. The rank in life which dispenses with their fulfilling this duty necessarily degrades them by making them mere dolls.

. . . To render her really virtuous and useful, she must not, if she discharge her civil duties, want individually the protection of civil laws; she must not be dependent on her husband's bounty for her subsistence during his life or support after his death. For how can a being be generous who has nothing of its own? Or virtuous who is not free? The wife, in the present state of things, who is faithful to her husband and neither suckles nor educates her children scarcely deserves the name of a wife and has no right to that of a citizen. But take away natural rights, and duties become null. . . .

Besides, when poverty is more disgraceful than even vice, is not morality cut to the quick? Still to avoid misconstruction, though I consider that women in the common walks of life are called to fulfill the duties of wives and mothers by religion and reason, I cannot help lamenting that women of a superior cast have not a road open by which they can pursue more extensive plans of usefulness and independence. I may excite laughter by dropping a hint . . . for I really think that women ought to have representatives, instead of being arbitrarily governed without having any direct share allowed them in the deliberations of government.

But as the whole system of representation is now in this country only a convenient handle for despotism, they need not complain, for they are as well represented as a numerous class of hard-working mechanics, who pay for the support of royalty when they can scarcely stop their children's mouths with bread. How are they represented whose very sweat supports the splendid stud of an heir apparent or varnishes the chariot of some female favorite who looks down on shame? Taxes on the very necessaries of life enable an endless tribe of idle princes and princesses to pass with stupid pomp before a gaping crowd, who almost worship the very parade which costs them so dear. . . .

In the superior ranks of life every duty is done by deputies, as if duties could ever be waived, and the vain pleasures which consequent idleness forces the rich to pursue appear so enticing to the next rank that the numerous scramblers for wealth sacrifice everything to tread on their heels. The most sacred trusts are then considered as sinecures because they were procured by interest and only sought to enable a man to keep *good company*. Women in particular all want to be ladies—which is simply to have nothing to do but listlessly to go they scarcely care where for they cannot tell what.

But what have women to do in society, I may be asked, but to loiter with easy grace? Surely you would not condemn them all to suckle fools and chronicle small beer! No. Women might certainly study the art of healing and be physicians as well as nurses. And midwifery, decency seems to allot to them. . . .

They might also study politics and settle their benevolence on the broadest basis; for the reading of history will scarcely be more useful than the perusal of romances if read as mere biography, if the character of the times, the political improvements, arts, &c, be not observed. . . .

Business of various kinds they might likewise pursue, if they were educated in a more orderly manner, which might save many from common and legal prostitution. Women would not then marry for a support, as men accept of places under government, and neglect the implied duties; nor would an attempt to earn their own subsistence—a most laudable one!—sink them almost to the level of those poor abandoned creatures who live by prostitution. For are not milliners and mantua-makers reckoned the next class? The few employments open to women, so far from being liberal, are menial; and when a superior education enables them to take charge of the education of children as governesses, they are not treated like the tutors of sons, though even clerical tutors are not always treated in a manner calculated to render them respectable in the eyes of their pupils, to say nothing of the private comfort of the individual. But as women educated like gentlewomen are never designed for the humiliating situation which necessity sometimes forces them to fill, these situations are considered in the light of a degradation; and they know little of the human heart who need to be told that nothing so painfully sharpens sensibility as such a fall in life.

Some of these women might be restrained from marrying by a proper spirit or delicacy, and others may not have had it in their power to escape in this pitiful way from servitude. Is not that government then very defective and very unmindful of the happiness of one-half of its members that does not provide for honest, independent women by encouraging them to fill respectable stations? But in order to render their private virtue a public benefit, they must have a civil existence in the state, married or single; else we shall continually see some worthy woman, whose sensibility has been rendered painfully acute by undeserved contempt, droop like "the lily broken down by a plow-share."

It is a melancholy truth—yet such is the blessed effect of civilization!—the most respectable women are the most oppressed; and unless they have understandings far superior to the common run of understandings, taking in both sexes, they must, from being treated like contemptible beings, become contemptible. How many women thus waste life away, the prey of discontent, who might have practised as physicians, regulated a farm, managed a shop, and stood erect, supported by their own industry, instead of hanging their heads surcharged with the dew of sensibility that consumes the beauty to which it at first gave luster. . . .

Would men but generously snap our chains and be content with rational fellowship instead of slavish obedience, they would find us more observant daughters, more affectionate sisters, more faithful wives, more reasonable mothers—in a word, better citizens. We should then love them with true affection because we should learn to respect ourselves; and the peace of mind of a worthy man would not be interrupted by the idle vanity of his wife, nor the babes sent to nestle in a strange bosom, having never found a home in their mother's.

XII. ON NATIONAL EDUCATION.

. . . A taste for the fine arts requires great cultivation, but not more than a taste for the virtuous affections; and both suppose that enlargement of mind which opens so many sources of mental pleasure. . . . With what a languid yawn have I seen an admirable poem thrown down that a man of true taste returns to again and again with rapture; and, whilst melody has almost suspended respiration, a lady has asked me where I bought my gown. I have seen also an eye [which] glanced coldly over a most exquisite picture rest sparkling with pleasure on a caricature rudely sketched; and whilst some terrific feature in nature has spread a sublime stillness through my soul, I have been desired to observe the pretty tricks of a lapdog that my perverse fate forced me to travel with. Is it surprising that such a tasteless being should rather caress this dog than her children? Or that she should prefer the rant of flattery to the simple accents of sincerity? . . .

True taste is ever the work of the understanding employed in observing natural effects; and till women have more understanding, it is vain to expect them to possess domestic taste. Their lively senses will ever be at work to harden their hearts, and the emotions struck out of them will continue to be vivid and transitory unless a proper education store their mind with knowledge. . . .

History brings forward a fearful catalogue of the crimes which their cunning has produced, when the weak slaves have had sufficient address to overreach their masters. In France, and in how many other countries, have men been the luxurious despots and women the crafty ministers? Does this prove that ignorance and dependence domesticate them? Is not their folly the by-word of the libertines who relax in their society, and do not men of sense continually lament that an immoderate fondness for dress and dissipation carries the mother of a family forever from home? Their hearts have not been debauched by knowledge, or their minds led astray by scientific pursuits; yet they do not fulfill the peculiar duties which as women they are called upon by nature to fulfill. On the contrary, the state of warfare which subsists between the sexes makes them employ those wiles that often frustrate the more open designs of force.

When therefore I call women slaves, I mean in a political and civil sense; for indirectly they obtain too much power and are debased by their exertions to obtain illicit sway.

Let an enlightened nation then try what effect reason would have to bring them back to nature and their duty and, allowing them to share the advantages of education and government with man, see whether they will become better as they grow wiser and become free. They cannot be injured by the experiment, for it is not in the power of man to render them more insignificant than they are at present.

To render this practicable, day schools for particular ages should be established by government in which boys and girls might be educated together. The school for the younger children, from five to nine years of age, ought to be absolutely free and open to all classes. A sufficient number of masters should also be chosen by a select committee in each parish to whom any complaint of negligence, etc., might be made if signed by six of the children's parents. . . .

. . . Boys and girls, the rich and poor should meet together. And to prevent any of the distinctions of vanity, they should be dressed alike and all obliged to submit to the same discipline or leave the school. The school room ought to be surrounded by a large piece of ground in which the children might be usefully exercised, for at this age they should not be confined to any sedentary employment for more than an hour at a time. But these relaxations might all be rendered a part of elementary education, for many things improve and amuse the senses, when introduced as a kind of show, to the principles of which, dryly laid down, children would turn a deaf ear. For instance, botany, mechanics, and astronomy. Reading, writing, arithmetic, natural history, and some simple experiments in natural philosophy might fill up the day; but these pursuits should never encroach on gymnastic plays in the open air. The elements of religion, history, the history of man, and politics might also be taught by conversations in the socratic form.

After the age of nine, girls and boys intended for domestic employments or mechanical trades ought to be removed to other schools and receive instruction in some measure appropriate to the destination of each individual, the two sexes being still together in the morning; but in the afternoon the girls should attend a school where plain-work, mantua-making, millinery, etc., would be their employment.

The young people of superior abilities or fortune might now be taught in another school the dead and living languages, the elements of science, and continue the study of history and politics on a more extensive scale, which would not exclude polite literature.

"Girls and boys still together?" I hear some readers ask. Yes. And I should not fear any other consequence than that some early attachment might take place, which, whilst it had the best effect on the moral character of the young people, might not perfectly agree with the views of the parents; for it will be a long time, I fear, before the world will be so far enlightened that parents, only anxious to render their children virtuous, shall allow them to choose companions for life themselves. . . . In this plan of education the constitution of boys would not be ruined by the early debaucheries which now make men so selfish or girls rendered weak and vain by indolence and frivolous pursuits. But I presuppose that such a degree of equality should be established between the sexes as would shut out gallantry and coquetry, yet allow friendship and love to temper the heart for the discharge of higher duties.

These would be schools of morality—and the happiness of man allowed to flow from the pure springs of duty and affection. . . . Society can only be happy and free in proportion as it is virtuous; but the present distinctions established in society corrode all private and blast all public virtue.

I have already inveighed against the custom of confining girls to their needle and shutting them out from all political and civil employments; for by thus narrowing their minds, they are rendered unfit to fulfill the peculiar duties which nature has assigned them.

Only employed about the little incidents of the day, they necessarily grow up cunning. My very soul has often sickened at observing the sly tricks practised by women to gain some foolish thing on which their silly hearts were set. Not allowed to dispose of money or call anything their own, they learn to turn the market penny; or should a husband offend by staying from home or give rise to some emotions of jealousy, a new gown or any pretty bauble smooths Juno's angry brow.

But these *littlenesses* would not degrade their character if women were led to respect themselves, if political and moral subjects were opened to them; and I will venture to affirm that this is the only way to make them properly attentive to their domestic duties. An active mind embraces the whole circle of its duties and finds time enough for all. It is not, I assert, a bold attempt to emulate masculine virtues, . . . [nor is it] the enchantment of literary pursuits or the steady investigation of scientific subjects that leads women astray from duty. No, it is indolence and vanity—the love of pleasure and the love of sway—that will reign paramount in an empty mind. I say empty emphatically because the education which women now receive scarcely deserves the name. For the little knowledge that they are led to acquire during the important years of youth is merely relative to accomplishments, and accomplishments without a bottom; for unless the understanding be cultivated, superficial and monotonous is every grace. Like the charms of a made-up face, they only strike the senses in a crowd; but at home, wanting mind, they want variety. The consequence is obvious; in gay scenes of dissipation we meet the artificial mind and face, for those who fly from solitude dread, next to solitude, the domestic circle; not having it in their power to amuse or interest, they feel their own insignificance or find nothing to amuse or interest themselves.

Besides, what can be more indelicate than a girl's *coming out* in the fashionable world? Which, in other words, is to bring to market a marriageable miss whose person is taken from one public place to another, richly caparisoned. Yet mixing in the giddy circle under restraint, these butterflies long to flutter at large, for the first affection of their souls is their own persons, to which their attention has been called with the most sedulous care whilst they were preparing for the period that decides their fate for life. Instead of pursuing this idle routine, sighing for tasteless show and heartless state, with what dignity would the youths of both sexes form attachments in the schools that I have cursorily pointed out, in which, as life advanced, dancing, music, and drawing might be admitted as relaxations; for at these schools young people of fortune ought to remain, more or less, till they were of age. Those who were designed for particular professions might attend, three or four mornings in the week, the schools appropriate for their immediate instruction. . . .

I know that libertines will . . . exclaim that woman would be unsexed by acquiring strength of body and mind and that beauty, soft bewitching beauty, would no longer adorn the daughters of men. I am of a very different opinion, for I think that, on the contrary, we should then see dignified beauty and true grace, to produce which many powerful physical and moral causes would concur. Not relaxed beauty, it is true, or the graces of helplessness, but such as appears to make us respect the human body as a majestic pile fit to receive a noble inhabitant in the relics of antiquity. . . .

. . . Exercise and cleanliness appear to be not only the surest means of preserving health but of promoting beauty, the physical causes only considered; yet this is not sufficient. Moral ones must concur, or beauty will be merely of that rustic kind which blooms on the innocent, wholesome countenances of some country people whose minds have not been exercised. To render the person perfect, physical and moral beauty ought to be attained at the same time, each lending and receiving force by the combination. Judgment must reside on the brow, affection and fancy beam in the eye, and humanity curve the cheek, or vain is the sparkling of the finest eye or the elegantly turned finish of the fairest features; whilst in every motion that displays the active limbs and well-knit joints, grace and modesty should appear. But this fair assemblage is not to be brought together by chance; it is the reward of exertions calculated to support each other; for judgment can only be acquired by reflection, affection by the discharge of duties, and humanity by the exercise of compassion to every living creature. . . .

The libertinism and even the virtues of superior men will always give women, of some description, great power over them. . . . Men of fancy and those sanguine characters who mostly hold the helm of human affairs in general relax in the society of women; and surely I need not cite to the most superficial reader of history the numerous examples of vice and oppression which the private intrigues of female favorites have produced, not to dwell on the mischief that naturally arises from the blundering interposition of well-meaning folly. For in the transactions of business it is much better to have to deal with a knave than a fool, because a knave adheres to some plan; and any plan of reason may be seen through much sooner than a sudden flight of folly. The power which vile and foolish women have had over wise men who possessed sensibility is notorious; I shall only mention one instance.

Who ever drew a more exalted female character than Rousseau, though in the lump he constantly endeavored to degrade the sex? And why was he thus anxious? Truly to justify to himself the affection which weakness and virtue had made him cherish for that fool Theresa. He could not raise her to the common level of her sex, and therefore he labored to bring woman down to hers. He found her a convenient humble companion, and pride made him determine to find some superior virtues in the being whom he chose to live with; but did not her conduct during his life and after his death clearly show how grossly he was mistaken who called her a celestial innocent. Nay, in the bitterness of his heart he himself laments that when his bodily infirmities made him no longer treat her like a woman, she ceased to have an affection for him. And it was very natural that she should, for having so few sentiments in common, when the sexual tie was broken, what was to hold her? To hold her affection whose sensibility was confined to one sex, nay, to one man, it requires sense to turn sensibility into the broad channel of humanity; many women have not mind enough to have an affection for a woman or a friendship for a man. But the sexual weakness that makes woman depend upon a man for subsistence produces a kind of cattish affection which leads a wife to purr about her husband as she would about any man who fed and caressed her.

Men are, however, often gratified by this kind of fondness, which is confined in a beastly manner to themselves; but should they ever become more virtuous, they will wish to converse at their fireside with a friend after they cease to play with a mistress. . . .

I speak of the improvement and emancipation of the whole sex, for I know that the behavior of a few women who by accident or following a strong bent of nature have acquired a portion of knowledge superior to that of the rest of their sex has often been overbearing; but there have been instances of women who, attaining knowledge, have not discarded modesty, nor have they always pedantically appeared to despise the ignorance which they labored to disperse in their own minds. The exclamations then which any advice respecting female learning commonly produces, especially from pretty women, often arise from envy. When they chance to see that even the luster of their eyes and the flippant sportiveness of refined coquetry will not always secure them attention during a whole evening should a woman of a more cultivated understanding endeavor to give a rational turn to the conversation, the common source of consolation is that such women seldom get husbands. What arts have I not seen silly women use to interrupt by *flirtation* . . . a rational conversation which made the men forget that they were pretty women.

But allowing what is very natural to man, that the possession of rare abilities is really calculated to excite overweening pride disgusting in both men and women, in what a state of inferiority must the female faculties have rusted when such a small portion of knowledge as those women attained, who have sneeringly been termed learned women, could be singular? Sufficiently so to puff up the possessor and excite envy in her contemporaries and some of the other sex. Nay, has not a little rationality exposed many women to the severest censure? I advert to well-known facts, for I have frequently heard women ridiculed and every little weakness exposed only because they adopted the advice of some medical men and deviated from the beaten track in their mode of treating their infants. I have actually heard this barbarous aversion to innovation carried still further and a sensible woman stigmatized as an unnatural mother who has thus been wisely solicitous to preserve the health of her children when in the midst of her care she has lost one by some of the casualties of infancy, which no prudence can ward off. Her acquaintance has observed that this was the consequence of new-fangled notions—the new-fangled notions of ease and cleanliness. And those, who pretending to experience though they have long adhered to prejudices that have, according to the opinions of the most sagacious physicians, thinned the human race, almost rejoiced at the disaster that gave a kind of sanction to prescription.

Indeed, if it were only on this account, the national education of women is of the utmost consequence, for what a number of human sacrifices are made to that moloch prejudice! And in how many ways are children destroyed by the lasciviousness of man? The want of natural affection in many women who are drawn from their duty by the admiration of men and the ignorance of others renders the infancy of man a much more perilous state than that of brutes; yet men are unwilling to place women in situations proper to enable them to acquire sufficient understanding to know how even to nurse their babes.

So forcibly does this truth strike me that I would rest the whole tendency of my reasoning upon it, for whatever tends to incapacitate the maternal character takes woman out of her sphere. . . . The weakness of the mother will be visited on the children! And whilst women are educated to rely on their husbands for judgment, this must ever be the consequence, for there is no improving an understanding by halves, nor can any being act wisely from imitation because in every circumstance of life there is a kind of individuality which requires an exertion of judgment to modify general rules. The being who can think justly in one track will soon extend its intellectual empire; and she who has sufficient judgment to manage her children will not submit, right or wrong, to her husband or, patiently, to the social laws which make a nonentity of a wife.

In public schools women, to guard against the errors of ignorance, should be taught the elements of anatomy and medicine, not only to enable them to take proper care of their own health, but to make them rational nurses of their infants, parents, and husbands; for the bills of mortality are swelled by the blunders of self-willed old women who give nostrums of their own without knowing anything of the human frame. It is likewise proper only in a domestic view to make women acquainted with the anatomy of the mind by allowing the sexes to associate together in every pursuit: and by leading them to observe the progress of the human understanding in the improvement of the sciences and arts, never forgetting the science of morality or the study of the political history of mankind. . . .

Discussing the advantages which a public and private education combined, as I have sketched, might rationally be expected to produce, I have dwelt most on such as are particularly relative to the female world because I think the female world oppressed; yet the gangrene which the vices engendered by oppression have produced is not confined to the morbid part but pervades society at large, so that when I wish to see my sex become more like moral agents, my heart bounds with the anticipation of the general diffusion of that sublime contentment which only morality can diffuse.

XIII. SOME INSTANCES OF THE FOLLY WHICH THE IGNORANCE OF WOMEN GENERATES; WITH CONCLUDING REFLECTIONS ON THE MORAL IMPROVEMENT THAT A REVOLUTION IN FEMALE MANNERS MIGHT NATURALLY BE EXPECTED TO PRODUCE.

There are many follies in some degree peculiar to women: sins against reason of commission as well as of omission; but all flowing from ignorance or prejudice, I shall only point out such as appear to be particularly injurious to their moral character. And in animadverting on them, I wish especially to prove that the weakness of mind and body which men have endeavored, impelled by various motives, to perpetuate prevents their discharging the peculiar duty of their sex; for when weakness of body will not permit them to suckle their children, and weakness of mind makes them spoil their tempers, is woman in a natural state? . . .

III.

Ignorance and the mistaken cunning that nature sharpens in weak heads as a principle of self-preservation render women very fond of dress and produce all the vanity which such a fondness may naturally be expected to generate to the exclusion of emulation and magnanimity.

I agree with Rousseau that the physical part of the art of pleasing consists in ornaments, and for that very reason I should guard girls against the contagious fondness for dress, so common to weak women, that they may not rest in the physical part. Yet weak are the women who imagine that they can long please without the aid of the mind or, in other words, without the moral art of pleasing. But the moral art . . . is never to be found with ignorance; the sportiveness of innocence, so pleasing to refined libertines of both sexes, is widely different in its essence from this superior gracefulness.

. . . When men meet, they converse about business, politics, or literature; but, says Swift, "how naturally do women apply their hands to each other's lappets and ruffles." And very natural is it, for they have not any business to interest them, have not a taste for literature, and they find politics dry because they have not acquired a love for mankind by turning their thoughts to the grand pursuits that exalt the human race and promote general happiness.

Besides various are the paths to power and fame which by accident or choice men pursue, and though they jostle against each other—for men of the same profession are seldom friends—yet there is a much greater number of their fellow-creatures with whom they never clash. But women are very differently situated with respect to each other—for they are all rivals.

Before marriage it is their business to please men; and after, with a few exceptions, they follow the same scent with all the persevering pertinacity of instinct. Even virtuous women never forget their sex in company, for they are forever trying to make themselves *agreeable*. A female beauty, and a male wit appear to be equally anxious to draw the attention of the company to themselves, and the animosity of contemporary wits is proverbial.

Is it then surprising that when the sole ambition of woman centers in beauty, and interest gives vanity additional force, perpetual rivalships should ensue? They are all running the same race and would rise above the virtue of mortals if they did not view each other with a suspicious and even envious eye.

An immoderate fondness for dress, for pleasure, and for sway are the passions of savages, the passions that occupy those uncivilized beings who have not yet extended the dominion of the mind or even learned to think with the energy necessary to concatenate that abstract train of thought which produces principles. And that women, from their education and the present state of civilized life, are in the same condition cannot, I think, be controverted. To laugh at them then or satirize the follies of a being who is never to be allowed to act freely from the light of her own reason is as absurd as cruel; for that they who are taught blindly to obey authority will endeavor cunningly to elude it is most natural and certain.

Yet let it be proved that they ought to obey man implicitly, and I shall immediately agree that it is woman's duty to cultivate a fondness for dress, in order to please and [to develop] a propensity to cunning for her own preservation. . . .

IV.

Women are supposed to possess more sensibility, and even humanity, than men, and their strong attachments and instantaneous emotions of compassion are given as proofs; but the clinging affection of ignorance has seldom anything noble in it and may mostly be resolved into selfishness. . . I have known many weak women whose sensibility was entirely engrossed by their husbands;

and as for their humanity, it was very faint indeed, or rather it was only a transient emotion of compassion. . . .

But this kind of exclusive affection, though it degrades the individual, should not be brought forward as a proof of the inferiority of the sex because it is the natural consequence of confined views; for even women of superior sense, having their attention turned to little employments and private plans, rarely rise to heroism unless when spurred on by love! And love, as an heroic passion like genius, appears but once in an age. I therefore agree with the moralist who asserts "that women have seldom so much generosity as men" and that their narrow affections, to which justice and humanity are often sacrificed, render the sex apparently inferior, especially as they are commonly inspired by men; but I contend that the heart would expand as the understanding gained strength if women were not depressed from their cradles.

I know that a little sensibility and great weakness will produce a strong sexual attachment and that reason must cement friendship; consequently I allow that more friendship is to be found in the male than the female world and that men have a higher sense of justice. . . .

Besides, how can women be just or generous when they are the slaves of injustice?

V.

As the rearing of children—that is, the laying a foundation of sound health both of body and mind in the rising generation—has justly been insisted on as the peculiar destination of woman, the ignorance that incapacitates them must be contrary to the order of things. And I contend that their minds can take in much more and ought to do so, or they will never become sensible mothers. Many men attend to the breeding of horses and oversee the management of the stable who would—strange want of sense and feeling! —think themselves degraded by paying any attention to the nursery; yet how many children are absolutely murdered by the ignorance of women! But when they escape and are destroyed neither by unnatural negligence nor blind fondness, how few are managed properly with respect to the infant mind! So that to break the spirit allowed to become vicious at home, a child is sent to school; and the methods taken there, which must be taken to keep a number of children in order, scatter the seeds of almost every vice in the soil thus forcibly torn up.

I have sometimes compared the struggles of these poor children, who ought never to have felt restraint nor would, had they been always held in with an even hand, to the despairing plunges of a spirited filly which I have seen breaking on a strand: its feet sinking deeper and deeper in the sand every time it endeavored to throw its rider, till at last it sullenly submitted. . . . I am, however, certain that a child should never be thus forcibly tamed after it has injudiciously been allowed to run wild; for every violation of justice and reason in the treatment of children weakens their reason. And so early do they catch a character that the base of the moral character, experience leads me to infer, is fixed before their seventh year, the period during which women are allowed the sole management of children. Afterwards it too often happens that half the business of education is to correct—and very imperfectly is it done if done hastily—the faults which they would never have acquired if their mothers had had more understanding.

. . . A child should always be made to receive assistance from a man or woman as a favor; and as the first lesson of independence, they should practically be taught by the example of their mother not to require that personal attendance which it is an insult to humanity to require when in health; and instead of being led to assume airs of consequence, a sense of their own weakness should first make them feel the natural equality of man. Yet how frequently have I indignantly heard servants imperiously called to put children to bed and sent away again and again because master or miss hung about mamma to stay a little longer. Thus made slavishly to attend the little idol, all those most disgusting humors were exhibited which characterize a spoiled child.

In short, speaking of the majority of mothers, they leave their children entirely to the care of servants or, because they are their children, treat them as if they were little demi-gods, though I have always observed that the women who thus idolize their children seldom show common humanity to servants or feel the least tenderness for any children but their own.

It is, however, these exclusive affections and an individual manner of seeing things produced by ignorance which keep women forever at a stand with respect to improvement and make many of them dedicate their lives to their children only to weaken their bodies and spoil their tempers, frustrating also any plan of education that a more rational father may adopt; for unless a mother concur, the father who restrains will ever be considered as a tyrant.

But fulfilling the duties of a mother, a woman with a sound constitution may still keep her person scrupulously neat and assist to maintain her family if necessary or, by reading and conversations with both sexes indiscriminately, improve her mind. For nature has so wisely ordered things that did women suckle their children, they would preserve their own health, and there would be such an interval between the birth of each child that we should seldom see a houseful of babes. And did they pursue a plan of conduct and not waste their time in following the fashionable vagaries of dress, the management of their household and children need not shut them out from literature or prevent their attaching themselves to a science with that steady eye which strengthens the mind or practising one of the fine arts that cultivate the taste.

But visiting to display finery, card-playing, and balls, not to mention the idle bustle of morning trifling, draw women from their duty to render them insignificant, to render them pleasing according to the present acceptation of the word to every man but their husband. For a round of pleasures in which the affections are not exercised cannot be said to improve the understanding, though it be erroneously called seeing the world; yet the heart is rendered cold and averse to duty by such a senseless intercourse, which becomes necessary from habit even when it has ceased to amuse.

But we shall not see women affectionate till more equality be established in society, till ranks are confounded and women freed; neither shall we see that dignified domestic happiness, the simple grandeur of which cannot be relished by ignorant or vitiated minds; nor will the important task of education ever be properly begun till the person of a woman is no longer preferred to her mind. For it would be as wise to expect corn from tares or figs from thistles as that a foolish, ignorant woman should be a good mother.

VI.

. . . Moralists have unanimously agreed that unless virtue be nursed by liberty, it will never attain due strength—and what they say of man I extend to mankind, insisting that in all cases morals must be fixed on immutable principles and that the being cannot be termed rational or virtuous who obeys any authority but that of reason.

To render women truly useful members of society, I argue that they should be led, by having their understandings cultivated on a large scale, to acquire a rational affection for their country, founded on knowledge, because it is obvious that we are little interested about what we do not understand. And to render this general knowledge of due importance, I have endeavored to show that private duties are never properly fulfilled unless the understanding enlarges the heart and that public virtue is only an aggregate of private. But the distinctions established in society undermine both by beating out the solid gold of virtue till it becomes only the tinsel covering of vice; for whilst wealth renders a man more respectable than virtue, wealth will be sought before virtue; and whilst women's persons are caressed when a childish simper shows an absence of mind, the mind will lie fallow. . . .

That women at present are by ignorance rendered foolish or vicious is, I think, not to be disputed; and that the most salutary effects tending to improve mankind might be expected from a REVOLUTION in female manners appears, at least with a face of probability, to rise out of the observation. For as marriage has been termed the parent of those endearing charities which draw man from the brutal herd, the corrupting intercourse that wealth, idleness, and folly produce between the sexes is more universally injurious to morality than all the other vices of mankind collectively considered. To adulterous lust the most sacred duties are sacrificed because before marriage men, by a promiscuous intimacy with women, learned to consider love as a selfish gratification—learned to separate it not only from esteem but from the affection merely built on habit, which mixes a little humanity with it. Justice and friendship are also set at defiance, and that purity of taste is vitiated which would naturally lead a man to relish an artless display of affection rather than affected airs. But that noble simplicity of affection which dares to appear unadorned has few attractions for the libertine, though it be the charm which, by cementing the matrimonial tie, secures to the pledges of a warmer passion the necessary parental attention; for children will never be properly educated till friendship subsists between parents. . . .

The affection of husbands and wives cannot be pure when they have so few sentiments in common and when so little confidence is established at home as must be the case when their pursuits are so different. That intimacy from which tenderness should flow will not, cannot subsist between the vicious.

Contending, therefore, that the sexual distinction which men have so warmly insisted upon is arbitrary, I have dwelt on an observation . . . that the little chastity to be found amongst men and consequent disregard of modesty tend to degrade both sexes and, further, that the modesty of women, characterized as such, will often be only the artful veil of wantonness instead of being the natural reflection of purity till modesty be universally respected.

From the tyranny of man I firmly believe the greater number of female follies proceed; and the cunning, which I allow makes at present a part of their character, I likewise have repeatedly endeavored to prove is produced by oppression. . . .

Asserting the rights which women in common with men ought to contend for, I have not attempted to extenuate their faults but to prove them to be the natural consequence of their education and station in society. If so, it is reasonable to suppose that they will change their character and correct their vices and follies when they are allowed to be free in a physical, moral, and civil sense.

Let woman share the rights and she will emulate the virtues of man, for she must grow more perfect when emancipated or justify the authority that chains such a weak being to her duty. If the latter, it will be expedient to open a fresh trade with Russia for whips, a present which a father should always make to his son-in-law on his wedding day that a husband may keep his whole family in order by the same means and without any violation of justice reign, wielding this scepter, sole master of his house because he is the only being in it who has reason—the divine, indefeasible, earthly sovereignty breathed into man by the Master of the universe. Allowing this position, women have not any inherent rights to claim; and by the same rule their duties vanish, for rights and duties are inseparable.

Be just then, O ye men of understanding! And mark not more severely what women do amiss than the vicious tricks of the horse or the ass for whom ye provide provender—and allow her the privileges of ignorance to whom ye deny the rights of reason, or ye will be worse than Egyptian task-masters, expecting virtue where nature has not given understanding!

PART II

Sarah Grimké:

Radical Sectarian

Sarah Moore Grimké (1792–1873) escaped her destiny as a South Carolina gentlewoman by embracing first Quakerism, then a series of radical causes including feminism. The tidewater planter aristocracy probably did not expect one of its daughters to write a treatise like *Letters on the Equality of the Sexes and the Condition of Woman* (1837–1838), but perhaps no one else could have written it.[1] White women had considerable first-hand experience with the American social system's entrapment of blacks and women in the South, where it was most blatant, and that experience was not lost on Sarah Grimké.

Noted since ancient times, the similarities between slavery and patriarchy were widely understood in the antebellum South.[2] Traditionally, Southern women and children, as well as slaves, recognized the male head of the family as lord and master. It was no accident, therefore, that apologists for slavery espoused the subordination of women or that many antislavery Southerners were female. Plantation ladies, who frequently taught, supervised, and ministered to a large and demanding retinue of slaves, bore a physical and psychological burden which bred both affection for and antagonism towards slaves. The double standard which permitted the master interracial sexual freedom and insisted upon chastity for the mistress, the lady's fear that the lord might carry venereal disease back from the slave cabin, and the mortal danger of constant pregnancies for white as well as black mothers led many Southern women to sense that slavery and patriarchy were reinforcing oppressions. But it took an unusual combination of circumstances to produce a woman who could translate a generalized sense of injustice into the articulate feminism which Sarah Grimké voiced.

Sixth of fourteen children, Sarah—along with her youngest sister, Angelina—understood these related discriminations of the planter society and escaped their grasp.[3] Her parents belonged to the state's ruling elite by virtue of their families' established wealth and position. Trained at Cambridge University and Middle Temple in London, her father, John F. Grimké, fought in the American Revolution, served in the South Carolina legislature and on the state's highest court, supported ratification of the federal constitution, and administered the family's sizeable plantations.

Judge Grimké and his wife emphasized classical aristocratic and Enlightenment values in an age when Southern rationalism, republicanism, and gentility were more memory than reality. He insisted that his sons acquire the traditional education of gentlemen in the finest Anglo-American universities, and he provided his daughters with the best education usual for young ladies. But precocious and ambitious Sarah pursued even more. With the judge's acquiescence, she studied her brothers' college preparatory lessons and joined them in the debates which Grimké encouraged as training for the boys.

An increasingly aggressive provincialism accompanied the rapid extension of cotton culture into the Southern interior. Sensing that changing social trends were displacing the older traditions which Grimké and his wife valued, some of their children tried to renew public commitment to traditional values by supporting various reforms, including peace, temperance, and colonization—a scheme for solving the slavery problem by shipping blacks back to Africa.[4]

When Judge Grimké reprimanded Sarah for teaching a slave girl to read, he observed a state law designed to avert the dangers inherent in educating persons supposed to be kept in subjection. But when he partially indulged Sarah's appetite for education, he helped undermine female subordination. The latitude he granted her only encouraged her to seek more. After the judge refused to let her learn Latin along with her brother Thomas, Sarah felt some of those same social constraints which fettered slaves begin to narrow her own development. She concluded later that her intellectual powers had been "repressed by the false idea that a girl need not have the education I coveted."[5]

Sarah's requests to pursue a legal career were also apparently denied, but she studied law in secret, hoping for a parental reprieve that did not come. "Oh!" she exclaimed some years later, "had I received the education I desired, had I been bred to the profession of the law, I might have been a useful member of society, and instead of myself and my property being taken care of, I might have been a protector of the helpless, a pleader for the poor and unfortunate."[6] Sarah never completely abandoned her interest in or pursuit of the law. She systematically explored the Blackstone-based legal structure which discriminated against the single woman and pronounced the married woman civilly dead. Consequently the *Equality of the Sexes* paid more attention to woman's legal disabilities than any prior American feminist work.[7]

What little freedom she found or made for herself in her unusual family setting became difficult to preserve in adolescent and adult life. After her brother-companion Thomas left for Yale, she faced a Southern daughter's loneliness and intellectual stagnation. Reaching tentatively beyond the family, she fluttered briefly in Charleston society. But with neither beauty nor inclination to enter the ranks of the belles, Sarah found no fulfillment in the conventional life of the Southern woman. She discovered some solace in acting as substitute-mother for baby Angelina and in church work. Stunted in intellectual development, cut off from a coveted career, and possibly doomed to spinsterhood, Sarah felt increasingly entombed in an anachronistic Southern family that had instilled an unconventional will without providing a way for her to express it.

The superfluous spinster of twenty-six was most easily spared to accompany her ailing father to Philadelphia for medical consultation—a journey which ended Grimké's life and resurrected his daughter's. After completely depending upon Sarah for months, John Grimké died in the North. The circumstances of the judge's fatal illness both elevated and depressed Sarah by throwing her still more upon her internal resources, allowing her for once to give wholly of herself, and forcing her to shed the traditional filial role. Secure in her ability to serve usefully as a single woman, Sarah sailed for Carolina. On the voyage a Friend from Philadelphia gave her a copy of John Woolman's Quaker writings, where she found so much solace that she read and absorbed all the Quaker works which her brother Thomas could supply and plied her Philadelphia Friend with numerous inquiries by mail. After "an unmistakable call, not to be disregarded," Sarah embarked for Philadelphia and the Society of Friends in 1821.[8]

John Woolman's Quakerism offered Sarah Grimké an escape from the dead end of Charleston convention.[9] Woolman's total empathy induced him to explore the feelings of the downtrodden in a way that explicated Sarah's experiences with slavery and as a woman: "Suppose then, that our ancestors and we had been exposed to constant servitude, in the most servile and inferior employments of life; that we had been destitute of the help of reading and good company; that . . . being wholly at the command of others, [we] have generally been treated as a contemptible, ignorant part of mankind: Should we, in that case, be less abject than they now are?"[10] Woolman's environmentalist approach to the oppressed touched only one of the possible points of contact between Sarah and the Quakers: Her family's interest in colonization resembled Quaker antislavery views; Thomas' commitment to the peace society harmonized with Quaker nonresistance; and Sarah's latent feminism applauded the Quaker woman's freedom to speak and serve within the sect.

Still more important, the radical sectarian tradition which included Quakerism gave Sarah an ideological foundation which supported and unified reforms, including feminism.[11] The Judeo-Christian heritage, as recorded in the customary translations of the Old and New Testaments and elaborated in the institutions of the various Christian churches, provided crucial support for the subordination of women. One of the feminists' main tasks was to confront this religious ban upon equality. Few, however, found the resources which Sarah exploited to attack sexism from within the Christian tradition. By considering God a transforming energy rather than a fixed good, radical sectarians questioned traditional views that found the existing social order a necessary compromise with sin. The perfectionist's shift from the idea of nature as unchangeable to the idea of history as a creative process and the millenarian's faith in the imminent possibility of a heavenly equality on earth both colored Quaker thinking.

The key to Quaker reform lay in linking millennial and perfectionist strains with the doctrine of the Inner Light, a belief that God communed directly with each individual without benefit of theology, custom, or clerics. When Sarah followed the Quakers and reduced the search for truth to God, man, and the Bible, she set aside traditional Christian submission to temporal inequalities and hierarchies without questioning the existence of an absolute God whose plan for all mankind was enscribed in the Scriptures. That single plan, she felt, would emerge only through each individual's internal quest, although a majority might not take the trouble to seek it or to bring secular law into harmony with biblical law.

The *Equality of the Sexes* indicated that Sarah Grimké had little "superstitious reverence" for King James translators and no deference for ordained ministers. Christians who want to help a fellow human being relate properly to God should work to remove the barriers between the individual and his Maker, not interpose themselves, as ministers or magistrates usually do. Human interposition denies the equality of all human beings as potential recipients of the Inner Light.

Sarah's biblical interpretation emerged during fifteen years in Philadelphia, where she added the biblical scholarship of British sectarians (e.g., Adam Clarke and Joseph John Gurney) and Anglicans to the formative experiences of her Southern youth. Joined in 1829 by Angelina, who had also abandoned Charleston, Sarah lived quietly and happily among the orthodox Friends upon her modest paternal inheritance, reading and training for a career in the Quaker ministry.

The orthodox Friends had developed subtle institutional restraints to keep Quakers from following perfectionist, millenial, and inner impulses beyond the bounds of existing social realities.[12] When Friends rejected oaths, tithes, bearing arms, and trafficking in slaves, theirs was a symbolic social protest which protected the sectarian's soul without challenging the established order. Maintaining a sensitive balance between fundamental change and accommodation, Quakers avoided both fanaticism and worldly compromise. The principle of nonresistance precluded violent attempts to alter the basic structure of society. And the Quaker emphasis upon the Inner Light encouraged an introspection which sometimes consumed an individual's energies. A common memory of persecution, rules against marriage with nonmembers, special dress, and distinctive speech helped to mark Quakers as a people apart, more immediately concerned with ridding themselves of the moral taint of sin than with reforming others.

The Grimké sisters were, however, far more interested in the perfectionist possibilities of the sectarian tradition than in Quaker convention. Friends expected women to devote most of their energies to marriage, the family, and domestic pursuits. But neither sister hurried into marriage. Sarah refused one proposal, possibly because she did not wish to trade independence for stepmotherhood; and Angelina, who gave some of her other activities priority over courtship, lost a somewhat rebuffed suitor in an epidemic.

Orthodox Quakerism was uncomfortably limiting for the Grimkés in other ways also. Unlike most other contemporary sects, the Friends encouraged both men and women to minister, preach, and perform charitable works. But, as Angelina noted, Quakers regarded women "as equal to men on the ground of *spiritual gifts, not* on the broad ground of *humanity*. Woman may *preach;* this is a *gift;* but woman must *not* make the discipline by which *she herself* is to be governed."[13] Sarah prepared for nine years for the ministry without any encouragement from the elders. When the patriarch of orthodox Quakerism interrupted her in meeting in 1836, Sarah felt firmly rebuked and abandoned her ministerial quest. "No religious body," she concluded in a chapter on the ministry of women in the *Equality of the Sexes,* entertained "the Scripture doctrine of the perfect equality of man and woman."

The elders' efforts to contain social reform nudged the Grimké sisters beyond the orthodox pale. Sarah attempted to establish a peace society among the Philadelphia Friends, only to be effectively discouraged by the

Quaker leadership. Angelina, who drifted from the limited and personal antislavery position of orthodox Quakerism to the reform drive of abolitionism, was not so easily contained. She joined the Philadelphia Female Anti-Slavery Society, where she became better acquainted with Lucretia Mott, an adherent of the reform-minded Hicksite Quakers, who had successfully rebelled against the orthodox Friends.

Appalled by vitriolic attacks on William Lloyd Garrison and his associates, Angelina publicly endorsed abolitionism in an 1835 letter to the Boston *Liberator*. The Philadelphia orthodox deplored the publication of Angelina's views and her endorsement of a radical like Garrison. But enthusiastic support from other Quaker activists at the Friends Yearly Meeting in Providence, Rhode Island, dispelled whatever doubts the sisters had about the letter. Thus encouraged, they wrote a number of pamphlets for the nationwide abolitionist campaigns of the American Anti-Slavery Society (AASS). Angelina penned a widely read *Appeal to the Women of the South* (1836), which developed the parallels between the experiences of women and those of slaves. And Sarah produced an *Epistle to the Clergy of the Southern States* (1836) and an *Address to Free Colored Americans* (1837). Accepting the Anti-Slavery Society's invitation to visit New York, the Grimkés were immediately inundated with requests to speak of their South Carolina experiences, and they quickly accepted the many opportunities. Angelina and Sarah, who soon took part in an extensive and successful series of talks delivered to Female Anti-Slavery societies in the New York area, considered their writing and speaking in the best tradition of Quaker immortals such as George Fox and William Penn. But the sisters' activities distressed the Philadelphia Quaker overseers, who suggested that the Grimkés resign from the Meeting. Adhering to what they understood to be basic Friends' principles, both refused.

The Grimké sisters came into especially close contact with activist Quakers and evangelical reformers while in New York. The directorates of the great benevolent societies interlocked in New York City in the 1830's with those of the evangelical revivalists. Such philanthropists as Arthur and Lewis Tappan and such Midwestern reform revivalists as Theodore D. Weld, Charles G. Finney, and James G. Birney had abandoned the selective salvation, rituals, rationalism, and conservatism generally characteristic of American Protestantism.[14] They hoped to introduce some of the perfectionist impulses of the radical sectarian tradition into Presbyterianism and Congregationalism in particular. With Methodists, Baptists, and Hicksite Quakers, these philanthropists and revivalists preached the freedom of each human being to escape the bonds of original sin through a combination of good works and faith, and they acknowledged the power of disciplined human emotion as well as that of reason.

The philanthropists and revivalists took an equally moderate position toward social change. They argued that the abolition of slavery would eliminate the main deviation from the essential goodness of American society. Carrying their campaigns to sinners of many denominations, reform revivalists kept to that single main issue, slavery. They reached beyond orthodox Quaker restraints on perfectionism, but rarely far enough to incite or justify radical change.

Sarah and Angelina Grimké attended the AASS convention and participated in Theodore Weld's training of the Seventy, the agents who would carry abolitionism throughout the North with the same doctrines and by the same methods that the Great Revival had used to conquer the Midwest. Weld took special interest in the sisters' preparation. He prescribed an extensive reading program for the women, tutored them in standard antislavery arguments, coached the two in elements of public speaking, and refined their platform style. When their training ended, the sisters were more effective than many of Weld's male agents.

Invited to Boston in the spring of 1837, Angelina and Sarah opened a twenty-three week lecture tour at their own expense which took them to sixty-seven New England towns, exposed them to radical agitators, and provoked the writing and publication of the *Equality of the Sexes.* Maria Weston Chapman, secretary of the Boston Female Anti-Slavery Society, introduced the Grimkés to other New England abolitionist groups with the hope that the societies would "ask no one's sect, rank or color. Whosoever *will,* let them come."[15] For a woman to give formal public speeches to other women was novel enough, but the sisters went well beyond convention when they spoke to sexually mixed "promiscuous assemblies." These accomplished and genteel Southern women, whose description of slavery had an obvious authenticity, aroused a great deal of public curiosity. "One brother wanted to come and another thought he had a right, and now the door is wide open."[16] The more than 40,000 persons who came to hear the Grimkés accuse them of complicity in the sin of slavery helped to breach another barrier between the sexes. The sensational tour culminated in Angelina's three-day appearance in February 1838 before a committee of the Massachusetts legislature holding hearings on antislavery petitions. The Bostonians who crowded into the State House heard a moving attack on slavery, and for the first time in American history, a legislative body listened to a woman.

While in New England, the Grimké sisters came into contact with the radical agitators, whom they found more congenial abolitionists than the evangelical reformers.[17] There the Grimkés had easy access to the *Liberator* and its radical editor, William L. Garrison. Henry C. Wright, a radical agent of the AASS, escorted the Grimkés on the Massachusetts tour, exposed the sisters to the perfectionist theories of John Humphrey Noyes (later leader of the communitarian experiment at Oneida, New York), and discussed at length his belief in the equality of all persons without regard to race, sex, or age.

Considering slavery as only the worst evidence of a society relying on force rather than on love, agitators like Garrison and Wright supported a host of institutional and ideological changes that would have drastically altered the existing social order. The radicals argued that each human being was equally and individually responsible to do God's will as revealed in the Bible. They repudiated human governments for enforcing a group will upon the individual and substituting human for divine authority. When society established and government enforced racial and sexual inequalities, for example, they obstructed the essential relationships between the oppressed and the God to whom they were individually responsible. When a person surrendered to alcohol or submitted to the dictates of any church, he enslaved himself. The radicals were abolitionists, feminists, temperance supporters, anti-Sabbatarians, pacifists, nonresistants, and nonvoters; perfectionists, they believed in the ability of individuals to obey divine commands and therefore in their capability to base their social relationships on love from within rather than on coercion from without. Universal reform meant universal freedom on divine terms, and no single reform—not even abolition—could by itself achieve that result.

The Grimkés found the notions of Garrison, Noyes, and Wright so congenial to their own rampant individualism that Sarah integrated many of them into the feminist arguments of the *Equality of the Sexes*. Sarah found "in many respects a transcript of my heart" within the several issues of Noyes' *Perfectionist* which she read during the Massachusetts speaking tour. "Civil government, public worship, the ministry, the sabbath, and other points connected with religion have long been matters of enquiry and doubt, and . . . I can say with Milton 'We want new light and care not whence it comes; we want reformers worthy of the name; and we should rejoice in such a manifestation of Christianity, as would throw *all present* systems into obscurity.' "[18] The sisters had long viewed slavery, war, drink, and male chauvinism as similar forms of enslavement to sin. In Massachusetts the Grimkés spoke on "the peace question" to ladies' groups as well as addressing antislavery meetings, and when in New York, they had helped to form a temperance society. Sarah's thinking led her to agree with the radicals that "this sublime doctrine of acknowledging no government but God's, of loosing myself from all dominion of man both civil and ecclesiastical . . . is the only doctrine that can bring us into that liberty wherewith Christ hath made us free." She found indescribable "the blessed influence which my ultra peace principles have had upon my mind."[19]

More than any previous feminist writer, Sarah saw the subjugation of woman as only one—but *the first*—expression of the sin of slavery. Her Southern upbringing caused her to analyze slavery and feminine oppression as a unit. After visits to Lynn and Danvers, Massachusetts, Sarah was also implicitly able to recognize similarities between Southern chattel slavery and the wage slavery of women and children working in Northern mills and factories.

After briefly watching the radical abolitionists espouse one reform issue after another to build an increasingly broad, public attack upon American society, the defenders of the established order counterattacked. Advocates of African colonization, such as Catherine E. Beecher and the General Association of Congregational ministers in Massachusetts, attacked abolitionism at its weakest point—where reformers and radicals differed over the single- or multi-issue assault. They attacked feminist thought with the traditional Christian arguments for female subordination.

Catherine Beecher addressed *An Essay on Slavery and Abolitionism with Reference to the Duty of American Females* (1837) to Angelina Grimké. The *Essay,* an apology for the colonizationists, attacked women in political life, whether in female antislavery societies or circulating petitions for abolition, as well as any feminine influence outside the family circle. The Congregational ministers aimed their blast at both sisters in a famous pastoral letter which maintained that the duties and influence of women should be "unobtrusive and private," in keeping with the teachings of the New Testament. When woman "assumes the place and tone of man as a public reformer, . . . she yields the power which God has given her for protection, and her character becomes unnatural."[20] The ministers, for the most part supporters of colonization, had passed an antiabolitionist resolution in 1836 and found appalling the idea of female abolitionists' lecturing publicly to mixed audiences.

The New York-based AASS executives responded to the mounting attack by affirming support of single-issue reform. They sought only the abolition of slavery and deplored agent Henry C. Wright's columns in Garrison's *Liberator,* in which he associated abolitionism with what they considered peripheral and objectionable issues, such as no-government, nonresistance, and feminism. And they particularly rebelled against having two of their most successful speakers, the Grimké sisters, explicitly affiliated with these ideas. Thus, much to the displeasure of Sarah and

Angelina, the AASS quietly moved Wright's agency from Massachusetts to Pennsylvania and tried to dampen the public expressions of other radical abolitionists.

Both Theodore Weld, who exerted a continuing influence on the Grimkés through an extensive correspondence, and John Greenleaf Whittier, the Quaker abolitionist poet, counselled the sisters to practice feminism without preaching it.[21] They argued that the Grimkés' open espousal of woman's rights would detract from the abolition movement. Unlike many of the AASS leaders, neither Weld nor Whittier were antifeminist. Indeed Weld had encouraged women to preach when he was part of revivalist Albert Finney's Holy Band, and Whittier had attacked the pastoral letter scathingly in a poem applauding "Carolina's high-souled daughters." But both feared that the drift to universal reform or radicalism would sacrifice crucial public support for abolition and doom even moderate change.

The Grimké sisters felt that respecting the conventional role assigned to women could not contribute significantly to the abolition of anyone's slavery. They found the radical's linkage of the various reform doctrines too compelling for them to divorce one from another. Failure to meet conservative challenges in public debate, the sisters decided, would only result in a slow strangulation as the noose of social convention slipped gradually tighter and denied them access to public forums. Thus Angelina's *Letters to Catherine E. Beecher* responded at length to Beecher's attacks on abolition and briefly to her antifeminist arguments as well.[22] But Sarah undertook the full-scale discussion of the sisters' feminist convictions in the *Equality of the Sexes*. Each of these works, sharpened by the often stormy correspondence between Weld and the sisters, appeared in 1837 as a series of letters in Boston newspapers and were reprinted in book form in 1838.

The assault from without and the debates within abolitionism shook the movement into factions that increasingly attacked each other over the woman question. The sisters' stand and Sarah's *Equality of the Sexes* in particular helped to fuel the growing divisions. Not all of the arguments, however, caused dissension. Indeed, the sometimes bitter but determinedly honest exchange between Angelina and Theodore Weld led to their marriage and took the sisters away from the barricades. The Weld wedding brought leading radicals and reformers, blacks and whites, men and women together in peace, if only briefly, in May 1838. Those assembled witnessed a ceremony performed without benefit of clergy in which Weld renounced his legal rights over his wife's person and property and Angelina omitted the usual vow to obey her husband. Shortly thereafter the

Philadelphia Friends Meeting formally dismissed the Grimké sisters from membership—Angelina for marrying a non-Quaker and Sarah for attending the wedding. But Quakerism was not the only chapter closed in the sisters' lives, for the reform schism and nineteenth-century marriage gradually ended their public careers as well.

Considering such institutions divinely ordained, the sisters never attacked marriage, motherhood, or housewifery. Indeed Sarah had argued in the *Equality of the Sexes* that moral and intellectual equality enhanced rather than detracted from woman's abilities to fulfill traditional feminine "obligations" or "duties." "Let us remember," she advised her readers, "that our claim to stand on perfect equality with our brethren can only be substantiated by a scrupulous attention to our domestic duties." Daughters of wealth, the Grimkés had never had any housekeeping experience. But both were anxious to prove that public lecturing did not leave women unfit for domestic life and that they could keep house without outside help. To prevent Angelina's marriage and motherhood from drawing their energies away from matters of mind and soul to mundane concerns, the sisters kept a starkly simple house and dressed plainly, later in the Bloomer costume. For "emancipation of women from the toils of the kitchen," they adopted the plain, efficient health diet of Sylvester Graham, which was consistent with their own advice on cooking simply.[23] Yet with a meager income, with Angelina debilitated from successive pregnancies and ensuing complications, and with both sisters occupied with the Weld children, the women found it increasingly difficult to rise above physical needs and nearly impossible to work alongside Weld in public reform activities. As the Grimkés learned, it took something more than individual will power and domestic reform for the housewife and mother of moderate means to put feminism into effective practice in rural nineteenth-century America, given the existing state of medical and industrial development.

During the Welds' early married years and later when they and Sarah ran the school at the Raritan Bay Union, a Fourierist-inclined community, the sisters maintained their interest in and their ties with various reform movements. They also watched in dismay as the evangelical reformers split with the radical agitators in 1840 over whether to allow Abigail Kelley, an abolitionist-feminist directly inspired by the Grimkés, to assume a seat on an AASS national committee. And they regretted that as a result abolitionism was henceforth divided into two national organizations.

The abolitionists could not agree upon a multidimensional reform movement. The mid-nineteenth-century feminists, like latter-day feminists, agonized over which reform was most important to them. When forced to choose, the Grimké sisters put abolitionism before feminism. Sarah had described woman's position in terms of slavery on many occasions. But she "did not wish to intimate that the condition of free women can be compared to that of slaves in suffering or in degradation." The sisters therefore gave what little time they could to abolitionism, although they never conceded their feminist interests altogether. Their quandary over the great moral schism consumed important energy and further muted their reform activities.

Henry Stanton brought his new wife, Elizabeth Cady, on a long visit to the Weld-Grimké household before they sailed to London for the World Anti-Slavery Convention. The sisters learned from Mrs. Stanton's letters how women delegates had been barred from the convention and that female abolitionists planned to launch a separate woman's rights movement on their return to the United States. Mrs. Stanton also reported that the *Equality of the Sexes* was widely read in England.[24]

Sarah and Angelina supported the nascent woman's rights movement. Both attended various conventions, sent letters or addresses to be read, served on committees, and gave their names and at least moral support for the various projects that the feminists espoused. Their support elicited praise from, among others, Lucy Stone, Susan B. Anthony, and Harriet Kezia Hunt, America's first woman medical practitioner.

No longer considered merely a radical fanatic but rather commended as a pioneer in the struggle for equal rights for blacks and women, Sarah Grimké continued to act upon her convictions. In her seventy-eighth year, she and Angelina led a group of suffragists and their escorts through driving snow to a local polling place and in a symbolic gesture deposited their ballots in a specially prepared box. At seventy-nine, she peddled 150 copies of John Stuart Mills' *Subjection of Women* door to door. Appropriately eulogized at her funeral by the radical Garrison, Sarah had witnessed the abolition of slavery without the establishment of racial equality. She had also lived to see the issue of woman's rights raised, although the fourteenth amendment to ensure due process for black Americans wrote sexual discrimination into the federal constitution for the first time. In thought and action—on the lecture platform; in newspaper columns, pamphlets, and longer treatises; and within the confines of the Weld-Grimké household—Sarah Grimké helped to construct a feminism from the highly individualistic radical sectarian strains of Anglo-American Protestantism, and she lived out many of the perfectionist implications. "All I ask of our brethren," Sarah wrote, "is that they will take their feet from off our necks and permit us to stand upright on the ground which God designed us to occupy."

NOTES

1. Sarah M. Grimké, *Letters on the Equality of the Sexes, and the Condition of Woman* (Boston: Isaac Knapp, 1838; reissued in 1970 by Source Book Press, New York).

2. David Brion Davis, *Problems of Slavery in Western Culture* (Ithaca: Cornell University Press, 1966), 31, 92, 118, 188, 201, 298, 335, 338. For a well-documented, sensitive analysis of the interrelatedness of slavery and patriarchy in the antebellum American South, see Anne Firor Scott, *The Southern Lady from Pedestal to Politics, 1830–1930* (Chicago: University of Chicago Press, 1970), 4–79.

3. Gerda Lerner, *The Grimké Sisters from South Carolina: Pioneers for Woman's Rights and Abolition* (New York: Schocken Books, 1971 reissue of 1967 edition), offers the best modern biography from which much of the narrative information about the Grimkés was taken for this essay.

4. William R. Taylor, *Cavalier and Yankee: The Old South and American National Character* (London: W. H. Allen, 1963), 55–65, developed the theme of the social and political displacement of established, tidewater, and Enlightenment planters like the Grimkés, whom he labelled Southern mugwumps.

5. Quoted in Lerner, *Grimké Sisters,* 320.

6. Quoted in Catherine H. Birney, *The Grimké Sisters—Sarah and Angelina Grimké—the First American Women Advocates of Abolition and Woman's Rights* (Boston: Lee and Shepard Publishers, 1885), 38.

7. Sir William Blackstone, an ultraconservative English legal scholar who systematized the common law and provided it with a rational foundation, sealed woman's subordination in the law. For a study of Blackstone's influence upon woman's situation and the feminists' response to it, see Mary R. Beard, *Woman as Force in History: A Study in Traditions and Realities* (New York: Collier Books, 1962 reissue of 1946 edition).

8. Quoted in Lerner, *Grimké Sisters,* 57.

9. See Davis, *Slavery in Western Culture,* 483–493.

10. Quoted in Winthrop D. Jordan, *White over Black: American Attitudes toward the Negro, 1550–1812* (Chapel Hill: University of North Carolina Press, 1968), 273.

11. This discussion of Quakerism and the sectarian tradition is indebted to Davis, *Slavery in Western Culture,* 291–332, and Jordan, *White over Black,* 271–280, 356–365.

12. For Quaker restraint on the perfectionist impulse, see Davis, *Slavery in Western Culture,* 299–306.

13. Gilbert H. Barnes and Dwight L. Dumond (eds.), *Letters of Theodore Dwight Weld, Angelina Grimké Weld, and Sarah Grimké, 1822–1844* (2

volumes, Gloucester, Massachusetts: Peter Smith, 1965 reissue of 1934 edition), I, 429.

14. Fuller discussions of evangelical thought, benevolence, and reform activity can be found in Davis, *Slavery in Western Culture,* 382–390, and Gilbert H. Barnes, *The Anti-Slavery Impulse, 1830–1844* (New York: Harcourt, Brace & World, Inc., 1964 reissue with a new introduction of the 1933 edition). Barnes' sympathy for the evangelicals unfortunately prejudices his discussion of the radical agitators.

15. Barnes & Dumond, *Weld-Grimké Letters,* I, 397.

16. Barnes & Dumond, *Weld-Grimké Letters,* I, 410.

17. For a more extended analysis of the radical agitators, see Aileen S. Kraditor, *Means and Ends in American Abolitionism: Garrison and His Critics on Strategy and Tactics, 1834–1850* (New York: Random House, Inc., 1970).

18. Barnes & Dumond, *Weld-Grimké Letters,* I, 402.

19. Barnes & Dumond, *Weld-Grimké Letters,* I, 408.

20. Excerpts from the pastoral letter may be found in Aileen S. Kraditor, (ed.), *Up from the Pedestal: Selected Writings in the History of American Feminism* (Chicago: Quadrangle Books, Inc., 1968), 50–52.

21. Much of this correspondence can be found in Barnes & Dumond, *Weld-Grimké Letters,* I, 386–510.

22. Excerpts from the feminist portions of Angelina's rejoinder to Beecher are reprinted in Kraditor, *Up From the Pedestal,* 58–66.

23. Sarah Grimké, as quoted in Birney, *Grimké Sisters,* 245–246.

24. Eleanor Flexner, *Century of Struggle: The Woman's Rights Movement in the United States* (New York: Atheneum, 1968 reissue of 1959 edition), 344.

LETTERS ON THE EQUALITY OF THE SEXES, AND THE CONDITION OF WOMAN (1837–1838)

I. THE ORIGINAL EQUALITY OF WOMAN.*

In attempting to give my views on the Province of Woman, I feel that I am venturing on nearly untrodden ground and that I shall advance arguments in opposition to a corrupt public opinion and to the perverted interpretation of Holy Writ which has so universally obtained. But I am in search of truth; and no obstacle shall prevent my prosecuting that search because I believe the welfare of the world will be materially advanced by every new discovery we make of the designs of Jehovah in the creation of woman. It is impossible that we can answer the purpose of our being unless we understand that purpose. It is impossible that we should fulfill our duties unless we comprehend them or live up to our privileges unless we know what they are.

In examining this important subject, I shall depend solely on the Bible to designate the sphere of woman because I believe almost everything that has been written on this subject has been the result of a misconception of the simple truths revealed in the Scriptures, in consequence of the false translation of many passages of Holy Writ. My mind is entirely delivered from the superstitious reverence which is attached to the English version of the Bible. King James's translators certainly were not inspired. I therefore claim the original as my standard, *believing that to have been inspired,* and I also claim to judge for myself what is the meaning of the inspired writers because I believe it to be the solemn duty of every individual to search the Scriptures for themselves, with the aid of the Holy Spirit, and not be governed by the views of any man or set of men.

We must first view woman at the period of her creation. "And God said, Let us make man in our own image, after our likeness; and let them have dominion over the fish of the sea,

* The date, salutation, complimentary close, and signature of each letter have been omitted without further editorial notation.

and over the fowl of the air, and over the cattle, and over all the earth, and over every creeping thing that creepeth upon the earth. So God created man in his own image, in the image of God created he him, male and female created he them." In all this sublime description of the creation of man (which is a generic term including man and woman), there is not one particle of difference intimated as existing between them. They were both made in the image of God; dominion was given to both over every other creature but not over each other. Created in perfect equality, they were expected to exercise the vicegerence intrusted to them by their Maker in harmony and love.

Let us pass on now to the recapitulation of the creation of man. "The Lord God formed man of the dust of the ground, and breathed into his nostrils the breath of life; and man became a living soul. And the Lord God said, it is not good that man should be alone, I will make him an helpmeet for him." All creation swarmed with animated beings capable of natural affection, as we know they still are; it was not, therefore, merely to give man a creature susceptible of loving, obeying, and looking up to him, for all that the animals could do and did do. It was to give him a companion, *in all respects* his equal: one who was like himself *a free agent,* gifted with intellect and endowed with immortality, not a partaker merely of his animal gratifications but able to enter into all his feelings as a moral and responsible being. If this had not been the case, how could she have been an helpmeet for him? I understand this as applying not only to the parties entering into the marriage contract but to all men and women because I believe God designed woman to be an helpmeet for man in every good and perfect work. She was a part of himself, as if Jehovah designed to make the oneness and identity of man and woman perfect and complete; and when the glorious work of their creation was finished, "the morning stars sang together, and all the sons of God shouted for joy."

This blissful condition was not long enjoyed by our first parents. Eve, it would seem from the history, was wandering alone amid the bowers of Paradise when the serpent met with her. From her reply to Satan, it is evident that the command not to eat "of the tree that is in the midst of the garden" was given to both, although the term man was used when the prohibition was issued by God. "And the woman said unto the serpent, WE may eat of the fruit of the trees of the garden, but of the fruit of the tree which is in the midst of the garden, God hath said, YE shall not eat of it, neither shall YE touch it, lest YE die." Here the woman was exposed to temptation from a being with whom she was unacquainted. She had been accustomed to associate with her beloved partner and to hold communion with God and with angels, but of satanic intelligence she was in all probability entirely ignorant. Through the subtlety of the serpent, she was beguiled. And "when she saw that the tree was good for food, and that it was pleasant to the eyes, and a tree to be desired to make one wise, she took of the fruit thereof and did eat."

We next find Adam involved in the same sin, not through the instrumentality of a supernatural agent but through that of his equal, a being whom he must have known was liable to transgress the divine command because he must have felt that he was himself a free agent and that he was restrained from disobedience only by the exercise of faith and love towards his Creator. Had Adam tenderly reproved his wife and endeavored to lead her to repentance instead of sharing in her guilt, I should be much more ready to accord to man that superiority which he claims; but as the facts stand disclosed by the sacred historian, it appears to me that, to say the least, there was as much weakness exhibited by Adam as by Eve. They both fell from innocence and consequently from happiness, *but not from equality*.

Let us next examine the conduct of this fallen pair when Jehovah interrogated them respecting their fault. They both frankly confessed their guilt. "The man said, 'the woman whom thou gavest to be with me, she gave me of the tree and

I did eat.' And the woman said, 'the serpent beguiled me and I did eat.' And the Lord God said unto the woman, 'Thou wilt be subject unto thy husband, and he will rule over thee.'" That this did not allude to the subjection of woman to man is manifest, because the same mode of expression is used in speaking to Cain of Abel. The truth is that the curse, as it is termed, which was pronounced by Jehovah upon woman is a simple prophecy. The Hebrew, like the French language, uses the same word to express shall and will. Our translators, having been accustomed to exercise lordship over their wives and seeing only through the medium of a perverted judgment, very naturally, though I think not very learnedly or very kindly, translated it *shall* instead of *will* and thus converted a prediction to Eve into a command to Adam; for observe, it is addressed to the woman and not to the man. The consequence of the fall was an immediate struggle for dominion, and Jehovah foretold which would gain the ascendency; but as he created them in his image, as that image manifestly was not lost by the fall, . . . there is no reason to suppose that sin produced any distinction between them as moral, intellectual and responsible beings. . . .

Here then I plant myself. God created us equal; He created us free agents; He is our Lawgiver, our King and our Judge, and to Him alone is woman bound to be in subjection, and to Him alone is she accountable for the use of those talents with which her Heavenly Father has entrusted her. One is her Master even Christ.

II. WOMAN SUBJECT ONLY TO GOD.

. . . Adam's ready acquiescence with his wife's proposal does not savor much of that superiority *in strength of mind* which is arrogated by man. Even admitting that Eve was the greater sinner, it seems to me man might be satisfied with the dominion he has claimed and exercised for nearly six thousand years and that more true nobility would be manifested by endeavoring to raise the fallen and invigorate the weak than by keeping woman in subjection. But I ask no favors for my sex. I surrender not our claim to equality. All I ask of our brethren is that they will take their feet from off our necks and permit us to stand upright on that ground which God designed us to occupy. If he has not given us the rights which have, as I conceive, been wrested from us, we shall soon give evidence of our inferiority and shrink back into that obscurity which the high-souled magnanimity of man has assigned us as our appropriate sphere.

As I am unable to learn from sacred writ when woman was deprived by God of her equality with man, I shall touch upon a few points in the Scriptures which demonstrate that no supremacy was granted to man. When God had destroyed the world, except Noah and his family, by the deluge, He renewed the grant formerly made to man and again gave him dominion over every beast of the earth, every fowl of the air, over all that moveth upon the earth, and over all the fishes of the sea; into his hands they were delivered. But was woman, bearing the image of her God, placed under the dominion of her fellowman? Never! Jehovah could not surrender his authority to govern his own immortal creatures into the hands of a being whom He knew, and whom his whole history proved, to be unworthy of a trust so sacred and important. God could not do it because it is a direct contravention of his law, "Thou shalt worship the Lord thy God, and *him only* shalt thou serve." If Jehovah had appointed man as the guardian or teacher of woman, He would certainly have given some intimation of this surrender of his own prerogative. But so far from it, we find the commands of God invariably the same to man and woman; and not the slightest intimation is given in a single passage of the Bible that God designed to point woman to man as her instructor. The tenor of his language always is, "Look unto ME, and be ye saved, all the ends of the earth, for I am God, and there is none else."

The lust of dominion was probably the first effect of the fall, and as there was no other intelligent being over whom to exercise it, woman was the first victim of this unhallowed passion. We afterwards see it exhibited by Cain in the murder of his brother, by Nimrod in his becoming a mighty hunter of men and setting up a kingdom over which to reign. Here we see the origin of . . . slavery, which sprang up immediately after the fall and has spread its pestilential branches over the whole face of the known world. All history attests that man has subjected woman to his will, used her as a means to promote his selfish gratification, to minister to his sensual pleasures, to be instrumental in promoting his comfort; but never has he desired to elevate her to that rank she was created to fill. He has done all he could to debase and enslave her mind, and now he looks triumphantly on the ruin he has wrought and says the being he has thus deeply injured is his inferior.

Woman has been placed by John Quincy Adams side by side with the slave whilst he was contending for the right side of petition. I thank him for ranking us with the oppressed, for . . . in all ages and countries, not even excepting enlightened republican America, woman has more or less been made a *means* to promote the welfare of man, without due regard to her own happiness and the glory of God as the end of her creation.

During the *patriarchal* ages we find men and women engaged in the same employments. Abraham and Sarah both assisted in preparing the food which was to be set before the three men who visited them in the plains of Mamre; but although their occupations were similar, Sarah was not permitted to enjoy the society of the holy visitant; and as we learn from Peter that she "obeyed Abraham, calling him Lord," we may presume he exercised dominion over her. We shall pass on now to Rebecca. In her history we find another striking illustration of the low estimation in which woman was held. Eleazur is sent to seek a wife for Isaac. He finds Rebecca going down to the well to fill her pitcher. He accosts her, and she replies with all humility, "Drink, my lord." How does he endeavor to gain her favor and confidence? Does he approach her as a dignified creature whom he was about to invite to fill an important station in his master's family as the wife of his only son? No. He offered incense to her vanity, and "he took a golden earring of half a shekel weight, and two bracelets for her hands of ten shekels weight of gold" and gave them to Rebecca.

The cupidity of man soon led him to regard woman as property, and hence we find them sold to those who wished to marry them. . . . That women were a profitable kind of property we may gather from the description of a virtuous woman in the last chapter of Proverbs. To work willingly with her hands, to open her hands to the poor, to clothe herself with silk and purple, to look well to her household, to make fine linen and sell it, to deliver girdles to the merchant, and not to eat the bread of idleness seems to have constituted in the view of Solomon the perfection of a woman's character and achievements. . . .

III. THE PASTORAL LETTER OF THE GENERAL ASSOCIATION OF CONGREGATIONAL MINISTERS OF MASSACHUSETTS.

. . . I am persuaded that when the minds of men and women become emancipated from the thraldom of superstition and "traditions of men," the sentiments contained in the Pastoral Letter will be [referred] . . . to with as much astonishment as the opinions of Cotton Mather and other distinguished men of his day on the subject of witchcraft; nor will it be deemed less wonderful that a body of divines should gravely assemble and endeavor to prove that woman has no right to "open her mouth for the dumb" than it now is that judges should have sat on the trials of witches and solemnly condemned nineteen persons and one dog to death for witchcraft.

But to the letter. It says, "We invite your attention to the dangers which at present seem to threaten the FEMALE CHARACTER with widespread and permanent injury." I rejoice that they have called the attention of my sex to this subject because I believe if woman investigates it, she will soon discover that danger is impending, though from a totally different source from that which the Association apprehends—danger from those who, having long held the reins of *usurped* authority, are unwilling to permit us to fill that sphere which God created us to move in and who have entered into league to crush the immortal mind of woman. I rejoice because I am persuaded that the rights of woman, like the rights of slaves, need only be examined to be understood and asserted, even by some of those who are now endeavoring to smother the irrepressible desire for mental and spiritual freedom which glows in the breast of many who hardly dare to speak their sentiments.

"The appropriate duties and influence of women are clearly stated in the New Testament. Those duties are unobtrusive and private, but the sources of *mighty power*. When the mild, *dependent,* softening influence of woman upon the sternness of man's opinions is fully exercised, society feels the effects of it in a thousand ways." No one can desire more earnestly than I do that woman may move exactly in the sphere which her Creator has assigned her, and I believe her having been displaced from that sphere has introduced confusion into the world. It is therefore of vast importance to herself and to all the rational creation that she should ascertain what are her duties and her privileges as a responsible and immortal being. The New Testament has been referred to, and I am willing to abide by its decisions but must enter my protest against the false translation of some passages by the MEN who did that work and against the perverted interpretation by the MEN who undertook to write commentaries thereon. I am inclined to think [that] when we are admitted to the honor of studying Greek and Hebrew, we shall produce some various readings of the Bible a little different from those we now have.

The Lord Jesus defines the duties of his followers in his Sermon on the Mount. He lays down grand principles by which they should be governed, without any reference to sex or condition. "Ye are the light of the world. A city that is set on a hill cannot be hid. Neither do men light a candle and put it under a bushel, but on a candlestick, and it giveth light unto all that are in the house. Let your light so shine before men, that they may see your good works, and glorify your Father which is in Heaven." I follow him through all his precepts and find him giving the same directions to women as to men, never even referring to the distinction now so strenuously insisted upon between masculine and feminine virtues: This is one of the anti-Christian "traditions of men" which are taught instead of the "commandments of God." Men and women were CREATED EQUAL; they are both moral and accountable beings, and whatever is *right* for man to do is *right* for woman.

But the influence of woman, says the Association, is to be private and unobtrusive; her light is not to shine before man like that of her brethren; but she is passively to let the lords of the creation, as they call themselves, put the bushel over it, lest peradventure it might appear that the world has been benefited by the rays of *her* candle. So that her quenched light, according to their judgment, will be of more use than if it were set on the candlestick. "Her influence is the source of mighty power." This has ever been the flattering language of man since he laid aside the whip as a means to keep woman in subjection. He spares her body, but the war he has waged against her mind, her heart, and her soul has been no less destructive to her as a moral being. How monstrous, how anti-Christian is the doctrine that woman is to be dependent on man! Where in all the sacred Scriptures is this taught? Alas, she has too well learned the lesson which MAN has labored to teach her! She has surrendered her dearest RIGHTS and been satisfied with the privileges which man has assumed to grant her; she has been amused with the show of power, whilst man has absorbed all the reality into himself. He has adorned the creature whom God gave him as a companion with baubles and gewgaws, turned her attention to personal attractions, offered incense to her vanity, and made her the instrument of his selfish gratification, a plaything to please his eye and amuse his hours of leisure. "Rule by obedience and by submission sway"; or, in other words, study to be a hypocrite, pretend to submit, but gain your point has been the code of household morality which woman has been taught. The poet has sung in sickly strains the loveliness of woman's dependence upon man, and now we find it re-echoed by those who profess to teach the religion of the Bible. God says, "Cease ye from man, whose breath is in his nostrils, for wherein is he to be accounted of?" Man says, depend upon me. God says, "HE will teach us of his ways." Man says, believe it not; I am to be your teacher. This doctrine of dependence upon man is utterly at variance with the doctrine of the Bible. In that book I find nothing like the softness of woman nor the sternness of man: Both are equally commanded to bring forth the fruits of the Spirit—love, meekness, gentleness, &c.

But we are told, "The power of woman is in her dependence, flowing from a consciousness of that weakness which God has given her for her protection." If physical weakness is alluded to, I cheerfully concede the superiority; if brute force is what my brethren are claiming, I am willing to let them have all the honor they desire; but if they mean to intimate that mental or moral weakness belongs to woman more than to man, I utterly disclaim the charge. Our powers of mind have been crushed as far as man could do it; our sense of morality has been impaired by his interpretation of our duties; but nowhere does God say that he made any distinction between us as moral and intelligent beings.

"We appreciate," say the Association, "the *unostentatious* prayers and efforts of woman in advancing the cause of religion at home and abroad, in leading religious inquirers TO THE PASTOR for instruction." Several points here demand attention. If public prayers and public efforts are necessarily ostentatious, then "Anna the prophetess (or preacher), who departed not from the temple, but served God with fastings and prayers night and day . . . and spake of Christ to all them that looked for redemption in Israel," was ostentatious in her efforts. Then the apostle Paul encourages women to be ostentatious in their efforts to spread the gospel when he gives them directions how they should appear when engaged in praying or preaching in the public assemblies. . . .

But woman may be permitted to lead religious inquirers to the PASTORS for instruction. Now this is assuming that all pastors are better qualified to give instruction than woman. This I utterly deny. I have suffered too keenly from the teaching of man to lead anyone to him for instruction. The Lord Jesus says, "Come unto me and learn of me." He points his followers to no man; and when woman is made the favored instrument of rousing a sinner to his lost and helpless condition, she has no right to substitute any teacher for Christ; all she has to do is to turn the contrite inquirer to the "Lamb of God which taketh away the sins of the world." More souls have probably been lost by going down to Egypt for help and by trusting in man in the early stages of religious experience than by any other error. Instead of the petition being offered to God, . . . the young convert is directed to go to man, as if he were in the place of God and his instructions essential to an advancement in the path of righteousness. . . . The business of men and women, who are ORDAINED OF GOD to preach the unsearchable riches of Christ to a lost and perishing world, is to lead souls to Christ and not to pastors for instruction.

The General Association say that "when woman assumes the place and tone of man as a public reformer, our care and protection of her seem unnecessary; we put ourselves in self-defence against her, and her character becomes unnatural." Here again the unscriptural notion is held up that there is a distinction between the duties of men and women as moral beings, that what is virtue in man is vice in woman, and women who dare to obey the command of Jehovah, "Cry aloud, spare not, lift up thy voice like a trumpet, and show my people their transgression," are threatened with having the protection of the brethren withdrawn. If this is all they do, we shall not even know the time when our chastisement is inflicted; our trust is in the Lord Jehovah, and in him is everlasting strength. The motto of woman when she is engaged in the great work of public reformation should be, "The Lord is my light and my salvation; whom shall I fear? The Lord is the strength of my life; of whom shall I be afraid?" She must feel, if she feels rightly, that she is fulfilling one of the important duties laid upon her as an accountable being and that her character, instead of being "unnatural," is in exact accordance with the will of Him to whom, and to no other, she is responsible for the talents and the gifts confided to her. As to the pretty simile introduced into the Pastoral Letter —"If the vine whose strength and beauty is to lean upon the trellis work and half conceal its clusters thinks to assume the independence and the overshadowing nature of the elm," etc.—I shall only remark that it might well suit the poet's fancy who sings of sparkling eyes and coral lips and knights in armor clad; but it seems to me utterly inconsistent with the dignity of a Christian body to endeavor to draw such an antiscriptural distinction between men and women. Ah, how many of my sex feel in the dominion thus unrighteously exercised over them under the gentle appellation of *protection* that what they have leaned upon has proved a broken reed at best and oft a spear!

IV. SOCIAL INTERCOURSE OF THE SEXES.

. . . We approach each other and mingle with each other under the constant pressure of a feeling that we are of different sexes; and instead of regarding each other only in the light of immortal creatures, the mind is fettered by the idea, which is early and industriously infused into it, that we must never forget the distinction between male and female. Hence our intercourse, instead of being elevated and refined, is generally calculated to excite and keep alive the lowest propensities of our nature. Nothing, I believe, has tended more to destroy the true dignity of woman than the fact that she is approached by man in the character of a female. The idea that she is sought as an intelligent and heaven-born creature whose society will cheer, refine and elevate her companion, and that she will receive the same blessings she confers is rarely held up to her view. On the contrary, man almost always addresses himself to the weakness of woman. By flattery, by an appeal to her passions, he seeks access to her heart; and when he has gained her affections, he uses her as the instrument of his pleasure—the minister of his temporal comfort. He furnishes himself with a housekeeper, whose chief business is in the kitchen or the nursery. And whilst he goes abroad and enjoys the means of improvement afforded by collision of intellect with cultivated minds, his wife is condemned to draw nearly all her instruction from books, if she has time to peruse them, and if not, from her meditations whilst engaged in those domestic duties which are necessary for the comfort of her lord and master.

Surely no one who contemplates with the eye of a Christian philosopher the design of God in the creation of woman can believe that she is now fulfilling that design. The literal translation of the word "helpmeet" is a helper like unto himself; it is so rendered in the Septuagint and manifestly signifies a companion. Now I believe it will be impossible for woman to fill the station assigned her by God until her brethren mingle with her as an equal, as a moral being, and lose, in the dignity of her immortal nature and in the fact of her bearing like himself the image and superscription of her God, the idea of her being a female. The apostle beautifully remarks, "As many of you as have been baptized into Christ, have put on Christ. There is neither Jew nor Greek, there is neither bond nor free, there is neither *male* nor *female;* for ye are all one in Christ Jesus." Until our intercourse is purified by the forgetfulness of sex, until we rise above the present low and sordid views which entwine themselves around our social and domestic interchange of sentiment and feelings, we never can derive that benefit from each other's society which it is the design of our Creator that we should. Man has inflicted an unspeakable injury upon woman by holding up to her view her animal nature and placing in the background her moral and intellectual being. Woman has inflicted an injury upon herself by submitting to be thus regarded; and she is now called upon to rise from the station where *man*, not God, has placed her and claim those sacred and inalienable rights, as a moral and responsible being, with which her Creator has invested her.

What but these views so derogatory to the character of woman could have called forth the remark contained in the Pastoral Letter? "We especially deplore the intimate acquaintance and promiscuous conversation of *females* with regard to things 'which ought not to be named,' by which that modesty and delicacy, which is the charm of domestic life and which constitutes the true influence of woman, is consumed." How wonderful that the conceptions of man relative to woman are so low that he cannot perceive that she may converse on any subject connected with the improvement of her species without swerving in the least from that modesty which is one of her greatest virtues! Is it designed to insinuate that woman should possess a greater degree of modesty than man? This idea I utterly reprobate. Or is it supposed that woman cannot go into scenes of misery, the necessary result of those very things which the Pastoral Letter says ought not to be named, for the purpose of moral reform without becoming contaminated by those with whom she thus mingles?

This is a false position and I presume has grown out of the never-forgotten distinction of male and female. The woman who goes forth, clad in the panoply of God, to stem the tide of iniquity and misery which she beholds rolling through our land goes not forth to her labor of love as a female. She goes as the dignified messenger of Jehovah, and all she does and says must be done and said irrespective of sex. She is in duty bound to communicate with all who are able and willing to aid her in saving her fellow-creatures, both men and women, from that destruction which awaits them.

So far from woman losing anything of the purity of her mind by visiting the wretched victims of vice in their miserable abodes, by talking with them or of them, she becomes more and more elevated and refined in her feelings and views. While laboring to cleanse the minds of others from the malaria of moral pollution, her own heart becomes purified and her soul rises to nearer communion with her God. Such a woman is infinitely better qualified to fulfill the duties of a wife and a mother than the woman whose *false delicacy* leads her to shun her fallen sister and brother and shrink from *naming those sins* which she knows exist but which she is too fastidious to labor by deed and by word to exterminate. Such a woman feels, when she enters upon the marriage relation, that God designed that relation not to debase her to a level with the animal creation but to increase the happiness and dignity of his creatures. Such a woman comes to the important task of training her children in the nurture and admonition of the Lord with a soul filled with the greatness of the beings committed to her charge. She sees in her children creatures bearing the image of God; and she approaches them with reverence and treats them at all times as moral and accountable beings. . . .

VII. CONDITION IN SOME PARTS OF . . . AMERICA.

. . . The heathen philosophers doubtless wished to keep woman in her *"appropriate sphere"*; and we find our clerical brethren of the present day re-echoing these pagan sentiments and endeavoring to drive woman from the field of moral labor and intellectual culture to occupy her talents in the pursuit of those employments which will enable her to regale the palate of her lord with the delicacies of the table and in every possible way minister to his animal comfort and gratification. In my humble opinion, woman has long enough subserved the interests of man, and in the spirit of self-sacrifice submitted almost without remonstrance to his oppression; and now that her attention is solicited to the subject of her rights, her privileges and her duties, I would entreat her to double her diligence in the performance of all her obligations as a *wife*, a *mother*, a *sister*, and a *daughter*. Let us remember that our claim to stand on perfect equality with our brethren can only be substantiated by a scrupulous attention to our domestic duties as well as by aiding in the great work of moral reformation—a work which is now calling for the energies and consecrated powers of every man and woman who desires to see the Redeemer's kingdom established on earth. That man must indeed be narrow-minded and can have but a poor conception of the power of moral truth on the female heart who supposes that a correct view of her own rights can make woman *less solicitous to fill up every department of duty*. If it should have this effect, it must be because she has not taken a comprehensive view of the whole subject.

. . . A new and vast sphere of usefulness is opened to her, and she is pressed by surrounding circumstances to come up to the help of the Lord against the giant sins which desolate our beloved country. Shall woman shrink from duty in this exigency and, retiring within her own domestic circle, delight herself in the abundance of her own selfish enjoyments? Shall she rejoice in her home, her husband, her children, and forget her brethren and sisters in bondage, who know not what it is to call a spot of earth their own, whose husbands and wives are torn from them by relentless tyrants and whose children are snatched from their arms by their unfeeling task-masters whenever interest, or convenience, tempts them to this sacrilegious act? Shall woman disregard the situation of thousands of her fellow-creatures who are the victims of intemperance and licentiousness and, retreating to the privacy of her own comfortable home, be satisfied that her whole duty is performed when she can exhibit "her children well clad and smiling and her table neatly spread with wholesome provisions?" Shall she, because "her house is her *home*," refuse her aid and her sympathy to the down-trodden slave, to the poor, unhappy outcasts who are deprived of those blessings which she so highly prizes? Did God give her those blessings to steel her heart to the sufferings of her fellow-creatures? Did He grant her the possession of husband and children to dry up the fountains of feeling for those who know not the consolations of tenderness and reciprocal affection? Ah no! For every such blessing, God demands a grateful heart; and woman must be recreant to her duty if she can quietly sit down in the enjoyments of her own domestic circle and not exert herself to procure the same happiness for others. . . .

The page of history teems with woman's wrongs, and it is wet with woman's tears. For the sake of my degraded sex everywhere and for the sake of my brethren who suffer just in proportion as they place woman lower in the scale of creation than man, lower than her Creator placed her, I entreat my sisters to arise in all the majesty of moral power, in all the dignity of immortal beings, and plant themselves side by side on the platform of human rights with man, to whom they were designed to be companions, equals, and helpers in every good word and work.

VIII. ON THE CONDITION OF WOMEN IN THE UNITED STATES.

. . . During the early part of my life, my lot was cast among the butterflies of the *fashionable* world; and of this class of women I am constrained to say both from experience and observation that their education is miserably deficient, that they are taught to regard marriage as the one thing needful, the only avenue to distinction; hence to attract the notice and win the attentions of men by their external charms is the chief business of fashionable girls. They seldom think that men will be allured by intellectual acquirements because they find that where any mental superiority exists, a woman is generally shunned and regarded as stepping out of her "appropriate sphere," which in their view is to dress, to dance, to set out to the best possible advantage her person, to read the novels which inundate the press and which do more to destroy her character as a rational creature than anything else. Fashionable women regard themselves, and are regarded by men, as pretty toys or as mere instruments of pleasure; and the vacuity of mind, the heartlessness, the frivolity which is the necessary result of this false and debasing estimate of women can only be fully understood by those who have mingled in the folly and wickedness of fashionable life and who have been called from such pursuits by the voice of the Lord Jesus, inviting their weary and heavy-laden souls to come unto Him and learn of Him that they may find something worthy of their immortal spirit and their intellectual powers, that they may learn the high and holy purposes of their creation and consecrate themselves unto the service of God and not, as is now the case, to the pleasure of man.

There is another and much more numerous class in this country who are withdrawn by education or circumstances from the circle of fashionable amusements but who are brought up with the dangerous and absurd idea that *marriage* is a kind of preferment, and that to be able to keep their husband's house and render his situation comfortable is the end of her being. Much that she does and says and thinks is done in reference to this situation; and to be married is too often held up to the view of girls as the sine qua non of human happiness and human existence. For this purpose more than for any other, I verily believe the majority of girls are trained. This is demonstrated by the imperfect education which is bestowed upon them and the little pains taken to cultivate their minds after they leave school, by the little time allowed them for reading, and by the idea being constantly inculcated that although all household concerns should be attended to with scrupulous punctuality at particular seasons, the improvement of their intellectual capacities is only a secondary consideration and may serve as an occupation to fill up the odds and ends of time. In most families it is considered a matter of far more consequence to call a girl off from making a pie or a pudding than to interrupt her whilst engaged in her studies. This mode of training necessarily exalts, in their view, the animal above the intellectual and spiritual nature and teaches women to regard themselves as a kind of machinery, necessary to keep the domestic engine in order but of little value as the *intelligent* companions of men.

Let no one think from these remarks that I regard a knowledge of housewifery as beneath the acquisition of women. Far from it: I believe that a complete knowledge of household affairs is an indispensable requisite in a woman's education—that by the mistress of a family, whether married or single, doing her duty thoroughly and *understandingly,* the happiness of the family is increased to an incalculable degree as well as a vast amount of time and money [saved]. . . . I do long to see the time when it will no longer be necessary for women to expend so many precious hours in furnishing "a well-spread table" but that their husbands will forego some of their accustomed indulgences in this way and encourage their wives to devote some portion of their time to mental cultivation, even at the expense of having to dine sometimes on baked potatoes or bread and butter. . . .

There is another way in which the general opinion that women are inferior to men is manifested that bears with tremendous effect on the laboring class and indeed on almost all who are obliged to earn a subsistence, whether it be by mental or physical exertion—I allude to the disproportionate value set on the time and labor of men and of women. A man who is engaged in teaching can always, I believe, command a higher price for tuition than a woman—even when he teaches the same branches and is not in any respect superior to the woman. This I know is the case in boarding and other schools with which I have been acquainted, and it is so in every occupation in which the sexes engage indiscriminately. As, for example, in tailoring, a man has twice or three times as much for making a waistcoast or pantaloons as a woman, although the work done by each may be equally good. In those employments which are peculiar to women, their time is estimated at only half the value of that of men. A woman who goes out to wash works as hard in proportion as a wood sawyer or a coal heaver, but she is not generally able to make more than half as much by a day's work. The low remuneration which women receive for their work has claimed the attention of a few philanthropists, and I hope it will continue to do so until some remedy is applied for this enormous evil. I have known a widow, left with four or five children to provide for, unable to leave home because her helpless babes demand her attention, compelled to earn a scanty subsistence by making coarse shirts at 12½ cents apiece or by taking in washing for which she was paid by some wealthy persons 12½ cents per dozen. All these things evince the low estimation in which woman is held. . . .

There is another class of women in this country to whom I cannot refer without feelings of the deepest shame and sorrow. I allude to our female slaves. Our southern cities are whelmed beneath a tide of pollution; the virtue of female slaves is wholly at the mercy of irresponsible tyrants, and women are bought and sold in our slave markets to gratify the brutal lust of those who bear the name of Christians. In our slave States, if amid all her degradation and ignorance a woman desires to preserve her virtue unsullied, she is either bribed or whipped into compliance; or if she dares resist her seducer, her life by the laws of some of the slave states may be, and has actually been, sacrified to the fury of disappointed passion. Where such laws do not exist, the power which is necessarily vested in the master over his property leaves the defenseless slave entirely at his mercy, and the sufferings of some females on this account, both physical and mental, are intense. . . .

. . . Nor does the colored woman suffer alone: The moral purity of the white woman is deeply contaminated. In the daily habit of seeing the virtue of her enslaved sister sacrificed without hesitancy or remorse, she looks upon the crimes of seduction and illicit intercourse without horror, and although not personally involved in the guilt, she loses that value for innocence in her own as well as the other sex which is one of the strongest safeguards to virtue. She lives in habitual intercourse with men whom she knows to be polluted by licentiousness, and often is she compelled to witness in her own domestic circle those disgusting and heart-sickening jealousies and strifes which disgraced and distracted the family of Abraham. In addition to all this, the female slaves suffer every species of degradation and cruelty which the most wanton barbarity can inflict; they are indecently divested of their clothing, sometimes tied up and severely whipped, sometimes prostrated on the earth while their naked bodies are torn by the scorpion lash. . . . Can any American woman look at these scenes of shocking licentiousness and cruelty and fold her hands in apathy and say, "I have nothing to do with slavery"? *She cannot and be guiltless.*

I cannot close this letter without saying a few words on the benefits to be derived by men, as well as women, from the opinions I advocate relative to the equality of the sexes. Many women are now supported in idleness and extravagance by the industry of their husbands, fathers, or brothers, who are compelled to toil out their existence at the counting house or in the printing office or some other laborious occupation while the wife and daughters and sisters take no part in the support of the family and appear to think that their sole business is to spend the hard bought earnings of their male friends. I deeply regret such a state of things because I believe that if women felt their responsibility for the support of themselves or their families, it would add strength and dignity to their characters and teach them more true sympathy for their husbands than is now generally manifested, a sympathy which would be exhibited by actions as well as words. Our brethren may reject my doctrine because it runs counter to common opinions and because it wounds their pride; but I believe they would be "partakers of the benefit" resulting from the Equality of the Sexes and would find that woman as their equal was unspeakably more valuable than woman as their inferior, both as a moral and an intellectual being.

XI. DRESS OF WOMEN.

. . . Woman in all ages and countries has been the scoff and the jest of her lordly master. If she attempted, like him, to improve her mind, she was ridiculed as pedantic and driven from the temple of science and literature by coarse attacks and vulgar sarcasms. If she yielded to the pressure of circumstances and sought relief from the monotony of existence by resorting to the theatre and the ball-room, by ornamenting her person with flowers and with jewels while her mind was empty and her heart desolate, she was still the mark at which wit and satire and cruelty levelled their arrows.

"Woman," says Adam Clarke, "has been invidiously defined, *an animal of dress.* How long will they permit themselves to be thus degraded?" I have been an attentive observer of my sex, and I am constrained to believe that the passion for dress which so generally characterizes them is one cause why there is so little of that solid improvement and weight of character which might be acquired under almost any circumstances if the mind were not occupied by the love of admiration and the desire to gratify personal vanity. . . .

It must, however, be conceded that . . . there is a numerous class whose improvement of mind and devotion to the cause of humanity justly entitle them to our respect and admiration. One of the most striking characteristics of modern times is the tendency toward a universal dissemination of knowledge in all Protestant communities. But the character of woman has been elevated more by participating in the great moral enterprises of the day than by anything else. It would astonish us if we could see at a glance all the labor, the patience, the industry, the fortitude which woman has exhibited in carrying on the causes of Moral Reform, Anti-Slavery, &c. Still, even these noble and ennobling pursuits have not destroyed personal vanity. Many of those who are engaged in these great and glorious reformations watch with eager interest the ever varying freaks of the goddess of fashion and are not exceeded by the butterflies of the ball-room in their love of curls, artificial flowers, embroidery and gay apparel. Many a woman will ply her needle with ceaseless industry to obtain money to forward a favorite benevolent scheme, while at the same time she will expend on useless articles of dress more than treble the sum which she procures by the employment of her needle and which she might throw into the Lord's treasury and leave herself leisure to cultivate her mind and to mingle among the poor and the afflicted more than she can possibly do now.

I feel exceedingly solicitous to draw the attention of my sisters to this subject. I know that it is called trifling, and much is said about dressing fashionably and elegantly and becomingly without thinking about it. This I do not believe can be done. If we indulge our fancy in the chameleon caprices of fashion or in wearing ornamental and extravagant apparel, the mind must be in no small degree engaged in the gratification of personal vanity.

Lest anyone may suppose from my being a Quaker that I should like to see a uniform dress adopted, I will say that I have no partiality for their peculiar costume, except so far as I find it simple and convenient; and I have not the remotest desire to see it worn where one more commodious can be substituted. But I do believe one of the chief obstacles in the way of woman's elevation to the same platform of human rights and moral dignity and intellectual improvement with her brother . . . is her love of dress. . . . Those men who are superior to such a childish vanity in themselves are, nevertheless, ever ready to encourage it in women. They know that so long as we submit to be dressed like dolls, we never can rise to the stations of duty and usefulness from which they desire to exclude us; and they are willing to grant us paltry indulgences which forward their own design of keeping us out of our appropriate sphere while they deprive us of essential rights.

To me it appears beneath the dignity of woman to bedeck herself in gewgaws and trinkets, in ribbons and laces, to gratify the eye of man. I believe, furthermore, that we owe a solemn duty to the poor. Many a woman in what is called humble life spends nearly all her earnings in dress because she wants to be as well attired as her employer. . . . "Well," I am often asked, "where is the limitation?" This it is not my business to decide. Every woman . . . can best settle this on her knees before God. He has commanded her not to be conformed to this world but to be transformed by the renewing of her mind that she may know what is the good and acceptable and perfect will of God. . . . He has commanded them through his apostles not to adorn themselves with broidered hair or gold or pearls or costly array. Not to let their adorning be the "outward adorning of plaiting the hair or of wearing of gold or of putting on of apparel, but let it be the hidden man of the heart, in that which is not corruptible, even the ornament of a meek and quiet spirit, which is in the sight of God of great price"; yet we disregard these solemn admonitions. May we not form some correct estimate of dress by asking ourselves how we should feel if we saw ministers of the gospel rise to address an audience with earrings dangling from their ears, glittering rings on their fingers, and a wreath of artificial flowers on their brow, and the rest of their apparel in keeping? If it would be wrong for a minister, it is wrong for every professing Christian. God makes no distinction between the moral and religious duties of ministers and people. . . .

XII. LEGAL DISABILITIES OF WOMEN.

. . . There are few things which present greater obstacles to the improvement and elevation of woman to her appropriate sphere of usefulness and duty than the laws which have been enacted to destroy her independence and crush her individuality: laws which, although they are framed for her government, she has had no voice in establishing and which rob her of some of her *essential rights*. Woman has no political existence. With the single exception of presenting a petition to the legislative body, she is a cipher in the nation; or if not actually so in representative governments, she is only counted, like the slaves of the South, to swell the number of law-makers who form decrees for her government with little reference to her benefit, except so far as her good may promote their own. . . . These laws bear with peculiar rigor on married women. [Sir William] Blackstone in the chapter entitled "Of husband and wife" says:

> By marriage, the husband and wife are one person in law; that is, *the very being, or legal existence of the woman* is suspended during the marriage, or at least is incorporated and consolidated into that of the husband under whose wing, protection and cover she performs everything. . . .
>
> For this reason, a man cannot grant anything to his wife, or enter into covenant with her; for the grant would be to suppose her separate existence, and to covenant with her would be to covenant with himself; and therefore it is also generally true, that all compacts made between husband and wife when single, are voided by the intermarriage.

Here now, the very being of a woman, like that of a slave, is absorbed in her master. All contracts made with her, like those made with slaves by their owners, are a mere nullity. Our kind defenders have legislated away almost all our legal rights, and in the true spirit of such injustice and oppression have kept us in ignorance of those very laws by which we are governed. They have persuaded us that we have no right to investigate the laws and that, if we did, we could not comprehend them; they alone are capable of understanding the mysteries of Blackstone, &c. But they are not backward to make us feel the practical operation of their power over our actions.

> The husband is bound to provide his wife with necessaries by law, as much as himself; and if she contracts debts for them, he is obliged to pay for them; but for anything besides necessaries, he is not chargeable.

Yet a man may spend the property he has acquired by marriage at the ale-house, the gambling table, or in any other way that he pleases. Many instances of this kind have come to my knowledge; and women who have brought their husbands handsome fortunes have been left, in consequence of the wasteful and dissolute habits of their husbands, in straitened circumstances and compelled to toil for the support of their families. . . .

> If the wife be injured in her person or property, she can bring no action for redress without her husband's concurrence, and his name as well as her own: neither can she be sued, without making her husband a defendant.

This law that "a wife can bring no action," &c., is similar to the law respecting slaves. "A slave cannot bring a suit against his master, or any other person, for an injury—his master must bring it." So if any damages are recovered for an injury committed on a wife, the husband pockets it; in the case of the slave, the master does the same.

> In criminal prosecutions, the wife may be indicted and punished separately, unless there be evidence of coercion from the fact that the offence was committed in the presence, or by the command of her husband. A wife is excused from punishment for theft committed in the presence, or by the command of her husband.

It would be difficult to frame a law better calculated to destroy the responsibility of woman as a moral being or a free agent. Her husband is supposed to possess unlimited control over her; and if she can offer the flimsy excuse that he bade her steal, she may break the eighth commandment with impunity as far as human laws are concerned.

> Our law, in general, considers man and wife as one person; yet there are some instances in which she is separately considered, as inferior to him and acting by his compulsion. Therefore, all deeds executed, and acts done by her during her coverture (i.e., marriage,) are void, except it be a fine, or like matter of record, in which case she must be solely and secretly examined, to learn if her act be voluntary.

Such a law speaks volumes of the abuse of that power which men have vested in their own hands. Still the private examination of a wife, to know whether she accedes to the disposition of property made by her husband, is in most cases a mere form; a wife dares not do what will be disagreeable to one who is in his own estimation her superior and who makes her feel in the privacy of domestic life that she has thwarted him. . . .

> The husband, by the old law, might give his wife moderate correction, as he is to answer for her misbehavior. The law thought it reasonable to entrust him with this power of restraining her by domestic chastisement. The courts of law will still permit a husband to restrain a wife of her liberty, in case of any gross misbehavior.

What a mortifying proof this law affords of the estimation in which woman is held! She is placed completely in the hands of a being subject like herself to the outbursts of passion and therefore unworthy to be trusted with power. Perhaps I may be told respecting this law that it is a dead letter, as I am sometimes told about the slave laws; but this is not true in either case. The slaveholder does kill his slave by moderate correction, as the law allows; and many a husband among the poor exercises the right given him by the law of degrading woman by personal chastisement. And among the higher ranks, if actual imprisonment is not resorted to, women are not unfrequently restrained of the liberty of going to places of worship by irreligious husbands and of doing many other things about which, as moral and responsible beings, *they* should be the *sole* judges. . . .

A woman's personal property by marriage becomes absolutely her husband's, which, at his death, he may leave entirely away from her.

And farther, all the avails of her labor are absolutely in the power of her husband. All that she acquires by her industry is his so that she cannot with her own honest earnings become the legal purchaser of any property. If she expends her money for articles of furniture to contribute to the comfort of her family, they are liable to be seized for her husband's debts; and I know an instance of a woman who by labor and economy had scraped together a little maintenance for herself and a do-little husband who was left at his death, by virtue of his last will and testament, to be supported by charity. . . .

With regard to the property of women, there is taxation without representation; for they pay taxes without having the liberty of voting for representatives.

And this taxation without representation, be it remembered, was the cause of our Revolutionary war, a grievance so heavy that it was thought necessary to purchase exemption from it at an immense expense of blood and treasure, yet the daughters of New England, as well as of all the other states of this free Republic, are suffering a similar injustice; but for one, I had rather we should suffer any injustice or oppression than that my sex should have any voice in the political affairs of the nation. . . .

. . . That the laws which have generally been adopted in the United States for the government of women have been framed almost entirely for the exclusive benefit of men and with a design to oppress women by depriving them of all control over their property is too manifest to be denied. . . . As these abuses do exist and women suffer intensely from them, our brethren are called upon in this enlightened age by every sentiment of honor, religion, and justice to repeal these unjust and unequal laws and restore to woman those rights which they have wrested from her. Such laws approximate too nearly to the laws enacted by slaveholders for the government of their slaves and must tend to debase and depress the mind of that being whom God created as a helpmeet for man or "helper like unto himself" and designed to be his equal and his companion. Until such laws are annulled, woman never can occupy that exalted station for which she was intended by her Maker. And just in proportion as they are practically disregarded, which is the case to some extent, just so far is woman assuming that independence and nobility of character which she ought to exhibit. . . .

. . . I do not wish by any means to intimate that the condition of free women can be compared to that of slaves in suffering or in degradation; still I believe [that] the laws which deprive married women of their rights and privileges have a tendency to lessen them in their own estimation as moral and responsible beings and that their being made by civil law inferior to their husbands has a debasing and mischievous effect upon them, teaching them practically the fatal lesson to look unto man for protection and indulgence.

Ecclesiastical bodies, I believe, without exception follow the example of legislative assemblies in excluding woman from any participation in forming the discipline by which she is governed. The men frame the laws and, with few exceptions, claim to execute them on both sexes. In ecclesiastical as well as civil courts woman is tried and condemned, not by a jury of her peers but by beings who regard themselves as her superiors in the scale of creation. Although looked upon as an inferior when considered as an intellectual being, woman is punished with the same severity as man when she is guilty of moral offenses. Her condition resembles in some measure that of the slave who, while he is denied the advantages of his more enlightened master, is treated with even greater rigor of the law. . . .

XIII. RELATION OF HUSBAND AND WIFE.

Perhaps some persons may wonder that I should attempt to throw out my views on the important subject of marriage and may conclude that I am altogether disqualified for the task because I lack experience. However, I shall not undertake to settle the specific duties of husbands and wives but only to exhibit opinions based on the word of God and formed from a little knowledge of human nature and close observation of the working of generally received notions respecting the dominion of man over woman.

When Jehovah ushered into existence man created in his own image, He instituted marriage as a part of paradisiacal happiness: It was a *divine ordination,* not a civil contract. God established it, and man, except by special permission, has no right to annul it. There can be no doubt that the creation of Eve perfected the happiness of Adam; hence, our all-wise and merciful Father made her as He made Adam, in His own image after His likeness, crowned her with glory and honor, and placed in her hand, as well as in his, the scepter of dominion over the whole lower creation. . . .

"Previous to the introduction of the religion of Jesus Christ, the state of society was wretchedly diseased. The relation of the sexes to each other had become so gross in its manifested forms that it was difficult to perceive the pure conservative principle in its inward essence." Christianity came in at this juncture with its hallowed influence and has without doubt tended to lighten the yoke of bondage, to purify the manners, and give the spiritual in some degree an empire over the animal nature. Still, that state which was designed by God to increase the happiness of woman as well as man often proves the means of lessening her comfort and degrading her into the mere machine of another's convenience and pleasure. Woman, instead of being elevated by her union with man, which might be expected from an alliance with a superior being, is in reality lowered. She generally loses her individuality, her independent character, her moral being. She becomes absorbed into him and henceforth is looked at and acts through the medium of her husband.

In the wealthy classes of society and those who are in comfortable circumstances, women are exempt from great corporeal exertion and are protected by public opinion and by the genial influence of Christianity from much physical ill treatment. Still, there is a vast amount of secret suffering endured from the forced submission of women to the opinions and whims of their husbands. Hence they are frequently driven to use deception to compass their ends. They are early taught that to appear to yield is the only way to govern. Miserable sophism! I deprecate such sentiments as being peculiarly hostile to the dignity of woman. If she submits, let her do it openly, honorably, not to gain her point but as a matter of Christian duty. But let her beware how she permits her husband to be her conscience-keeper. On all moral and religious subjects she is bound to think and to act for herself. Where confidence and love exist, a wife will naturally converse with her husband as with her dearest friend on all that interests her heart, and there will be a perfectly free interchange of sentiment; but *she is no more bound to be governed by his judgment* than he is by hers. They are standing on the same platform of human rights, are equally under the government of God and accountable to Him, and Him alone.

I have sometimes been astonished and grieved at the servitude of women and at the little idea many of them seem to have of their own moral existence and responsibilities. A woman who is asked to sign a petition for the abolition of slavery in the District of Columbia or to join a society for the purpose of carrying forward the annihilation of American slavery or any other great reformation not unfrequently replies, "My husband does not approve of it." She merges her rights and her duties in her husband and thus virtually chooses him for a savior and a king and rejects Christ as her Ruler and Redeemer. I know some women are very glad of so convenient a pretext to shield themselves from the performance of duty; but there are others who, under a mistaken view of their obligations as wives, submit conscientiously to this species of oppression and go mourning on their way for want of that holy fortitude which would enable them to fulfill their duties as moral and responsible beings without reference to poor fallen man. . . .

There is, perhaps, less bondage of mind among the poorer classes because their sphere of duty is more contracted and they are deprived of the means of intellectual culture and of the opportunity of exercising their judgment on many moral subjects of deep interest and of vital importance. Authority is called into exercise by resistance, and hence there will be mental bondage only in proportion as the faculties of mind are evolved and woman feels herself as a rational and intelligent being on a footing with man. But women among the lowest classes of society, so far as my observation has extended, suffer intensely from the brutality of their husbands. Duty, as well as inclination, has led me for many years into the abodes of poverty and sorrow, and I have been amazed at the treatment which women receive at the hands of those who arrogate to themselves the epithet of *protectors*. Brute force, the law of violence, rules to a great extent in the poor man's domicile, and woman is little more than his drudge. They are less under the supervision of public opinion, less under the restraints of education, and unaided or unbiased by the refinements of polished society. Religion, wherever it exists, supplies the place of all these; but the real cause of woman's degradation and suffering in married life is to be found in the erroneous notion of her inferiority to man; and never will she be rightly regarded by herself or others until this opinion, so derogatory to the wisdom and mercy of God, is exploded and woman arises in all the majesty of her womanhood to claim those rights which are inseparable from her existence as an immortal, intelligent, and responsible being.

Independent of the fact that Jehovah could not—consistently with his character as the King, the Lawgiver, and the Judge of his people—give the reins of government over woman into the hands of man, I find that all His commands, all His moral laws, are addressed to women as well as to men. When He assembled Israel at the foot of Mount Sinai to issue His commandments, we may reasonably suppose He gave all the precepts which He considered necessary for the government of moral beings. Hence we find that God says, "Honor thy father and thy mother," and He enforces this command by severe penalties upon those who transgress it. . . . But in the decalogue there is no direction given to women to obey their husbands: Both are commanded to have no other God but Jehovah and not to bow down or serve any other. When the Lord Jesus delivered his sermon on the Mount, full of the practical precepts of religion, He did not issue any command to wives to obey their husbands. When He is speaking on the subject of divorce, Mark 16: 11, 12, He places men and women on the same ground. And the Apostle, 1st Cor[inthians] 7: 12, 13, speaking of the duties of the Corinthian wives and husbands who had embraced Christianity to their unconverted partners, points out the same path to both, although our translators have made a distinction. "Let him not put her away," 12—"Let her not leave him," 13—is precisely the same in the original. If man is constituted the governor of woman, he must be her god; and the sentiment expressed to me lately by a married man is perfectly correct: "In my opinion," said he, "the greatest excellence to which a married woman can attain is to worship her husband." He was a professor of religion—his wife, a lovely and intelligent woman. He only spoke out what thousands think and act. . . .

This much admired sentimental nonsense is fraught with absurdity and wickedness. If it were true, the commandment of Jehovah should have run thus: Man shall have no other gods before ME, and woman shall have no other gods before MAN.

The principal support of the dogma of woman's inferiority and consequent submission to her husband is found in some passages of Paul's epistles. I shall proceed to examine those passages, premising first that the antiquity of the opinions based on the false construction of those passages has no weight with me: They are the opinions of interested judges, and I have no particular reverence for them *merely* because they have been regarded with veneration from generation to generation. So far from this being the case, I examine any opinions of centuries' standing with as much freedom and investigate them with as much care as if they were of yesterday. I was educated to think for myself, and it is a privilege I shall always claim to exercise. Second, notwithstanding my full belief that the apostle Paul's testimony respecting himself is true, "I was not a whit behind the chiefest of the apostles," yet I believe his mind was under the influence of Jewish prejudices respecting women, just as Peter's and the apostles were about the uncleanness of the Gentiles. "The Jews," says Clarke, "would not suffer a woman to read in the synagogue, although a servant or even a child had this permission." When I see Paul shaving his head for a vow and offering sacrifices and circumcising Timothy to accommodate himself to the prepossessions of his countrymen, I do not conceive that I derogate in the least from his character as an inspired apostle to suppose that he may have been imbued with the prevalent prejudices against women.

In 1st Cor[inthians] 11: 3, after praising the Corinthian converts because they kept the "ordinances" or "traditions," as the margin reads, the apostle says, "I would have you know that the head of every man is Christ, and the head of the woman is the man; and the head of Christ is God," Eph[esians] 5: 23 is a parallel passage. "For the husband is the head of the wife, even as Christ is the head of the Church." The apostle closes his remarks on this subject by observing, "This is a great mystery, but I speak concerning Christ and the Church." I shall pass over this with simply remarking that God and Christ are one. "I and my Father are one," and there can be no inferiority where there is no divisibility. . . .

. . . The idea that man as man is superior to woman involves an absurdity so gross that I really wonder how any man of reflection can receive it as of divine origin; and I can only account for it by that passion for supremacy which characterizes man as a corrupt and fallen creature. If it be true that he is more excellent than she as man, independent of his moral and intellectual powers, then every man is superior by virtue of his manship to every woman. The man who sinks his moral capacities and spiritual powers in his sensual appetites is still, as a man, simply by the conformation of his body a more dignified being than the woman whose intellectual powers are highly cultivated and whose approximation to the character of Jesus Christ is exhibited in a blameless life and conversation.

But it is strenuously urged by those who are anxious to maintain their usurped authority that wives are in various passages of the New Testament commanded to obey their husbands. Let us examine these texts.

> Eph[esians] 5: 22. Wives, submit yourselves unto your own husbands as unto the Lord. . . . As the church is subject unto Christ, so let the wives be to their own husbands in every thing.

Col[ossians] 3: 18. Wives, submit yourselves unto your own husbands, as it is fit in the Lord.

1st Pet[er] 3: 2. Likewise ye wives, be in subjection to your own husbands; that if any obey not the word, they may also without the word be won by the conversation of the wives.

Accompanying all these directions to wives are commands to husbands.

Eph[esians] 5: 25. Husbands, love your wives even as Christ loved the Church, and gave himself for it. . . . So ought men to love their wives as their own bodies. He that loveth his wife, loveth himself.

Col[ossians] 3: 19. Husbands, love your wives, and be not bitter against them.

1st Pet[er] 3: 7. Likewise ye husbands, dwell with them according to knowledge, giving honor unto the wife as unto the weaker vessel, and as being heirs together of the grace of life.

I may just remark in relation to the expression "weaker vessel" that the word in the original has no reference to intellect: It refers to physical weakness merely.

The apostles were writing to Christian converts and laying down rules for their conduct towards their unconverted consorts. It no doubt frequently happened that a husband or a wife would embrace Christianity while their companions clung to heathenism, and husbands might be tempted to dislike and despise those who pertinaciously adhered to their pagan superstitions. And wives who, when they were pagans, submitted as a matter of course to their heathen husbands might be tempted, knowing that they were superior as moral and religious characters, to assert that superiority by paying less deference to them than heretofore. Let us examine the context of these passages and see what are the grounds of the directions here given to husbands and wives. The whole epistle to the Ephesians breathes a spirit of love. The apostle beseeches the converts to walk, worthy of the vocation wherewith they are called, with all lowliness and meekness, with long suffering, forbearing one another in love. The verse preceding 5: 22, is "SUBMITTING YOURSELVES ONE TO ANOTHER IN THE FEAR OF GOD." Colossians 3: from 11 to 17, contains similar injunctions. The 17th verse says, "Whatsoever ye do in word, or in deed, do all in the name of the Lord Jesus." Peter, after drawing a most touching picture of Christ's sufferings for us and reminding the Christians that he had left us an example that we should follow his steps "who did no sin, neither was guile found in his mouth," exhorts wives to be in subjection, &c.

From an attentive consideration of these passages and of those in which the same words "submit" [and] "subjection" are used, I cannot but believe that the apostles designed to recommend to wives, as they did to subjects and to servants, to carry out the holy principle laid down by Jesus Christ, "Resist not evil." And this without in the least acknowledging the right of the governors, masters, or husbands to exercise the authority they claimed. The recognition of the existence of evils does not involve approbation of them. God tells the Israelites he gave them a king in his wrath, but nevertheless as they chose to have a king, he laid down directions for the conduct of that king and had him anointed to reign over them. According to the generally received meaning of the passages I have quoted, they directly contravene the laws of God as given in various parts of the Bible. Now I must understand the sacred Scriptures as harmonizing with themselves, or I cannot receive them as the word of God. . . . Now if God ordained man the governor of woman, he must be able to save her and to answer in her stead for all those sins which she commits by his direction. Awful responsibility. Do husbands feel able and willing to bear it? And what becomes of the solemn affirmation of Jehovah? "Hear this, all ye people, give ear all ye inhabitants of the world, both low and high, rich and poor." "None can by any means redeem his brother or give to God a ransom for him, for the redemption of the soul is precious, and man cannot accomplish it."—*French Bible.*

XIV. MINISTRY OF WOMEN.

. . . If it is the duty of man to preach the unsearchable riches of Christ, it is the duty also of woman. I am aware that I have the prejudices of education and custom to combat both in my own and the other sex as well as "the traditions of men," which are taught for the commandments of God. I feel that I have no sectarian views to advance; for although among the Quakers, Methodists, and Christians, women are permitted to preach the glad tidings of peace and salvation, yet I know of no religious body who entertain the Scripture doctrine of the perfect equality of man and woman which is the fundamental principle of my argument in favor of the ministry of women. . . .

That women were called to the prophetic office I believe is universally admitted. Miriam, Deborah, and Huldah were prophetesses. The judgments of the Lord are denounced by Ezekiel on false prophetesses as well as false prophets. And if Christian ministers are, as I apprehend, successors of the prophets and not of the priests, then of course women are now called to that office as well as men because God has nowhere withdrawn from them the privilege of doing what is the great business of preachers, viz., to point the penitent sinner to the Redeemer. . . .

Surely there is nothing either astonishing or novel in the gifts of the Spirit being bestowed on woman: nothing astonishing because there is no respect of persons with God; the soul of the woman in his sight is as the soul of the man, and both are alike capable of the influence of the Holy Spirit. Nothing novel because, as has been already shown, in the sacred records there are found examples of women, as well as of men, exercising the gift of prophecy.

We attach to the word prophecy the exclusive meaning of foretelling future events, but this is certainly a mistake, for the apostle Paul defines it to be "speaking to edification, exhortation and comfort." And there appears no possible reason why women should not do this as well as men. At the time that the Bible was translated into English, the meaning of the word prophecy was delivering a message from God, whether it was to predict future events or to warn the people of the consequences of sin. . . .

Let us now examine whether women actually exercised the office of minister under the gospel dispensation. Philip had four daughters who prophesied or preached. Paul calls Priscilla as well as Aquila his helpers or, as in the Greek, his fellow laborers in Christ Jesus. Divers other passages might be adduced to prove that women continued to be preachers and that *many* of them filled this dignified station.

We learn also from ecclesiastical history that female ministers suffered martyrdom in the early ages of the Christian church. In ancient councils mention is made of deaconesses; and in an edition of the New Testament printed in 1574, a woman is spoken of as minister of a church. The same word which in our common translation is now rendered a servant of the church in speaking of Phebe, Rom[ans] 16: 1, is rendered minister, Eph[esians] 6: 21, when applied to Tychicus. A minister with whom I had lately the pleasure of conversing remarked, "My rule is to expound scripture by scripture, and I cannot deny the ministry of women because the apostle says, 'help those women who labored with me IN THE GOSPEL.' He certainly meant something more than pouring out tea for him."

In the 11th Ch[apter] of 1 Cor[inthians], Paul gives directions to women and men how they should appear when they prophesy or pray in public assemblies. It is evident that the design of the apostle, in this and the three succeeding chapters is to rectify certain abuses which had crept into the Christian church. He therefore admonishes women to pray with their heads covered because according to the fashion of that day it was considered immodest and immoral to do otherwise. He says "that were all one as if she were shaven"; and shaving the head was a disgraceful punishment that was inflicted on women of bad character. . . .

But there are certain passages in the Epistles of St. Paul which seem to be of doubtful interpretation, at which we cannot much marvel seeing that his brother Peter says there are some things in them hard to be understood. Most commentators, having their minds preoccupied with the prejudices of education, afford little aid; they rather tend to darken the text by the multitude of words. One of these passages occurs in 1 Cor[inthians]: 14. I have already remarked that this chapter, with several of the preceding, was evidently designed to correct abuses which had crept into the assemblies of Christians in Corinth. Hence we find that the men were commanded to be silent as well as the women when they were guilty of anything which deserved reprehension. The apostle says, "If there be no interpreter, let him keep silence in the church." The men were doubtless in the practice of speaking in unknown tongues when there was no interpreter present, and Paul reproves them because this kind of preaching conveyed no instruction to the people. Again he says, "If anything be revealed to another that sitteth by, let the first hold his peace." We may infer from this that two men sometimes attempted to speak at the same time, and the apostle rebukes them and adds, "Ye may ALL prophesy one by one, for God is not the author of confusion but of peace." He then proceeds to notice the disorderly conduct of the women who were guilty of other improprieties. They were probably in the habit of asking questions on any points of doctrine which they wished more thoroughly explained. This custom was common among the men in the Jewish synagogues, after the pattern of which the meetings of the early Christians were in all probability conducted. And the Christian women, presuming on the liberty which they enjoyed under the new religion, interrupted the assembly by asking questions. The apostle disapproved of this, because it disturbed the solemnity of the meeting: He therefore admonishes the women to keep silence in the churches. That the apostle did not allude to preaching is manifest because he tells them, "If they will *learn* anything, let them ask their husbands at home." Now a person endowed with a gift in the ministry does not ask questions in the public exercise of that gift for the purpose of gaining information: She is instructing others. Moreover, the apostle in closing his remarks on this subject says, "Wherefore, brethren (a generic term, applying equally to men and women), covet to prophesy and forbid not to speak with tongues. Let all things be done decently and in order." . . .

The other passage on which the opinion that women are not called to the ministry is founded is 1 Tim[othy] second ch[apter]. The apostle speaks of the duty of prayer and supplication, mentions his own ordination as a preacher, and then adds, "I will, therefore, that men pray everywhere, lifting up holy hands, without wrath and doubting. In like manner also, that women adorn themselves in modest apparel," &c. I shall here premise that, as the punctuation and division into chapters and verses is no part of the original arrangement, they cannot determine the sense of a passage. Indeed, every attentive reader of the Bible must observe that the injudicious separation of sentences often destroys their meaning and their beauty. Joseph John Gurney, whose skill as a biblical critic is well known in England, commenting on this passage, says,

> It is worded in a manner somewhat obscure; but appears to be best construed according to the opinion of various commentators . . . as conveying an injunction, that women as well as men should pray everywhere, lifting up holy hands without wrath and doubting. 1 Tim[othy] 2: 8, 9. 'I will therefore that men pray everywhere, &c.; likewise also the women in a modest dress.' . . .

I have no doubt this is the true meaning of the text and that the translators would never have thought of altering it had they not been under the influence of educational prejudice.

The apostle proceeds to exhort the women who thus publicly made intercession to God not to adorn themselves with braided hair or gold or pearls or costly array, but (which becometh women professing godliness) with good works. The word in this verse translated "professing" would be more properly rendered preaching godliness or enjoining piety to the gods or conducting public worship. After describing the duty of female ministers about their apparel, the apostle proceeds to correct some improprieties which probably prevailed in the Ephesian church similar to those which he had reproved among the Corinthian converts. He says, "Let the women LEARN in silence with all subjection; but I suffer not a woman to teach, nor to usurp authority over the man, but to be in silence," or quietness. Here again it is evident that the women of whom he was speaking were admonished to learn in silence, which could not refer to their public ministrations to others. The verb to teach, verse 12, is one of very general import and may in this place more properly be rendered dictate. It is highly probable that women who had long been in bondage, when set free by Christianity from the restraints imposed upon them by Jewish traditions and heathen customs, ran into an extreme in their public assemblies and interrupted the religious services by frequent interrogations which they could have had answered as satisfactorily at home.

On a candid examination and comparison of the passages which I have endeavored to explain, viz., 1 Cor[inthians] chap[ters] 11 and 14 and 1 Tim[othy chapter] 2:8–12, I think we must be compelled to adopt one of two conclusions: either that the apostle grossly contradicts himself on a subject of great practical importance and that the fulfillment of the prophecy of Joel was a shameful infringement of decency and order or that the directions given to women not to speak or to teach in the congregations had reference to some local and peculiar customs which were then common in religious assemblies and which the apostle thought inconsistent with the purpose for which they were met together. No one, I suppose, will hesitate which of these two conclusions to adopt. . . .

XV. MAN EQUALLY GUILTY WITH WOMAN IN THE FALL.

It is said that "modern Jewish women light a lamp every Friday evening, half an hour before sunset, which is the beginning of their Sabbath, in remembrance of their original mother, who first extinguished the lamp of righteousness, to remind them of their obligation to rekindle it." I am one of those who always admit to its fullest extent the popular charge that woman brought sin into the world. I accept it as a powerful reason why woman is bound to labor with double diligence for the regeneration of that world she has been instrumental in ruining. . . .

My present object is to show that as woman is charged with all the sin that exists in the world, it is her solemn duty to labor for its extinction and that this she can never do effectually and extensively until her mind is disenthralled of those shackles which have been riveted upon her by a *"corrupt public opinion and a perverted interpretation of the holy Scriptures."* Woman must feel that she is the equal and is designed to be the fellow-laborer of her brother, or she will be studying to find out the *imaginary* line which separates the sexes and divides the duties of men and women into two distinct classes, a separation not even hinted at in the Bible, where we are expressly told "there is neither male nor female, for ye are all one in Christ Jesus."

My views on this subject are so much better embodied in the language of a living author [Angelina Grimké] than I can express them that I quote the passage entire: "Woman's rights and man's rights are *both* contained in the *same* charter and held by the *same* tenure. *All rights* spring out of the *moral* nature: They are both the root and the offspring of *responsibilities.* The physical constitution is the mere *instrument* of the *moral* nature; sex is a mere *incident* of this constitution, a provision necessary to this *form* of existence; its *only* design, not to give nor to take away, nor in any respect to modify or even *touch* rights or responsibilities in any sense, except so far as the peculiar offices of each sex may afford less or more *opportunity* and ability for the exercise of rights and the discharge of responsibilities, but merely to continue and enlarge the human department of God's government. Consequently, I know nothing of *man's* rights or *woman's* rights; *human* rights are all that I recognize. The doctrine that the *sex of the body* presides over and administers upon the rights and responsibilities of the moral, immortal nature is to my mind a doctrine kindred to blasphemy *when seen in its intrinsic nature.* It breaks up utterly the *relations* of the two natures and reverses their functions, exalting the animal nature into a monarch and humbling the moral into a slave, making the former a proprietor and the latter its property."

To perform our duties, we must comprehend our rights and responsibilities; and it is because we do not understand that we now fall so far short in the discharge of our obligations. Unaccustomed to think for ourselves and to search the sacred volume to see how far we are living up to the design of Jehovah in our creation, we have rested satisfied with the sphere marked out for us by man, never detecting the fallacy of that reasoning which forbids woman to exercise some of her noblest faculties and stamps with the reproach of indelicacy those actions by which women were formerly dignified and exalted in the church.

I should not mention this subject again if it were not to point out to my sisters what seems to me an irresistible conclusion from the literal interpretation of St. Paul without reference to the context and the peculiar circumstances and abuses which drew forth the expressions, "I suffer not a woman to teach" [and] "Let your women keep silence in the church," i.e., congregation. It is manifest that if the apostle meant what his words imply when taken in the strictest sense, then women have no right to *teach* Sabbath or day schools or to open their lips to sing in the assemblies of the people; yet young and delicate women are engaged in all these offices; they are expressly trained to exhibit themselves and raise their voices to a high pitch in the choirs of our places of worship. I do not intend to sit in judgment on my sisters for doing these things; I only want them to see that they are as really infringing a *supposed* divine command by instructing their pupils in the Sabbath or day schools, and by singing in the congregation as if they were engaged in preaching the unsearchable riches of Christ to a lost and perishing world. Why then are we permitted to break this injunction in some points and so sedulously warned not to overstep the bounds set for us by our *brethren* in another? Simply, as I believe, because in the one case we subserve *their* views and *their* interests and act *in subordination to them* whilst in the other we come in contact with their interests and claim to be on an equality with them in the highest and most important trust ever committed to man, namely, the ministry of the word. It is manifest that if women were permitted to be ministers of the gospel, as they unquestionably were in the primitive ages of the Christian church, it would interfere materially with the present organized system of spiritual power and ecclesiastical authority which is now vested solely in the hands of men. It would either show that all the paraphernalia of theological seminaries, &c., &c., to prepare men to become evangelists is wholly unnecessary, or it would create a necessity for similar institutions in order to prepare women for the same office; and this would be an encroachment on that learning, which our kind brethren have so ungenerously monopolized. I do not ask anyone to believe my statements or adopt my conclusions because they are mine; but I do earnestly entreat my sisters to lay aside their prejudices and examine these subjects *for themselves,* regardless of the "traditions of men," because they are intimately connected with their duty and their usefulness in the present important crisis.

All who know anything of the present system of benevolent and religious operations, know that women are performing an important part in them, in *subserviency to men,* who guide our labors, and are often the recipients of those benefits of education we toil to confer and which we rejoice they can enjoy, although it is their mandate which deprives us of the same advantages. Now whether our brethren have defrauded us intentionally or unintentionally, the wrong we suffer is equally the same. For years they have been spurring us up to the performance of our duties. The immense usefulness and the vast influence of woman have been eulogized and called into exercise, and many a blessing has been lavished upon us and many a prayer put up for us because we have labored by day and by night to clothe and feed and educate young men whilst our own bodies sometimes suffer for want of comfortable garments and our minds are left in almost utter destitution of that improvement which we are toiling to bestow upon the brethren. . . .

If the sewing societies, the avails of whose industry are now expended in supporting and educating young men for the ministry, were to withdraw their contributions to these objects and give them where they are *more needed,* to the advancement of their *own sex* in useful learning, the next generation might furnish sufficient proof that in intelligence and ability to master the whole circle of sciences woman is not inferior to man. . . . I confess, considering the high claim men in this country make to great politeness and deference to women, it does seem a little extraordinary that we should be urged to work for the brethren. I should suppose it would be more in character with "the generous promptings of chivalry and the poetry of romantic gallantry," for which Catherine E. Beecher gives them credit, for them to form societies to educate their sisters, seeing our inferior capacities require more cultivation to bring them into use and qualify us to be helpmeets for them. However, though I think this would be but a just return for all our past kindnesses in this way, I should be willing to balance our accounts and begin a new course. Henceforth, let the benefit be reciprocated, or else let each sex provide for the education of their own poor whose talents ought to be rescued from the oblivion of ignorance. . . .

DUTIES OF WOMEN.

One of the duties which devolve upon women in the present interesting crisis is to prepare themselves for more extensive usefulness by making use of those religious and literary privileges and advantages that are within their reach if they will only stretch out their hands and possess them. By doing this, they will become better acquainted with their rights as moral beings and with their responsibilities growing out of those rights: They will regard themselves as they really are, FREE AGENTS, immortal beings, amenable to no tribunal but that of Jehovah, and bound not to submit to any restriction imposed for selfish purposes or to gratify that love of power which has reigned in the heart of man from Adam down to the present time. In contemplating the great moral reformations of the day and the part which they are bound to take in them instead of puzzling themselves with the harassing, because unnecessary, inquiry [of] how far they may go without overstepping the bounds of propriety, which separate male and female duties, they will only inquire, "Lord, what wilt thou have us to do?" They will be enabled to see the simple truth: that God has made no distinction between men and women as moral beings, that the distinction now so much insisted upon between male and female virtues is as absurd as it is unscriptural and has been the fruitful source of much mischief—granting to man a license for the exhibition of brute force and conflict on the battle field, for sternness, selfishness, and the exercise of irresponsible power in the circle of home and [granting] to woman a permit to rest on an arm of flesh and to regard modesty and delicacy, and all the kindred virtues as peculiarly appropriate to her. Now to me it is perfectly clear that WHATSOEVER IT IS MORALLY RIGHT FOR A MAN TO DO, IT IS MORALLY RIGHT FOR A WOMAN TO DO and that confusion must exist in the moral world until woman takes her stand on the same platform with man and feels that she is clothed by her Maker with the *same rights* and, of course, that upon her devolve the *same duties*.

It is not my intention, nor indeed do I think it is in my power, to point out the precise duties of women. To him who still teacheth by his Holy Spirit as never man taught I refer my beloved sisters. There is a vast field of usefulness before them. The signs of the times give portentous evidence that a day of deep trial is approaching. . . .

CONCLUSION.

I have now, my dear sister, completed my series of letters. I am aware they contain some new views; but I believe they are based on the immutable truths of the Bible. All I ask for them is the candid and prayerful consideration of Christians. If they strike at some of our bosom sins, our deep-rooted prejudices, our long cherished opinions, let us not condemn them on that account but investigate them fearlessly and prayerfully and not shrink from the examination because, if they are true, they place heavy responsibilities upon women. In throwing them before the public, I have been actuated solely by the belief that if they are acted upon, they will exalt the character and enlarge the usefulness of my own sex and contribute greatly to the happiness and virtue of the other. That there is a root of bitterness continually springing up in families and troubling the repose of both men and women must be manifest to even a superficial observer; and I believe it is the mistaken notion of the inequality of the sexes. As there is an assumption of superiority on the one part, which is not sanctioned by Jehovah, there is an incessant struggle on the other to rise to that degree of dignity which God designed women to possess in common with men and to maintain those rights and exercise those privileges which every woman's common sense, apart fom the prejudices of education, tells her are inalienable; they are a part of her moral nature and can only cease when her immortal mind is extinguished.

One word more. I feel that I am calling upon my sex to sacrifice what has been, what is still dear to their hearts, the adulation, the flattery, the attentions of trifling men. I am asking them to repel these insidious enemies whenever they approach them, to manifest by their conduct that, although they value highly the society of pious and intelligent men, they have no taste for idle conversation. . . . In lieu of these flattering but injurious attentions yielded to her as an inferior, as a mark of benevolence and courtesy, I want my sex to claim nothing from their brethren but what their brethren may justly claim from them in their intercourse as Christians. I am persuaded woman can do much in this way to elevate her own character. And that we may become duly sensible of the dignity of our nature, only a little lower than the angels, and bring forth fruit to the glory and honor of Emanuel's name is the fervent prayer of

Thine in the bonds of womanhood,

SARAH M. GRIMKÉ.

PART III

Margaret Fuller:

Romantic Idealist

The feminism of Sarah Margaret Fuller (1810–1850), the "most educated woman" America had produced, emerged from a different tradition than that of either Mary Wollstonecraft or Sarah Grimké.[1] Although well instructed in the Enlightenment thought of Mary Wollstonecraft and her heroes, Fuller was among the leaders of the American Romantic movement. And while, like Grimké, concerned about religious and moral values, she was too influenced by idealism to confine herself to the sectarian tradition. Margaret was born into an established New England family whose social position gave her great assurance. Naturally gifted and well-schooled, she rebelled against the encrusted social, intellectual, and religious doctrines of the past and denounced the mediocrity and materialism of the present. Although rebellious, she never embraced Jacksonian democracy or the social reform movements often associated with it. Rather she endorsed the transcendentalist's rejection of conventional Yankee thought and society for a fully developed Romantic idealism. The fullest expression of her feminist ideas—*Woman in the Nineteenth Century* (1844–1845)—came as she left the New England intellectual rebellion for still more heady European movements.[2]

Margaret, the eldest child of Timothy and Margaret Crane Fuller, grew up among the most elite and intellectual citizens of America's most elite and intellectual city, Boston. The Fuller ancestors first came to America in the mid-seventeenth century, and by the early nineteenth Harvard-educated Timothy Fuller had achieved prominence as a member of Congress and speaker of the Massachusetts House of Representatives. His daughter thus spent her formative years among stimulating and important people, including President John Quincy Adams, whom Fuller supported politically.[3]

In a thinly veiled autobiographical passage in *Woman in the Nineteenth Century*, Margaret Fuller credits her father with developing her self-reliance and encouraging her originality of thought and character, a paternal influence that Mary Wollstonecraft and Sarah Grimké would have envied. His belief in the equality of the sexes consequently affected her education and established an inner sense of worth which sexual discrimination could not shake. Only later did she discover that "this self-dependence, which was honored in me, is deprecated as a fault in most women. They are taught to learn their rule from without, not to unfold it from within." Most women "are so overloaded with precepts by guardians . . . they lose their chance of fair, free proportions." Luckily she had escaped such a guardian.

An intelligent and determined man, Timothy Fuller early decided that Margaret would have the best education available and proceeded to administer it himself. At age six, before reading English, she was reading Latin, the language forbidden to Sarah Grimké. In the ensuing years she digested an amazing variety of literature as well as mathematics, music, and history. Her education and inclinations were overwhelmingly literary. So steeped was she in the classics, she later recalled, "that when she was first old enough to think about Christianity, she cried out for her dear old Greek gods." By contrast Christian "spirituality seemed nakedness."[4]

Few people of the time had been so prepared for the intellectual life, but young Margaret paid for her father's rigorous tutoring and high expectations with insomnia, nightmares, and loneliness.[5] In time, however, she met and conversed with young male students of Harvard College and shared the revolt of the avant-garde against the intellectual currents of the day. She had women friends as well, but there were very few women who had either the scholarly interests or the intellectual preparation that Margaret had. Nor did they enjoy her sharp wit. Her talents led her to people similarly gifted, and most of these in the first part of the nineteenth century were necessarily men. Her Harvard friends included Frederic Henry Hedge, James Freeman Clarke, and William Henry Channing, all transcendentalists and her life-long confidants. With them she discussed French and Italian literature as well as philosophy and Greek. Intrigued by the increasing attention British Romantics, such as Thomas Carlyle, were paying to German writers, Margaret began to study the German language. She and Clarke jointly translated works by Johann Wolfgang von Goethe, Johann Christoph von Schiller, Jean Paul Richter, and others.

Her father, whose political opportunities had ended with the presidency of Andrew Jackson, gave up his law office and removed his family to a Groton farm forty miles from Cambridge. Here Margaret had the responsibility of tutoring her younger siblings and assisting her ailing mother. While she read American history with her father, she continued her work in European history and literature.

By this time Margaret Fuller had endorsed the European Romantic's reaction against both an Enlightenment rationalism that neglected imagination and a materialism that emphasized the external instead of the inner and the esthetic. She welcomed the Romantic's rejection of any restraint on the free spirit of the individual. The Romantic thought, and she agreed, that by working intuitively, the artist could elicit a deeper truth than could the scientist or "objectifier." Rejecting a mechanistic universe which mankind could observe but not alter, supporters of Romanticism argued for subjectivism, believing that the human mind affected the external reality it grasped. Thus the individual freed from rules, moral conventions, and external restraints could become a creative genius.

In her translation of *Tasso,* Margaret Fuller had become acquainted with the first in a series of Goethe's noble feminine characters. She felt that the German Romantics expressed "the idea of woman in their literature both to a greater height and depth" than other writers did. They designated the ideal toward which her feminism reached. Not immediately interested in material conditions or social station, Fuller did not embrace the Jacksonian democrat's dogmas of equal access to material goods and concern for bodily comfort. Focusing on the intellect and soul more than the body and the individual rather than the group, Margaret approved Goethe's attention to the "pure and perfected intelligence," "pure self-subsistence," and "the lyrical element in Woman." Goethe's women, she noted, "are units, addressed as souls. Accordingly the meeting between Man and Woman, as represented in him, is equal and noble."

In the fall of 1835 Margaret Fuller's intellectual work was suddenly curtailed. Her father died unexpectedly, leaving an ill wife, a very small estate, and several children to the care of his oldest child, who complained, "I have often had reason to regret being of the softer sex and never more than now. If I were an eldest son, I could be guardian to my brothers and sister, administer the estate, and really become the head of the family."[6] The law would not recognize her as such and her education had lacked practicality. But Margaret was nevertheless the head of the family.

On one of her occasional escapes to Cambridge, Margaret met Ralph Waldo Emerson, who shared her enthusiasm for the English and Scottish Romantics. He later introduced her to Amos Bronson Alcott, who offered her the position in his experimental Temple School in Boston which in 1836 ended her Groton exile and brought her into closer contact with Emerson. Along with their mutual friends, Fuller and Emerson constituted not only the best of the then current American literati and philosophers but the cultural avant-garde of the 1830's and 1840's. Emerson, who found Margaret "quite an extraordinary person for her apprehensiveness, her acquisitions, and her powers of conversation," declared that being in the presence of such an intelligence was like "being set in a large place. You stretch your limbs and dilate to your utmost size."[7]

At the time Emerson was beginning his close friendship with Margaret Fuller, he was also finishing the manuscript of his first book, *Nature*.[8] Influenced by Plato, Plotinus, other Neoplatonists, and the Kantians as well as the English Romantics, Emerson found in nature a reflection of the universal soul. Although he later modified his views somewhat, he then shared with Margaret the Romantic belief in nature as a link between man and the "world spirit," a means to commune with a higher reality. Emerson, like Fuller, embraced the Romantic's preference for an artistic grasp of nature rather than a scientific or objective analysis of the physical world.

Emerson, Fuller, and their friends absorbed the Neoplatonic and Kantian dualisms that distinguished the world of matter from that of spirit. The German philosopher Immanuel Kant, who "made the best catalogue of the human faculties and the best analysis of the mind," had separated reality into the phenomenal and the noumenal.[9] The phenomenal denoted the world of science, the realm of appearance, and the properties of things discernable by the senses. The human mind, Kant argued, contains principles which participate in the organizing of experience, imposing order on them and giving them meaning. Hence, human perception does not mirror physical reality but reflects pre-existing constructs within the mind. Kant also hailed the noumenal realm of value, of moral and esthetic experience, which deals with substantive reality: The soul might in moments of moral or esthetic revelation glimpse the divine. The New England transcendentalists followed Kant in finding science and religion qualitatively distinct, with different kinds of cognition appropriate to each.

Implementing religious cognition, Emerson put the material world aside for that of the mind or the ideal and postulated a universal soul or Oversoul in his famous Harvard Divinity School address. The guardians of rationalism in New England became alarmed at this "hyper-Germanized" apostasy and scolded the "New School in Literature and Religion" on the front page of the Boston *Daily Advertiser* and elsewhere.[10] Martin

Luther had declared that every man is his own priest, but Emerson carried the logic further; every man, as a part of nature, has within him some of the Oversoul, the divine. From this, reasoned his startled opponents, Emerson had concluded that every man is his own God. But the avant-garde did not acknowledge the traditionalists. William Henry Channing felt that Emerson and his other friends "on the somewhat stunted stock of Unitarianism—whose characteristic dogma was trust in individual reason as correlative to Supreme Wisdom—had . . . grafted German Idealism . . . and the result was a vague yet exalting conception of the godlike nature of the human spirit."[11]

Emerson, Fuller, and their friends considered the religious dimension of their new school as an improvement on the Quakers' Inner Light and the Swedenborgians' subscription to the primacy of the spirit. Emanuel Swedenborg, an eighteenth-century Swedish scientist, philosopher, and theologian read by the Emersonians, postulated that "God is a man."[12] Strongly distinguishing the material from the spiritual world, as did the Neoplatonists and Kantians, Swedenborg thought of God as a spiritually divine man or as infinite love and wisdom, not as body and blood.

While never inclined to philosophy, Margaret Fuller had learned enough of Kant and the Platonists both to grasp and to accept their fundamental distinction between matter and idea, body and soul, and to base her feminism upon it. "Male and female," she pronounced, "represent the two sides of the great radical dualism." Where many feminists before and after her tried to minimize differences between the sexes, Margaret built boldly upon ideal sexual distinctions, although she recognized, as did most Romantics, that in the world of matter the characteristics of individuals varied widely. She attributed characteristics of the male-dominated, materialist world around her to the physically stronger sex—energy, power, and intellect—which she thought developed first in time. To the second sex she attributed those emotional and spiritual characteristics—harmony, beauty, and love—that followed and refined masculine virtue. "The especial genius of Woman I believe to be electrical in movement, intuitive in function, spiritual in tendency." Because she believed that the feminine characteristics were precisely what the world now needed more of, Margaret thought the freeing of feminine spiritual power would develop women and improve society. If the masculine and feminine attributes were once brought into "perfect harmony, they would correspond to and fulfill one another, like hemispheres or the tenor and bass in music."

Dr. William Ellery Channing, founder of American Unitarianism and "bishop" to his younger colleagues like Emerson, tried to initiate regular gatherings of "cultivated, thoughtful people."[13] Although original attempts to do so failed, Frederic Henry Hedge urged Emerson to try again. And in September 1836 Hedge's "club of speculative students, who found the air in America getting a little close and stagnant," came into being. Except for Alcott, that "God-made priest," all the original members were ordained Unitarians, radical theologically even for that sect. During the following summer "the wise men . . . crave[d] the aid of wise and blessed women at their session," and Emerson, on behalf of "Mr. Hedge's Club," invited Margaret Fuller to join them.[14]

The little club of scholars, informal and varied in membership, met haphazardly at best. But word of their meetings gradually spread abroad in Boston, and they found themselves labelled transcendentalists or the Transcendental Club. An old philosophical term, "transcendental" had been applied to the philosophy of the post-Kantians. Among these major German philosophers, Johann Fichte and Friedrich von Schelling moved beyond Kant's system in two somewhat overlapping directions, both of which interested Emerson, Fuller, and the rest of the club. Fichte emphasized idealism, the proposition that the world is a mental construct or, more particularly, that the universe consists of an absolute Ego of which human consciousness is a manifestation. This Ego, or idea, makes up reality and strives in mankind for perfect self-awareness. Fichte considered the individual's effort to participate in the totality as a moral endeavor to attain fullest humanity.

Schelling, Fichte's disciple and Georg Hegel's friend, developed a transcendental idealism that, like Romanticism and mysticism, emphasized the poetic imagination in exploring reality by nonscientific methods. Stressing the dualistic nature of reality more than either Kant or Fichte, Schelling drew a sharp distinction between the objective, physical world and the subjective, ideal forces. His interest in the positive and negative poles of electricity, for example, may have sparked Margaret Fuller's consideration of the electrical properties of the sexes. Schelling reached out in all directions to deal with totality. But only in artistic creation, the act of esthetic intuition, did he find the objective and subjective, the negative and the positive, fused into synthesis. It is in art that the infinite manifests itself in the finite, that form and matter join, and that spirit and experience combine.

Margaret was particularly welcome to the transcendentalist group because of her conversational powers. Her friends found that she had them "at her mercy when she pleased to make us laugh," and she was very adept at drawing people out and placing all their various comments into meaningful patterns.[15] In an age which prized conversation, her acquaintances declared Margaret the supreme artist, and she complained that she found writing a poor second to discussion. "I shall write better, but never, I think, so well as I talk; for then I feel inspired."[16] "The club of clubs" gave her the opportunity to sharpen her conversational talent, which she then found to be a saleable commodity.[17]

Teaching in Boston and later in Providence, when added to tutoring, writing, and translating, led Fuller to physical exhaustion. Thus in 1839 she resigned her Providence position and moved to Boston's environs. But she could not support her family on her teacher's savings. Faced with the need to earn additional money, Margaret made necessity serve her own peculiarly feminist ends: She decided to hold conversation classes for those educated women of Boston who wished to subscribe. Convinced that each human being had an internal spark of soul or divinity which allowed him to transcend the commonplace, Margaret believed that women could be at least the moral equals of men—if women would develop their full intellectual and spiritual potential. She hoped that her subscribers might learn by example and direction to give precision, clarity, and system to their thought. She regretted that women "have so few inducements to test and classify what they receive" or "to ascertain what pursuits are best suited to us . . . and how we may make best use of our means for building up the life of thought upon the life of action."[18]

The first group of twenty-five women met to discuss Greek mythology. Fuller opened this initial series by complaining that "men are called on . . . to reproduce all that they learn. Their college exercises, their political duties, their professional studies, the first actions of life in any direction, call on them to put to use what they have learned. But women learn without any attempt to reproduce. Their only reproduction is for purposes of display."[19]

For five years she conducted her discussions, focusing on such topics as art, culture, literature, and women and life. The "gorgeous pedants" who returned yearly included the abolitionist-feminist Lydia Maria Child, Anna B. Shaw of woman's rights fame, the Peabody sisters (Elizabeth, the bookdealer; Mary, who married Horace Mann; and the artist Sophia, later Nathaniel Hawthorne's wife), Maria White (James Russell Lowell's fiancée), and the wives of Emerson, the transcendentalist minister Theodore Parker, and the historian George Bancroft.[20] Indeed men became so interested that Margaret held a series of coeducational conversations, but these she found less successful and did not repeat.

The conversations, along with her belief in intuition and the artist as revealer of reality, quickened her youthful interest in music and art. But basically her interest lay with the literary, particularly the poetic, as did the interests of most transcendentalists. In poetry they saw "the perpetual endeavor to express the spirit of the thing."[21] Fuller, Emerson, Thoreau, and several lesser luminaries all attempted, with varying degrees of success, to write verse. Like their translations, diaries, and copies of foreign periodicals, their poetry passed from hand to hand among themselves.

For several years Hedge's Club, dissatisfied with the journals of the day, had considered starting a transcendentalist periodical. Contemporary American criticism supported the literary status quo and rejected many of the new ideas which the Boston group espoused. The Enlightenment had not yet made way for Romanticism in American periodicals. But the *Dial,* a short-lived quarterly, emerged in the autumn of 1839, when Fuller agreed to be editor. Emerson, who had pledged "my own ink to fill it up," obtained promises of help from John Sullivan Dwight, the music critic; Theodore Parker, the brilliant Unitarian cleric, editor, philosopher, and master of twenty languages; art student Samuel Gray Ward; and Henry Thoreau, then resident in a hut outside of Concord.[22]

For the duration of the periodical, correspondence between Fuller and Emerson became even more extended, intense, and frequent than before. The two discussed the magazine and its contents as well as their own particular literary interests. Together, they prepared the editors' introductory statement for the *Dial.* In the late summer and fall of 1840, they exchanged several letters about friendship that provided Emerson with ideas for an essay later published in the *Dial.* The correspondence allowed the introspective Margaret to compare her "need of manifold being" to Emerson's "simple force." Her own inclination as well as lack of money led her to embrace life in the wider geographical and emotional world which he sought to escape by dint of his "arctic habits" and his belief that Spirit was readily attainable in a Concord apple orchard. But he, who kept both feet firmly on the ground, became distressed at times by her mystical ideas.[23]

For its initial two years the *Dial*'s financial difficulties caused Margaret Fuller to forgo the salary promised her. After fighting the bankrupt publisher to retain both the title *Dial* and the subscription list, she declared herself exhausted. Emerson, unwilling to see the journal expire, assumed the editorship. Fuller continued to supply pieces to keep the pages full, but the *Dial* was unable to pay its way. Emerson reluctantly ended its short life in April 1844. And as he later noted, "All its papers were unpaid contributions, and it was rather a work of friendship among the narrow circle of students than the organ of any party. Perhaps its writers were its chief readers: yet it contained some noble papers by Margaret Fuller."[24]

The many "papers" contributed to the *Dial* by Fuller varied in quality. She wrote on some of her favorite topics, sometimes rushing things into print which she had been considering for later use. Her article on Goethe praised his earlier Romantic works—*Tasso, Iphigenia,* etc.—and indicated her reservations about his later, somewhat more classical efforts. His women characters again attracted her attention, and she dwelled at length on Iphigenia, "solitary but tender, wise and innocent, sensitive and self-collected."[25] While editing and writing for the *Dial,* Margaret also translated and published correspondence that passed between two German women, Bettina von Arnim, a Romantic intellectual, and Karoline von Gunderode, the poet, and she printed an article in the *Dial* comparing Arnim as nature with Gunderode as the ideal. Although literary criticism was her main forte, Margaret also contributed verse, art and music criticism, fictional pieces of various kinds, and nonfictional essays to the magazine.

The *Dial* articles, other writings, and intellectual conversations seemed paramount in the lives of most of the transcendentalists. Fuller, Emerson, Thoreau, and their foremost poet, Margaret's brother-in-law, William Ellery Channing, wanted to transcend politics, among other mundane things. Like Fuller, the other transcendentalists generally came from long-established, native New England families that gloried in the classical republican days of Federalism and National Republicanism and found Jacksonian democracy vulgar and Whiggery plutocratic. Except for minister-publisher George Ripley, Parker, Alcott, and a few others, transcendentalists kept aloof from the various reform movements of the 1830's and early 1840's. Abolitionism, the temperance crusade, and the other great reforms focused upon the social and material conditions of mankind, and each of these movements seemed obsessed with only a small slice of life. None worried primarily about the spiritual dimension, and that was what concerned Fuller and other transcendentalists most. The Cambridge coterie generally abhorred slavery, but they would not divert their energies from spiritual concerns in order to work in any social movement.

Margaret Fuller always spoke approvingly of feminists and abolitionists, such as Abigail Kelley and the Grimké sisters, although she rarely associated with these reformers. Abolitionism commanded her "respect," but the movement was too partisan for her tastes. She sympathized with the aims of the abolitionists but not with their "measures."[26] The creative genius, striving for assimilation with God, Beauty, and Perfection, might do more for human uplift by example than could the multitude of reformers working for limited social and material improvements. She thought it vain to "clear away all the bad forms of society, . . . unless the individual begin to be ready for better." All "the rules left by Moses availed less to further the best life than the living example of one Messiah."

Aside from this spiritual bias, Fuller and her friends were so individualistic that they had little aptitude for judging or reconciling the diverse intuitions of widely different human beings—feminist or male supremacist, slaveholder or abolitionist, one transcendentalist or another. Unlike the Quaker reformers, they did not believe that the Bible reveals a single, immutable divine plan for the universe, nor did they think that social reform necessarily benefits the reformer's spirit.

George Ripley's creation of Brook Farm forced Hedge's Club to consider seriously the virtues of a community of "united individuals" patterned somewhat after the communalism of Charles Fourier.[27] But Fuller and most others found even this modified Fourierist phalanx distasteful. She disdained Brook Farm because she wished to belong to "a constellation, not a phalanx."[28] While recognizing the feminist implications of contemporary utopian communities and studying the writings of Charles Fourier, she nevertheless remained unenthusiastic about communalism. Such utopians, she thought, seemed to dwell upon material and social conditions and assumed that human beings were prisoners of their environment.

Margaret Fuller recognized the existence of burdensome poverty and discrimination, although she considered these injustices more a matter of individual than of institutional failure. She sought reform first from each person rather than from society. She accepted the institution of conventional marriage, while noting its abuses, offering a plea for the single adult, and seeking wider vocational outlets for women. She did not reject the traditional "functions" or duties assigned to women, as long as they were performed "in thought and love, willingly." She knew "no fairer, holier relation than that of a mother," provided that women "not be treated with an exclusive view to any one relation," including maternity. And she did not rail loudly against the political and civil death of her sex, though she considered such disabilities unfair. "What Woman needs is not as a woman to act or rule but as a nature to grow, as an intellect to discern, as a soul to live freely." Restraints upon women prove "insuperable only to those who think them so or who noisily strive to break them."

Reared to intellectual superiority, forced to head a household, and associated with and minister to America's most self-assured intellectuals, Margaret Fuller expected nothing short of equal treatment or consideration from her peers. While she was teaching in Providence, novelist John Neal spoke on the destiny and vocation of women in America and encouraged her thinking along explicitly feminist lines. Her reading of Charles Brockden Brown and William Godwin also contributed to the development of her feminist thought. She explored the woman question further in her Boston conversations and in July 1843 contributed a feminist piece to the *Dial.* The *Dial* essay—cumbersomely entitled "The Great Lawsuit: Man versus Men. Woman versus Women"—formed the nucleus of her argument in *Woman in the Nineteenth Century.* Emerson, Thoreau, Sophia Ripley, and Ellery Channing found it "to be a piece of life."[29]

Margaret's increasing concern with sexism crept into her correspondence with Emerson. When he announced the birth of a friend's child with "though no son, yet a sacred event," she demanded to know, "Why is not the advent of a daughter as 'sacred' a fact as that of a son? I do believe, O Waldo, . . . that you are at heart a sinner on this point. I entreat you to seek light in prayer upon it."[30] And when Lidian Emerson's delivery was approaching, Fuller wrote Emerson, "I hope you will have another son, for I perceive that men do not feel themselves represented to the next generation by *daughters.*"[31] Margaret, whom Timothy Fuller had valued more than any of his sons, found the commonly held view of the second sex difficult to accept.

Shortly after she submitted the "Great Lawsuit" to the *Dial,* she accepted James Clarke's invitation for a trip to the West and sailed from Buffalo through the Great Lakes to Chicago. With Clarke and his sister, Margaret visited northern Illinois and southern Wisconsin, where she found the feminine situation especially difficult. She talked with many of the women whose "unfitness . . . for their new lot" seemed to her the "great drawback upon the lives of these settlers." Going West, she decided, was generally "the choice of the men, and the women follow as women will . . . too often in heart-sickness and weariness." The women's part was the more difficult, little help was available to them, their education was inadequate for the job at hand, their bodily strength was less than that of the men, and their opportunities for pleasure and recreation were much scarcer. She found one contented woman, "the only one I heard of out there," who had suffered so much in her native England that she was prepared for frontier life. But even those most fit, such as farm women from western New York, did not like the change. They accepted it only because "it might be best for the young folks."[32]

Nevertheless, the lot of white women was attractive compared to that of Indian women. Margaret had read whatever was available about the Indians, whose cause she championed. She found that the women were little other than servants and beasts of burden, and while she knew that the life of the Indian male also was scarcely an easy one, she despaired for the women of the tribes. They too had little choice but to follow.

Upon her return home, Margaret revised her journal of the Western trip, which was published as *Summer on the Lakes* (1844). The book reached the crusading editor of the *New York Tribune,* Horace Greeley, who offered her a position as literary critic on his staff.

Before becoming the first woman on the regular staff of a major American newspaper, Fuller turned her *Dial* article, "The Great Lawsuit," into *Woman in the Nineteenth Century,* which Greeley and his partner published. Underestimating its impact, she felt a thousand copies disposed of in two or three years would be a gratifying accomplishment and was even willing to undertake the printing expense herself. When the book came out in February 1845, the entire first edition sold to bookdealers within a week and earned for its author an unexpected $85. Steeped in mythology and literary allusion, Margaret's view of what woman should be in the nineteenth century created both delight and dismay. William Cullen Bryant, editor of the *New York Evening Post,* declared the book's "language . . . pretty strong," but its thoughts were "so important that we should rejoice to know it read by every man and woman in America."[33] And while Margaret noted that "abuse public and and private is lavished upon its views," she considered the returns from the book's sale as the "signet of success. If one can be heard that is enough."[34]

Margaret's feminist volume, like her conversations and her philosophy, was designed for the educated fraction of American women who could make sense of the multitude of classical and literary references. Knowing her manuscript required "too much culture in the reader," Fuller hoped it might move "a mind here and there and through that others."[35] Neither mill girl, washerwoman, seamstress, nor farm wife would understand, empathize with, or profit immediately from her feminism, although there was always the distant hope that some benefit would trickle down from the intellectual elite.

While praising the book, Horace Greeley acknowledged that "many have closed it with but vague and dim ideas of what ought to be done." The transcendental Margaret was "a philanthropist, a critic, a relentless destroyer of shams and traditions; not a creator, a legislator." Edgar Allen Poe, who admired her abilities as a literary critic and praised *Summer on the Lakes,* was less enamored of her feminist volume. He found *Woman in the Nineteenth Century* "nervous, forcible, thoughtful, suggestive, brilliant, and to a certain extent scholar-like." He suggested, however, that she erred "through her own excessive subjectiveness. She judges woman by the heart and intellect of Miss Fuller, but there are not more than one or two dozen Miss Fullers on the whole face of the earth." Poe saw that "her acts are bookish, and her books are less thoughts than acts."[36] As a Romantic idealist, Margaret Fuller did indeed entwine thought with act and, in striving for genius, sought social reform through the power of example.

By 1845 Margaret, who had deserted New England the previous summer for her Western trip, abandoned Boston altogether and left for New

York. Her restless spirit and the need for income launched her upon a new career that left transcendentalism behind. She relished the adventure of demonstrating to readers of the *Tribune* that the woman who could write a feminist treatise could pen newspaper columns as well. Emerson disapproved of her move: "The muses have feet, to be sure, but it is an odd arrangement that selects them for the treadmill."[37] However, Margaret was happy with New York, with her lodging at the Greeleys', and with the three columns she wrote each week, two of which concerned literature while the third frequently branched out into a discussion of governmental matters or social institutions. Her education, interests, and contributions to the *Western Messenger* (which James Clarke published in Ohio) and the *Dial* had amply prepared her to write criticism. In New York she had the time, inclination, and freedom to develop these powers. She was remarkably shrewd in judging the literary talent of her day, declaring such popular poetry as Longfellow's and James Russell Lowell's to be mediocre while praising the work of the little-known Poe and Hawthorne. When she left New York for Europe in 1846 after an abortive romance, the days of arguing with Emerson about his retirement into a "cave" were forever gone, as were her close ties to the Cambridge world.[38]

Margaret spent her last years far from her native New England in a manner few would have predicted. After extensive visits in England and Scotland with some of her heroes—Carlyle, the Romantic poet William Wordsworth, and the exiled Italian republican Giuseppe Mazzini—she went to France, where she met the female novelist George Sand and examined Rousseau's manuscripts. By October 1847 she had reached Rome, the most familiar city of her childhood reading. There she became deeply involved in Italian politics and participated in the short-lived Roman Republic, a social activism that her American friends in the abolitionist movement never elicited.

Margaret had started to change even before she left America. Her columns in the *Tribune* often focused on one of the city's institutions or asylums which she had toured. Her interest in reform movements had increased, and her thoughts returned to Fourierism and other social schemes. She read about and discussed the communalism of Charles Fourier with greater interest and sympathy. After seeing the material deprivation and social degradation of people living in American cities, on the frontier, and throughout Europe, she developed increasing appreciation of the importance of the phenomenal realm. Shortly after she arrived in Italy, she wrote Henry Channing, "Art is not important to me now . . . I take interest in the state of the people, their manners. . . . I see the future dawning; it is in important aspects Fourier's future."[39]

Caught in Rome during the republican rising, she assumed supervision of a hospital for the wounded republican troops. Garibaldi's men regarded her as something of an angel. She also clandestinely married Giovanni Angelo, Marquis Ossoli, a lesser Italian nobleman fighting in the republican cause, and bore their son. After the fall of Mazzini's Republic of Rome, the Ossolis took refuge in other Italian cities until they sailed for America in the summer of 1850. Their ship grounded and sank within sight of Long Island, and Margaret, her husband, and the child perished with it. Henry Thoreau, William Henry Channing, and others rushed to Fire Island to salvage anything they could, but local scavengers had arrived first and few of Margaret's effects were found. The manuscript history of the Roman Republic, which Fuller had considered her best work, was lost forever with its author. All her friends and relatives could claim were a few assorted papers and the body of her child.

The transcendentalist circle, the New York literati, and her European friends were shocked by Margaret's death. Although her candid, forthright personality and critical reviews did not always endear her to people, she had vast numbers of admirers. Some, such as Greeley, went on to become active in the woman's rights movement organized after Margaret had left for Europe. At the Worcester National Convention a few months after Margaret's death, Henry Channing effectively offered organizational plans and principles for the fledgling national movement. Theodore Parker; Elizabeth Peabody; Caroline Healy Dall, one of the "gorgeous pedants" who recorded her impressions of the conversations; Rebecca Spring, who with her husband had taken Margaret on her fateful European trip; James Freeman Clarke; and Bronson Alcott—all supported the national women's rights movement in various ways. Even Emerson obliged the ladies with letters of support and eventually an address.

Probably many of these friends would have supported the feminist drive without having for "our watchword the language of Margaret Fuller."[40] But Paulina Wright Davis, the president of the new woman's rights national organization, bemoaned the movement's "one great disappointment. . . . Margaret Fuller, toward whom many eyes were turned as the future leader in this movement, was not with us . . . and we were left to mourn her guiding hand—her royal presence. To her, I, at least, had hoped to confide the leadership of this movement. It can never be known if she would have accepted it; the desire had been expressed to her by letter; but be that as it may, she was, and still is, a leader of thought; a position far more desirable than a leader of numbers."[41]

NOTES

1. Ralph W. Emerson, as quoted in Barbara M. Cross (ed.), *The Educated Woman in America: Selected Writings of Catharine Beecher, Margaret Fuller, and M. Carey Thomas* (New York: Teachers College Press, Columbia University, 1965), 30.

2. Margaret Fuller, *Woman in the Nineteenth Century, with Kindred Papers Relating to the Sphere, Condition and Duties of Woman* (New York: Tribune Press, 1845). The 1855 edition was reissued in 1971 by Source Book Press, New York. The other accessible unabridged edition of the text (without the lengthy appendices) can be found in Mason Wade (ed.), *The Writings of Margaret Fuller* (New York: The Viking Press, 1941), 109–218.

3. Mason Wade, *Margaret Fuller: Whetstone of Genius* (New York: The Viking Press, 1940), and Arthur W. Brown, *Margaret Fuller* (New York: Twayne Publishers, 1964), offer the best modern biographies from which much of the narrative information about Margaret Fuller was drawn for this essay. For the direct assessment of her New England friends, see R. W. Emerson, W. H. Channing, and J. F. Clarke, *Memoirs of Margaret Fuller Ossoli* (2 volumes, New York: The Tribune Association, 1869).

4. Cross, *Educated Woman,* 122.

5. For a somewhat fictionalized account of her boarding-school experiences, see "Mariana," as reprinted in Perry Miller (ed.), *Margaret Fuller: American Romantic* (Ithaca: Cornell University Press, 1970 reissue of 1963 edition), 5–24, which also offers the most accessible selection of Fuller's writings and correspondence. See also Emerson et al., *Fuller Memoirs,* I, 42–52.

6. Emerson et al., *Fuller Memoirs,* I, 157.

7. Ralph L. Rusk (ed.), *The Letters of Ralph Waldo Emerson* (6 volumes, New York: Columbia University Press, 1939), II, 32.

8. For an introduction to Emerson's ideas, see Loren Baritz, *City on a Hill: A History of Ideas and Myths in America* (New York: John Wiley & Sons, Inc., 1964), 205–269, and Paul M. Conkin, *Puritans and Pragmatists: Eight Eminent American Thinkers* (New York: Dodd, Mead & Co., 1968), 151–190.

9. Emerson, as quoted in Perry Miller (ed.), *The American Transcendentalists: Their Prose and Poetry* (New York: Doubleday & Company, Inc., 1957), 7.

10. Brown, *Fuller,* 46.

11. Miller, *American Transcendentalists,* 36–37.

12. L. B. DeBeaumont, "Swedenborg," in James Hastings (ed.), *Encyclopedia of Religion and Ethics* (12 volumes, New York: Charles Scribner's Sons, 1908–1922), XII, 129–132.

13. Miller, *American Transcendentalists,* 13.

14. Emerson et al., *Fuller Memoirs,* I, 322; Rusk, *Emerson Letters,* II, 29, 95.

15. Rusk, *Emerson Letters,* II, 47.

16. Quoted in Wade, *Fuller,* 89.

17. Rusk, *Emerson Letters,* II, 293.

18. Cross, *Educated Woman,* 113.

19. Cross, *Educated Woman,* 117.

20. Harriet Martineau, as quoted in Brown, *Fuller,* 54.

21. Emerson, "Poetry and Imagination," as quoted in Miller, *American Transcendentalists,* 204.

22. Rusk, *Emerson Letters,* II, 229.

23. Rusk, *Emerson Letters,* II, 340n–341n.

24. Miller, *American Transcendentalists,* 15.

25. Wade, *Fuller Writings,* 272.

26. Wade, *Fuller Writings,* 556.

27. For a consideration of the relationship between transcendentalism and the social reform movements, see Stanley M. Elkins, *Slavery: A Problem in American Institutional and Intellectual Life,* second edition (Chicago: University of Chicago Press, 1969), 140–193, and Aileen S. Kraditor, *Means and Ends in American Abolitionism: Garrison and His Critics on Strategy and Tactics, 1834–1850* (New York: Random House, Inc., 1970), 12–38.

28. Quoted in Brown, *Fuller,* 66.

29. Rusk, *Emerson Letters,* III, 183.

30. Rusk, *Emerson Letters,* III, 170.

31. Rusk, *Emerson Letters,* III, 235.

32. *Summer on the Lakes* is conveniently reprinted in Wade, *Fuller Writings,* 5–104. For specific quotations, see pp. 44–45, 58, 64.

33. Quoted in Brown, *Fuller,* 132.

34. Wade, *Fuller Writings,* 575.

35. Wade, *Fuller Writings,* 567.

36. Horace Greeley, as quoted in Wade, *Fuller,* 142–143; Edgar Allen Poe, "Sarah Margaret Fuller," as reprinted in Edmund Wilson (ed.), *The Shock of Recognition* (2 volumes, New York: Grosset and Dunlap, 1955), I, 146–154.

37. Rusk, *Emerson Letters,* III, 268.

38. Rusk, *Emerson Letters,* III, 252–254.

39. Wade, *Fuller Writings,* 203.

40. Sarah Grimké, as quoted in Elizabeth Cady Stanton, Susan B. Anthony, Matilda J. Gage, and Ida H. Harper, (eds.), *History of Woman Suffrage,* (6 volumes, Rochester, New York, and New York, 1881–1922), I, 355.

41. Stanton et al., *Woman Suffrage,* I, 217.

WOMAN IN THE NINETEENTH CENTURY, WITH KINDRED PAPERS RELATING TO THE SPHERE, CONDITION AND DUTIES OF WOMAN (1844–1845)

"Frailty, thy name is WOMAN.*"*

"The Earth waits for her Queen."

The connection between these quotations may not be obvious, but it is strict. Yet would any contradict us if we made them applicable to the other side and began also,

Frailty, thy name is MAN.

The Earth waits for its King?

Yet Man, if not yet fully installed in his powers, has given much earnest of his claims. Frail he is indeed—how frail, how impure! Yet often has the vein of gold displayed itself amid the baser ores, and Man has appeared before us in princely promise worthy of his future.

If oftentimes we see the prodigal son feeding on the husks in the fair field no more his own, anon we raise the eyelids, heavy from bitter tears, to behold in him the radiant apparition of genius and love, demanding not less than the all of goodness, power, and beauty. We see that in him the largest claim finds a due foundation. That claim is for no partial sway, no exclusive possession. He cannot be satisfied with any one gift of life, any one department of knowledge or telescopic peep at the heavens. He feels himself called to understand and aid Nature that she may through his intelligence be raised and interpreted, to be a student of and servant to the universe-spirit and king of his planet that as an angelic minister he may bring it into conscious harmony with the law of that spirit. . . .

Sages and lawgivers have bent their whole nature to the search for truth and thought themselves happy if they could buy, with the sacrifice of all temporal ease and pleasure, one seed for the future Eden. Poets and priests have strung the lyre with the heartstrings, poured out their best blood upon the altar which, reared anew from age to age, shall at last sustain the flame pure enough to rise to highest heaven. Shall we not name with as deep a benediction those who, if not so immediately or so consciously in connection with the eternal truth, yet led and fashioned by a divine instinct serve no less to develop and interpret the open secret of love passing into life, energy creating for the purpose of happiness: the artist whose hand, drawn by a pre-existent harmony to a certain medium, molds it to forms of life more highly and completely organized than are seen elsewhere and by carrying out the intention of Nature reveals her meaning to those who are not yet wise enough to divine it; the philosopher who listens steadily for laws and causes and from those obvious infers those yet unknown; the historian who, in faith that all events must have their reason and their aim, records them and thus fills archives from which the youth of prophets may be fed; the man of science dissecting the statements, testing the facts, and demonstrating order, even where he cannot [demonstrate] its purpose?

Lives, too, which bear none of these names have yielded tones of no less significance. The candlestick set in a low place has given light as faithfully where it was needed as that upon the hill. . . . So great has been from time to time the promise that in all ages men have said the gods themselves came down to dwell with them, that the All-Creating wandered on the earth to taste in a limited nature the sweetness of virtue. . . . And the dwellers in green pastures and natural students of the stars were selected to hail first among men the holy child, whose life and death were to present the type of excellence which has sustained the heart of so large a portion of mankind in these later generations.

Such marks have been made by the footsteps of *man* (still, alas, to be spoken of as the *ideal* man) wherever he has passed through the wilderness of *men;* and whenever the pygmies stepped in one of those, they felt dilate within the breast somewhat that promised nobler stature and purer blood. They were impelled to forsake their evil ways of decrepit skepticism and covetousness of corruptible possessions. Convictions flowed in upon them. They, too, raised the cry: God is living now, today; and all beings are brothers, for they are his children. Simple words enough, yet which only angelic natures can use or hear in their full, free sense. These were the triumphant moments; but soon the lower nature took its turn, and the era of a truly human life was postponed.

Thus is Man still a stranger to his inheritance, still a pleader, still a pilgrim. Yet his happiness is secure in the end. And now no more a glimmering consciousness but assurance begins to be felt and spoken that the highest ideal Man can form of his own powers is that which he is destined to attain. Whatever the soul knows how to seek, it cannot fail to obtain. This is the Law and the Prophets. Knock and it shall be opened; seek and ye shall find. It is demonstrated; it is a maxim. Man no longer paints his proper nature in some form and says, "Prometheus had it; it is Godlike"; but "Man must have it; it is human." However disputed by many, however ignorantly used or falsified by those who do receive it, the fact of a universal, unceasing revelation has been too clearly stated in words to be lost sight of in thought; and sermons preached from the text, "Be ye perfect," are the only sermons of a pervasive and deep-searching influence. . . .

. . . The idea of Man, however imperfectly brought out, has been far more so than that of Woman; that she, the other half of the same thought, the other chamber of the heart of life, needs now take her turn in the full pulsation, and that improvement in the daughters will best aid in the reformation of the sons of this age.

It should be remarked that as the principle of liberty is better understood and more nobly interpreted, a broader protest is made in behalf of Woman. As men become aware that few men have had a fair chance, they are inclined to say that no women have had a fair chance. The French Revolution, that strangely disguised angel, bore witness in favor of Woman but interpreted her claims no less ignorantly than those of Man. Its idea of happiness did not rise beyond outward enjoyment, unobstructed by the tyranny of others. The title it gave was *citoyen, citoyenne;*

and it is not unimportant to Woman that even this species of equality was awarded her. Before, she could be condemned to perish on the scaffold for treason, not as a citizen but as a subject. The right with which this title then invested a human being was that of bloodshed and license. The Goddess of Liberty was impure. . . . Yes! Man, born to purify and animate the unintelligent and the cold, can in his madness degrade and pollute no less the fair and the chaste. Yet truth was prophesied in the ravings of that hideous fever caused by long ignorance and abuse. Europe is conning a valued lesson from the bloodstained page.

The same tendencies further unfolded will bear good fruit in this country. . . . Though the national independence be blurred by the servility of individuals, though freedom and equality have been proclaimed only to leave room for a monstrous display of slavedealing and slavekeeping, though the free American so often feels himself free like the Roman only to pamper his appetites and his indolence through the misery of his fellow-beings, still it is not in vain that the verbal statement has been made, "All men are born free and equal." . . . It is inevitable that an external freedom, an independence of the encroachments of other men such as has been achieved for the nation, should be so also for every member of it. That which has once been clearly conceived in the intelligence cannot fail sooner or later to be acted out. It has become a law as irrevocable as that of the Medes in their ancient dominion; men will privately sin against it, but the law . . . cannot fail of universal recognition. . . . We have waited here long in the dust; we are tired and hungry, but the triumphal procession must appear at last.

Of all its banners, none has been more steadily upheld, and under none have more valor and willingness for real sacrifices been shown, than that of the champions of the enslaved African. And this band it is which, partly from a natural following out of principles, partly because many women have been prominent in that cause, makes just now the warmest appeal in behalf of Woman. . . .

"Is it not enough," cries the irritated [slave] trader, "that you have done all you could to break up the national union and thus destroy the prosperity of our country, but now you must be trying to break up family union, to take my wife away from the cradle and the kitchen-hearth to vote at polls and preach from a pulpit? Of course if she does such things, she cannot attend to those of her own sphere. She is happy enough as she is. She has more leisure than I have—every means of improvement, every indulgence."

"Have you asked her whether she was satisfied with these *indulgences?*"

"No, but I know she is. She is too amiable to desire what would make me unhappy and too judicious to wish to step beyond the sphere of her sex. I will never consent to have our peace disturbed by any such discussions."

"Consent—you? It is not consent from you that is in question—it is assent from your wife."

"Am not I the head of my house?"

"You are not the head of your wife. God has given her a mind of her own."

"I am the head, and she the heart."

"God grant you play true to one another then! I suppose I am to be grateful that you did not say she was only the hand. If the head represses no natural pulse of the heart, there can be no question as to your giving your consent. Both will be of one accord, and there needs but to present any question to get a full and true answer. There is no need of precaution, of indulgence, nor consent. But our doubt is whether the heart *does* consent with the head or only obeys its decrees with a passiveness that precludes the exercise of its natural powers or a repugnance that turns sweet qualities to bitter or a doubt that lays waste the fair occasions of life. It is to ascertain the truth that we propose some liberating measures." . . .

It may well be an Anti-Slavery party that pleads for Woman, if we consider merely that she does not hold property on equal terms with men; so that if a husband dies without making a will, the wife, instead of taking at once his place as head of the family, inherits only a part of his fortune, often brought him by herself, as if she were a child or ward only, not an equal partner.

We will not speak of the innumerable instances in which profligate and idle men live upon the earnings of industrious wives or if the wives leave them and take with them the children to perform the double duty of mother and father, follow from place to place and threaten to rob them of the children; if deprived of the rights of a husband . . ., [these men] plant . . . themselves in their [wives'] poor lodgings, frightening them into paying tribute by taking from them the children, running into debt at the expense of these otherwise so overtasked helots. Such instances count up by scores within my own memory.

. . . The public opinion of their own sex is already against such men, and where cases of extreme tyranny are made known, there is private action in the wife's favor. But she ought not to need this, nor, I think, can she long. Men must soon see that as on their own ground Woman is the weaker party, she ought to have legal protection which would make such oppression impossible. But I would not deal with "atrocious instances," except in the way of illustration, neither demand from men a partial redress in some one matter but go to the root of the whole. If principles could be established, particulars would adjust themselves aright. Ascertain the true destiny of Woman; give her legitimate hopes and a standard within herself; marriage and all other relations would by degrees be harmonized with these.

But to return to the historical progress of this matter. Knowing that there exists in the minds of men a tone of feeling toward women as toward slaves, such as is expressed in the common phrase, "Tell that to women and children"—that the infinite soul can only work through them in already ascertained limits; that the gift of reason, Man's highest prerogative, is allotted to them in much lower degree; that they must be kept from mischief and melancholy by being constantly engaged in active labor which is to be furnished and directed by those better able to think, etc., etc.—we need not multiply instances, for who can review the experience of last week without recalling words which imply, whether in jest or earnest, these views or views like these. Knowing this, can we wonder that many reformers think that measures are not likely to be taken in behalf of women unless their wishes could be publicly represented by women?

"That can never be necessary," cry the other side. "All men are privately influenced by women; each has his wife, sister, or female friends and is too much biased by these relations to fail of representing their interests; and if this is not enough, let them propose and enforce their wishes with the pen. The beauty of home would be destroyed, the delicacy of the sex be violated, the dignity of halls of legislation degraded by an attempt to introduce them there. Such duties are inconsistent with those of a mother"; and then we have ludicrous pictures of ladies in hysterics at the polls and senate chambers filled with cradles.

But if in reply we admit as truth that Woman seems destined by nature rather for the inner circle, we must add that the arrangements of civilized life have not been as yet such as to secure it to her. Her circle, if the duller, is not the quieter. If kept from "excitement," she is not from drudgery. Not only the Indian squaw carries the burdens of the camp, but the favorites of Louis XIV accompany him in his journeys, and the washerwoman stands at her tub and carries home her work at all seasons and in all states of health. Those who think the physical circumstances of Woman would make a part in the affairs of national government unsuitable are by no means those who think it impossible for Negresses to endure field work even during pregnancy or for seamstresses to go through their killing labors.

As to the use of the pen, there was quite as much opposition to Woman's possessing herself of that help to free agency as there is now to her seizing on the rostrum or the desk; and she is likely to draw, from a permission to plead her cause that way, opposite inferences to what might be wished by those who now grant it.

As to the possibility of her filling with grace and dignity any such position, we should think those who had seen the great actresses and heard the Quaker preachers of modern times would not doubt that Woman can express publicly the fullness of thought and creation without losing any of the peculiar beauty of her sex. What can pollute and tarnish is to act thus from any motive except that something needs to be said or done. Woman could take part in the processions, the songs, the dances of old religion; no one fancied her delicacy was impaired by appearing in public for such a cause.

As to her home, she is not likely to leave it more than she now does for balls, theaters, meetings for promoting missions, revival meetings, and others to which she flies in hope of an animation for her existence commensurate with what she sees enjoyed by men. Governors of ladies' fairs are no less engrossed by such a charge than the governor of a state by his; presidents of Washingtonian societies no less away from home than presidents of conventions. If men look straitly to it, they will find that unless their lives are domestic, those of the women will not be. A house is no home unless it contain food and fire for the mind as well as for the body. The female Greek of our day is as much in the street as the male to cry, "What news?" We doubt not it was the same in Athens of old. The women, shut out from the marketplace, made up for it at the religious festivals. For human beings are not so constituted that they can live without expansion. If they do not get it in one way, they must in another or perish.

As to men's representing women fairly at present, while we hear from men who owe to their wives not only all that is comfortable or graceful but all that is wise in the arrangement of their lives the frequent remark, "You cannot reason with a woman," when from those of delicacy, nobleness, and poetic culture falls the contemptuous phrase "women and children" and that in no light sally of the hour but in works intended to give a permanent statement of the best experiences, [and] when not one man in the million, . . . in the hundred million, can rise above the belief that Woman was made *for Man*—when such traits as these are daily forced upon the attention, can we feel that Man will always do justice to the interests of Woman? Can we think that he takes a sufficiently discerning and religious view of her office and destiny *ever* to do her justice except when prompted by sentiment—accidentally or transiently, that is, for the sentiment will vary according to the relations in which he is placed? The lover, the poet, the artist are likely to view her nobly. The father and the philosopher have some chance of liberality; the man of the world, the legislator for expediency, none.

Under these circumstances, without attaching importance in themselves to the changes demanded by the champions of Woman, we hail them as signs of the times. We would have every arbitrary barrier thrown down. We would have every path laid open to Woman as freely as to Man. Were this done and a slight temporary fermentation allowed to subside, we should see crystallizations more pure and of more various beauty. We believe the divine energy would pervade nature to a degree unknown in the history of former ages and that no discordant collision but a ravishing harmony of the spheres would ensue.

Yet then and only then will mankind be ripe for this—when inward and outward freedom for Woman as much as for Man shall be acknowledged as a *right,* not yielded as a concession. As the friend of the Negro assumes that one man cannot by right hold another in bondage, so should the friend of Woman assume that Man cannot by right lay even well-meant restrictions on Woman. If the Negro be a soul, if the woman be a soul, appareled in flesh, to one Master only are they accountable. There is but one law for souls, and if there is to be an interpreter of it, he must come not as man or son of man but as son of God.

Were thought and feeling once so far elevated that Man should esteem himself the brother and friend, but nowise the lord and tutor, of Woman —were he really bound with her in equal worship—arrangements as to function and employment would be of no consequence. What Woman needs is not as a woman to act or rule but as a nature to grow, as an intellect to discern, as a soul to live freely and unimpeded to unfold such powers as were given her when we left our common home. If fewer talents were given her, yet if allowed the free and full employment of these so that she may render back to the giver his own with usury, she will not complain; nay, I dare to say she will bless and rejoice in her earthly birthplace, her earthly lot. Let us consider what obstructions impede this good era and what signs give reason to hope that it draws near.

I was talking on this subject with Miranda, a woman who, if any in the world could, might speak without heat and bitterness of the position of her sex. Her father was a man who cherished no sentimental reverence for Woman but a firm belief in the equality of the sexes. She was his eldest child and came to him at an age when he needed a companion. From the time she could speak and go alone, he addressed her not as a plaything but as a living mind. . . . He called on her for clear judgment, for courage, for honor and fidelity—in short, for such virtues as he knew. In so far as he possessed the keys to the wonders of this universe, he allowed free use of them to her, and by the incentive of a high expectation he forbade, so far as possible, that she should let the privilege lie idle.

Thus this child was early led to feel herself a child of the spirit. She took her place easily not only in the world of organized being but in the world of mind. A dignified sense of self-dependence was given as all her portion, and she found it a sure anchor. Herself securely anchored, her relations with others were established with equal security. She was fortunate in a total absence of those charms which might have drawn to her bewildering flatteries and in a strong electric nature which repelled those who did not belong to her and attracted those who did. With men and women her relations were noble—affectionate without passion, intellectul without coldness. The world was free to her, and she lived freely in it. Outward adversity came and inward conflict, but that faith and self-respect had early been awakened which must always lead at last to an outward serenity and an inward peace.

Of Miranda I had always thought as an example that the restraints upon the sex were insuperable only to those who think them so or who noisily strive to break them. She had taken a course of her own, and no man stood in her way. Many of her acts had been unusual but excited no uproar. Few helped but none checked her; and the many men who knew her mind and her life showed to her confidence as to a brother, gentleness as to a sister. And not only refined but very coarse men approved and aided one in whom they saw resolution and clearness of design. Her mind was often the leading one, always effective.

When I talked with her upon these matters and had said very much what I have written, she smilingly replied: "And yet we must admit that I have been fortunate, and this should not be. My good father's early trust gave the first bias, and the rest followed of course. It is true that I have had less outward aid in after years than most women, but that is of little consequence. Religion was early awakened in my soul—a sense that what the soul is capable to ask it must attain and that though I might be aided and instructed by others, I must depend on myself as the only constant friend. This self-dependence which was honored in me is deprecated as a fault in most women. They are taught to learn their rule from without, not to unfold it from within.

"This is the fault of Man, who is still vain and wishes to be more important to Woman than by right he should be."

"Men have not shown this disposition toward you," I said.

"No, because the position I early was enabled to take was one of self-reliance. And were all women as sure of their wants as I was, the result would be the same. But they are so overloaded with precepts by guardians who think that nothing is so much to be dreaded for a woman as originality of thought or character that their minds are impeded by doubts till they lose their chance of fair, free proportions. The difficulty is to get them to the point from which they shall naturally develop self-respect and learn self-help.

"Once I thought that men would help to forward this state of things more than I do now. I saw so many of them wretched in the connections they had formed in weakness and vanity. They seemed so glad to esteem women whenever they could.

" 'The soft arms of affection,' said one of the most discerning spirits, 'will not suffice for me, unless on them I see the steel bracelets of strength.'

"But early I perceived that men never in any extreme of despair wished to be women. On the contrary, they were ever ready to taunt one another at any sign of weakness with,

Art thou not like the women, who—

The passage ends various ways according to the occasion and rhetoric of the speaker. When they admired any woman, they were inclined to speak of her as 'above her sex.' Silently I observed this and feared it argued a rooted skepticism which for ages had been fastening on the heart and which only an age of miracles could eradicate. Ever I have been treated with great sincerity; and I look upon it as a signal instance of this that an intimate friend of the other sex said in a fervent moment that I 'deserved in some star to be a man.' He was much surprised when I disclosed my view of my position and hopes, when I declared my faith that the feminine side, the side of love, of beauty, of holiness, was now to have its full chance, and that if either were better, it was better now to be a woman; for even the slightest achievement of good was furthering an especial work of our time. He smiled incredulously. 'She makes the best she can of it,' thought he. 'Let Jews believe the pride of Jewry, but I am of the better sort and know better.' " . . .

[I]

. . . Not only is Man vain and fond of power, but the same want of development which thus affects him morally prevents his intellectually discerning the destiny of Woman. The boy wants no woman but only a girl to play ball with him and mark his pocket handkerchief.

Thus in Schiller's "Dignity of Woman," beautiful as the poem is, there is no "grave and perfect man" but only a great boy to be softened and restrained by the influence of girls. Poets—the elder brothers of their race—have usually seen further; but what can you expect of everyday men if Schiller was not more prophetic as to what women must be? Even with Richter, one foremost thought about a wife was that she would "cook him something good." But as this is a delicate subject and we are in constant danger of being accused of slighting what are called "the functions," let me say in behalf of Miranda and myself that we have high respect for those who "cook something good," who create and preserve fair order in houses and prepare therein the shining raiment for worthy inmates, worthy guests. Only these "functions" must not be a drudgery or enforced necessity but a part of life. Let Ulysses drive the beeves home while Penelope there piles up the fragrant loaves; they are both well employed if these be done in thought and love, willingly. But Penelope is no more meant for a baker or weaver solely than Ulysses for a cattleherd. . . .

No, Man is not willingly ungenerous. He wants faith and love because he is not yet himself an elevated being. He cries with sneering skepticism, "Give us a sign." But if the sign appears, his eyes glisten and he offers not merely approval but homage.

The severe nation which taught that the happiness of the race was forfeited through the fault of a Woman and showed its thought of what sort of regard Man owed her by making him accuse her on the first question to his God—who gave her to the patriarch as a handmaid and by the Mosaical law bound her to allegiance like a serf—even they greeted with solemn rapture all great and holy women as heroines, prophetesses, judges in Israel; and if they made Eve listen to the serpent, [they] gave Mary as a bride to the Holy Spirit. In other nations it has been the same down to our day. To the Woman who could conquer, a triumph was awarded. And not only those whose strength was recommended to the heart by association with goodness and beauty, but those who were bad, if they were steadfast and strong, had their claims allowed. In any age a Semiramis, an Elizabeth of England, a Catherine of Russia makes her place good, whether in a large or small circle. How has a little wit, a little genius, been celebrated in a Woman! . . .

Whatever may have been the domestic manners of the ancients, the idea of Woman was nobly manifested in their mythologies and poems where she appears as Sita in the "Ramayana," a form of tender purity, [and] as the Egyptian Isis, of divine wisdom never yet surpassed. In Egypt, too, the Sphinx, walking the earth with lion tread, looked out upon its marvels in the calm, inscrutable beauty of a virgin's face, and the Greek could only add wings to the great emblem. In Greece, Ceres and Proserpine, significantly termed the "great goddesses," were seen seated side by side. They needed not to rise for any worshiper or any change; they were prepared for all things, as those initiated to their mysteries knew. . . . I cannot complain of the age and nation which represents its thought by such a symbol as I see before me at this moment. It is a zodiac of the busts of gods and goddesses, arranged in pairs. The circle breathes the music of a heavenly order. Male and female heads are distinct in expression, but equal in beauty, strength, and calmness. Each male head is that of a brother and a king—each female of a sister and a queen. Could the thought thus expressed be lived out, there would be nothing more to be desired. There would be unison in variety, congeniality in difference.

Coming nearer our own time, we find religion and poetry no less true in their revelations. The rude man just disengaged from the sod, the Adam, accuses Woman to his God and records her disgrace to their posterity. He is not ashamed to write that he could be drawn from heaven by one beneath him—one made, he says, from but a small part of himself. But in the same nation educated by time, instructed by a succession of prophets, we find Woman in as high a position as she has ever occupied. No figure that has ever arisen to greet our eyes has been received with more fervent reverence than that of the Madonna. . . .

And not only this holy and significant image was worshiped by the pilgrim and the favorite subject of the artist, but it exercised an immediate influence on the destiny of the sex. The empresses who embraced the cross converted sons and husbands. . . . Nor, however imperfect may be the action in our day of the faith thus expressed and though we can scarcely think it nearer this ideal than that of India or Greece was near their ideal, is it in vain that the truth has been recognized that Woman is not only a part of Man, bone of his bone and flesh of his flesh, born that men might not be lonely—but that women are in themselves possessors of and possessed by immortal souls. This truth undoubtedly received a greater outward stability from the belief of the church that the earthly parent of the Saviour of souls was a woman. . . .

It is not the transient breath of poetic incense that women want; each can receive that from a lover. It is not lifelong sway; it needs but to become a coquette, a shrew, or a good cook to be sure of that. It is not money nor notoriety nor the badges of authority which men have appropriated to themselves. If demands made in their behalf lay stress on any of these particulars, those who make them have not searched deeply into the need. . . . It is for that which is the birthright of every being capable of receiving it—the freedom, the religious, the intelligent freedom of the universe to use its means, to learn its secret as far as Nature has enabled them with God alone for their guide and their judge.

Ye cannot believe it, men, but the only reason why women ever assume what is more appropriate to you is because you prevent them from finding out what is fit for themselves. Were they free, were they wise fully to develop the strength and beauty of Woman, they would never wish to be men or manlike. The well-instructed moon flies not from her orbit to seize on the glories of her partner. No, for she knows that one law rules, one heaven contains, one universe replies to them alike. It is with women as with the slave. . . .

In slavery, acknowledged slavery, women are on a par with men. Each is a worktool, an article of property—no more! In perfect freedom, such as is painted in Olympus, in Swedenborg's angelic state, in the heaven where there is no marrying nor giving in marriage, each is a purified intelligence, an enfranchised soul—no less. . . .

That an era approaches which shall approximate nearer to such a temper than any has yet done, there are many tokens, indeed so many that only a few of the most prominent can here be enumerated.

The reigns of Elizabeth of England and Isabella of Castile forboded this era. They expressed the beginning of the new state while they forwarded its progress. These were strong characters and in harmony with the wants of their time. One showed that this strength did not unfit a woman for the duties of a wife and a mother; the other, that it could enable her to live and die alone, a wide, energetic life, a courageous death. . . . We may accept as an omen for ourselves that it was Isabella who furnished Columbus with the means of coming hither. This land must pay back its debt to Woman, without whose aid it would not have been brought into alliance with the civilized world. . . .

[II]

Centuries have passed since, but civilized Europe is still in a transition state about marriage, not only in practice but in thought. It is idle to speak with contempt of the nations where polygamy is an institution or seraglios a custom while practices far more debasing haunt, well-nigh fill, every city and every town; and so far as union of one with one is believed to be the only pure form of marriage, a great majority of societies and individuals are still doubtful whether the earthly bond must be a meeting of souls or only supposes a contract of convenience and utility. Were Woman established in the rights of an immortal being, this could not be. She would not in some countries be given away by her father with scarcely more respect for her feelings than is shown by the Indian chief who sells his daughter for a horse and beats her if she runs away from her new home. Nor in societies where her choice is left free would she be perverted by the current of opinion that seizes her into the belief that she must marry, if it be only to find a protector and a home of her own. Neither would Man, if he thought the connection of permanent importance, form it so lightly. He would not deem it a trifle that he was to enter into the closest relations with another soul which, if not eternal in themselves, must eternally affect his growth. Neither, did he believe Woman capable of friendship, would he by rash haste lose the chance of finding a friend in the person who might probably live half a century by his side. Did love to his mind stretch forth into infinity, he would not miss his chance of its revelations that he might the sooner rest from his weariness by a bright fireside and secure a sweet and graceful attendant "devoted to him alone." Were he a step higher, he would not carelessly enter into a relation where he might not be able to do the duty of a friend, as well as a protector from external ill, to the other party and have a being in his power pining for sympathy, intelligence, and aid that he could not give.

What deep communion, what real intercourse is implied in sharing the joys and cares of parentage when any degree of equality is admitted between the parties! It is true that in a majority of instances the man looks upon his wife as an adopted child and places her to the other children in the relation of nurse or governess rather than that of parent. Her influence with them is sure, but she misses the education which should enlighten that influence by being thus treated. It is the order of nature that children should complete the education, moral and mental, of parents by making them think what is needed for the best culture of human beings, and [parents should] conquer all faults and impulses that interfere with their giving this to these dear objects who represent the world to them. Father and mother should assist one another to learn what is required for this sublime priesthood of Nature. But for this a religious recognition of equality is required.

Where this thought of equality begins to diffuse itself, it is shown in four ways.

First: The household partnership. In our country the woman looks for a "smart but kind" husband, the man for a "capable, sweet-tempered" wife. The man furnishes the house; the woman regulates it. Their relation is one of mutual esteem, mutual dependence. Their talk is of business; their affection shows itself by practical kindness. . . .

Next comes a closer tie, which takes the form either of mutual idolatry or of intellectual companionship. The first, we suppose, is to no one a pleasing subject of contemplation. The parties weaken and narrow one another; they lock the gate against all the glories of the universe that they may live in a cell together. To themselves they seem the only wise, to all others, steeped in infatuation. . . .

The other form—of intellectual companionship—has become more and more frequent. Men engaged in public life, literary men, and artists have often found in their wives companions and confidantes in thought no less than in feeling. And as the intellectual development of Woman has spread wider and risen higher, they have not unfrequently shared the same employment. . . .

. . . I would put . . . on the shelf a little volume, containing . . . [an] appeal from the verdict of contemporaries to that of mankind made by Godwin in behalf of his wife, the celebrated, the by most men detested Mary Wollstonecraft. In his view it was an appeal from the injustice of those who did such wrong in the name of virtue. Were this little book interesting for no other cause, it would be so for the generous affection evinced under the peculiar circumstances. This man had courage to love and honor this woman in the face of the world's sentence and of all that was repulsive in her own past history. He believed he saw of what soul she was and that the impulses she had struggled to act out were noble, though the opinions to which they had led might not be thoroughly weighed. He loved her, and he defended her for the meaning and tendency of her inner life. It was a good fact.

Mary Wollstonecraft, like Madame Dudevant (commonly known as George Sand) in our day, was a woman whose existence better proved the need of some new interpretation of Woman's Rights than anything she wrote. Such beings as these, rich in genius, of most tender sympathies, capable of high virtue and a chastened harmony, ought not to find themselves by birth in a place so narrow that in breaking bonds they become outlaws. . . . They find their way at last to light and air, but the world will not take off the brand it has set upon them. The champion of the Rights of Woman found in Godwin one who would plead that cause like a brother. . . . This form of appeal rarely fails to touch the basest man: "Are you acting toward other women in the way you would have men act toward your sister?" George Sand smokes, wears male attire, wishes to be addressed as "*Mon frère.*" Perhaps if she found those who were as brothers indeed, she would not care whether she were brother or sister. . . .

This author, beginning like the many in assault upon bad institutions and external ills yet deepening the experience through comparative freedom, sees at last that the only efficient remedy must come from individual character. These bad institutions indeed, it may always be replied, prevent individuals from forming good character; therefore we must remove them. Agreed; yet keep steadily the higher aim in view. Could you clear away all the bad forms of society, it is vain unless the individual begin to be ready for better. There must be a parallel movement in these two branches of life. And all the rules left by Moses availed less to further the best life than the living example of one Messiah.

Still the mind of the age struggles confusedly with these problems, better discerning as yet the ill it can no longer bear than the good by which it may supersede it. But women like Sand will speak now and cannot be silenced; their characters and their eloquence alike foretell an era when such as they shall easier learn to lead true lives. But though such forebode, not such shall be parents of it. Those who would reform the world must show that they do not speak in the heat of wild impulse; their lives must be unstained by passionate error; they must be severe lawgivers to themselves. They must be religious students of the divine purpose with regard to man if they would not confound the fancies of a day with the requisitions of eternal good. Their liberty must be the liberty of law and knowledge. . . . Wherever abuses are seen, the timid will suffer; the bold will protest. But society has a right to outlaw them till she has revised her law, and this she must be taught to do by one who speaks with authority, not in anger or haste. . . .

We might mention instances . . . of minds, partners in work and in life, . . . [which share] together on equal terms public and private interests and which wear not on any side the aspect of offense shown by those last-named: persons who steer straight onward, yet in our comparatively free life have not been obliged to run their heads against any wall. But the principles which guide them might under petrified and oppressive institutions have made them warlike, paradoxical, and in some sense pariahs. The phenomena are different; the law is the same in all these cases. Men and women have been obliged to build up their house anew from the very foundation. If they found stone ready in the quarry, they took it peaceably; otherwise they alarmed the country by pulling down old towers to get materials.

These are all instances of marriage as intellectual companionship. The parties meet mind to mind, and a mutual trust is produced which can buckler them against a million. They work together for a common purpose and in all these instances with the same implement—the pen. The pen and the writing-desk furnish forth as naturally the retirement of Woman as of Man.

. . . I do not mean to imply that community of employment is essential to the union of husband and wife more than to the union of friends. Harmony exists in difference no less than in likeness if only the same keynote govern both parts. Woman the poem, Man the poet! Woman the heart, Man the head! Such divisions are only important when they are never to be transcended. If nature is never bound down nor the voice of inspiration stifled, that is enough. We are pleased that women should write and speak, if they feel need of it from having something to tell; but silence for ages would be no misfortune if that silence be from divine command and not from Man's tradition. . . .

The fourth and highest grade of marriage union is the religious, which may be expressed as pilgrimage toward a common shrine. This includes the others: home sympathies and household wisdom, for these pilgrims must know how to assist each other along the dusty way; intellectual communion, for how sad it would be on such a journey to have a companion to whom you could not communicate your thoughts and aspirations as they sprang to life, who would have no feeling for the prospects that open more and more glorious as we advance, who would never see the flowers that may be gathered by the most industrious traveller! It must include all these. . . .

[III]

The influence has been such that the aim certainly is now, in arranging school instruction for girls, to give them as fair a field as boys. As yet, indeed, these arrangements are made with little judgment or reflection; just as the tutors of Lady Jane Grey and other distinguished women of her time taught them Latin and Greek because they knew nothing else themselves, so now the improvement in the education of girls is to be made by giving them young men as teachers who only teach what has been taught themselves at college, while methods and topics need revision for these new subjects which could better be made by those who had experienced the same wants. Women are often at the head of these institutions, but they have as yet seldom been thinking women capable of organizing a new whole for the wants of the time and choosing persons to officiate in the departments. And when some portion of instruction of a good sort is got from the school, the far greater proportion which is infused from the general atmosphere of society contradicts its purport. Yet books and a little elementary instruction are not furnished in vain. Women are better aware how great and rich the universe is, not so easily blinded by narrowness or partial views of a home circle. "Her mother did so before her" is no longer a sufficient excuse. Indeed it was never received as an excuse to mitigate the severity of censure but was adduced as a reason, rather, why there should be no effort made for reformation.

Whether much or little has been done or will be done—whether women will add to the talent of narration the power of systematizing—whether they will carve marble as well as draw and paint—is not important. But that it should be acknowledged that they have intellect which needs developing—that they should not be considered complete if beings of affection and habit alone—is important.

Yet even this acknowledgment, rather conquered by Woman than proffered by Man, has been sullied by the usual selfishness. Too much is said of women being better educated that they may become better companions and mothers *for men*. They should be fit for such companionship, and we have mentioned with satisfaction instances where it has been established. Earth knows no fairer, holier relation than that of a mother. It is one which rightly understood must both promote and require the highest attainments. But a being of infinite scope must not be treated with an exclusive view to any one relation. Give the soul free course, let the organization both of body and mind be freely developed, and the being will be fit for any and every relation to which it may be called. The intellect, no more than the sense of hearing, is to be cultivated merely that Woman may be a more valuable companion to Man but because the Power who gave a power by its mere existence signifies that it must be brought out toward perfection.

In this regard of self-dependence and a greater simplicity and fullness of being, we must hail as a preliminary the increase of the class contemptuously designated as "old maids."

We cannot wonder at the aversion with which old bachelors and old maids have been regarded. Marriage is the natural means of forming a sphere, of taking root in the earth; it requires more strength to do this without such an opening; very many have failed, and their imperfections have been in everyone's way. They have been more partial, more harsh, more officious and impertinent than those compelled by severer friction to render themselves endurable. Those who have a more full experience of the instincts have a distrust as to whether the unmarried can be thoroughly human and humane, such as is hinted in the saying, "Old maids' and bachelors' children are well cared for," which derides at once their ignorance and their presumption.

Yet the business of society has become so complex that it could now scarcely be carried on without the presence of these despised auxiliaries, and detachments from the army of aunts and uncles are wanted to stop gaps in every hedge. They rove about, mental and moral Ishmaelites, pitching their tents amid the fixed and ornamented homes of men. In a striking variety of forms, genius of late, both at home and abroad, has paid its tribute to the character of the aunt and the uncle, recognizing in these personages the spiritual parents who have supplied defects in the treatment of the busy or careless actual parents. Thev also gain a wider, if not so deep, experience. Those who are not intimately and permanently linked with others are thrown upon themselves; and if they do not there find peace and incessant life, there is none to flatter them that they are not very poor and very mean.

A position which so constantly admonishes may be of inestimable benefit. The person may gain, undistracted by other relationships, a closer communion with the one. Such a use is made of it by saints and sibyls. Or she may be one of the lay sisters of charity, a canoness bound by an inward vow; or the useful drudge of all men, the Martha, much sought, little prized; or the intellectual interpreter of the varied life she sees, the Urania of a half-formed world's twilight.

Or she may combine all these. Not "needing to care that she may please a husband," a frail and limited being, her thoughts may turn to the center, and she may, by steadfast contemplation entering into the secret of truth and love, use it for the good of all men instead of a chosen few and interpret through it all the forms of life. It is possible, perhaps, to be at once a priestly servant and a loving muse. . . .

Perhaps the next generation . . . will find that contempt is put upon old maids or old women at all merely because they do not use the elixir which would keep them always young. Under its influence, a gem brightens yearly which is only seen to more advantage through the fissures Time makes in the casket. No one thinks of Michelangelo's "Persican Sibyl" or St. Theresa or Tasso's Leonora or the Greek Electra as an old maid, more than of Michelangelo or Canova as old bachelors, though all had reached the period in life's course appointed to take that degree. . . .

If larger intellectual resources begin to be deemed needful to Woman, still more is a spiritual dignity in her, or even the mere assumption of it, looked upon with respect. . . . Mysticism, which may be defined as the brooding soul of the world, cannot fail of its oracular promise as to Woman. "The mothers," "the mother of all things" are expressions of thought which lead the mind towards this side of universal growth. . . . If it be true as the legend says that Humanity withers through a fault committed by and a curse laid upon Woman, through her pure child or influence shall the new Adam, the redemption, arise. Innocence is to be replaced by virtue, dependence, by a willing submission in the heart of the Virgin Mother of the new race.

The spiritual tendency is toward the elevation of Woman, but the intellectual by itself is not so. Plato sometimes seems penetrated by that high idea of love which considers Man and Woman as the twofold expression of one thought. This the angel of Swedenborg, the angel of the coming age, cannot surpass but only explain more fully. But then again Plato, the man of intellect, treats Woman in the *Republic* as property and in the *Timæus* says that Man, if he misuse the privileges of one life, shall be degraded into the form of Woman and then, if he do not redeem himself, into that of a bird. This . . . expresses most happily how antipoetical is this state of mind. For the poet contemplating the world of things selects various birds as the symbols of his most gracious and ethereal thoughts, just as he calls upon his genius as muse rather than as God. But the intellect, cold, is ever more masculine than feminine; warmed by emotion, it rushes toward mother-earth and puts on the forms of beauty.

The electrical, the magnetic element in Woman has not been fairly brought out at any period. Everything might be expected from it; she has far more of it than Man. This is commonly expressed by saying that her intuitions are more rapid and more correct. . . . Women who combine this organization with creative genius are very commonly unhappy at present. They see too much to act in conformity with those around them, and their quick impulses seem folly to those who do not discern the motives. This is a usual effect of the apparition of genius whether in Man or Woman but is more frequent with regard to the latter because a harmony, an obvious order and self-restraining decorum, is most expected from her. . . .

. . . To this region, however misunderstood or interpreted with presumptuous carelessness, belong the phenomena of magnetism, or mesmerism as it is now often called, where the trance of the Ecstatica purports to be produced by the agency of one human being on another, instead of as in her case direct from the spirit. The worldling has his sneer at this as at the services of religion: "The churches can always be filled with women"; "Show me a man in one of your magnetic states, and I will believe."

Women are indeed the easy victims both of priestcraft and self-delusion, but this would not be if the intellect was developed in proportion to the other powers. They would then have a regulator and be more in equipoise yet must retain the same nervous susceptibility while their physical structure is such as it is. It is with just that hope that we welcome everything that tends to strengthen the fiber and develop the nature on more sides. When the intellect and affections are in harmony, when intellectual consciousness is calm and deep, inspiration will not be confounded with fancy. . . .

In our own country women are in many respects better situated than men. Good books are allowed, with more time to read them. They are not so early forced into the bustle of life nor so weighed down by demands for outward success. The perpetual changes incident to our society make the blood circulate freely through the body politic; and if not favorable at present to the grace and bloom of life, they are so to activity, resource, and would be to reflection but for a low materialist tendency from which the women are generally exempt in themselves, though its existence among the men has a tendency to repress their impulses and make them doubt their instincts, thus often paralyzing their action during the best years.

But they have time to think; and no traditions chain them, and few conventionalities, compared with what must be met in other nations. There is no reason why they should not discover that the secrets of nature are open, the revelations of the spirit waiting for whoever will seek them. When the mind is once awakened to this consciousness, it will not be restrained by the habits of the past, but fly to seek the seeds of a heavenly future.

Their employments are more favorable to meditation than those of men.

Woman is not addressed religiously here more than elsewhere. She is told that she should be worthy to be the mother of a Washington or the companion of some good man. But in many, many instances, she has already learned that all bribes have the same flaw, that truth and good are to be sought solely for their own sakes. And already an ideal sweetness floats over many forms, shines in many eyes.

Already deep questions are put by young girls on the great theme: What shall I do to enter upon the eternal life?

Men are very courteous to them. They praise them often, check them seldom. There is chivalry in the feeling toward the "ladies" which gives them the best seats in the stagecoach, frequent admission not only to lectures of all sorts but to courts of justice, halls of legislature, reform conventions. The newspaper editor "would be better pleased that the Lady's Book should be filled up exclusively by ladies. It would then indeed be a true gem, worthy to be presented by young men to the mistress of their affections." Can gallantry go further? . . .

Women who speak in public, if they have a moral power such as has been felt from Angelina Grimké and Abby Kelley—that is, if they speak for conscience' sake to serve a cause which they hold sacred—invariably subdue the prejudices of their hearers and excite an interest proportionate to the aversion with which it had been the purpose to regard them. . . .

For Woman, if by a sympathy as to outward condition she is led to aid the enfranchisement of the slave, must be no less so by inward tendency to favor measures which promise to bring the world more thoroughly and deeply into harmony with her nature. When the lamb takes place of the lion as the emblem of nations, both women and men will be as children of one spirit, perpetual learners of the word and doers thereof, not hearers only.

A writer in the New York *Pathfinder,* in two articles headed "Femality," has uttered a still more pregnant word than any we have named. . . . He views the feminine nature as a harmonizer of the vehement elements, and this has often been hinted elsewhere; but what he expresses most forcibly is the lyrical, the inspiring and inspired apprehensiveness of her being. . . .

There are two aspects of Woman's nature, represented by the ancients as Muse and Minerva. It is the former to which the writer in the *Pathfinder* looks. It is the latter which Wordsworth has in mind when he says,

> *With a placid brow,*
> *Which woman ne'er should forfeit, keep thy vow.*

The especial genius of Woman I believe to be electrical in movement, intuitive in function, spiritual in tendency. She excels not so easily in classification or recreation as in an instinctive seizure of causes and a simple breathing out of what she receives that has the singleness of life, rather than the selecting and energizing of art.

More native is it to her to be the living model of the artist than to set apart from herself any one form in objective reality, more native to inspire and receive the poem than to create it. In so far as soul is in her completely developed, all soul is the same; but in so far as it is modified in her as Woman, it flows, it breathes, it sings, rather than deposits soil or finishes work; and that which is especially feminine flushes in blossom the face of earth and pervades like air and water all this seeming solid globe, daily renewing and purifying its life. Such may be the especially feminine element spoken of as Femality. But it is no more the order of nature that it should be incarnated pure in any form than that the masculine energy should exist unmingled with it in any form.

Male and female represent the two sides of the great radical dualism. But in fact they are perpetually passing into one another. Fluid hardens to solid; solid rushes to fluid. There is no wholly masculine man, no purely feminine woman.

History jeers at the attempts of physiologists to bind great original laws by the forms which flow from them. They make a rule; they say from observation what can and cannot be. In vain! Nature provides exceptions to every rule. She sends women to battle and sets Hercules spinning; she enables women to bear immense burdens, cold, and frost; she enables the man who feels maternal love to nourish his infant like a mother. Of late she plays still gayer pranks. Not only she deprives organizations but organs of a necessary end. She enables people to read with the top of the head and see with the pit of the stomach. Presently she will make a female Newton and a male siren.

Man partakes of the feminine in the Apollo, Woman of the masculine as Minerva.

What I mean by the Muse is that unimpeded clearness of the intuitive powers which a perfectly truthful adherence to every admonition of the higher instincts would bring to a finely organized human being. It may appear as prophecy or as poesy. . . . Sight must be verified by light before it can deserve the honors of piety and genius. Yet sight comes first, and of this sight of the world of causes, this approximation to the region of primitive motions, women I hold to be especially capable. Even without equal freedom with the other sex, they have already shown themselves so; and should these faculties have free play, I believe they will open new, deeper, and purer sources of joyous inspiration than have as yet refreshed the earth.

Let us be wise and not impede the soul. Let her work as she will. Let us have one creative energy, one incessant revelation. Let it take what form it will, and let us not bind it by the past to man or woman, black or white. . . .

If it has been the tendency of these remarks to call Woman rather to the Minerva side—if I, unlike the more generous writer, have spoken from society no less than the soul—let it be pardoned! It is love that has caused this—love for many incarcerated souls that might be freed could the idea of religious self-dependence be established in them, could the weakening habit of dependence on others be broken up. . . .

When the same community of life and consciousness of mind begin among men, humanity will have positively and finally subjugated its brute elements and Titanic childhood; criticism will have perished; arbitrary limits and ignorant censure be impossible; all will have entered upon the liberty of law and the harmony of common growth. Then Apollo will sing to his lyre what Vulcan forges on the anvil, and the Muse weave anew the tapestries of Minerva.

It is therefore only in the present crisis that the preference is given to Minerva. The power of continence must establish the legitimacy of freedom, the power of self-poise, the perfection of motion. Every relation, every gradation of nature is incalculably precious, but only to the soul which is poised upon itself and to whom no loss, no change, can bring dull discord, for it is in harmony with the central soul.

If any individual live too much in relations so that he becomes a stranger to the resources of his own nature, he falls after a while into a distraction or imbecility from which he can only be cured by a time of isolation which gives the renovating fountains time to rise up. With a society it is the same. Many minds, deprived of the traditionary or instinctive means of passing a cheerful existence, must find help in self-impulse or perish. It is therefore that, while any elevation in the view of union is to be hailed with joy, we shall not decline celibacy as the great fact of the time. It is one from which no vow, no arrangement can at present save a thinking mind. For now the rowers are pausing on their oars; they wait a change before they can pull together. All tends to illustrate the thoughts of a wise contemporary. Union is only possible to those who are units. To be fit for relations in time, souls, whether of Man or Woman, must be able to do without them in the spirit.

It is therefore that I would have Woman lay aside all thought, such as she habitually cherishes, of being taught and led by men. I would have her . . . dedicate herself to the Sun, the Sun of Truth, and go nowhere if his beams did not make clear the path. I would have her free from compromise, from complaisance, from helplessness, because I would have her good enough and strong enough to love one and all beings from the fullness, not the poverty, of being. . . .

Grant her then for a while the armor and the javelin. Let her put from her the press of other minds and meditate in virgin loneliness. The same idea shall reappear in due time as Muse, or Ceres, the all-kindly, patient Earth Spirit.

[IV]

Among the throng of symptoms which denote the present tendency to a crisis in the life of Woman —which resembles the change from girlhood with its beautiful instincts but unharmonized thoughts, its blind pupilage and restless seeking, to self-possessed, wise, and graceful womanhood —I have attempted to select a few.

One of prominent interest is the unison upon the subject of three male minds which for width of culture, power of self-concentration, and dignity of aim take rank as the prophets of the coming age, while their histories and labors are rooted in the past. . . .

Swedenborg approximated to that harmony between the scientific and poetic lives of mind which we hope from the perfected man. The links that bind together the realms of nature, the mysteries that accompany her births and growths, were unusually plain to him. He seems a man to whom insight was given at a period when the mental frame was sufficiently matured to retain and express its gifts.

His views of Woman are in the main satisfactory. In some details we may object to them; as in all his system there are still remains of what is arbitrary and seemingly groundless—fancies that show the marks of old habits and a nature as yet not thoroughly leavened with the spiritual. . . . His idea of Woman is sufficiently large and noble to interpose no obstacle to her progress. His idea of marriage is consequently sufficient. Man and Woman share an angelic ministry; the union is of one with one, permanent and pure. . . .

Quakerism also establishes Woman on a sufficient equality with Man. But though the original thought of Quakerism is pure, its scope is too narrow, and its influence, having established a certain amount of good and made clear some truth, must by degrees be merged in one of wider range. The mind of Swedenborg appeals to the various nature of Man and allows room for aesthetic culture and the free expression of energy.

As apostle of the new order, of the social fabric that is to rise from love and supersede the old that was based on strife, Charles Fourier comes next, expressing in an outward order many facts of which Swedenborg saw the secret springs. The mind of Fourier, though grand and clear, was in some respects superficial. He was a stranger to the highest experiences. His eye was fixed on the outward more than the inward needs of Man. Yet he too was a seer of the divine order in its musical expression, if not in its poetic soul. He has filled one department of instruction for the new era, and the harmony in action and freedom for individual growth, he hopes, shall exist; and if the methods he proposes should not prove the true ones, yet his fair propositions shall give many hints and make room for the inspiration needed for such.

He, too, places Woman on an entire equality with Man and wishes to give to one as to the other that independence which must result from intellectual and practical development.

Those who will consult him for no other reason might do so to see how the energies of Woman may be made available in the pecuniary way. The object of Fourier was to give her the needed means of self-help that she might dignify and unfold her life for her own happiness and that of society. . . .

On the opposite side of the advancing army leads the great apostle of individual culture, Goethe. Swedenborg makes organization and union the necessary results of solitary thought. Fourier, whose nature was above all constructive, looked to them too exclusively. Better institutions, he thought, will make better men. Goethe expressed in every way the other side. If one man could present better forms, the rest could not use them till ripe for them.

Fourier says, as the institutions, so the men! All follies are excusable and natural under bad institutions. Goethe thinks, as the man, so the institutions! There is no excuse for ignorance and folly. A man can grow in any place, if he will.

Aye! But, Goethe, bad institutions are prison walls and impure air that make him stupid so that he does not will. And thou, Fourier, do not expect to change mankind at once, or even "in three generations," by arrangement of groups and series or flourish of trumpets for attractive industry. If these attempts are made by unready men, they will fail.

Yet we prize the theory of Fourier no less than the profound suggestion of Goethe. Both are educating the age to a clearer consciousness of what Man needs, what Man can be, and better life must ensue.

Goethe, proceeding on his own track, elevating the human being in the most imperfect states of society by continual efforts at self-culture, takes as good care of women as of men. His mother, the bold, gay Frau Aja, with such playful freedom of nature; the wise and gentle maiden known in his youth over whose sickly solitude the "Holy Ghost brooded as a dove"; his sister, the intellectual woman *par excellence;* [his friend and patroness,] the Duchess Amelia; Lili, who combined the character of the woman of the world with the lyrical sweetness of the shepherdess . . . —all these had supplied abundant suggestions to his mind as to the wants and the possible excellences of Woman. And from his poetic soul grew up forms new and more admirable than life has yet produced, for whom his clear eye marked out paths in the future.

In *Faust* Margaret represents the redeeming power which at present upholds Woman while waiting for a better day. The lovely little girl, pure in instinct, ignorant in mind, is misled and profaned by man abusing her confidence. To the Mater Dolorosa she appeals for aid. It is given to the soul, if not against outward sorrow; and the maiden, enlightened by her sufferings, refusing to receive temporal salvation by the aid of an evil power, obtains the eternal in its stead.

In the second part, the intellectual man, [Faust], after all his manifold strivings owes to the interposition of her whom he had betrayed *his* salvation. She intercedes, this time herself a glorified spirit, with the Mater Gloriosa.

Leonora [in *Tasso*], too, is Woman as we see her now, pure, thoughtful, refined by much acquaintance with grief.

Iphigenia he speaks of in his journals as his "daughter," and she is the daughter whom a man will wish, even if he has chosen his wife from very mean motives. She is the virgin, steadfast soul to whom falsehood is more dreadful than any other death.

But it is to *Wilhelm Meister's Apprenticeship* and *Wandering Years* that I would especially refer, as these volumes contain the sum of the Sage's observations during a long life as to what Man should do under present circumstances to obtain mastery over outward through an initiation into inward life and severe discipline of faculty.

As Wilhelm advances into the upward path, he becomes acquainted with better forms of Woman by knowing how to seek and how to prize them when found. For the weak and immature man will often admire a superior woman, but he will not be able to abide by a feeling which is too severe a tax on his habitual existence. But with Wilhelm the gradation is natural and expresses ascent in the scale of being. At first he finds charm in Mariana and Philina, very common forms of feminine character, not without redeeming traits no less than charms but without wisdom or purity. Soon he is attended by Mignon, the finest expression ever yet given to what I have called the lyrical element in Woman. She is a child, but too full-grown for this man; he loves but cannot follow her; yet is the association not without an enduring influence. Poesy has been domesticated in his life; and though he strives to bind down her heavenward impulse as art or apothegm, these are only the tents beneath which he may sojourn for a while but which may be easily struck and carried on limitless wanderings.

Advancing into the region of thought, he encounters a wise philanthropy in Natalia (instructed, let us observe, by an *uncle*); practical judgment and the outward economy of life in Theresa; pure devotion in the Fair Saint.

Further and last, he comes to the house of Macaria, the soul of a star—that is, a pure and perfected intelligence embodied in feminine form —and the center of a world whose members revolve harmoniously around her. She instructs him in the archives of a rich human history and introduces him to the contemplation of the heavens.

From the hours passed by the side of Mariana to these with Macaria is a wide distance for human feet to traverse. Nor has Wilhelm travelled so far, seen and suffered so much, in vain. He now begins to study how he may aid the next generation; he sees objects in harmonious arrangement and from his observations deduces precepts by which to guide his course as a teacher and a master, "help-full, comfort-full."

In all these expressions of Woman, the aim of Goethe is satisfactory to me. He aims at a pure self-subsistence and a free development of any powers with which they may be gifted by nature as much for them as for men. They are units addressed as souls. Accordingly the meeting between Man and Woman, as represented by him, is equal and noble; and if he does not depict marriage, he makes it possible. . . . Their different characters have fair play, and each is beautiful in its minute indications, for nothing is enforced or conventional; but everything, however slight, grows from the essential life of the being. . . . All things are in their places in this little world because all is natural and free, just as "there is room for everything out of doors." Yet all is rounded in by natural harmony, which will always arise where Truth and Love are sought in the light of Freedom.

Goethe's book bodes an era of freedom, like its own, of "extraordinary, generous seeking" and new revelations. New individualities shall be developed in the actual world which shall advance upon it as gently as the figures come out upon his canvas.

I have indicated on this point the coincidence between his hopes and those of Fourier, though his are directed by an infinitely higher and deeper knowledge of human nature. But for our present purpose it is sufficient to show how surely these different paths have conducted to the same end two earnest thinkers. . . .

[v]

O men! I speak not to you. It is true that your wickedness . . . is its own punishment. Your forms degraded and your eyes clouded by secret sin, natural harmony broken and fineness of perception destroyed in your mental and bodily organization, God and love shut out from your hearts by the foul visitants you have permitted there, incapable of pure marriage, incapable of pure parentage, incapable of worship—O wretched men, your sin is its own punishment! You have lost the world in losing yourselves. . . .

But to you women, American women, a few words may not be addressed in vain. . . . My advice may be classed under three heads:

Clear your souls from the taint of vanity.

Do not rejoice in conquests either that your power to allure may be seen by other women or for the pleasure of rousing passionate feelings that gratify your love of excitement.

It must happen no doubt that frank and generous women will excite love they do not reciprocate, but in nine cases out of ten, the woman has half consciously done much to excite. In this case she shall not be held guiltless either as to the unhappiness or injury of the lover. Pure love inspired by a worthy object must ennoble and bless, whether mutual or not; but that which is excited by coquettish attraction of any grade of refinement must cause bitterness and doubt as to the reality of human goodness as soon as the flush of passion is over. . . .

I find the whole of what I want in this relation in the two epithets by which Milton makes Adam address *his* wife. In the intercourse of every day he begins:

> *Daughter of God and man,* accomplished *Eve.*

In a moment of stronger feeling:

> *Daughter of God and man,* IMMORTAL *Eve.*

What majesty in the cadence of the line; what dignity, what reverence in the attitude both of giver and receiver!

The woman who permits in her life the alloy of vanity, the woman who lives upon flattery coarse or fine, . . . is *not* immortal so far as her will is concerned; and every woman who does so creates miasma whose spread is indefinite. The hand which casts into the waters of life a stone of offense knows not how far the circles thus caused may spread their agitations.

A little while since, I was at one of the most fashionable places of public resort. I saw there many women dressed without regard to the season or the demands of the place in apery or, as it looked, in mockery of European fashions. I saw their eyes restlessly courting attention. I saw the way in which it was paid, the style of devotion, almost an open sneer, which it pleased those ladies to receive from men whose expression marked their own low position in the moral and intellectual world. . . . These were American *ladies;* that is, they were of that class who have wealth and leisure to make full use of the day and confer benefits on others. They were of that class whom the possession of external advantages makes of pernicious example to many if these advantages be misused.

Soon after, I met a circle of women stamped by society as among the most degraded of their sex. "How," it was asked of them, "did you come here?" for by the society that I saw in the former place they were shut up in a prison. The causes were not difficult to trace: love of dress, love of flattery, love of excitement. They had not dresses like the other ladies, so they stole them; they could not pay for flattery by distinctions and the dower of a worldly marriage, so they paid by the profanation of their persons. In excitement, more and more madly sought from day to day, they drowned the voice of conscience.

Now I ask you, my sisters, if the women at the fashionable house be not answerable for those women being in the prison?

As to position in the world of souls, we may suppose the women of the prison stood fairest, both because they had misused less light and because loneliness and sorrow had brought some of them to feel the need of better life, nearer truth and good. . . . Do not forget the unfortunates who dare not cross your guarded way. If it does not suit you to act with those who have organized measures of reform, then hold not yourself excused from acting in private. Seek out these degraded women, give them tender sympathy, counsel, employment. Take the place of mothers, such as might have saved them originally.

If you can do little for those already under the ban of the world, . . . you will at least leave a sense of love and justice in their hearts that will prevent their becoming utterly embittered and corrupt. And you may learn the means of prevention for those yet uninjured. These will be found in a diffusion of mental culture, simple tastes best taught by your example, a genuine self-respect, and above all, what the influence of Man tends to hide from Woman, the love and fear of a divine in preference to a human tribunal.

But suppose you save many who would have lost their bodily innocence (for as to mental, the loss of that is incalculably more general) through mere vanity and folly; there still remain many, the prey and spoil of the brute passions of Man; for the stories frequent in our newspapers outshame antiquity and vie with the horrors of war.

As to this, it must be considered that as the vanity and proneness to seduction of the imprisoned women represented a general degradation in their sex, so do these acts a still more general and worse [degradation] in the male. Where so many are weak, it is natural there should be many lost; where legislators admit that ten thousand prostitutes are a fair proportion to one city and husbands tell their wives that it is folly to expect chastity from men, it is inevitable that there should be many monsters of vice. . . .

. . . Men have indeed been for more than a hundred years rating women for countenancing vice. But at the same time they have carefully hid from them its nature, so that the preference often shown by women for bad men arises rather from a confused idea—that they are bold and adventurous, acquainted with regions which women are forbidden to explore—and the curiosity that ensues than a corrupt heart in the woman. As to marriage, it has been inculcated on women for centuries that men have not only stronger passions than they but of a sort that it would be shameful for them to share or even understand; that therefore they must "confide in their husbands," that is, submit implicitly to their will; that the least appearance of coldness or withdrawal, from whatever cause, in the wife is wicked because liable to turn her husband's thoughts to illicit indulgence; for a man is so constituted that he must indulge his passions or die!

Accordingly, a great part of women look upon men as a kind of wild beast but "suppose they are all alike"; the unmarried are assured by the married that "if they knew men as they do," that is, by being married to them, "they would not expect continence or self-government from them." . . .

Since the sliding and backsliding men of the world, no less than the mystics, declare that as through Woman Man was lost so through Woman must Man be redeemed, the time must be at hand. When she knows herself indeed as "accomplished," still more as "immortal Eve," this may be. . . .

[VI]

And now I have designated in outline, if not in fullness, the stream which is ever flowing from the heights of my thought. . . .

Man is a being of twofold relations, to nature beneath and intelligences above him. The earth is his school, if not his birthplace; God his object; life and thought his means of interpreting nature and aspiring to God.

Only a fraction of this purpose is accomplished in the life of any one man. Its entire accomplishment is to be hoped only from the sum of the lives of men, or Man considered as a whole. As this whole has one soul and one body, any injury or obstruction to a part or to the meanest member affects the whole. Man can never be perfectly happy or virtuous till all men are so.

To address Man wisely, you must not forget that his life is partly animal, subject to the same laws with Nature. But you cannot address him wisely unless you consider him still more as soul and appreciate the conditions and destiny of soul.

The growth of Man is twofold, masculine and feminine.

So far as these two methods can be distinguished, they are so as

Energy and Harmony,
Power and Beauty,
Intellect and Love,

or by some such rude classification; for we have not language primitive and pure enough to express such ideas with precision.

These two sides are supposed to be expressed in Man and Woman, that is, as the more and the less, for the faculties have not been given pure to either but only in preponderance. There are also exceptions in great number, such as men of far more beauty than power and the reverse. But as a general rule it seems to have been the intention to give a preponderance on the one side that is called masculine and, on the other, one that is called feminine.

There cannot be a doubt that if these two developments were in perfect harmony, they would correspond to and fulfill one another like hemispheres or the tenor and bass in music.

But there is no perfect harmony in human nature, and the two parts answer one another only now and then; or if there be a persistent consonance, it can only be traced at long intervals instead of discoursing an obvious melody.

What is the cause of this?

Man in the order of time was developed first; as energy comes before harmony, power before beauty. Woman was therefore under his care as an elder. He might have been her guardian and teacher. But as human nature goes not straight forward but by excessive action and then reaction in an undulated course, he misunderstood and abused his advantages and became her temporal master instead of her spiritual sire.

On himself came the punishment. He educated Woman more as a servant than a daughter and found himself a king without a queen. The children of this unequal union showed unequal natures, and more and more men seemed sons of the handmaid rather than princess.

At last there were so many Ishmaelites that the rest grew frightened and indignant. They laid the blame on Hagar and drove her forth into the wilderness. But there were none the fewer Ishmaelites for that.

At last men became a little wiser and saw that the infant Moses was in every case saved by the pure instincts of Woman's breast. For as too much adversity is better for the moral nature than too much prosperity, Woman in this respect dwindled less than Man, though in other respects still a child in leading-strings. So Man did her more and more justice and grew more and more kind.

But yet—his habits and his will corrupted by the past—he did not clearly see that Woman was half himself, that her interests were identical with his, and that by the law of their common being he could never reach his true proportions while she remained in any wise shorn of hers.

And so it has gone on to our day: both ideas developing, but more slowly than they would under a clearer recognition of truth and justice which would have permitted the sexes their due influence on one another and mutual improvement from more dignified relations.

Wherever there was pure love, the natural influences were for the time restored.

Wherever the poet or artist gave free course to his genius, he saw the truth and expressed it in worthy forms, for these men especially share and need the feminine principle. The divine birds need to be brooded into life and song by mothers.

Wherever religion (I mean the thirst for truth and good, not the love of sect and dogma) had its course, the original design was apprehended in its simplicity. . . .

I have aimed to show that no age was left entirely without a witness of the equality of the sexes in function, duty, and hope.

Also that when there was unwillingness or ignorance which prevented this being acted upon, women had not the less power for their want of light and noble freedom. But it was power which hurt alike them and those against whom they made use of the arms of the servile—cunning, blandishment, and unreasonable emotion.

That now the time has come when a clearer vision and better action are possible—when Man and Woman may regard one another as brother and sister, the pillars of one porch, the priests of one worship. I have believed and intimated that this hope would receive an ampler fruition than ever before in our own land. And it will do so if this land carry out the principles from which sprang our national life.

I believe that at present women are the best helpers of one another. Let them think, let them act, till they know what they need. We only ask of men to remove arbitrary barriers. Some would like to do more. But I believe it needs that Woman show herself in her native dignity to teach them how to aid her; their minds are so encumbered by tradition. . . .

You ask what use will she make of liberty when she has so long been sustained and restrained?

I answer, in the first place, this will not be suddenly given. I read yesterday a debate of this year on the subject of enlarging women's rights over property. It was a leaf from the classbook that is preparing for the needed instruction. The men learned visibly as they spoke. The champions of Woman saw the fallacy of arguments on the opposite side and were startled by their own convictions. With their wives at home and the readers of the paper, it was the same. And so the stream flows on: thought urging action, and action leading to the evolution of still better thought.

But were this freedom to come suddenly, I have no fear of the consequences. Individuals might commit excesses, but there is not only in the sex a reverence for decorums and limits inherited and enhanced from generation to generation which many years of other life could not efface but a native love in Woman as Woman of proportion, of "the simple art of not too much"—a Greek moderation which would create immediately a restraining party, the natural legislators and instructors of the rest, and would gradually establish such rules as are needed to guard without impeding life.

. . . If you ask me what offices they may fill, I reply—any. I do not care what case you put; let them be sea captains, if you will. I do not doubt there are women well fitted for such an office. . . .

I think women need especially at this juncture a much greater range of occupation than they have to rouse their latent powers. A party of travellers lately visited a lonely hut on a mountain. There they found an old woman who told them she and her husband had lived there forty years. "Why," they said, "did you choose so barren a spot?" She "did not know; *it was the man's notion.*" And during forty years she had been content to act, without knowing why, upon the "man's notion." I would not have it so.

In families that I know, some little girls like to saw wood, others to use carpenters' tools. Where these tastes are indulged, cheerfulness and good-humor are promoted. Where they are forbidden because "such things are not proper for girls," they grow sullen and mischievous.

Fourier had observed these wants of women, as no one can fail to do who watches the desires of little girls or knows the ennui that haunts grown women, except where they make to themselves a serene little world by art of some kind. He therefore, in proposing a great variety of employments in manufactures or the care of plants and animals, allows for one-third of women as likely to have a taste for masculine pursuits, one-third of men for feminine.

Who does not observe the immediate glow and serenity that is diffused over the life of women before restless or fretful by engaging in gardening, building, or the lowest department of art? Here is something that is not routine, something that draws forth life towards the infinite.

I have no doubt, however, that a large proportion of women would give themselves to the same employments as now because there are circumstances that must lead them. Mothers will delight to make the nest soft and warm. Nature would take care of that; no need to clip the wings of any bird that wants to soar and sing or finds in itself the strength of pinion for a migratory flight unusual to its kind. The difference would be that *all* need not be constrained to employments for which *some* are unfit.

I have urged upon the sex self-subsistence in its two forms of self-reliance and self-impulse because I believe them to be the needed means of the present juncture.

I have urged on Woman independence of Man, not that I do not think the sexes mutually needed by one another, but because in Woman this fact has led to an excessive devotion which has cooled love, degraded marriage, and prevented either sex from being what it should be to itself or the other.

I wish Woman to live *first* for God's sake. Then she will not make an imperfect man her god and thus sink to idolatry. Then she will not take what is not fit for her from a sense of weakness and poverty. Then if she finds what she needs in Man embodied, she will know how to love and be worthy of being loved. By being more a soul she will not be less Woman, for nature is perfected through spirit.

Now there is no woman, only an overgrown child.

That her hand may be given with dignity, she must be able to stand alone. I wish to see men and women capable of such relations . . . where grace is the natural garb of strength and the affections are calm because deep. . . .

A profound thinker has said, "No married woman can represent the female world, for she belongs to her husband. The idea of Woman must be represented by a virgin."

But that is the very fault of marriage and of the present relation between the sexes—that the woman *does* belong to the man instead of forming a whole with him. Were it otherwise, there would be no such limitation to the thought.

Woman, self-centered, would never be absorbed by any relation; it would be only an experience to her as to man. It is a vulgar error that love, *a* love, to Woman is her whole existence; she also is born for Truth and Love in their universal energy. Would she but assume her inheritance, Mary would not be the only virgin mother. . . . The soul is ever young, ever virgin.

And will not she soon appear? The woman who shall vindicate their birthright for all women, who shall teach them what to claim and how to use what they obtain? . . .

An idea not unknown to ancient times has of late been revived, that in the metamorphoses of life the soul assumes the form first of Man, then of Woman, and takes the chances and reaps the benefits of either lot. Why then, say some, lay such emphasis on the rights or needs of Woman? What she wins not as Woman will come to her as Man.

That makes no difference. It is not Woman but the law of right, the law of growth that speaks in us and demands the perfection of each being in its kind—apple as apple, Woman as Woman. Without adopting your theory, I know that I, a daughter, live through the life of Man; but what concerns me now is that my life be a beautiful, powerful, in a word, a complete life in its kind. Had I but one more moment to live I must wish the same.

Suppose at the end of your cycle, your great world-year, all will be completed whether I exert myself or not (and the supposition is *false*—but suppose it true), am I to be indifferent about it? Not so! I must beat my own pulse true in the heart of the world; for *that* is virtue, excellence, health. . . .

I stand in the sunny noon of life. Objects no longer glitter in the dews of morning neither are yet softened by the shadows of evening. Every spot is seen, every chasm revealed. Climbing the dusty hill, some fair effigies that once stood for symbols of human destiny have been broken; those I still have with me show defects in this broad light. Yet enough is left, even by experience, to point distinctly to the glories of that destiny, faint but not to be mistaken streaks of the future day. . . .

PART IV

John Stuart Mill:

Utilitarian Liberal

John Stuart Mill (1806–1873), whose fame generally rests upon his utilitarian liberal philosophy and his great essay, *On Liberty,* appealed to Sarah Grimké, Susan B. Anthony, Paulina Davis, and their co-workers in the American woman's rights movement because of his unequivocal support of equality for women. The youth of twenty who found chivalric "courtesy to woman a barrier to her self-development and her self-respect" continued his crusade for woman's rights through the major part of the nineteenth century, moving as an elderly Member of Parliament to change the word "man" in a franchise bill to "person" and publishing a few years before his death his arguments against sexism in *The Subjection of Women* (1869).[1] Quite apart from its well-developed and reasoned argument, his feminist essay became famous as the product of one of the world's pre-eminent thinkers and writers, a man whose fame could rest on any of several other works or on his editorial and political activity.

The currents which ran through Mill's feminist thought were not exclusive to it: They ran through all his thought. And the emphasis which he placed on woman's rights grew out of his concern for women as a part of humanity. Many of the advantages which he saw accruing to women were similar to those which he would, and indeed at times did, urge for minority groups, including blacks and Irish peasants.

Mill was an unusually precocious child, whose Scottish father, James Mill, had early imbibed the ideas of the Scottish Enlightenment and of Jeremy Bentham. Benthamism, or what John Mill would later call utilitarianism, developed the idea of an equation between usefulness and goodness which defined the general welfare as the greatest good for the greatest number. Bentham had charged all institutions, including government, with the responsibility of being as productive of the general welfare or happiness as possible. To measure individual and group effectiveness, he sought a gauge for happiness, which he outlined in *Principles of Morals and Legislation.* His democratic, secular philosophy sought a surplus of pleasure and a minimization of pain for as many individuals as possible—black, white, rich, poor, male, female.[2]

James Mill, then a London journalist, became the instrument for both radicalizing and publicizing Bentham's attacks on a variety of political institutions—particularly the courts, the legal code, and the penal system—culminating in a press for representative government, always an important element in utiliarian programs. Bentham and James Mill, unlike some of the earlier Enlightenment thinkers and later socialist ones, believed not only that justice and expediency were both possible but that the achievement of justice would be secured in the pursuit of expediency.

The elder Mill felt that the brain was simply another organ of the body and that most infants started out with similar cerebral capacities. The experiences available to them in childhood made some, like himself and Bentham, superior to their contemporaries, and such experiences could presumably do the same for any child. Thus while Timothy Fuller was teaching Latin to young Margaret on one side of the Atlantic, on the other James Mill instructed young John in Greek.

Philosophical heir to his father and Bentham, the adolescent Mill composed verse, delighted in chemistry, and surpassed his father in calculus. But more important were the studies he undertook at twelve, when his father rigorously drilled him in scholastic logic, instilling in him the ability not only to build a rational argument but to dissect an illogical one. Simultaneously he encountered the Socratic method, with its "perpetual testing of all general statements by particular instances." As "an education for precise thinking," Mill found the Socratic method's empirical test, as well as its insistence on definite terms, "inestimable."[3] His father's belief in negative as well as positive influences deprived John of playmates. And although John supervised his sisters' instruction, his father remained his closest companion. On their daily walks they discussed John's reading, utilizing the logical and empirical techniques which would later surface in all of John Stuart Mill's work, including the *Subjection.*

Unusual in its time, James Mill's curriculum emphasized the empirical, scientific method and applied it to society. Thus his son read the limited works then available in psychology along with materials of a sociological nature. And he was early exposed to the study of political economy, a broad field which included the present discipline of economics. David Ricardo, James Mill's "intimate friend" and fellow Benthamite, spent much time at the Mill house, helping John to master laissez-faire economics.[4] Ricardo was a devotee of the great Adam Smith, economist-author of *Wealth of Nations* (1776). Smith and Ricardo wanted each individual to develop his own talents and pursue his own interests on the assumption that this course of action would guarantee the greatest total product for society, therefore promoting the general welfare. Left alone, the division of labor and the demands of the market would ensure that whatever was useful was produced at the lowest possible cost. Anything, including government, which interfered with the operations of the marketplace hampered the greatest happiness of the greatest number.

During these early decades of the nineteenth century, reform forces began to surface after having been decimated in reaction to the French Revolution. Armed by Adam Smith, the newly emerging industrialists and their supporters, largely Whigs, thundered away at the aristocratic, land-holding Tories. Now in Parliament, Ricardo joined the Whig attack on the landlords, whose famous Corn Laws maintained artificially high food prices by keeping imported grain out of a hungry England. But the Whigs generally pressed laissez-faire argument only to force English agrarianism to accommodate English industrialism. Enraged by the comfort that conventional Whigs and Tories enjoyed inside Parliament and in the pages of the *Edinburgh* and *Quarterly Reviews,* respectively, the reforming Benthamites decided it was time for both a new party and a new review. Overrepresentation of the aristocratic governing classes and underrepresentation of everyone else were leading the utilitarians to consider reforms which approached democracy.

When the *Westminster Review,* bankrolled by Bentham, appeared, the Mills were major contributors. James Mill attacked the established parties and the institutions which they supported or which supported them—Parliament, the law, the church. His son aided him, contributing many articles, including some commentary on the unfortunate position of women. Although his contacts with women were generally limited to those within his family, John Mill nonetheless early believed in sexual equality and shared this remarkable position with Jeremy Bentham and an earlier utilitarian, William Godwin, Wollstonecraft's husband. Other radical writers in the *Review* offered new challenges to established customs, and Mill particularly liked the argument of his legal tutor, John Austin, against primogeniture, the doctrine which favored inheritance by the firstborn and by the male line.[5]

Until 1823, when he accepted a position under his father on the administrative staff of the East India Company, John Mill's circle had been so completely confined to his immediate family and his father's friends that when he wished to start a "utilitarian" society emulating the intellectual stimulation of his father's Political Economy Club and the Cambridge Union, he had few acquaintances to include. This small society, which reorganized in 1825 as a larger discussion group, read texts on political economy, logic, and analytical psychology. These young men and most of the London Debating Society, which Mill had also initiated, formed a new force on the British political scene, philosophical radicalism.

The philosophic radicals revered James Mill, whose opinions gave "color and character to" the movement and who possessed "an almost unbounded confidence in the efficacy of two things: representative government and complete freedom of discussion."[6] Their Benthamite emphasis upon the equal worth of each individual and their Ricardian distrust of governmental interference soon transformed the "philosophical radicals" into "liberals." They were partisans of free speech and a free press, supporters of a wider franchise (including women), and champions of freedom from governmental controls.

When James Mill's *Essay on Government and Other Essays* (1828) appeared supporting a broader male franchise, it occasioned an attack by Thomas Babington Macaulay, one of England's best young writers, in the *Edinburgh Review*. Macaulay singled out Mill's statement that almost all of women's interests are involved in those of their husbands or fathers and that they are thus automatically represented, although indirectly, when their men vote. Although Mill did not endorse a restricted franchise but rather assumed it, Macaulay nevertheless accused him of "dogmatiz[ing] away the interest of one-half of the human race." Rising to champion women, Macaulay asserted that they "have always been, and still are, over the greater part of the globe, humble companions, playthings, captives, menials, beasts of burden. Except in a few happy and highly civilized communities, they are strictly in a state of personal slavery. Even in those countries where they are best treated, the laws are generally unfavorable to them."[7]

John Mill avidly read Macaulay's audacious attack on his father's proposed Parliamentary reforms. Neither he nor his friends supported the position on women's enfranchisement which Macaulay attacked, although at a time when only a select few could vote and any extension of that privilege seemed dangerously radical to the country at large, James Mill's assumption was not surprising. The Benthamites nonetheless saw freedom and salvation in the ballot. And John Mill's circle believed "that every reason which exists for giving the suffrage to anybody demands it should not be withheld from women."[8] The younger Mill in much of his later writing, including the *Subjection,* used Macaulay's assertion of a world half-enslaved and reiterated his comparison of the male to a king and the female to a subject.

As Mill passed into his twentieth year, he developed an internal despair. Reflecting on the narrowness of his father's Benthamism, he found "the fabric" of his "old and taught opinions giving way in many fresh places" so that he was "incessantly occupied with weaving it anew." Later he would write that the description of a Benthamite as "a mere reasoning machine" might well have applied to himself for two or three years.[9] An ordained Presbyterian himself, the older Mill generally dismissed religious questions. He also maintained some of the eighteenth century's suspicion of the arts, so his son had taken little time to pursue them. James Mill disdained novels, and although he did encourage John to read such poets as John Milton and Robert Burns, he never cared for the Romantics of the early nineteenth century. His was the world of the obvious, not the intuitive, of "things as they are," not the poetic or transcendental. If James Mill's curriculum and temperament left little room for emotional expression, neither did John's radical circle care about cultivating or showing feeling. So while continuing his usual pursuits, John struggled with his depression alone. He was an intellectual still living and working with his teacher, an adult son yet in the family home, a person with a need to confide who found his single confidant now unapproachable, and a man who had yet to form any meaningful relationship with a woman outside of his family.

Emerging from his depression, John Mill did not disown eighteenth-century rationalism for nineteenth-century Romanticism, nor logic for intuition. But he was now ready to admit a place in life for feeling, to allow Wordsworth and even Samuel Taylor Coleridge their reasonable due, and to read that great exponent of the post-Kantians, Carlyle; from his newly broadened outlook he cautioned against substituting one piece of truth for another when combining the two would produce a greater piece of the whole.[10]

After disagreeing with most of his Benthamite friends on poetry, John Stuart Mill left the London Debating Society. Disillusionment with the editor of the *Westminster Review* also caused both Mills to cease writing for it. No longer immersed in work, Mill visited Paris to investigate the Citizen King and applaud the greater role the common citizen had assumed after the 1830 revolution. And he also found time for social events. At one of these he met John Taylor, a radical businessman, and his lovely wife, Harriet Hardy Taylor.

John Mill was then twenty-five and Harriet Taylor twenty-three. She already had two sons and the following year bore a daughter, Helen. Nevertheless, an un-Victorian friendship developed between Mill and Mrs. Taylor. By the fall of 1833 the Taylors had agreed to a trial separation, which ended in the arrangement that came to be the trio's way of life. The marriage of Harriet and John Taylor stayed legally intact. She continued to live with him and their children with frequent, long absences at a variety of houses he rented for her in the country, where Mill often visited. Her relationship with Mill was probably platonic, as thereafter was that with her husband. If no one was really happy, Harriet at least felt their arrangement the best available answer to an insoluble problem.

Thus hopelessly entangled, Mill and Mrs. Taylor in 1831 and 1832 wrote papers for each other on marriage and divorce. John Stuart Mill later asserted that "the honor and chief blessing of . . . [his] existence," the "most valuable friendship" of his life had not given him his "strong convictions on the complete equality in all legal, political, social and domestic relations which ought to exist between men and women."[11] Before he met Harriet, he held these beliefs as a matter of "abstract principle," drawn from his conclusion that any viable society except a slavocracy would need to consult the interests of all adults. She gave him the "practical bearings of women's disabilities," an exposure to the multitude of barriers and indignities sexism promoted, and an example of woman's substantial capabilities.[12]

Both agreed that marriage was the keystone to woman's lot. Mill found it absurd and immoral that a woman's social position depended on her marital state. Such a situation meant not only that a single woman must establish her usefulness but also that marriage would seldom take place between equals. They found that woman was trained only for marriage, an education woefully inadequate for a full life. For, as Mill pointed out, woman had started with the single disadvantage of lesser physical strength until man had introduced the pecuniary factor. And as long as woman remained unable to support herself, she would deliver her body for bread. If woman were well educated, as she ought to be for her own happiness and that of those around her, she could maintain her independence. Such a woman would enter marriage as an equal, improving that relationship immeasurably, or she would have the realistic option of remaining single.[13]

John Mill's and Harriet Taylor's comments on marriage and divorce reflected their personal situation. Both felt a mistake once made should not be perpetuated, nor should social custom limit the private lives of adults. Mill suggested, however, that people should not resort to divorce too readily. But he saw the chances against happiness in a first marriage as "many to one," for it occurred when the participants had neither the age nor the experience on which to base a judgment. Accepting Robert Owen's definition of chastity as sexual intercourse with love and of prostitution as intercourse without love, he would define any marriage where one of the partners no longer loved the other as a prostitution. In the case of one partner's passionate attachment to a third person or the positive discomfort of either spouse, divorce should follow. In utilitarian fashion Mill allowed, however, that one should forebear in a bad marriage if divorce would be purchased at the expense of others' greater happiness. Although he never discussed the question of divorce so fully again, Mill did note in the *Subjection* that to train a woman only for servitude in marriage and then allow her no opportunity to change masters was to make slavery out of servitude.

Mrs. Taylor declared in her essay that were things as they should be, marriage law would disappear—matrimony, divorce, and all. Educated women and higher natures would see no possible need for a legal "tie that binds." Her essay looked to the future; his dealt also with the present. Without a "regulated community of living among persons intimately acquainted," Mill found no ready solution for the problem of children after divorce. And since Harriet Taylor already had her three, like herself well provided for by her husband, divorce seemed likely to remain a matter for essays.

While John Mill and Harriet Taylor were engrossed in their personal lives and thoughts, the fortunes of the philosophical radicals had reached their zenith in a restive England. The northern industrial workers, as well as the dispossessed southern peasants, were facing starvation. Favorably impressed by the French Revolution of 1830, the middle classes, who feared violence, disliked the aristocracy, and hated George IV, demanded Parliamentary reforms. When the ascension of William IV in 1830 forced a new general election, the country returned liberals numerous enough to turn out the Tories, establish a liberal Whig government, and carry the great reform bill of 1832, which broadened the franchise. The bill set England firmly on the path to democracy and a steady widening of the franchise until it included women.

The *Westminster Review*, founded to further political reform, had languished under its last editors. As a result, in 1835 a wealthy, radical Member of Parliament underwrote the *London Review*, which John Mill clandestinely edited and which "Old Mill" launched with a biting lead article.[14] Bentham's "spirit was scouring the country, armed with the force of government and of public opinion, inquiring into every local authority or endowment, and pertly asking, 'What is the use of it?' "[15] But the only enemy who had the power to still James Mill's pen soon did. "As Brutus was called the last of the Romans, so was he the last of the eighteenth century," his son sadly commented.[16]

His father's death freed Mill to widen the scope of the journal beyond a limited Benthamism, opening its pages to Thomas Carlyle, among others, and to points of view not only different from his father's but from his own. Mill also introduced Alexis de Tocqueville to English readers, recognizing *Democracy in America* as the classic it has since been acclaimed. Tocqueville's analysis of the American experience led Mill to reconsider pure democracy and contributed to his later belief in a modified representative democracy. Moreover, Tocqueville's description of the tyranny which the majority can inflict upon minorities influenced Mill's thinking on the limits to personal liberty, a question which was one of his great concerns, the subject of his most famous essay, and complementary to his attitudes on the poor, the slave, and woman.

Although widely circulated—Margaret Fuller read it in America—the combined *London and Westminster Review* could not counter the renewed popularity of the Tories. Most of the radicals who survived the election of 1837 became "a mere appendage of the Whigs," and a time without a radical party needed no *Westminster Review*.[17] Thus at thirty-four John Mill turned to finishing his *System of Logic.*

The *Logic* is a massive work which attempts to systematize all thought, or rather all experience, for Mill excluded discussion of nondemonstrable truths. Here he posited that man arrives at general laws by organizing the many impressions and events his mind absorbs and that from these general laws he deduces or predicts certain results. Initially, then, the laws are not intuitive, infallible absolutes but rather the result of observations and the attempt to fit these observations into patterns, therefore the result of induction. Although modern social scientific techniques were unknown to him, Mill was an empiricist who consistently tried to rest his conclusions on observation, experience, and/or copious historical examples. He had little use for the idealist's and Romantic's emphasis on intuition or the earlier rationalist's commitment to innate ideas. He considered nineteenth-century German idealism "the greatest speculative hindrance to the regeneration so urgently required of man and society, which can never be effected under the influences of a philosophy which makes opinions their own proof and feelings their own justifications."[18]

Mill's emphasis on induction, on verifying conclusions by specific experience, was shared by the French logician, Auguste Comte, whose *Cours de Philosophie Positive* in six volumes Mill read avidly. But gradually he found himself in basic disagreement with Comte about his relegation of the science of the mind, psychology, to a rather fancy phrenology dependent upon physiology. Comte felt that particular geographical areas of the brain governed particular faculties and that the size of the area determined the amount of competence. Thus those with bigger heads presumably had larger brains and therefore greater mental powers. Comte's thesis worked to the disadvantage of women, for their slighter builds presumably allotted them less brain and therefore limited their possibilities for infinite improvement. With this premise Mill could not agree. He believed not only in the importance of the psychological science but also in the "unlimited possibility of improving the moral and intellectual condition of mankind by education."[19]

In 1841 John Stuart Mill began a lengthy correspondence with the French philosopher, applauding Comte's treatise and approaching their differences gingerly. Although he did not dispute Comte's analysis of social organization including an unchanging social static and variable social dynamic, Mill challenged particular assumptions about the static. While he recognized that the existing institutions of property and marriage probably fulfilled a social need, he felt both of them, particularly marriage, needed to undergo serious modification, and he questioned Comte's insistence on the necessity of subordinating women.[20]

The correspondence, which soon dwelt upon the relationship of men and women, provided a basis for important parts of Mill's argument in the *Subjection*. In the third and final stage of Comte's positivist society, philosophers would govern, much like medieval Roman Catholic bishops. Mill observed that such beneficent philosopher-rulers would require knowledge of woman's experience, knowledge they could not possess in a state of sexual inequality. Although man was likely to learn more about woman, his information would be limited, for few women would write or speak out; most of those who did would do so for men or at least would fear men's judgments. And those women openly in rebellion would not offer reliable testimony, so the male superior would never understand the life of the female dependent. Thus Mill argued the need for a knowledge of women—which no man could possess either in the contemporary society or in the positivist one which Comte proposed.

Comte continued to maintain that women, with their obviously smaller brains, were merely in a state of prolonged childhood. He also thought that a stable society necessitated dependent females. Allowing that women's muscular, cellular, and nervous systems, as well as their cerebral structures, might possibly be closer organically to those of children than were those of men, Mill continued to dispute. To test the assumption that children's brains, and also women's, were inferior to men's would necessitate keeping the brain unchanged while undergoing education and exercise—an impossible task. Without empirical evidence Mill could not dismiss the theory of "several eminent physiologists" that women's brains were smaller and less vigorous, but more active, than men's. This state might, he noted, make them less suited for prolonged intellectual work but better suited to tasks which demanded quickness.

As in the *Subjection,* however, Mill did not wish to attribute to physiology whatever might be explained by social conditioning. And he cautioned Comte that it was easy to exaggerate the degree of real diversity between the sexes if one did not consider the yet unmeasured differences in education and social position. He hoped that ethology, a word he first used to designate the study of the individual character and how environmental differences affect it, would provide an answer. Perhaps because he lacked adequate empirical techniques, he abandoned his own projected ethological study; but such studies, related to possible sexual differences, have currently assumed some importance.[21]

Mill chose to base his argument with Comte on conditioning rather than anatomy. He pointed out that very few men possess the ability to sustain intellectual pursuits or the consistency necessary to manage important industrial enterprises. And one could hardly accuse women of lacking such ability when they seem to show patience and forbearance in those matters which permanently concern them. As for Comte's judgment that women are less able to control their passions, Mill thought that most English men would find males incapable of as much moral restraint as women. English women, if not others, seemed to possess more scrupulous consciences than men. And what is conscience, Mill asked, but submission of the passions to reason?

Citing the emancipation of slaves and serfs over the centuries, Comte attributed women's continued social subordination to their organic inferiority. Mill faulted Comte for not taking into account all the important variables. Mill preferred at least to limit the analogy to domestic slaves, who had achieved freedom mainly by the efforts of nondomestic slaves and/or the acquiescence of their masters. Unlike male serfs or slaves, women were educated from infancy to accept subjection and to find happiness in the favor and affection of the other sex, accorded to them on condition of dependence. Women had never possessed the semi-independence of the male serf, who at least assumed responsibility for himself and his family. Although women's lives might be sweeter, the serf or slave had some time at his own disposal, while feminine servitude remained servitude without intermission. And the intimacy in which men and women coexist, as well as male physical superiority, must bind women all the more tightly to their subordinate position.

Unlike the serfs, who built towns, women would never form a separate society. Their recourse must be an individual one. They must prove themselves one at a time in the careers open to them; and as individual women became eminent, all women would profit, until eventually they gained the franchise, which to Mill, as to other Benthamites, was tantamount to gaining freedom. Mill felt that women had progressed in this regard, and while they had yet to sustain creativity of the highest sort in the arts, perhaps with the advent of female professionalism that endeavor too would be forthcoming. Certainly, he believed, they had performed extraordinarily well in the one exalted opening available to them in human affairs—that of monarch—a point he expanded in the *Subjection.* Recognizing an impasse, he closed his discussion with Comte and had copies of their exchange bound for Harriet Taylor.

Mrs. Taylor had become increasingly central to much of Mill's work. Success with a volume on economic questions encouraged Mill to begin his *Principles of Political Economy,* the universal economics textbook of the nineteenth century. Although this volume bore a modest imprint of Mrs. Taylor's sympathy for socialism, her major interest was "justice for women." She felt human progress awaited "the emancipation of women from their present degraded slavery to the *necessity* of marriage or to modes of earning their living which . . . consist only of poorly paid and hardly worked occupations." Certainly woman's "emancipation would relieve the character of men from the deadening and degrading influences of life passed in intimacy with inferiors." But "domestic slaves cannot organize themselves—each one owns a master, and this mastery which is normally passive would assert itself if they attempted it."[22]

In the summer of 1848 she complained to Mill about the French Assembly's exclusion of women from debates, suggesting he might use this occasion to prepare an article asserting the principle of woman suffrage. Perhaps she considered attempting the task herself. In 1849 Mill vigorously objected to the doctrine "that women always are and must always be what men make them." He felt that "only two things . . . tend at all to shake this nonsensical prejudice: a better psychology and theory of human nature for the few and for the many, more and greater proofs by example of what women can do." And he urged Mrs. Taylor to get on with a pamphlet on the subject—"published it *must be,* and next season too."[23] But meantime the projected work on women gave way to more pressing matters. John Taylor, that long suffering man, was suffering his last, freeing his widow to marry Mill.

In their early essays written for each other, Mill and Mrs. Taylor had seriously questioned marriage laws, and Mill's youngest brother seemed surprised that they would deem marriage either necessary or desirable. For his part, John Mill formally registered their disapproval of "the marriage relation as constituted by law." He noted that it conferred upon one of the parties "legal power and control over the person, property, and freedom of action of the other party." With no means of legally divesting himself of these powers, before his wedding in 1851 Mill signed a disclaimer to any such rights.[24] Throughout his married life he refused to administer or invest any of his wife's estate. And later in the *Subjection* he paraphrased this renunciation of his interest in her property, deploring the "what is mine is yours but what is yours is not mine" doctrine.

Between the time of John Taylor's death and Harriet Taylor's marriage to Mill, the latter published an article, the "Enfranchisement of Women," in the July 1851 edition of the *Westminster Review*. Later, when giving credit to his wife for her help in his articles, Mill pointed out the "Enfranchisement" as "hers in a peculiar sense, my share in it being little more than that of an editor and amanuensis." And later yet he wrote to Mrs. Paulina Wright Davis about the service rendered by his "dear wife . . . by her essay in the *Westminster Review*."[25] Always generous in giving credit, Mill, the "amanuensis," probably wrote the article himself, using some of his wife's ideas or possibly incorporating sections written by her.

In the autumn of 1850 Mill had "been put in spirits" by the Women's Rights Convention held at Worcester, Massachusetts, a meeting without "the least iota of compromise—asserting the whole of the principle and claiming the whole of the consequences."[26] The "Enfranchisement" attempted to bring this argument for female suffrage to an English audience. The article immediately embraced the goals of the American organization: sexual equality in education, production, and legislation. The case, the author claimed, could rest on justice and expediency, both important considerations for a utilitarian and considerations which he employed in the *Subjection*.

The "Enfranchisement" opened with a summary of the history of sexual discrimination, the initial problem of physical advantage and the ensuing one of custom. Mill thereafter dropped anatomical arguments, as he had in his letters to Comte, to deal solely with the relationship of women and politics. Also as in the letters he singled out the great political women of history—notably queens—to prove the competence of women for political life. It was proof by example, the only possible proof of female competence, as Mill had told Comte, until proof by ethology became a reality.[27]

But even if women were suited for politics, was politics suitable for women? Answering this query, the "Enfranchisement" considered three points commonly raised against woman suffrage. The first, if it existed—the incompatibility of active life with maternity—would resolve itself naturally without legislation, as there is no need to compel women to be mothers or to be mothers only, "to devote their lives to one animal function and its consequences."[28] Improvement in their education and enlargement of their faculties would certainly make them competent for other jobs.

The "Enfranchisement" next attacked the argument against increasing the labor supply. Mill had written in his early essay on marriage and divorce that women should be able to support themselves, should have an alternative to economic dependence on men and an opportunity for expression outside the home. Nonetheless, he felt most women would not need to support themselves, although their education would enrich life for themselves, their husbands, and their children. His overriding concern in the days of reform lay with raising the wages of the lower classes, a move incompatible with increasing the labor supply. Mrs. Taylor in her essay had supported opening the labor market equally to men and women. In the "Enfranchisement" they concluded that even though the joint effort of husband and wife would net no more real income than husbands without competition would provide, wives in the labor market were partners, not servants. With the possibility of a socialist state and the recognition of the consequences of "improvident multiplication," remedies for the labor surplus would be found.[29] Mill in the *Subjection* took a stand somewhat nearer to his original position, advocating opening all employment to women but hoping that most would find a family their occupation.

As for the third destructive influence that life outside the home would have upon women, that of "hardening" them, the question belonged to the past, when life was considerably rougher. The only way to exclude women from such influences as remained was to remove them from men's society altogether, an obviously infeasible approach.

Having found the reasons for insulating women from public life inadequate, the "Enfranchisement" held men and their power responsible for the subjection of women. Might had made right, but a costly right it had been, for associating with "disciples" and submissive creatures, as Mill had previously informed Comte, both limits men and makes them servile minded. The influence which women exert over men is often a negative one, an attempt for favors. Therefore, for their own good as well as that of women, men should abolish legal disabilities victimizing women. If that sex naturally prefers these disabilities, the laws concerning marriage, property, and the vote would be unnecessary anyway. The only just and rational action would be to admit women to all social privileges, to give them equal rights—"not a position apart, [nor] a sort of sentimental priesthood."[30]

Certainly the marriage of John Stuart and Harriet Taylor Mill allowed for no "position apart." Mill, who commonly criticized the abilities of his fellowmen and never overestimated his own, classed his wife with Percy Bysshe Shelley as possessors of "both great genius and great experience."

He was convinced that hers was the better, more original mind—that he was the translator and editor and she the creative intellectual of their relationship.[31] Increasingly he came to rely on her judgment, although the advancing pulmonary consumption of both frequently kept them separated while one or the other sought health abroad. During one of their separations Mill decided to expand an essay he had written on liberty to counteract the *"liberticide"* tendencies of contemporary social reformers—most notably Comte.[32]

The resulting famous treatise, *On Liberty,* posited his belief in the importance of "human development in its richest diversity."[33] In order for man to develop as much and as well as possible, the power of society needs to be limited. This position also underlay Mill's reasoning in the *Subjection of Women.* In *On Liberty* he pointed out the social powers that interfere with man's development: the power of authorities, of tyrannical majorities, of prevailing opinion and mores. He saw the need to define the limits of those powers. And he did so in a general way when he claimed self-protection as the only reason for society or an individual to interfere with any other individual or group. An individual should have control over his/her own soul and body and should be restricted only from infringing upon others. Mill recognized a distinction between thought and action: It is one thing to believe something, another to act upon it. Exciting an emotional mob could harm others, could trespass on the liberty of others. Action, therefore, necessarily must be more restricted than opinion; but when the question of protecting others from harm is not pertinent, then men and women should be free to act on their opinions. For, Mill believed, the well-being of mankind rests on pursuing the truth and often in acting upon it.

On Liberty, Mill noted, "was more directly and literally" the "joint production" of himself and his wife than any of the other writings ascribed to him.[34] Together they had examined each sentence, planning to revise it further before its publication. However, Harriet Taylor Mill fell dangerously ill while travelling, dying in Avignon in 1858. A disconsolate Mill returned to the topics which he and his wife had hoped to work on together, writing *Considerations on Representative Government,* which extended some of his ideas from *On Liberty* and included an argument for woman suffrage. Addressing the woman question more fully in 1861, he drafted the *Subjection of Women,* the major feminist document of the nineteenth century.[35]

The *Subjection* incorporated much of his earlier thought. He found sexual subordination both unjust and inexpedient and therefore not utilitarian. After tracing its historical roots, he began to demonstrate it to be sø. In his logical manner he despaired of nineteenth-century reliance on intuition instead of reason and assumed that subordination of women would continue until "a sound psychology" could dislodge it scientifically. He argued that sexual equality had never been tried and that, lacking such an empirical test and without any considered plan, the world had probably adopted a mistaken system. Endorsing once again the process of laissez-faire liberalism—that government does not and should not prescribe the conduct of industrial and social operation but leave it to individuals—he argued that personal conduct as well should reside with the individual, echoing his sentiments in *On Liberty*.

Much of the first chapter, in which he discussed the relationship of men to women, men's knowledge of women, and women's gradual emergence in the literary and public worlds, is an elaboration of ideas first outlined in his letters to Auguste Comte and touched upon in the later "Enfranchisement of Women." As he had when deploring his father's concessions on the franchise, Mill again asserted that the choice of "those by whom one is to be governed is a means of self-protection due to everyone."

His plea for liberty instead of power and for the ideal marriage "of two persons of cultivated faculties, identical in opinions and purposes, between whom there exists that best kind of equality, similarity of powers and capacities with reciprocal superiority in them—so that each can enjoy the luxury of looking up to the other" is a more fitting tribute to his beloved Harriet than the expensive marble monument engraved with effusive praise which marks her Avignon grave.

While waiting for the right time to publish his *Subjection,* Mill wrote on other topics and gradually began to emerge from the social retirement which he had self-imposed during his intimacy with Mrs. Taylor. "Political instructor to the nation" since his *Westminster Review* days, he had been a "tribune" for the emerging Liberal party of the 1860's. His "unparalleled intellectual ascendency" had helped to bring the support of radicals, reformers, intellectuals, and workingmen to the party and in 1865 prompted the request that he stand for Parliament.[36] His speeches and votes in the House of Commons reflected his life-long interests—the Irish peasants, land reform, the 1867 Reform Bill, proportional representation, and of course votes for women. When during debate on the Reform Bill he moved that the word "man" be amended to read "person," his speech for the amendment contained many of the arguments of the *Subjection* and helped to convince almost a third of the Members present to support him. Encouraged by the vote, Mill organized a woman suffrage society and eventually released the *Subjection.* English feminists hailed him because he carried the suffrage question "into the arena of practical politics and gave it the weight of an honored name."[37] And in 1868 they submitted many thousands of signatures on petitions for the vote to Mill to present to Parliament.

His fight for woman suffrage and the *Subjection* endeared him to Americans active in woman's rights work. Already valued as the author of the earlier "Enfranchisement," Mill became one of their "able champions."[38] Although he declined Mrs. Davis's invitation to the Women's Suffrage Convention in Washington in 1870, he kept abreast of the American movement. American feminists reciprocated his interest. Sarah Grimké was not alone in peddling Mill's *Subjection*. The National Suffrage Convention of 1884 recommended that every local society should own a copy of it "to furnish ammunition for arguments and debates."[39] In England, where two editions of the *Subjection of Women* sold rapidly, Mill's constituency turned him out in the election of 1868. With his stepdaughter, Helen Taylor, he retired to Avignon, where he died in 1873.

Mill's fame, unlike that of many other feminists, did not depend primarily upon his feminism. He was, one newspaper reported, the "first spirit of his age."[40] George Macaulay Trevelyan, the historian whose uncle had attacked James Mill, noted that John Stuart Mill's philosophy stood "behind the statesmen of the transition" of Britain into a democracy. When his influence was at its height in the sixties and seventies, he had used it to popularize the idea of sexual equality. To Mill, Trevelyan attributed a change in social thought and custom which even before Mill's death materialized in legislative reform regarding the property and personal rights of women.[41] Although the *Subjection* is not the best known of Mill's works, Mill's was the most formidable reputation yet enlisted actively in the cause of feminism. As such, his thought formed an important platform for later feminists, English and American.

NOTES

1. Emery Neff, *Carlyle and Mill: An Introduction to Victorian Thought* (New York: Columbia University Press, 1926), 342.

2. John Plamenatz, *Mill's Utilitarianism Reprinted with a Study of the English Utilitarians* (Oxford: Basil Blackwell, 1949), 22. This book is a useful introduction to the utilitarians and the roots of their doctrines.

3. John Stuart Mill, *Autobiography* (New York: Henry Holt and Company, 1887), 18–22. In addition to Mill's *Autobiography*, the other major biographical source is the comprehensive study of Michael St. John Packe, *The Life of John Stuart Mill* (New York: The Macmillan Company, 1954).

4. Mill, *Autobiography*, 27–29. A useful summary of utilitarian economic thought, including Mill, can be found in Robert L. Heilbroner, *The Worldly*

Philosophers: The Lives, Times, and Ideas of the Great Economic Thinkers (New York: Simon and Schuster, Inc., 1953).

5. Packe, *Mill,* 63; Mill, *Autobiography,* 96, 97.

6. Mill, *Autobiography,* 105–108.

7. Packe, *Mill,* 89.

8. Mill, *Autobiography,* 104–105.

9. Mill, *Autobiography,* 156, 109.

10. Francis E. Mineka (ed.), *Collected Works of John Stuart Mill,* volumes XII and XIII: *The Earlier Letters of John Stuart Mill, 1812–1848* (Toronto: University of Toronto Press, 1963), XII, 37–38.

11. Mill, *Autobiography,* 244n. Particularly informative about Harriet Taylor Mill and her relationship with John Stuart Mill is Friedrich A. Hayek, *John Stuart Mill and Harriet Taylor: Their Correspondence and Subsequent Marriage* (Chicago: University of Chicago Press, 1951), which includes much of their extant correspondence.

12. Mill, *Autobiography,* 244n; Elizabeth Cady Stanton, Susan B. Anthony, Matilda J. Gage, and Ida H. Harper, (eds.), *History of Woman Suffrage* (6 volumes, Rochester, New York, and New York, 1881–1922), II, 419; Mill, *Utilitarianism,* as reprinted in Plamenatz, *Utilitarianism,* 194.

13. These early essays on marriage and divorce are readily available in Hayek, *Mill and Taylor,* 58–78, and in John Stuart Mill and Harriet Taylor Mill, *Essays on Sex Equality,* edited by Alice S. Rossi (Chicago: University of Chicago Press, 1970), 67–87.

14. Packe, *Mill,* 197.

15. George Macaulay Trevelyan, *British History in the Nineteenth Century and After (1782–1919),* second edition (London: Longmans, Green and Co. Ltd., 1941), 243.

16. Mill, *Autobiography,* 204.

17. Quoted in Packe, *Mill,* 234.

18. Quoted in Packe, *Mill,* 252–253.

19. Mill, *Autobiography,* 108.

20. Mill's letters to Comte on the woman question are reprinted in the original French in Mineka (ed.), *Mill Letters,* XIII, 584–595, 604–611.

21. For example, the work of Konrad Lorenz, including *On Aggression* (London: Methuen, 1966).

22. Quoted in Hayek, *Mill and Taylor,* 122–123.

23. Quoted in Hayek, *Mill and Taylor,* 138.

24. Quoted in Hayek, *Mill and Taylor,* 168.

25. Mill and Mill, *Essays,* 91; Hayek, *Mill and Taylor,* 167; Stanton et al., *Woman Suffrage,* I, 219.

26. Quoted in Hayek, *Mill and Taylor,* 166.

27. The "Enfranchisement of Women" is reprinted in full in Mill and Mill, *Essays,* 91–121.

28. Mill and Mill, *Essays,* 104.

29. Mill and Mill, *Essays,* 105.

30. Mill and Mill, *Essays,* 120.

31. Hayek, *Mill and Taylor,* 145, 185.

32. Quoted in Hayek, *Mill and Taylor,* 216.

33. Wilhelm von Humboldt, as quoted on the title page in John Stuart Mill, *On Liberty.* Modern reprints are available in John M. Robson (ed.), *John Stuart Mill: A Selection of His Works* (New York: Odyssey Press, 1966), 13–147, and in Max Lerner (ed.), *Essential Works of John Stuart Mill* (New York: Bantam Books, Inc., 1961), 255–360.

34. Mill, *Autobiography,* 251.

35. For a readily available, unabridged text of *The Subjection of Women,* see Mill and Mill, *Essays,* 125–242, or John Stuart Mill, *The Subjection of Women,* edited by Wendell Robert Carr (Cambridge, Massachusetts, and London: The M.I.T. Press, 1970).

36. For an assessment of Mill's role as a Liberal party leader, see John Vincent, *The Formation of the British Liberal Party* (New York: Charles Scribner's Sons, 1966), 141–142, 149–158.

37. Stanton et al., *Woman Suffrage,* III, 853.

38. Stanton et al., *Woman Suffrage,* II, 378n.

39. Stanton et al., *Woman Suffrage,* IV, 26n.

40. Quoted in Packe, *Mill,* 326.

41. Trevelyan, *British History in the Nineteenth Century,* 340–341.

THE SUBJECTION OF WOMEN (1869)

I.

The object of this essay is to explain . . . that the principle which regulates the existing social relations between the two sexes—the legal subordination of one sex to the other—is wrong in itself and now one of the chief hindrances to human improvement, and that it ought to be replaced by a principle of perfect equality, admitting no power or privilege on the one side nor disability on the other. . . .

In every respect the burden is hard on those who attack an almost universal opinion. . . . The *a priori* presumption is in favor of freedom and impartiality. It is held that there should be no restraint not required by the general good and that the law should be no respecter of persons, but should treat all alike, save where dissimilarity of treatment is required by positive reasons, either of justice or of policy. But of none of these rules of evidence will the benefit be allowed to those who maintain the opinion I profess. It is useless for me to say that those who maintain the doctrine that men have a right to command and women are under an obligation to obey or that men are fit for government and women unfit are on the affirmative side of the question and that they are bound to show positive evidence for the assertions, or submit to their rejection. It is equally unavailing for me to say that those who deny to women any freedom of privilege rightly allowed to men, having the double presumption against them that they are opposing freedom and recommending partiality, must be held to the strictest proof of their case, and unless their success be such as to exclude all doubt, the judgment ought to go against them. These would be thought good pleas in any common case, but they will not be thought so in this instance. Before I could hope to make any impression, I should be expected not only to answer all that has ever been said by those who take the other side of the question but to imagine all that could be said by them, . . . as well as answer all I find; and besides refuting all arguments for the affirmative, I shall be called upon for invincible positive arguments to prove a negative. And even if I could do all this and leave the opposite party with a host of unanswered arguments against them and not a single unrefuted one on their side, I should be thought to have done little; for a cause supported on the one hand by universal usage and on the other by so great a preponderance of popular sentiment is supposed to have a presumption in its favor superior to any conviction which an appeal to reason has power to produce in any intellects but those of a high class. . . .

. . . It is one of the characteristic prejudices of the reaction of the nineteenth century against the eighteenth to accord to the unreasoning elements in human nature the infallibility which the eighteenth century is supposed to have ascribed to the reasoning elements. For the apotheosis of Reason we have substituted that of Instinct; and we call everything instinct which we find in ourselves and for which we cannot trace any rational foundation. This idolatry, infinitely more degrading than the other and the most pernicious of the false worships of the present day, of all of which it is now the main support, will probably hold its ground until it gives way before a sound psychology, laying bare the real root of much that is bowed down to as the intention of Nature and the ordinance of God. . . .

The generality of a practice is in some cases a strong presumption that it is, or at all events once was, conducive to laudable ends. This is the case when the practice was first adopted or afterwards kept up as a means to such ends and was grounded on experience of the mode in which they could be most effectually attained. . . . But the state of the case is in every respect the reverse of this. In the first place, the opinion in favor of the present system, which entirely subordinates the weaker sex to the stronger, rests upon theory only; for there never has been trial made of any other: so that experience, in the sense in which it is vulgarly opposed to theory, cannot be pretended to have pronounced any verdict. And in the second place, the adoption of this system of inequality never was the result of deliberation or forethought or any social ideas or any notion whatever of what conduced to the benefit of humanity or the good order of society. It arose simply from the fact that from the very earliest twilight of human society, every woman (owing to the value attached to her by men, combined with her inferiority in muscular strength) was found in a state of bondage to some man. Laws and systems of polity always begin by recognizing the relations they find already existing between individuals. They convert what was a mere physical fact into a legal right, give it the sanction of society, and principally aim at the substitution of public and organized means of asserting and protecting these rights instead of the irregular and lawless conflict of physical strength. Those who had already been compelled to obedience became in this manner legally bound to it.

. . . People flatter themselves that the rule of mere force is ended, that the law of the strongest cannot be the reason of existence of anything which has remained in full operation down to the present time. However any of our present institutions may have begun, it can only, they think, have been preserved to this period of advanced civilization by a well-grounded feeling of its adaptation to human nature and conduciveness to the general good. They do not understand the great vitality and durability of institutions which place right on the side of might; how intensely they are clung to; . . . how slowly these bad institutions give way, one at a time, the weakest first, beginning with those which are least interwoven with the daily habits of life; and how very rarely those who have obtained legal power because they first had physical have ever lost their hold of it until the physical power had passed over to the other side. Such shifting of the physical force not having taken place in the case of women, this fact . . . made it certain from the first that this branch of the system of right founded on might, though softened in its most atrocious features at an earlier period than several of the others, would be the very last to disappear. . . .

The truth is that people of the present and the last two or three generations have lost all practical sense of the primitive condition of humanity; and only the few who have studied history accurately or have much frequented the parts of the world occupied by the living representatives of ages long past are able to form any mental picture of what society then was. People are not aware how entirely in former ages the law of superior strength was the rule of life, how publicly and openly it was avowed. . . . Less than forty years ago, Englishmen might still by law hold human beings in bondage as saleable property. Within the present century they might kidnap them and carry them off and work them literally to death. This absolutely extreme case of the law of force, condemned by those who can tolerate almost every other form of arbitrary power, and which of all others presents features the most revolting to the feelings of all who look at it from an impartial position, was the law of civilized and Christian England within the memory of persons now living. And in one-half of Anglo-Saxon America three or four years ago, not only did slavery exist, but the slave trade and the breeding of slaves expressly for it was a general practice between slave states. . . . So extreme an instance makes it almost superfluous to refer to any other, but consider the long duration of absolute monarchy. In England at present it is the almost universal conviction that military despotism is a case of the law of force having no other origin or justification. Yet in all the great nations of Europe except England, it either still exists or has only just ceased to exist and has even now a strong party favorable to it in all ranks of the people, especially among persons of station and consequence. Such is the power of an established system, even when far from universal, when not only in almost every period of history there have been great and well-known examples of the contrary system but these have almost invariably been afforded by the most illustrious and most prosperous communities. In this case, too, the possessor of the undue power, the person directly interested in it, is only one person, while those who are subject to it and suffer from it are literally all the rest. The yoke is naturally and necessarily humiliating to all persons, except the one who is on the throne together with, at most, the one who expects to succeed to it. How different are these cases from that of the power of men over women! I am not now prejudging the question of its justifiableness. I am showing how vastly more permanent it could not but be, even if not justifiable, than these other dominations which have nevertheless lasted down to our own time. Whatever gratification of pride there is in the possession of power and whatever personal interest in its exercise is in this case not confined to a limited class but common to the whole male sex. . . . It comes home to the person and hearth of every male head of a family and of everyone who looks forward to being so. The clodhopper exercises, or is to exercise, his share of the power equally with the highest nobleman. And the case is that in which the desire of power is the strongest: For everyone who desires power desires it most over those who are nearest to him, with whom his life is passed, with whom he has most concerns in common, and in whom any independence of his authority is oftenest likely to interfere with his individual preferences. . . . We must consider, too, that the possessors of the power have facilities in this case, greater than in any other, to prevent any uprising against it. Every one of the subjects lives under the very eye and almost, it may be said, in the hands of one of the masters—in closer intimacy with him than with any of her fellow-subjects, with no means of combining against him, no power of even locally overmastering him, and, on the other hand, with the strongest motives for seeking his favor and avoiding to give him offense. In struggles for political emancipation, everybody knows how often its champions are bought off by bribes or daunted by terrors. In the case of women, each individual of the subject class is in a chronic state of bribery and intimidation combined. In setting up the standard of resistance, a large number of the leaders and still more of the followers must make an almost complete sacrifice of the pleasures of the alleviations of their own individual lot. If ever any system of privilege and enforced subjection had its yoke tightly riveted on the necks of those who are kept down by it, this has. . . .

Some will object that a comparison cannot fairly be made between the government of the male sex and the forms of unjust power which I have adduced in illustration of it, since these are arbitrary and the effect of mere usurpation, while it on the contrary is natural. But was there ever any domination which did not appear natural to those who possessed it? There was a time when the division of mankind into two classes, a small one of masters and a numerous one of slaves, appeared even to the most cultivated minds to be a natural, and the only natural, condition of the human race. . . . The subjection of women to men being a universal custom, any departure from it quite naturally appears unnatural. But how entirely, even in this case, the feeling is dependent on custom appears by ample experience. Nothing so much astonishes the people of distant parts of the world when they first learn anything about England as to be told that it is under a queen: The thing seems to them so unnatural as to be almost incredible. To Englishmen this does not seem in the least degree unnatural because they are used to it; but they do feel it unnatural that women should be soldiers or Members of Parliament. . . .

But, it will be said, the rule of men over women differs from all these others in not being a rule of force: It is accepted voluntarily; women make no complaint and are consenting parties to it. In the first place, a great number of women do not accept it. Ever since there have been women able to make their sentiments known by their writings (the only mode of publicity which society permits to them), an increasing number of them have recorded protests against their present social condition; and recently many thousands of them, headed by the most eminent women known to the public, have petitioned Parliament for their admission to the parliamentary suffrage. The claim of women to be educated as solidly and in the same branches of knowledge as men is urged with growing intensity and with a great prospect of success, while the demand for their admission into professions and occupations hitherto closed against them becomes every year more urgent. . . . How many more women there are who silently cherish similar aspirations no one can possibly know; but there are abundant tokens how many *would* cherish them were they not so strenuously taught to repress them as contrary to the proprieties of their sex. It must be remembered, also, that no enslaved class ever asked for complete liberty at once. . . . It is a political law of nature that those who are under any power of ancient origin never begin by complaining of the power itself but only of its oppressive exercise. There is never any want of women who complain of ill usage by their husbands. There would be infinitely more if complaint were not the greatest of all provocatives to a repetition and increase of the ill usage. It is this which frustrates all attempts to maintain the power but protect the woman against its abuses. In no other case (except that of a child) is the person who has been proved judicially to have suffered an injury replaced under the physical power of the culprit who inflicted it. Accordingly wives, even in the most extreme and protracted cases of bodily ill usage, hardly ever dare avail themselves of the laws made for their protection; and if, in a moment of irrepressible indignation or by the interference of neighbors, they are induced to do so, their whole effort afterwards is to disclose as little as they can and to beg off their tyrant from his merited chastisement.

All causes, social and natural, combine to make it unlikely that women should be collectively rebellious to the power of men. They are so far in a position different from all other subject classes that their masters require something more from them than actual service. Men do not want solely the obedience of women; they want their sentiments. All men, except the most brutish, desire to have in the woman most nearly connected with them not a forced slave but a willing one, not a slave merely but a favorite. They have therefore put everything in practice to enslave their minds. The masters of all other slaves rely for maintaining obedience on fear, either fear of themselves or religious fears. The masters of women wanted more than simple obedience, and they turned the whole force of education to effect their purpose. All women are brought up from the very earliest years in the belief that their ideal of character is the very opposite to that of men: not self-will and government by self-control but submission and yielding to the control of others. All the moralities tell them that it is the duty of women, and all the current sentimentalities that it is their nature, to live for others, to make complete abnegation of themselves and to have no life but in their affections. And by their affections are meant the only ones they are allowed to have —those to the men with whom they are connected or to the children who constitute an additional and indefeasible tie between them and a man. When we put together three things—first, the natural attraction between opposite sexes; secondly, the wife's entire dependence on the husband, every privilege or pleasure she has being either his gift or depending entirely on his will; and lastly, [the fact] that the principal object of human pursuit, consideration, and all objects of social ambition can in general be sought or obtained by her only through him—it would be a miracle if the object of being attractive to men had not become the polar star of feminine education and formation of character. . . .

The preceding considerations are amply sufficient to show that custom, however universal it may be, affords in this case no presumption and ought not to create any prejudice in favor of the arrangements which place women in social and political subjection to men. But I may go farther and maintain that the course of history and the tendencies of progressive human society afford not only no presumption in favor of this system of inequality of rights but a strong one against it; and . . . so far as the whole course of human improvement up to this time, the whole stream of modern tendencies, warrants any inference on the subject, it is that this relic of the past is discordant with the future and must necessarily disappear.

For what is the peculiar character of the modern world—the difference which chiefly distinguishes modern institutions, modern social ideas, modern life itself, from those of times long past? It is that human beings are no longer born to their place in life and chained down by an inexorable bond to the place they are born to but are free to employ their faculties and such favorable chances as offer to achieve the lot which may appear to them most desirable. . . . Law and government do not undertake to prescribe by whom any social or industrial operation shall or shall not be conducted or what modes of conducting them shall be lawful. These things are left to the unfettered choice of individuals. . . . The old theory was that the least possible should be left to the choice of the individual agent, that all he had to do should, as far as practicable, be laid down for him by superior wisdom. Left to himself, he was sure to go wrong. The modern conviction, the fruit of a thousand years of experience, is that things in which the individual is the person directly interested never go right but as they are left to his own discretion and that any regulation of them by authority, except to protect the rights of others, is sure to be mischievous. This conclusion, slowly arrived at and not adopted until almost every possible application of the contrary theory had been made with disastrous result, now (in the industrial department) prevails universally in the most advanced countries, almost universally in all that have pretensions to any sort of advancement. It is not that all processes are supposed to be equally good or all persons to be equally qualified for everything but that freedom of individual choice is now known to be the only thing which procures the adoption of the best processes and throws each operation into the hands of those who are best qualified for it. . . .

If this general principle of social and economical science . . . is true, we ought to act as if we believed it and not to ordain that to be born a girl instead of a boy, any more than to be born black instead of white or a commoner instead of a nobleman, shall decide the person's position through all life—shall interdict people from all the more elevated social positions and from all, except a few, respectable occupations. Even were we to admit the utmost that is ever pretended as to the superior fitness of men for all the functions now reserved to them, the same argument applies which forbids a legal qualification for Members of Parliament. If only once in a dozen years the conditions of eligibility exclude a fit person, there is a real loss, while the exclusion of thousands of unfit persons is no gain; for if the constitution of the electoral body disposes them to choose unfit persons, there are always plenty of such persons to choose from. In all things of any difficulty and importance, those who can do them well are fewer than the need, even with the most unrestricted latitude of choice; and any limitation of the field of selection deprives society of some chances of being served by the competent without ever saving it from the incompetent.

At present in the more improved countries, the disabilities of women are the only case, save one, in which laws and institutions take persons at their birth and ordain that they shall never in all their lives be allowed to compete for certain things. The one exception is that of royalty. Persons still are born to the throne; no one not of the reigning family can ever occupy it, and no one even of that family can by any means but the course of hereditary succession attain it. All other dignities and social advantages are open to the whole male sex; many indeed are only attainable by wealth, but wealth may be striven for by anyone and is actually obtained by many men of the very humblest origin. The difficulties to the majority are indeed insuperable without the aid of fortunate accidents, but no male human being is under any legal ban; neither law nor opinion superadd artificial obstacles to the natural ones. . . .

The social subordination of women thus stands out an isolated fact in modern social institutions, a solitary breach of what has become their fundamental law. . . . This entire discrepancy between one social fact and all those which accompany it . . . raises a prima facie presumption on the unfavorable side far outweighing any which custom and usage could in such circumstances create on the favorable and should at least suffice to make this, like the choice between republicanism and royalty, a balanced question.

The least that can be demanded is that the question should not be considered as prejudged by existing fact and existing opinion but open to discussion on its merits as a question of justice and expediency, the decision on this . . . depending on what an enlightened estimate of tendencies and consequences may show to be most advantageous to humanity in general without distinction of sex. And the discussion must be a real discussion, descending to foundations and not resting satisfied with vague and general assertions. It will not do, for instance, to assert in general terms, that the experience of mankind has pronounced in favor of the existing system. Experience cannot possibly have decided between two courses so long as there has only been experience of one. . . . Experience does say that every step in improvement has been so invariably accompanied by a step made in raising the social position of women that historians and philosophers have been led to adopt their elevation or debasement as on the whole the surest test and most correct measure of the civilization of a people or an age. Through all the progressive periods of human history, the condition of women has been approaching nearer to equality with men. This does not of itself prove that the assimilation must go on to complete equality, but it assuredly affords some presumption that such is the case.

Neither does it avail anything to say that the *nature* of the two sexes adapts them to their present functions and position and renders these appropriate to them. Standing on the ground of common sense and the constitution of the human mind, I deny that anyone knows, or can know, the nature of the two sexes as long as they have only been seen in their present relation to one another. If men had ever been found in society without women, or women without men, or if there had been a society of men and women in which the women were not under the control of the men, something might have been positively known about the mental and moral differences which may be inherent in the nature of each. What is now called the nature of women is an eminently artificial thing—the result of forced repression in some directions, unnatural stimulation in others. It may be asserted without scruple that [members of] no other class of dependents have had their characters so entirely distorted from [their] natural proportions by their relations with their masters; for, if conquered and slave races have been in some respects more forcibly repressed, whatever in them has not been crushed down by an iron heel has generally been let alone, and, if left with any liberty of development, it has developed itself according to its own laws; but in the case of women, a hot-house and stove cultivation has always been carried on of some of the capabilities of their nature, for the benefit and pleasure of their masters. . . .

Of all difficulties which impede the progress of thought and the formation of well-grounded opinions on life and social arrangements, the greatest is now the unspeakable ignorance and inattention of mankind in respect to the influences which form human character. Whatever any portions of the human species now are or seem to be, such, it is supposed, they have a natural tendency to be—even when the most elementary knowledge of the circumstances in which they have been placed clearly points out the causes that made them what they are. Because a cotter deeply in arrears to his landlord is not industrious, there are people who think that the Irish are naturally idle. Because constitutions can be overthrown when the authorities appointed to execute them turn their arms against them, there are people who think the French incapable of free government. . . . And because women, as is often said, care nothing about politics except their personalities, it is supposed that the general good is naturally less interesting to women than to men.

. . . While almost everybody dogmatizes upon it, almost all neglect and make light of the only means by which any partial insight can be obtained into it. This is an analytic study of the most important department of psychology, the laws of the influence of circumstances on character. For however great and apparently ineradicable the moral and intellectual differences between men and women might be, the evidence of their being natural differences could only be negative. Those only could be inferred to be natural which could not possibly be artificial—the residuum after deducting every characteristic of either sex which can admit of being explained [by] . . . education or external circumstances. The profoundest knowledge of the laws of the formation of character is indispensable to entitle anyone to affirm even that there is any difference, much more what the difference is, between the two sexes considered as moral and rational beings; and since no one as yet has that knowledge . . . , no one is thus far entitled to any positive opinion on the subject. Conjectures are all that can at present be made. . . .

Even the preliminary knowledge [of] what the differences between the sexes now are, apart from all questions as to how they are made what they are, is still in the crudest and most incomplete state. Medical practitioners and physiologists have ascertained to some extent the differences in bodily constitution, and this is an important element to the psychologist; but hardly any medical practitioner is a psychologist. Respecting the mental characteristics of women, their observations are of no more worth than those of common men. It is a subject on which nothing final can be known so long as those who alone can really know it, women themselves, have given but little testimony and that little, mostly suborned. . . . It is only a man here and there who has any tolerable knowledge of the character even of the women of his own family. I do not mean of their capabilities; these nobody knows, not even themselves, because most of them have never been called out. I mean their actually existing thoughts and feelings. Many a man thinks he perfectly understands women because he has had amatory relations with several, perhaps with many, of them. If he is a good observer and his experience extends to quality as well as quantity, he may have learnt something of one narrow department of their nature—an important department, no doubt. But of all the rest of it, few persons are generally more ignorant because there are few from whom it is so carefully hidden. The most favorable case which a man can generally have for studying the character of a woman is that of his own wife, for the opportunities are greater and the cases of complete sympathy not so unspeakably rare. And in fact, this is the source from which any knowledge worth having on the subject has, I believe, generally come. But most men have not had the opportunity of studying in this way more than a single case; accordingly one can, to an almost laughable degree, infer what a man's wife is like from his opinions about women in general. To make even this one case yield any result, the woman must be worth knowing and the man not only a competent judge but of a character so sympathetic in itself and so well adapted to hers that he can either read her mind by sympathetic intuition or has nothing in himself which makes her shy of disclosing it. Hardly anything, I believe, can be more rare than this conjunction. It often happens that there is the most complete unity of feeling and community of interests as to all external things, yet the one has as little admission into the internal life of the other as if they were common acquaintances. Even with true affection, authority on the one side and subordination on the other prevent perfect confidence. Though nothing may be intentionally withheld, much is not shown. . . . The truth is that the position of looking up to another is extremely unpropitious to complete sincerity and openness with him. The fear of losing ground in his opinion or in his feelings is so strong that even in an upright character there is an unconscious tendency to show only the best side or the side which, though not the best, is that which he most likes to see. And it may be confidently said that thorough knowledge of one another hardly ever exists but between persons who, besides being intimates, are equals. How much more true, then, must all this be when the one is not only under the authority of the other but has it inculcated on her as a duty to reckon everything else subordinate to his comfort and pleasure and to let him neither see nor feel anything coming from her except what is agreeable to him. All these difficulties stand in the way of a man's obtaining any thorough knowledge even of the one woman whom alone, in general, he has sufficient opportunity of studying. When we further consider that to understand one woman is not necessarily to understand any other woman, that even if he could study many women of one rank or of one country, he would not thereby understand women of other ranks or countries—and even if he did, they are still only the women of a single period of history—we may safely assert that the knowledge which men can acquire of women, even as they have been and are without reference to what they might be, is wretchedly imperfect and superficial and always will be so, until women themselves have told all that they have to tell.

And this time has not come; nor will it come otherwise than gradually. It is but of yesterday that women have either been qualified by literary accomplishments or permitted by society to tell anything to the general public. As yet very few of them dare tell anything which men, on whom their literary success depends, are unwilling to hear. Let us remember in what manner up to a very recent time the expression, even by a male author, of uncustomary opinions or what are deemed eccentric feelings usually was, and in some degree still is, received; and we may form some faint conception under what impediments a woman, who is brought up to think custom and opinion her sovereign rule, attempts to express in books anything drawn from the depths of her own nature. . . . Literary women are becoming more freespoken and more willing to express their real sentiments. Unfortunately, in this country especially they are themselves such artificial products that their sentiments are compounded of a small element of individual observation and consciousness and a very large one of acquired associations. This will be less and less the case, but it will remain true to a great extent as long as social institutions do not admit the same free development of originality in women which is possible to men. When that time comes and not before, we shall see, and not merely hear, as much as it is necessary to know of the nature of women and the adaptation of other things to it.

I have dwelt so much on the difficulties which at present obstruct any real knowledge by men of the true nature of women because in this as in so many other things . . . there is little chance of reasonable thinking on the matter while people flatter themselves that they perfectly understand a subject of which most men know absolutely nothing and of which it is at present impossible that any man, or all men taken together, should have knowledge which can qualify them to lay down the law to women as to what is, or is not, their vocation. . . .

One thing we may be certain of—that what is contrary to women's nature to do, they never will be made to do by simply giving their nature free play. The anxiety of mankind to interfere in behalf of nature, for fear lest nature should not succeed in effecting its purpose, is an altogether unnecessary solicitude. What women by nature cannot do, it is quite superfluous to forbid them from doing. What they can do, but not so well as the men who are their competitors, competition suffices to exclude them from, since nobody asks for protective duties and bounties in favor of women; it is only asked that the present bounties and protective duties in favor of men should be recalled. . . .

The general opinion of men is supposed to be that the natural vocation of a woman is that of a wife and mother. I say "is supposed to be" because judging from acts—from the whole of the present constitution of society—one might infer that their opinion was the direct contrary. They might be supposed to think that the alleged natural vocation of women was of all things the most repugnant to their nature, insomuch that if they are free to do anything else—if any other means of living or occupation of their time and faculties is open which has any chance of appearing desirable to them—there will not be enough of them who will be willing to accept the condition said to be natural to them. . . . It is not a sign of one's thinking the boon one offers very attractive when one allows only Hobson's choice, "that or none." And here, I believe, is the clue to the feelings of those men who have a real antipathy to the equal freedom of women. I believe they are afraid, not lest women should be unwilling to marry, for I do not think that anyone in reality has that apprehension, but lest they should insist that marriage should be on equal conditions, lest all women of spirit and capacity should prefer doing almost anything else, not in their own eyes degrading, rather than marry when marrying is giving themselves a master, and a master too of all their earthly possessions. And truly, if this consequence were necessarily incident to marriage, I think that the apprehension would be very well founded. I agree in thinking it probable that few women capable of anything else would . . . choose such a lot when any other means were open to them of filling a conventionally honorable place in life; and if men are determined that the law of marriage shall be a law of despotism, they are quite right, in point of mere policy, in leaving to women only Hobson's choice. But in that case all that has been done in the modern world to relax the chain on the minds of women has been a mistake. They never should have been allowed to receive a literary education. Women who read, much more women who write, are in the existing constitution of things a contradiction and a disturbing element; and it was wrong to bring women up with any acquirements but those of an odalisque or of a domestic servant.

II.

It will be well to commence the detailed discussion of the subject by the particular branch of it to which the course of our observations has led us: the conditions which the laws of this and all other countries annex to the marriage contract, marriage being the destination appointed by society for women. . . . The wife is the actual bond-servant of her husband: no less so, as far as legal obligation goes, than slaves commonly so called. She vows a lifelong obedience to him at the altar and is held to it all through her life by law. . . . The two are called "one person in law," for the purpose of inferring that whatever is hers is his, but the parallel inference is never drawn that whatever is his is hers; the maxim is not applied against the man, except to make him responsible to third parties for her acts, as a master is for the acts of his slaves or of his cattle. . . . Hardly any slave, except one immediately attached to the master's person, is a slave at all hours and all minutes; in general he has, like a soldier, his fixed task, and when it is done or when he is off duty, he disposes within certain limits of his own time and has a family life into which the master rarely intrudes. . . . Not so the wife: However brutal a tyrant she may unfortunately be chained to—though she may know that he hates her, though it may be his daily pleasure to torture her, and though she may feel it impossible not to loathe him—he can claim from her and enforce the lowest degradation of a human being, that of being made the instrument of an animal function contrary to her inclinations. . . . It is only legal separation by a decree of a court of justice which entitles her to live apart without being forced back into the custody of an exasperated jailer—or which empowers her to apply any earnings to her own use without fear that a man whom perhaps she has not seen for twenty years will pounce upon her some day and carry all off. . . . Surely if a woman is denied any lot in life but that of being the personal body-servant of a despot and is dependent for everything upon the chance of finding one who may be disposed to make a favorite of her instead of merely a drudge, it is a very cruel aggravation of her fate that she should be allowed to try this chance only once. The natural sequel and corollary from this state of things would be that since her all in life depends upon obtaining a good master, she should be allowed to change again and again until she finds one. . . . All I now say is that to those to whom nothing but servitude is allowed, the free choice of servitude is the only, though a most insufficient, alleviation. Its refusal completes the assimilation of the wife to the slave. . . .

. . . I have described the wife's legal position, not her actual treatment. The laws of most countries are far worse than the people who execute them, and many of them are only able to remain laws by being seldom or never carried into effect. If married life were all that it might be expected to be looking to the laws alone, society would be a hell upon earth. Happily there are both feelings and interests which in many men exclude and in most greatly temper the impulses and propensities which lead to tyranny; and of those feelings, the tie which connects a man with his wife affords, in a normal state of things, incomparably the strongest example. The only tie which at all approaches to it, that between him and his children, tends, in all save exceptional cases, to strengthen instead of conflicting with the first. Because this is true, because men in general do not inflict nor women suffer all the misery which could be inflicted and suffered if the full power of tyranny with which the man is legally invested were acted on, the defenders of the existing form of the institution think that all its iniquity is justified and that any complaint is merely quarrelling with the evil which is the price paid for every great good. But the mitigations in practice, which are compatible with maintaining in full legal force this or any other kind of tyranny, instead of being any apology for despotism, only serve to prove what power human nature possesses of reacting against the vilest institutions and with what vitality the seeds of good as well as those of evil in human character diffuse and propagate themselves. . . .

Whether the institution to be defended is slavery, political absolutism, or the absolutism of the head of a family, we are always expected to judge of it from its best instances. . . . Who doubts that there may be great goodness and great happiness and great affection under the absolute government of a good man? Meanwhile, laws and institutions require to be adapted not to good men but to bad. Marriage is not an institution designed for a select few. Men are not required as a preliminary to the marriage ceremony to prove by testimonials that they are fit to be trusted with the exercise of absolute power. The tie of affection and obligation to a wife and children is very strong with those whose general social feelings are strong and with many who are little sensible to any other social ties; but there are all degrees of sensibility and insensibility to it, as there are all grades of goodness and wickedness in men, down to those whom no ties will bind and on whom society has no action but through . . . the penalties of the law. In every grade of this descending scale are men to whom are committed all the legal powers of a husband. The vilest malefactor has some wretched woman tied to him against whom he can commit any atrocity except killing her and, if tolerably cautious, can do that without much danger of the legal penalty. . . . The law, which till lately left even these atrocious extremes of domestic oppression practically unpunished, has within these few years made some feeble attempts to repress them. But its attempts have done little and cannot be expected to do much because it is contrary to reason and experience to suppose that there can be any real check to brutality consistent with leaving the victim still in the power of the executioner. . . .

. . . Absolute fiends are as rare as angels, perhaps rarer. Ferocious savages, with occasional touches of humanity, are, however, very frequent; and in the wide interval which separates these from any worthy representatives of the human species, how many are the forms and gradations of animalism and selfishness, often under an outward varnish of civilization and even cultivation, living at peace with the law, maintaining a creditable appearance to all who are not under their power, yet sufficient often to make the lives of all who are so a torment and a burden to them! . . . Even the commonest men reserve the violent, the sulky, the undisguisedly selfish side of their character for those who have no power to withstand it. The relation of superiors to dependents is the nursery of these vices of character which, wherever else they exist, are an overflowing from that source. A man who is morose or violent to his equals is sure to be one who has lived among inferiors whom he could frighten or worry into submission. If the family in its best forms is, as it is often said to be, a school of sympathy, tenderness, and loving forgetfulness of self, it is still oftener, as respects its chief, a school of willfulness, overbearingness, unbounded self-indulgence, and a double-dyed and idealized selfishness, of which sacrifice itself is only a particular form: the care for the wife and children being only care for them as parts of the man's own interests and belongings and their individual happiness being immolated in every shape to his smallest preferences. What better is to be looked for under the existing form of the institution? . . .

What . . . tempers the corrupting effects of the power and makes it compatible with such amount of good as we actually see? Mere feminine blandishments, though of great effect in individual instances, have very little effect in modifying the general tendencies of the situation; for their power only lasts while the woman is young and attractive, often only while her charm is new and not dimmed by familiarity; and on many men they have not much influence at any time. The real mitigating causes are the personal affection which is the growth of time, in so far as the man's nature is susceptible of it and the woman's character sufficiently congenial with his to excite it; their common interests as regards the children and their general community of interest as concerns third persons (to which, however, there are very great limitations); the real importance of the wife to his daily comforts and enjoyments and the value he consequently attaches to her on his personal account, which, in a man capable of feeling for others, lays the foundation of caring for her on her own; and lastly, the influence naturally acquired over almost all human beings by those near to their persons (if not actually disagreeable to them). . . . Through these various means the wife frequently exercises even too much power over the man; she is able to affect his conduct in things in which she may not be qualified to influence it for good—in which her influence may be not only unenlightened but employed on the morally wrong side and in which he would act better if left to his own prompting. But neither in the affairs of families nor in those of states is power a compensation for the loss of freedom. Her power often gives her what she has no right to but does not enable her to assert her own rights. . . . By entirely sinking her own existence in her husband, by having no will (or persuading him that she has no will) but his in anything which regards their joint relation, and by making it the business of her life to work upon his sentiments, a wife may gratify herself by influencing and very probably perverting his conduct in those of his external relations which she has never qualified herself to judge or in which she is herself wholly influenced by some personal [inclination] or other partiality or prejudice. Accordingly, as things now are, those who act most kindly to their wives are quite as often made worse as better by the wife's influence in respect to all interests extending beyond the family. She is taught that she has no business with things out of that sphere; and accordingly she seldom has any honest and conscientious opinion on them and therefore hardly ever meddles with them for any legitimate purpose but generally for an interested one. She neither knows nor cares which is the right side in politics, but she knows what will bring in money or invitations, give her husband a title, her son a place, or her daughter a good marriage.

But how, it will be asked, can any society exist without government? In a family, as in a state, some one person must be the ultimate ruler. Who shall decide when married people differ in opinion? Both cannot have their way, yet a decision one way or the other must be come to.

It is not true that in all voluntary association between two people, one of them must be absolute master, still less that the law must determine which of them it shall be. The most frequent case of voluntary association next to marriage is partnership in business; and it is not found or thought necessary to enact that in every partnership one partner shall have entire control over the concern and the others shall be bound to obey his orders. . . . The law never does this, nor does experience show it to be necessary that any theoretical inequality of power should exist between the partners or that the partnership should have any other conditions than what they may themselves appoint by their articles of agreement. Yet it might seem that the exclusive power might be conceded with less danger to the rights and interests of the inferior in the case of partnership than in that of marriage, since he is free to cancel the power by withdrawing from the connection. The wife has no such power, and even if she had, it is almost always desirable that she should try all measures before resorting to it.

It is quite true that things which have to be decided every day and cannot adjust themselves gradually or wait for a compromise ought to depend on one will: One person must have their sole control. But it does not follow that this should always be the same person. The natural arrangement is a division of powers between the two, each being absolute in the executive branch of [his or her] . . . own department and any change of system and principle requiring the consent of both. The division neither can nor should be pre-established by the law, since it must depend on individual capacities and suitabilities. If the two persons chose, they might pre-appoint it by the marriage contract, as pecuniary arrangements are now often pre-appointed. . . .

The real, practical decision of affairs, to whichever may be given the legal authority, will greatly depend, as it even now does, upon comparative qualifications. The mere fact that he is usually the eldest will in most cases give the preponderance to the man, at least until they both attain a time of life at which the difference in their years is of no importance. There will naturally also be a more potential voice on the side, whichever it is, that brings the means of support. Inequality from this source does not depend on the law of marriage but on the general conditions of human society as now constituted. The influence of mental superiority, either general or special, and of superior decision of character will necessarily tell for much. It always does so at present. And this fact shows how little foundation there is for the apprehension that the powers and responsibilities of partners in life (as of partners in business) cannot be satisfactorily apportioned by agreement between themselves. They always are so apportioned, except in cases in which the marriage institution is a failure. Things never come to an issue of downright power on one side and obedience on the other, except where the connection altogether has been a mistake and it would be a blessing to both parties to be relieved from it. . . . The despotic power which the law gives to the husband may be a reason to make the wife assent to any compromise by which power is practically shared between the two, but it cannot be the reason why the husband does. That there is always among decently conducted people a practical compromise, though one of them at least is under no physical or moral necessity of making it, shows that the natural motives which lead to a voluntary adjustment of the united life of two persons in a manner acceptable to both do on the whole, except in unfavorable cases, prevail. The matter is certainly not improved by laying down as an ordinance of law that the superstructure of free government shall be raised upon a legal basis of despotism on one side and subjection on the other and that every concession which the despot makes may, at his mere pleasure and without any warning, be recalled. . . .

The equality of married persons before the law is not only the sole mode in which that particular relation can be made consistent with justice to both sides and conducive to the happiness of both, but it is the only means of rendering the daily life of mankind, in any high sense, a school of moral cultivation. Though the truth may not be felt or generally acknowledged for generations to come, the only school of genuine moral sentiment is society between equals. The moral education of mankind has hitherto emanated chiefly from the law of force and is adapted almost solely to the relations which force creates. . . . Already in modern life, and more and more as it progressively improves, command and obedience become exceptional facts in life, equal association its general rule. The morality of the first ages rested on the obligation to submit to power, that of the ages next following, on the right of the weak to the forbearance and protection of the strong. How much longer is one form of society and life to content itself with the morality made for another? We have had the morality of submission and the morality of chivalry and generosity; the time is now come for the morality of justice. . . . Institutions, books, education, society, all go on training human beings for the old long after the new has come—much more when it is only coming. But the true virtue of human beings is fitness to live together as equals; claiming nothing for themselves but what they as freely concede to everyone else; regarding command of any kind as an exceptional necessity and in all cases a temporary one; and preferring, whenever possible the society of those with whom leading and following can be alternate and reciprocal. To these virtues, nothing in life as at present constituted gives cultivation by exercise. The family is a school of despotism in which the virtues of despotism, but also its vices, are largely nourished. Citizenship in free countries is partly a school of society in equality, but citizenship fills only a small place in modern life and does not come near the daily habits or inmost sentiments. The family . . . should be a school of sympathy in equality, of living together in love, without power on one side or obedience on the other. This it ought to be between the parents. It would then be an exercise of those virtues which each requires to fit them for all other association and a model to the children of the feelings and conduct which their temporary training by means of obedience is designed to render habitual, and therefore natural, to them. The moral training of mankind will never be adapted to the conditions of the life for which all other human progress is a preparation until they practise in the family the same moral rule which is adapted to the normal constitution of human society.

. . . It is almost superfluous to say anything concerning the more special point included in the general one—a woman's right to her own property. For I need not hope that this treatise can make any impression upon those who need anything to convince them that a woman's inheritance or gains ought to be as much her own after marriage as before. The rule is simple: Whatever would be the husband's or wife's if they were not married should be under their exclusive control during marriage, which need not interfere with the power to tie up property by settlement in order to preserve it for children. Some people are sentimentally shocked at the idea of a separate interest in money matters as inconsistent with the ideal fusion of two lives into one. For my own part, I am one of the strongest supporters of community of goods when resulting from an entire unity of feeling in the owners which makes all things common between them. But I have no relish for a community of goods resting on the doctrine that what is mine is yours but what is yours is not mine, and I should prefer to decline entering into such a compact with anyone, though I were myself the person to profit by it. . . .

. . . When the support of the family depends not on property but on earnings, the common arrangement, by which the man earns the income and the wife superintends the domestic expenditure, seems to me in general the most suitable division of labor between the two persons. If, in addition to the physical suffering of bearing children and the whole responsibility of their care and education in early years, the wife undertakes the careful and economical application of the husband's earnings to the general comfort of the family, she takes not only her fair share, but usually the larger share, of the bodily and mental exertion required by their joint existence. If she undertakes any additional portion, it seldom relieves her from this but only prevents her from performing it properly. The care which she is herself disabled from taking of the children and the household nobody else takes; those of the children who do not die grow up as they best can, and the management of the household is likely to be so bad as even in point of economy to be a great drawback from the value of the wife's earnings. In an otherwise just state of things, it is not therefore, I think, a desirable custom that the wife should contribute by her labor to the income of the family. . . . The *power* of earning is essential to the dignity of a woman if she has not independent property. But if marriage were an equal contract not implying the obligation of obedience, if the connection were no longer enforced to the oppression of those to whom it is purely a mischief but a separation on just terms (I do not now speak of a divorce) could be obtained by any woman who was morally entitled to it, and if she would then find all honorable employments as freely open to her as to men—it would not be necessary for her protection that during marriage she should make this particular use of her faculties. Like a man when he chooses a profession, so, when a woman marries, it may in general be understood that she makes choice of the management of a household and the bringing up of a family as the first call upon her exertions during as many years of her life as may be required for the purpose and that she renounces, not all other objects and occupations, but all which are not consistent with the requirements of this. . . . But the utmost latitude ought to exist for the adaptation of general rules to individual suitabilities, and there ought to be nothing to prevent faculties exceptionally adapted to any other pursuit from obeying their vocation notwithstanding marriage, due provision being made for supplying otherwise any falling short which might become inevitable in her full performance of the ordinary functions of mistress of a family. These things, if once opinion were rightly directed on the subject, might with perfect safety be left to be regulated by opinion without any interference of law.

III.

On the other point which is involved in the just equality of women, their admissibility to all the functions and occupations hitherto retained as the monopoly of the stronger sex, . . . I believe that their disabilities elsewhere are only clung to in order to maintain their subordination in domestic life because the generality of the male sex cannot yet tolerate the idea of living with an equal. Were it not for that, I think that almost everyone in the existing state of opinion in politics and political economy would admit the injustice of excluding half the human race from the greater number of lucrative occupations and from almost all high social functions, ordaining from their birth either that they are not and cannot by any possibility become fit for employments which are legally open to the stupidest and basest of the other sex or else that however fit they may be, those employments shall be interdicted to them in order to be preserved for the exclusive benefit of males. . . . When anything is forbidden to women, it is thought necessary to say and desirable to believe that they are incapable of doing it and that they depart from their real path of success and happiness when they aspire to it. But to make this reason plausible (I do not say valid), those by whom it is urged must be prepared to carry it to a much greater length than anyone ventures to do in the face of present experience. It is not sufficient to maintain that women on the average are less gifted than men on the average with certain of the higher mental faculties or that a smaller number of women than of men are fit for occupations and functions of the highest intellectual character. It is necessary to maintain that no women at all are fit for them and that the most eminent women are inferior in mental faculties to the most mediocre of the men on whom those functions at present devolve. For if the performance of the function is decided either by competition or by any mode of choice which secures regard to the public interest, there needs to be no apprehension that any important employments will fall into the hands of women inferior to average men or to the average of their male competitors. The only result would be that there would be fewer women than men in such employments, a result certain to happen in any case, if only from the preference always likely to be felt by the majority of women for the one vocation in which there is nobody to compete with them. Now the most determined depreciator of women will not venture to deny that when we add the experience of recent times to that of ages past, women, and not a few merely but many women, have proved themselves capable of everything, perhaps without a single exception, which is done by men and of doing it successfully and creditably. The utmost that can be said is that there are many things which none of them have succeeded in doing as well as they have been done by some men—many in which they have not reached the very highest rank. But there are extremely few dependent only on mental faculties in which they have not attained the rank next to the highest. Is not this enough and much more than enough to make it a tyranny to them and a detriment to society that they should not be allowed to compete with men for the exercise of these functions? . . . Is there so great a superfluity of men fit for high duties that society can afford to reject the service of any competent person? Are we so certain of always finding a man made to our hands for any duty or function of social importance which falls vacant that we lose nothing by putting a ban upon one-half of mankind and refusing beforehand to make their faculties available, however distinguished they may be? And even if we could do without them, would it be consistent with justice to refuse to them their fair share of honor and distinction or to deny to them the equal moral right of all human beings to choose their occupation (short of injury to others) according to their own preferences, at their own risk? Nor is the injustice confined to them: It is shared by those who are in a position to benefit by their services. To ordain that any kind of persons shall not be physicians or shall not be advocates or shall not be Members of Parliament is to injure not them only but all who employ physicians or advocates or elect Members of Parliament and who are deprived of the stimulating effect of greater competition on the exertions of the competitors as well as restricted to a narrower range of individual choice.

It will perhaps be sufficient if I confine myself in the details of my argument to functions of a public nature, since, if I am successful as to those, it probably will be readily granted that women should be admissible to all other occupations to which it is at all material whether they are admitted or not. And here let me begin by marking out one function, broadly distinguished from all others, their right to which is entirely independent of any question which can be raised concerning their faculties. I mean the suffrage. . . . The right to share in the choice of those who are to exercise a public trust is altogether a distinct thing from that of competing for the trust itself. If no one could vote for a Member of Parliament who was not fit to be a candidate, the government would be a narrow oligarchy indeed. To have a voice in choosing those by whom one is to be governed is a means of self-protection due to everyone, though he were to remain forever excluded from the function of governing. . . . Under whatever conditions and within whatever limits men are admitted to the suffrage, there is not a shadow of justification for not admitting women under the same. . . .

With regard to the fitness of women, not only to participate in elections but themselves to hold offices or practice professions involving important public responsibilities, I have already observed that this consideration is not essential to the practical question in dispute, since any woman who succeeds in an open profession proves by that very fact that she is qualified for it. . . .

. . . What they have done, that at least, if nothing else, it is proved that they can do. When we consider how sedulously they are all trained away from instead of being trained towards any of the occupations or objects reserved for men, it is evident that I am taking a very humble ground for them when I rest their case on what they have actually achieved. For in this case negative evidence is worth little, while any positive evidence is conclusive. It cannot be inferred to be impossible that a woman should be a Homer or an Aristotle or a Michelangelo or a Beethoven because no woman has yet actually produced works comparable to theirs in any of those lines of excellence. This negative fact at most leaves the question uncertain and open to psychological discussion. But it is quite certain that a woman can be a Queen Elizabeth or a Deborah or a Joan of Arc, since this is not inference but fact. Now it is a curious consideration that the only things which the existing law excludes women from doing are the things which they have proved that they are able to do. There is no law to prevent a woman from having written all the plays of Shakespeare or composed all the operas of Mozart. But Queen Elizabeth or Queen Victoria, had they not inherited the throne, could not have been intrusted with the smallest of the political duties of which the former showed herself equal to the greatest.

If anything conclusive could be inferred from experience without psychological analysis, it would be that the things which women are not allowed to do are the very ones for which they are peculiarly qualified, since their vocation for government has made its way and become conspicuous through the very few opportunities which have been given, while in the lines of distinction which apparently were freely open to them, they have by no means so eminently distinguished themselves. We know how small a number of reigning queens history presents. . . . They have, in a great number of instances, been distinguished by merits the most opposite to the imaginary and conventional character of women: They have been as much remarked for the firmness and vigor of their rule as for its intelligence. . . .

Is it reasonable to think that those who are fit for the greater functions of politics are incapable of qualifying themselves for the less? Is there any reason in the nature of things that the wives and sisters of princes should, whenever called on, be found as competent as the princes themselves to *their* business but that the wives and sisters of statesmen and administrators and directors of companies and managers of public institutions should be unable to do what is done by their brothers and husbands? The real reason is plain enough; it is that princesses, being more raised above the generality of men by their rank than placed below them by their sex, have never been taught that it was improper for them to concern themselves with politics but have been allowed to feel the liberal interest natural to any cultivated human being in the great transactions which took place around them and in which they might be called on to take a part. The ladies of reigning families are the only women who are allowed the same range of interests and freedom of development as men; and it is precisely in their case that there is not found to be any inferiority.

. . . Looking at women as they are known in experience, it may be said of them with more truth than belongs to most other generalizations on the subject that the general bent of their talents is towards the practical. This statement is conformable to all the public history of women. . . . It is no less borne out by common and daily experience. Let us consider the special nature of the mental capacities most characteristic of a woman of talent. They are all of a kind which fits them for practice and makes them tend towards it. What is meant by a woman's capacity of intuitive perception? It means a rapid and correct insight into present fact. It has nothing to do with general principles. Nobody ever perceived a scientific law of nature by intuition nor arrived at a general rule of duty or prudence by it. These are results of slow and careful collection and comparison of experience; and neither the men nor the women of intuition usually shine in this department, unless, indeed, the experience necessary is such as they can acquire by themselves. . . . Men who have been much taught are apt to be deficient in the sense of present fact; they do not see in the facts which they are called upon to deal with what is really there but what they have been taught to expect. This is seldom the case with women of any ability. Their capacity of "intuition" preserves them from it. With equality of experience and of general faculties, a woman usually sees much more than a man of what is immediately before her. Now this sensibility to the present is the main quality on which the capacity for practice, as distinguished from theory, depends. To discover general principles belongs to the speculative faculty; to discern and discriminate the particular cases in which they are and are not applicable constitutes practical talent; and for this women as they now are have a peculiar aptitude. I admit that there can be no good practice without principles and that the predominant place which quickness of observation holds among a woman's faculties makes her particularly apt to build over-hasty generalizations upon her own observation, though at the same time no less ready in rectifying those generalizations as her observation takes a wider range. But the corrective to this defect is access to the experience of the human race, general knowledge—exactly the thing which education can best supply. . . .

But this gravitation of women's minds to the present, to the real, to actual fact, while in its exclusiveness it is a source of errors, is also a most useful counteractive of the contrary error. The principal and most characteristic aberration of speculative minds, as such, consists precisely in the deficiency of this lively perception and ever present sense of objective fact. For want of this, they often not only overlook the contradiction which outward facts oppose to their theories but lose sight of the legitimate purpose of speculation altogether and let their speculative faculties go astray into regions not peopled with real beings, animate or inanimate, even idealized, but with personified shadows created by the illusions of metaphysics or by the mere entanglement of words and think these shadows the proper objects of the highest, the most transcendant, philosophy. . . . A woman seldom runs wild after an abstraction. The habitual direction of her mind to dealing with things as individuals rather than in groups and (what is closely connected with it) her more lively interest in the present feelings of persons . . . make her extremely unlikely to put faith in any speculation which loses sight of individuals and deals with things as if they existed for the benefit of some imaginary entity, some mere creation of the mind, not resolvable into the feelings of living beings. Women's thoughts are thus as useful in giving reality to those of thinking men as men's thoughts [are] in giving width and largeness to those of women. In depth, as distinguished from breadth, I greatly doubt if even now women, compared with men, are at any disadvantage. . . .

It will be said, perhaps, that the greater nervous susceptibility of women is a disqualification for practice, in anything but domestic life, by rendering them mobile, changeable, too vehemently under the influence of the moment, incapable of dogged perseverance, unequal and uncertain in the power of using their faculties. I think that these phrases sum up the greater part of the objections commonly made to the fitness of women for the higher class of serious business. Much of all this is the mere overflow of nervous energy run to waste and would cease when the energy was directed to a definite end. Much is also the result of conscious or unconscious cultivation, as we see by the almost total disappearance of "hysterics" and fainting fits since they have gone out of fashion. Moreover, when people are brought up, like many women of the higher classes, . . . shielded from the wholesome vicissitudes of air and temperature and untrained in any of the occupations and exercises which give stimulus and development to the circulatory and muscular system while their nervous system, especially in its emotional department, is kept in unnaturally active play, it is no wonder if those of them who do not die of consumption grow up with constitutions liable to derangement from slight causes, both internal and external, and without stamina to support any task, physical or mental, requiring continuity of effort. But women brought up to work for their livelihood show none of these morbid characteristics, unless indeed they are chained to an excess of sedentary work in confined and unhealthy rooms. Women who in their early years have shared in the healthful physical education and bodily freedom of their brothers and who obtain a sufficiency of pure air and exercise in after-life very rarely have any excessive susceptibility of nerves which can disqualify them for active pursuits. . . . Are men of nervous temperament found to be unfit for the duties and pursuits usually followed by men? If not, why should women of the same temperament be unfit for them? . . . It is the character of the nervous temperament to be capable of *sustained* excitement, holding out through long continued efforts. It is what is meant by *spirit.* It is what makes the highbred racehorse run without slackening speed till he drops down dead. It is what has enabled so many delicate women to maintain the most sublime constancy not only at the stake but through a long preliminary succession of mental and bodily tortures. It is evident that people of this temperament are particularly apt for what may be called the executive department of the leadership of mankind. They are the material of great orators, great preachers, impressive diffusers of moral influences. Their constitution might be deemed less favorable to the qualities required from a statesman in the cabinet or from a judge. It would be so if the consequence necessarily followed that because people are excitable, they must always be in a state of excitement. But this is wholly a question of training. Strong feeling is the instrument and element of strong self control, but it requires to be cultivated in that direction. When it is, it forms not the heroes of impulse only but those also of self-conquest. History and experience prove that the most passionate characters are the most fanatically rigid in their feelings of duty, when their passion has been trained to act in that direction. . . .

Supposing it, however, to be true that women's minds are by nature more mobile than those of men, less capable of persisting long in the same continuous effort, more fitted for dividing their faculties among many things than for travelling in any one path to the highest point which can be reached by it; . . . this difference is one which can only affect the kind of excellence, not the excellence itself or its practical worth; and it remains to be shown whether this exclusive working of a part of the mind, this absorption of the whole thinking faculty in a single subject and concentration of it on a single work, is the normal and healthful condition of the human faculties, even for speculative uses. I believe that what is gained in special development by this concentration is lost in the capacity of the mind for the other purposes of life; and even in abstract thought, it is my decided opinion that the mind does more by frequently returning to a difficult problem than by sticking to it without interruption. For the purposes . . . of practice, from its highest to its humblest departments, the capacity of passing promptly from one subject of consideration to another without letting the active spring of the intellect run down between the two is a power far more valuable; and this power women pre-eminently possess by virtue of the very mobility of which they are accused. They perhaps have it from nature, but they certainly have it by training and education; for nearly the whole of the occupations of women consist in the management of small but multitudinous details, on each of which the mind cannot dwell even for a minute but must pass on to other things and, if anything requires longer thought, must steal time at odd moments for thinking of it.

. . . It cannot now be known how much of the existing mental differences between men and women is natural and how much artificial; . . . but doubt does not forbid conjecture, and where certainty is unattainable, there may yet be the means of arriving at some degree of probability. The first point, the origin of the differences actually observed, is the one most accessible to speculation. . . . We cannot isolate a human being from the circumstances of his condition so as to ascertain experimentally what he would have been by nature; but we can consider what he is and what his circumstances have been and whether the one would have been capable of producing the other.

Let us take, then, the only marked case which observation affords of apparent inferiority of women to men, if we except the merely physical one of bodily strength. No production in philosophy, science, or art entitled to the first rank has been the work of a woman. Is there any mode of accounting for this without supposing that women are naturally incapable of producing them?

In the first place, we may fairly question whether experience has afforded sufficient grounds for an induction. It is scarcely three generations since women, saving very rare exceptions, have begun to try their capacity in philosophy, science, or art. It is only in the present generation that their attempts have been at all numerous, and they are even now extremely few. . . . It is a relevant question whether a mind possessing the requisites of first-rate eminence in speculation or creative art could have been expected, on the mere calculation of chances, to turn up during that lapse of time among the women whose tastes and personal position admitted of their devoting themselves to these pursuits. In all things which there has yet been time for—in all but the very highest grades in the scale of excellence—especially in the department in which they have been longest engaged, literature (both prose and poetry), women have done quite as much, have obtained fully as high prizes [and] as many of them, as could be expected from the length of time and the number of competitors. . . .

If we consider the works of women in modern times and contrast them with those of men, either in the literary or the artistic department, such inferiority as may be observed resolves itself essentially into one thing, but that is a most material one, deficiency of originality. . . . Thoughts original, in the sense of being unborrowed—of being derived from the thinker's own observations or intellectual processes—are abundant in the writings of women. But they have not yet produced any of those great and luminous new ideas which form an era in thought nor those fundamentally new conceptions in art which open a vista of possible effects not before thought of and found a new school. Their compositions are mostly grounded on the existing fund of thought, and their creations do not deviate widely from existing types. This is the sort of inferiority which their works manifest; for in point of execution, in the detailed application of thought and the perfection of style, there is no inferiority. Our best novelists in point of composition and of the management of detail have mostly been women. . . .

. . . Never since any considerable number of women have begun to cultivate serious thought has originality been possible on easy terms. Nearly all the thoughts which can be reached by mere strength of original faculties have long since been arrived at; and originality, in any high sense of the word, is now scarcely ever attained but by minds which have undergone elaborate discipline and are deeply versed in the results of previous thinking. . . . How many women are there who have gone through any such process? . . . When women have had the preparation which all men now require to be eminently original, it will be time enough to begin judging by experience of their capacity for originality.

It no doubt often happens that a person who has not widely and accurately studied the thoughts of others on a subject has by natural sagacity a happy intuition which he can suggest but cannot prove, which yet when matured may be an important addition to knowledge; but even then, no justice can be done to it until some other person who does possess the previous acquirements takes it in hand, tests it, gives it a scientific or practical form, and fits it into its place among the existing truths of philosophy or science. . . . Who can tell how many of the most original thoughts put forth by male writers belong to a woman by suggestion, to themselves only by verifying and working out? If I may judge by my own case, a very large proportion indeed.

If we turn from pure speculation to literature in the narrow sense of the term and the fine arts, there is a very obvious reason why women's literature is, in its general conception and in its main features, an imitation of men's. . . . If women lived in a different country from men and had never read any of their writings, they would have had a literature of their own. As it is, they have not created one because they found a highly advanced literature already created. . . . What years are to a gifted individual, generations are to a mass. If women's literature is destined to have a different collective character from that of men, depending on any difference of natural tendencies, much longer time is necessary than has yet elapsed before it can emancipate itself from the influence of accepted models and guide itself by its own impulses. But if, as I believe, there will not prove to be any natural tendencies common to women and distinguishing their genius from that of men, yet every individual writer among them has her individual tendencies, which at present are still subdued by the influence of precedent and example; and it will require generations more before their individuality is sufficiently developed to make head against that influence.

It is in the fine arts, properly so called, that the *prima facie* evidence of inferior original powers in women at first sight appears the strongest, since opinion (it may be said) does not exclude them from these but rather encourages them; and their education, instead of passing over this department, is in the affluent classes mainly composed of it. Yet in this line of exertion they have fallen still more short than in many others of the highest eminence attained by men. This shortcoming, however, needs no other explanation than the familiar fact, more universally true in the fine arts than in anything else: the vast superiority of professional persons over amateurs. . . . The exceptions are only of the kind which confirm the general truth. Women are taught music, but not for the purpose of composing, only of executing it; and accordingly, it is only as composers that men in music are superior to women. The only one of the fine arts which women do follow to any extent as a profession and an occupation for life is the histrionic, and in that they are confessedly equal, if not superior, to men. To make the comparison fair, it should be made between the productions of women in any branch of art and those of men not following it as a profession. In musical composition, for example, women surely have produced fully as good things as have ever been produced by male amateurs. There are now a few women, a very few, who practise painting as a profession, and these are already beginning to show quite as much talent as could be expected. . . .

There are other reasons besides those which we have now given that help to explain why women remain behind men even in the pursuits which are open to both. For one thing, very few women have time for them. This may seem a paradox; it is an undoubted social fact. The time and thoughts of every woman have to satisfy great previous demands on them for things practical. There is, first, the superintendence of the family and the domestic expenditure, which occupies at least one woman in every family, generally the one of mature years and acquired experience, unless the family is so rich as to admit of delegating that task to hired agency. . . . If a woman is of a rank and circumstances which relieve her in a measure from these cares, she has still devolving on her the management for the whole family of its intercourse with others—of what is called society—and the less the call made on her by the former duty, the greater is always the development of the latter: the dinner parties, concerts, evening parties, morning visits, letter writing, and all that goes with them. All this is over and above the engrossing duty, which society imposes exclusively on women, of making themselves charming. A clever woman of the higher ranks finds nearly a sufficient employment of her talents in cultivating the graces of manner and the arts of conversation. To look only at the outward side of the subject: the great and continual exercise of thought which all women who attach any value to dressing well . . . must bestow upon their own dress, perhaps also upon that of their daughters, would alone go a great way towards achieving respectable results in art or science or literature and does actually exhaust much of the time and mental power they might have to spare for either. . . . Independently of the regular offices of life which devolve upon a woman, she is expected to have her time and faculties always at the disposal of everybody. If a man has not a profession to exempt him from such demands, still, if he has a pursuit, he offends nobody by devoting his time to it; occupation is received as a valid excuse for his not answering to every casual demand which may be made on him. Are a woman's occupations, especially her chosen and voluntary ones, ever regarded as excusing her from any of what are termed the calls of society? . . .

There is another consideration to be added to all these. In the various arts and intellectual occupations, there is a degree of proficiency sufficient for living by it and there is a higher degree on which depend the great productions which immortalize a name. . . . The love of fame in men is encouraged by education and opinion: To "scorn delights and live laborious days" for its sake is accounted the part of "noble minds," even if spoken of as their "last infirmity," and is stimulated by the access which fame gives to all objects of ambition, including even the favor of women, while to women themselves all these objects are closed and the desire of fame itself considered daring and unfeminine. . . . The natural desire of consideration from our fellow creatures is as strong in a woman as in a man; but society has so ordered things that public consideration is, in all ordinary cases, only attainable by her through the consideration of her husband or of her male relations, while her private consideration is forfeited by making herself individually prominent or appearing in any other character than that of an appendage to men. Whoever is in the least capable of estimating the influence on the mind of the entire domestic and social position and the whole habit of a life must easily recognise in that influence a complete explanation of nearly all the apparent differences between women and men, including the whole of those which imply any inferiority.

As for moral differences considered as distinguished from intellectual, the distinction commonly drawn is to the advantage of women. They are declared to be better than men, an empty compliment which must provoke a bitter smile from every woman of spirit, since there is no other situation in life in which it is the established order and considered quite natural and suitable that the better should obey the worse. If this piece of idle talk is good for anything, it is only as an admission by men of the corrupting influence of power; for that is certainly the only truth which the fact, if it be a fact, either proves or illustrates. And it *is* true that servitude, except when it actually brutalizes, though corrupting to both, is less so to the slaves than to the slave-masters. It is wholesomer for the moral nature to be restrained, even by arbitrary power, than to be allowed to exercise arbitrary power without restraint. . . .

The complimentary dictum about women's superior moral goodness may be allowed to pair off with the disparaging one respecting their greater liability to moral bias. Women, we are told, are not capable of resisting their personal partialities: Their judgment in grave affairs is warped by their sympathies and antipathies. Assuming it to be so, it is still to be proved that women are oftener misled by their personal feelings than men by their personal interests. The chief difference would seem in that case to be that men are led from the course of duty and the public interest by their regard for themselves, women (not being allowed to have private interests of their own), by their regard for somebody else. It is also to be considered that all the education which women receive from society inculcates on them the feeling that the individuals connected with them are the only ones to whom they owe any duty—the only ones whose interest they are called upon to care for. . . .

The concessions of the privileged to the unprivileged are so seldom brought about by any better motive than the power of the unprivileged to extort them that any arguments against the prerogative of sex are likely to be little attended to by the generality as long as they are able to say to themselves that women do not complain of it. That fact certainly enables men to retain the unjust privilege some time longer but does not render it less unjust. . . .

IV.

. . . What good are we to expect from the changes proposed in our customs and institutions? Would mankind be at all better off if women were free? If not, why disturb their minds and attempt to make a social revolution in the name of an abstract right? . . .

To which let me first answer, the advantage of having the most universal and pervading of all human relations regulated by justice instead of injustice. . . . All the selfish propensities, the self-worship, the unjust self-preference which exist among mankind have their source and root in and derive their principal nourishment from the present constitution of the relation between men and women. Think what it is to a boy to grow up to manhood in the belief that without any merit or any exertion of his own, though he may be the most frivolous and empty or the most ignorant and stolid of mankind, by the mere fact of being born a male he is by right the superior of all and everyone of an entire half of the human race, including probably some whose real superiority to himself he has daily or hourly occasion to feel. . . . What must be the effect on his character of this lesson? . . .

The example afforded and the education given to the sentiments by laying the foundation of domestic existence upon a relation contradictory to the first principles of social justice must, from the very nature of man, have a perverting influence of such magnitude that it is hardly possible with our present experience to raise our imaginations to the conception of so great a change for the better as would be made by its removal. All that education and civilization are doing to efface the influences on character of the law of force and replace them by those of justice remains merely on the surface as long as the citadel of the enemy is not attacked. The principle of the modern movement in morals and politics is that conduct, and conduct alone, entitles to respect; that not what men are but what they do constitutes their claim to deference; that, above all, merit and not birth is the only rightful claim to power and authority. If no authority not in its nature temporary were allowed to one human being over another, society would not be employed in building up propensities with one hand which it has to curb with the other. . . .

The second benefit to be expected from giving to women the free use of their faculties, by leaving them the free choice of their employments and opening to them the same field of occupation and the same prizes and encouragements as to other human beings would be that of doubling the mass of mental faculties available for the higher service of humanity. Where there is now one person qualified to benefit mankind and promote the general improvement, as a public teacher or an administrator of some branch of public or social affairs, there would then be a chance of two. Mental superiority of any kind is at present everywhere so much below the demand, [and] there is such a deficiency of persons competent to do excellently anything which it requires any considerable amount of ability to do that the loss to the world by refusing to make use of one-half of the whole quantity of talent it possesses is extremely serious. It is true that this amount of mental power is not totally lost. Much of it is employed and would in any case be employed in domestic management and in the few other occupations open to women, and from the remainder indirect benefit is in many individual cases obtained through the personal influence of individual women over individual men. But these benefits are partial; their range is extremely circumscribed. . . .

This great accession to the intellectual power of the species and to the amount of intellect available for the good management of its affairs would be obtained partly through the better and more complete intellectual education of women. . . . The mere getting rid of the idea that all the wider subjects of thought and action, all the things which are of general and not solely of private interest, are men's business from which women are to be warned off—positively interdicted from most of it, coldly tolerated in the little which is allowed them—the mere consciousness a woman would then have of being a human being like any other, entitled to choose her pursuits, urged or invited by the same inducements as anyone else to interest herself in whatever is interesting to human beings, entitled to exert the share of influence on all human concerns which belongs to an individual opinion, whether she attempted actual participation in them or not—this alone would effect an immense expansion of the faculties of women, as well as enlargement of the range of their moral sentiments.

Besides the addition to the amount of individual talent available for the conduct of human affairs, . . . the opinion of women would then possess a more beneficial, rather than a greater, influence upon the general mass of human belief and sentiment. I say a more beneficial rather than a greater influence, for the influence of women over the general tone of opinion has always, or at least from the earliest known period, been very considerable. . . . The moral influence of women has had two modes of operation. First, it has been a softening influence. Those who were most liable to be the victims of violence have naturally tended as much as they could towards limiting its sphere and mitigating its excesses. . . . The other mode in which the effect of women's opinion has been conspicuous is by giving a powerful stimulus to those qualities in men which, not being themselves trained in, it was necessary for them that they should find in their protectors. Courage and the military virtues generally have at all times been greatly indebted to the desire which men felt of being admired by women; and the stimulus reaches far beyond this one class of eminent qualities, since, by a very natural effect of their position, the best passport to the admiration and favor of women has always been to be thought highly of by men. From the combination of the two kinds of moral influence thus exercised by women arose the spirit of chivalry: the peculiarity of which is to aim at combining the highest standard of the warlike qualities with the cultivation of a totally different class of virtues. . . . Modern society is able to repress wrong through all departments of life by a fit exertion of the superior strength which civilization has given it and thus to render the existence of the weaker members of society (no longer defenseless but protected by law) tolerable to them without reliance on the chivalrous feelings of those who are in a position to tyrannize. The beauties and graces of the chivalrous character are still what they were, but the rights of the weak and the general comfort of human life now rest on a far surer and steadier support; or rather they do so in every relation of life except the conjugal.

At present the moral influence of women . . . has more nearly merged in the general influence of public opinion. Both through the contagion of sympathy and through the desire of men to shine in the eyes of women, their feelings have great effect in keeping alive what remains of the chivalrous ideal—in fostering the sentiments and continuing the traditions of spirit and generosity. . . . But with the present education and position of women, the moral principles which have been impressed on them cover but a comparatively small part of the field of virtue and are, moreover, principally negative: forbidding particular acts but having little to do with the general direction of the thoughts and purposes. I am afraid it must be said that disinterestedness in the general conduct of life—the devotion of the energies to purposes which hold out no promise of private advantages to the family—is very seldom encouraged or supported by women's influence. . . .

Women have, however, some share of influence in giving the tone to public moralities, since their sphere of action has been a little widened and since a considerable number of them have occupied themselves practically in the promotion of objects reaching beyond their own family and household. The influence of women counts for a great deal in two of the most marked features of modern European life—its aversion to war and its addiction to philanthropy. Excellent characteristics both; but unhappily, if the influence of women is valuable in the encouragement it gives to these feelings in general, in the particular applications the direction it gives to them is at least as often mischievous as useful. In the philanthropic department more particularly, the two provinces chiefly cultivated by women are religious proselytism and charity. Religious proselytism at home is but another word for embittering of religious animosities; abroad, it is usually a blind running at an object without either knowing or heeding the fatal mischiefs—fatal to the religious object itself as well as to all other desirable objects—which may be produced by the means employed. As for charity, it is a matter in which the immediate effect on the persons directly concerned and the ultimate consequence to the general good are apt to be at complete war with one another. . . . A woman born to the present lot of women and content with it, how should she appreciate the value of self-dependence? She is not self-dependent; she is not taught self-dependence; her destiny is to receive everything from others, and why should what is good enough for her be bad for the poor? Her familiar notions of good are of blessings descending from a superior. She forgets that she is not free and that the poor are; that if what they need is given to them unearned, they cannot be compelled to earn it; that everybody cannot be taken care of by everybody but there must be some motive to induce people to take care of themselves; and that to be helped to help themselves, if they are physically capable of it, is the only charity which proves to be charity in the end.

These considerations show how usefully the part which women take in the formation of general opinion would be modified for the better by that more enlarged instruction and practical conversancy with the things which their opinions influence that would necessarily arise from their social and political emancipation. But the improvement it would work through the influence they exercise, each in her own family, would be still more remarkable.

It is often said that in the classes most exposed to temptation, a man's wife and children tend to keep him honest and respectable, both by the wife's direct influence and by the concern he feels for their future welfare. . . . But when we ascend higher in the scale, we come among a totally different set of moving forces. The wife's influence tends, as far as it goes, to prevent the husband from falling below the common standard of approbation of the country. It tends quite as strongly to hinder him from rising above it. The wife is the auxiliary of the common public opinion. A man who is married to a woman his inferior in intelligence finds her a perpetual dead weight or, worse than a dead weight, a drag upon every aspiration of his to be better than public opinion requires him to be. It is hardly possible for one who is in these bonds to attain exalted virtue. If he differs in his opinion from the mass —if he sees truths which have not yet dawned upon them or if, feeling in his heart truths which they nominally recognize, he would like to act up to those truths more conscientiously than the generality of mankind—to all such thoughts and desires, marriage is the heaviest of drawbacks, unless he be so fortunate as to have a wife as much above the common level as he himself is.

For in the first place, there is always some sacrifice of personal interest required, either of social consequence or of pecuniary means, perhaps the risk of even the means of subsistence. These sacrifices and risks he may be willing to encounter for himself, but he will pause before he imposes them on his family. . . . The man himself may be above opinion or may find sufficient compensation in the opinion of those of his own way of thinking. But to the women connected with him, he can offer no compensation. The almost invariable tendency of the wife to place her influence in the same scale with social consideration is sometimes made a reproach to women and represented as a peculiar trait of feebleness and childishness of character in them, surely with great injustice. Society makes the whole life of a woman in the easy classes a continued self-sacrifice; it exacts from her an unremitting restraint of the whole of her natural inclinations, and the sole return it makes to her for what often deserves the name of a martyrdom is consideration. Her consideration is inseparably connected with that of her husband, and after paying the full price for it, she finds that she is to lose it for no reason of which she can feel the cogency. . . . Many a woman flatters herself (nine times out of ten quite erroneously) that nothing prevents her and her husband from moving in the highest society of her neighborhood—society in which others well known to her and in the same class of life mix freely—except that her husband is unfortunately a Dissenter or has the reputation of mingling in low radical politics. That it is, she thinks, which hinders George from getting a commission or a place, Caroline from making an advantageous match, and prevents her and her husband from obtaining invitations, perhaps honors, which, for aught she sees, they are as well entitled to as some folks. With such an influence in every house, either exerted actively or operating all the more powerfully for not being asserted, is it any wonder that people in general are kept down in that mediocrity of respectability which is becoming a marked characteristic of modern times? . . .

. . . Intimate society between people radically dissimilar to one another is an idle dream. Unlikeness may attract, but it is likeness which retains; and in proportion to the likeness is the suitability of the individuals to give each other a happy life. . . . When each of two persons instead of being a nothing is a something [and] when they are attached to one another and are not too much unlike to begin with, the constant partaking in the same things, assisted by their sympathy, draws out the latent capacities of each for being interested in the things which were at first interesting only to the other and works a gradual assimilation of the tastes and characters to one another, partly by the insensible modification of each but more by a real enriching of the two natures, each acquiring the tastes and capacities of the other in addition to its own. This often happens between two friends of the same sex who are much associated in their daily life; and it would be a common, if not the commonest, case in marriage did not the totally different bringing-up of the two sexes make it next to an impossibility to form a really well-assorted union. Were this remedied, whatever differences there might still be in individual tastes, there would at least be, as a general rule, complete unity and unanimity as to the great objects of life. . . .

I have considered thus far the effects on the pleasures and benefits of the marriage union which depend on the mere unlikeness between the wife and the husband; but the evil tendency is prodigiously aggravated when the unlikeness is inferiority. . . . Even a really superior man almost always begins to deteriorate when he is habitually (as the phrase is) king of his company; and in his most habitual company the husband who has a wife inferior to him is always so. While his self-satisfaction is incessantly ministered to on the one hand, on the other he insensibly imbibes the modes of feeling and of looking at things which belong to a more vulgar or a more limited mind than his own. . . .

What marriage may be in the case of two persons of cultivated faculties, identical in opinions and purposes, between whom there exists that best kind of equality, similarity of powers and capacities with reciprocal superiority in them—so that each can enjoy the luxury of looking up to the other and can have alternately the pleasure of leading and of being led in the path of development—I will not attempt to describe. To those who can conceive it, there is no need; to those who cannot, it would appear the dream of an enthusiast. But I maintain with the profoundest conviction that this, and this only, is the ideal of marriage and that all opinions, customs, and institutions which favor any other notion of it or turn the conceptions and aspirations connected with it into any other direction, by whatever pretenses they may be colored, are relics of primitive barbarism. The moral regeneration of mankind will only really commence when the most fundamental of the social relations is placed under the rule of equal justice and when human beings learn to cultivate their strongest sympathy with an equal in rights and in cultivation.

Thus far, the benefits which it has appeared that the world would gain by ceasing to make sex a disqualification for privileges and a badge of subjection are social rather than individual, consisting in an increase of the general fund of thinking and acting power and an improvement in the general conditions of the association of men with women. But it would be a grievous understatement of the case to omit the most direct benefit of all, the unspeakable gain in private happiness to the liberated half of the species: the difference to them between a life of subjection to the will of others and a life of rational freedom. After the primary necessities of food and raiment, freedom is the first and strongest want of human nature. . . .

He who would rightly appreciate the worth of personal independence as an element of happiness should consider the value he himself puts upon it as an ingredient of his own. There is no subject on which there is a greater habitual difference of judgment between a man judging for himself and the same man judging for other people. . . . An active and energetic mind, if denied liberty, will seek for power: Refused the command of itself, it will assert its personality by attempting to control others. To allow to any human beings no existence of their own but what depends on others is giving far too high a premium on bending others to their purposes. Where liberty cannot be hoped for and power can, power becomes the grand object of human desire; those to whom others will not leave the undisturbed management of their own affairs will compensate themselves, if they can, by meddling for their own purposes with the affairs of others. . . . The love of power and the love of liberty are in eternal antagonism. Where there is least liberty, the passion for power is the most ardent and unscrupulous. The desire of power over others can only cease to be a depraving agency among mankind when each of them individually is able to do without it, which can only be where respect for liberty in the personal concerns of each is an established principle. . . .

There is nothing, after disease, indigence, and guilt, so fatal to the pleasurable enjoyment of life as the want of a worthy outlet for the active faculties. Women who have the cares of a family, and while they have the cares of a family have this outlet, . . . [find] it generally suffices for them; but what of the greatly increasing number of women who have had no opportunity of exercising the vocation which they are mocked by telling them is their proper one? What of the women whose children have been lost to them by death or distance or have grown up, married, and formed homes of their own? . . . If there is anything vitally important to the happiness of human beings, it is that they should relish their habitual pursuit. This requisite of an enjoyable life is very imperfectly granted or altogether denied to a large part of mankind; and by its absence many a life is a failure which is provided in appearance with every requisite of success. But if circumstances which society is not yet skillful enough to overcome render such failures often for the present inevitable, society need not itself inflict them. The injudiciousness of parents, a youth's own inexperience, or the absence of external opportunities for the congenial vocation and their presence for an uncongenial condemn numbers of men to pass their lives in doing one thing reluctantly and ill when there are other things which they could have done well and happily. But on women this sentence is imposed by actual law and by customs equivalent to law. What in unenlightened societies color, race, religion, or in the case of a conquered country, nationality, are to some men, sex is to all women: a peremptory exclusion from almost all honorable occupations but either such as cannot be fulfilled by others or such as those others do not think worthy of their acceptance. . . .

When we consider the positive evil caused to the disqualified half of the human race by their disqualification—first in the loss of the most inspiriting and elevating kind of personal enjoyment and next in the weariness, disappointment, and profound dissatisfaction with life which are so often the substitute for it—one feels that among all the lessons which men require for carrying on the struggle against the inevitable imperfections of their lot on earth, there is no lesson which they more need than not to add to the evils which nature inflicts by their jealous and prejudiced restrictions on one another. Their vain fears only substitute other and worse evils for those which they are idly apprehensive of, while every restraint on the freedom of conduct of any of their human fellow creatures . . . dries up *pro tanto* the principal fountain of human happiness and leaves the species less rich, to an inappreciable degree, in all that makes life valuable to the individual human being.

PART V

Charlotte Perkins Gilman:

Evolutionary Socialist

The America of Charlotte Perkins Gilman (1860–1935) differed drastically from that of the Grimké sisters or Margaret Fuller. By 1898, when Mrs. Gilman wrote *Women and Economics,* the Southern planter aristocracy was only a memory, the Northern commercial elite had fallen before the captains of oligopolistic industry, the nation's boundaries had closed, and cities burgeoning with non-English-speaking immigrants had replaced the countryside as the center of American population.[1] Labor, now mechanized, produced goods as never before; workers bound to an industrial business cycle were depressed as rarely occurred earlier; families engulfed in the expanding city lived in squalor and embraced machine politics in increasing numbers.

Intellectual currents had changed as well. Darwin had replaced Newton as the great interpreter of the universe; the social scientist supplanted the philosopher, theologian, and artist; socialists vied with atomistic individualists. Legions of reformers deluged the nation—some seeking to rehabilitate existing institutions, others proposing to discipline new forms according to old values. A contemporary feminist rationale had to take some account of swift social, economic, and intellectual currents.

Mrs. Gilman's efforts to build feminism into turn-of-the-century social thought achieved immediate success and secured her a place among America's foremost feminist theoreticians. Operating directly out of the rationalist tradition, she combined Enlightenment and classical liberal thought with the doctrines of reform Darwinism in a creative way that contributed to social thought in general as well as to feminism in particular.[2] With her unquestioning confidence in evolutionary science and her belief in inevitable progress, she maintained an abiding faith in human ability to understand the laws of social change through reason and experience and to bring the actions of mankind into harmony with the natural order. She therefore became an international publicist with the mission of encouraging humanity to hasten the inevitable advent of sexual equality.

Enthusiastically received, *Women and Economics* won special acclaim from the more militant and younger feminists as well as from the *Nation,* which declared it "the most significant utterance" on feminism since Mill's *Subjection of Women.* The "Bible of the student body" at Vassar, *Women and Economics* also received "long respectful reviews" in London, where Charlotte Gilman would become "quite a lion." The progressive historians, Mary and Charles Beard, reported that Gilman's feminist thought "sent reverberations as far afield as awakening Japan." Indeed in its seventh English edition by 1911 and available in eight languages, *Women and Economics* earned its author first place in suffragist Carrie Chapman Catt's list of the twelve greatest American women.[3]

Although born into a family with deep roots in the New England past, Charlotte Perkins Gilman faced a future that cast such tradition into a distinctly anachronistic light. Her close relatives included the renowned Beechers—Lyman, Henry Ward, Catherine, and Harriet Beecher Stowe—and Senator Edward Everett Hale. But Charlotte's upbringing was unconventional because of the changed times and the unusual circumstances within the household of Frederic and Mary Westcott Perkins.

Frederic Beecher Perkins—librarian, editor, author—left his wife and two children shortly after Charlotte's birth. "The word Father, in the sense of love, care, one to go to in trouble, means nothing to me," she later recalled, "save indeed in advice about books and the care of them—which seems more the librarian than the father." Pampered, popular, and beautiful in her youth, Mary Westcott Perkins withheld affection from her children to make them emotionally self-sufficient and thus spare them her own depressing fate. She allowed Charlotte no close girl friends and rigorously refused "all manner of invitations" for her daughter from young men. "I was denied so often that I found it saved emotion to . . . deny myself beforehand, and, strengthened by Emerson, Socrates, Epicetus and Marcus Aurelius, I became a genuine stoic."[4]

The near poverty and patchwork schooling which followed paternal neglect neither glossed the Gilded Age family nor trapped the willful young lady within its limits. Mother, son, and daughter moved nineteen times in eighteen years, usually from one New England city to another, often to escape the weight of mounting debts. Charlotte's formal education in seven different schools covered only four years and ended when she was fifteen. At sixteen she briefly attended the Rhode Island School of Design in Providence, where she learned enough craftsmanship to undertake minor projects in commercial art and to give elementary lessons.

Mary Wollstonecraft had read moral philosophy, Sarah Grimké studied theology, and Margaret Fuller consumed literature. But Charlotte Gilman embraced natural and social science. On once finding and proving an error in a teacher's manual, she claimed to have learned "a great lesson; science, law, was more to be trusted than authority." The "real study" which appealed deeply to her was physics or natural philosophy. "Here was law at last; not authority, not records of questionable truth or solemn tradition, but laws that could be counted on and *proved*." Before reaching her majority, she had decided that the laws of the physical universe "had parallels in psychology." She believed in a social science that was as infallible as natural science.[5]

Exposure to a cooperative housekeeping group of Swedenborgians that her mother once joined gave Charlotte "a settled distaste for anything smacking of the esoteric or occult," although she approved of their discussions of ideas "instead of gossip and personalities." Her response to a temperance meeting was similar. She was "not at all at home in that atmosphere of orthodox religion and strong emotion. My method was to approach a difficulty as if it [were] . . . a problem in physics, trying to invent the best solution." She particularly liked the household of Margaret Fuller's acquaintance, Dr. William F. Channing, where she witnessed "broad free-thinking, scientific thought, earnest promotion of great causes—life."[6]

Greatly concerned about physical health, Charlotte Gilman never wore a corset or any other clothing she considered unhealthful or restrictive. She approved of the growing late nineteenth-century European and American impulse toward a higher physical culture—expressed through the building of gymnasiums, practice of calisthenics, and development of college athletics—and championed physical fitness for women as well as men. As a young adult she successfully promoted the establishment of a gymnasium in Providence, where she and other women might vault and jump, climb ropes, work on the bars and rings, and run the mile to build a sound physique. She insisted on walking the streets of Providence and other cities without escort, admitting openly to being "absurdly vain of my physical strength and agility."[7]

When Charlotte Gilman consolidated her youthful beliefs in physical culture, natural philosophy, and social science into a "religion," the result bore an overall imprint of Charles Darwin's theory of evolution. Considering all plant and animal characteristics alterable over time, Darwin in the *Origin of Species* (1859) denied the permanence of every form of life.

In the struggle for survival, those plant and animal species best adapted or fitted to the ever changing environment tend to survive longer and to reproduce more, while those poorly adapted generally die earlier and produce less. The evolutionary process of "natural selection" continually tests the ability of all forms of life to make the necessary adjustments.

To adapt well to one's environment might be all that nature requires of mankind. Thus Charlotte accepted the new industrialization, welcomed technological change, worshipped scientific thought, and favored rapid human adjustment to the changing physical and social environment. "What does God want of earth?" the youthful Charlotte inquired. "To whirl and spin and keep its times and seasons. What of the vegetable world? To blossom and bear fruit. Of the animals? The same fulfillment of function. Of us? The same and more. We, with all life, are under the great law, Evolution." "Social evolution I easily saw to be in human work, in the crafts, trades, arts and sciences through which we are related, maintained and developed. Therefore . . . 'the first duty of a human being is to assume right functional relation to society'—more briefly to find your real job and do it."[8]

When she reached her majority in 1881, Charlotte Gilman set out to do her "real job." She would not squander her painfully developed intellectual abilities and physical fitness in the passive, dependent, and constricted functions traditionally assigned to women. Determined to test herself against the environment much as men might, she sought economic autonomy—the foundation of freedom and the basis of respect in American society—and declared herself independent of her mother's authority. Employing her intellectual abilities and artistic training, she eked out a livelihood through tutoring and occasional commercial art projects.

But within three years she nevertheless fell temporarily into woman's conventional lot—marriage, family, and housewifery. After a courtship filled with uncertainty and deep ambivalence, Charlotte married Charles Walter Stetson, a struggling Providence artist. Pregnancy followed almost immediately, and severe mental depression soon incapacitated the new mother. A visit with the Channings, who had moved to Pasadena, California, restored her mental health, although her return to married life in Providence undermined it once again. Understanding that continued marriage could lead to her insanity, the Stetsons reluctantly decided upon separation and ultimate divorce. With her little daughter, Charlotte abandoned the East for Pasadena, renewed independence, and better mental health. In her "first year of freedom" she drafted numerous short articles, poems, and children's verses, most of which she gave away or sold for modest sums to progressive periodicals.[9]

One Gilman poem published in the *Nationalist,* the chief organ of Edward Bellamy's socialism, interested William Dean Howells, the novelist, critic, and harbinger of literary realism.[10] By extolling certain evolutionary leaps which man had presumably taken willfully, the poet declared human nature open to progressive change. Most literary realists shared Charlotte Gilman's concern that the contemporary industrial-technological order would victimize the average American citizen unless non-economic aspects of society were appropriately adjusted or reformed. Howells, in particular, shared her general humanitarian and socialist sentiments and supported her interest in achieving social equality through evolutionary, democratic means.

The association of Charlotte Gilman and William Dean Howells through the auspices of the *Nationalist* was indicative of a more than passing common interest in Bellamyite socialism or "Nationalism," as its adherents preferred to label their movement. Before the publication of Edward Bellamy's *Looking Backward* (1888), no socialist had made government ownership of the means of production appealing to large numbers of Americans. But Bellamy convinced thousands of the feasibility and desirability of a home-grown system of social control. Placing utopia at the end of inexorable historical processes, Bellamy proposed no hasty reforms or revolution. Nationalism would result from natural social developments, which mankind might hasten or restrain but could not prevent. The ruthless consolidation of business in the nineteenth century would lead to the Great Trust of the twentieth, which government would ultimately nationalize without much ado. Nationalism would consolidate rather than abolish property rights merely by converting government into a large corporation in which everyone had an equal stake. The scientific methods of an organized and unified industrial system would wipe away the gigantic, wasteful struggle of the multitude of competing organizations and classes and establish an economic equality that would quickly blossom into political and social equality as well.

More than 160 Nationalist clubs claiming 6,000 members and at least half a million supporters had been organized in twenty-seven states by 1890.[11] Charlotte Gilman inaugurated another aspect of her career when in that year she spoke to the Nationalist Club of Pasadena. Her "socialism was of the early humanitarian kind, . . . with the American enthusiasm of Bellamy." She consistently rejected "the narrow and rigid 'economic determinism' of Marx, with its 'class consciousness' and 'class struggle,' " along with "the political methods pursued by Marxians." She later refused to attend the International Socialist and Labor Congress in London as a delegate of the Socialist party. She attended, instead, as the representative of a county Federation of Trade Unions. Gilman deplored bolshevism and its triumphs in the Russian Revolution of 1917, especially for its alleged crippling of non-Marxist social progress in the United States. Americans, she noted with deep regret, continually held domestic militants responsible for the actions of Europe-oriented anarchists, socialists, and Marxists. "Among the various unnecessary burdens of my life is that I have been discredited by conservative persons as a socialist, while to orthodox socialists themselves I was quite outside the ranks."[12]

The Nationalists and their fellow-travelers, such as Gilman and Howells, did not regard their movement as proletarian and, in fact, looked upon the industrial working class with indifference. The rural and nativist biases of the Nationalists only increased the distance. Gilman almost always spoke of Jews, Germans, and Italians in an urban-industrial context and as aliens, "fecund foreigners," or some other decidedly non-American designation. Returning in later years from New York City to Maine, she remarked, "I could have hugged the gaunt New England farmers and fishermen—I had forgotten what my people looked like!" Yet rising above her own feelings and adhering to principle, she never endorsed the more virulent nativist strains that ran through the Nationalist or the suffragist movement. In a convention of the National American Woman Suffrage Association, she was one of only five who spoke or voted against a proposed educational requirement for the franchise, designed as a slightly veiled attack on the non-English immigrants flooding American cities.[13]

Gilman's early articles and poems brought a modest reputation that helped to secure additional speaking opportunities in which she paid increasingly more attention to feminism. However, the struggle for economic autonomy during the Pasadena years was always waged at the brink of utter poverty. When in *Women and Economics* she wrote about the crucial importance and great difficulty of securing economic independence for women, not only could she draw on her mother's trials, a Darwinian emphasis on the physical environment, and a socialist's concern about the economic factor, but she could also speak from the depths of her own long climb towards economic autonomy. Her struggle had been much too onerous for this self-made woman not to raise the feminist issue out of the many other reforms she sought for American society.

Invited to deliver a paper to the Pacific Coast Woman's Press Association in 1891, Charlotte Gilman made new contacts which she used as an entrée when she moved to the San Francisco area soon thereafter. She lectured to a great number of Nationalist clubs in northern California, gave art lessons, and offered courses for women subscribers. Unlike Margaret Fuller's conversations, Mrs. Gilman preferred to read formal papers rather than conduct discussions. Although a deist, she preached on a variety of social issues to Unitarian, Universalist, Congregationalist, Methodist, Baptist, Spiritualist, and Mormon congregations. Yet she ultimately had to manage a boarding house, often filled with invalid women, to secure the means to support herself and her daughter. She still found time to write. Her first volume of poetry, *In This Our World* (1893), earned her a modest national and international reputation but very limited royalties.

California state women's congresses offered Mrs. Gilman the exposure necessary to become a full-time writer and national speaker, though her material resources were meager. She met and impressed the great suffragist-feminist leader, Susan B. Anthony, and the noted settlement-house reformer, Jane Addams, who invited Charlotte to visit her in Chicago. By this time Walter Stetson had married her closest friend, Grace Channing. Desperately poor, concerned about her daughter's education, and anxious for her own career, in 1894 Charlotte sent her nine-year-old daughter to live with the Stetsons for the next several years. With a half-price missionary ticket, she embarked for Chicago, hoping eventually to redeem her innumerable California debts. The matter of proving economic independence was of such consequence that she would pay every debt, however small, even if a decade late.

She attended her first national woman's rights convention in 1896—the beginning of her regular attendance at these meetings. The "delighted" *Woman's Journal* correspondent found her "still a young woman, tall, lithe and graceful, with fine dark eyes, and spirit and originality flashing from her at every turn like light from a diamond." The "delegates followed her around, as iron filings follow a magnet."[14] Speaking more regularly to woman's rights groups, she gave twenty-seven lectures in Kansas during the unsuccessful 1896 campaign to obtain the vote for women there.

In the next few years, Charlotte Gilman travelled to all but four of the United States and made two trips to England. She met the foremost reformers of the Anglo-American world, carried her various social messages across the country, and drafted her most noted works. In a decade filled with an upsurge of reform proposals in England and America, she finally achieved the status she sought as a social theorist. She made numerous and extended visits to Jane Addams; enjoyed the company of the great British Fabian socialists, Sydney and Beatrice Webb and George Bernard Shaw; talked with the noted antitrust reformer, Henry Demarest Lloyd; met literary realist, Hamlin Garlin; discussed reform with the colorful progressive mayor of Toledo, "Golden Rule" Jones; associated with the feminist stalwart, Elizabeth Cady Stanton; and met William Lloyd Garrison, "another link with the Great Lifters of earlier days."[15] She accepted membership in the British Fabian Society, addressed the Judiciary Committee of the House of Representatives on woman suffrage, and lectured to countless clubs, churches, and committees throughout the land. But during these most busy and profitable years, she continued to wear second-hand clothes and carried a near-empty pocketbook.

William Dean Howells reportedly commented that Charlotte Gilman was "the only optimist reformer he ever met." Perhaps, she replied, "I was not a reformer, but a philosopher." She might have more accurately described herself as an amateur social scientist or lay sociologist; for, like the other members of the Ethical Society she once joined, her primary concern was in studying "human conduct with a view to its improvement by scientific methods."

> My business was to find out what ailed society and how most easily and naturally to improve it. It might be called the effort of a social inventor, trying to advance human happiness by the introduction of better psychic machinery. I was not depressed by the local and temporary misery I saw in the world, any more than by the long centuries of worse misery behind us. When humanity is grasped as a growing thing, one long, unbroken process, one is more impressed by its new advances than by its old mistakes.

Of all her many reform-minded friends and acquaintances, Lester Frank Ward did most to integrate and inform her Darwinian, socialist, and feminist ideas. Like Howells, he had opened a correspondence with her after reading her early social Darwinian poem in the *Nationalist.* More than "an outstanding leader in sociology," Ward was also "the greatest man" she had ever known and a decided feminist.[16]

For many of the progressive thinkers of the twentieth century, and certainly for Charlotte Gilman, Ward single-handedly demolished the laissez-faire or conservative aspects of social Darwinism. In *Dynamic Sociology* (1883) Ward insisted that sociology, properly applied, permitted mankind to control the evolutionary process. Mrs. Gilman absorbed much of Ward's argument that psychic factors or collective human intellect counted more than natural factors in building civilization, for mind could regulate other matter. "The advent with man of the thinking, knowing, foreseeing, calculating, designing, inventing and constructing faculty, which is wanting in lower creatures, repealed . . . the law of nature and enacted in its stead the psychologic law, or law of mind," Ward wrote. "Thus far," he added, "social progress has in a certain awkward manner taken care of itself, but in the near future it will have to be cared for. To do this . . . is the real problem of sociology considered as an applied science."[17] Ward saw that while environment changes animals, mankind can transform environment. The transformation, he insisted, should be planned to establish material abundance and intellectual development. Uncontrolled nature is prodigal, ruthless, and indifferent to mankind's fortune; only when human beings channel nature's course can they release themselves from the slavery to which all other forms of life are condemned. Ward rejected laissez-faire as a denial of the past, a repudiation of present civilization, and a rejection of calculated progress in the future. Believing that mankind need not and ought not to be mere spectators of social evolution, he dismissed the concept of "survival of the fittest" as shibboleth.

Ward's sociology and reform Darwinism were most congenial to Gilman's evolutionary socialism. But his feminism—which stressed distinctions between the sexes and demanded equality for women on the basis of their alleged superiority—was of even greater import to the intellectual structure of her *Women and Economics.* Ward believed "that in the economy of organic nature the female sex is the primary, and the male a secondary, element." The major purpose of the male is to enable the female to reproduce, "after performing which function the male form is useless." Man, however, has employed brute force—"a *secondary sexual character*"—to alter the natural and primary arangement between the sexes by subjugating the female and treating women "as mere breeding-stock." The female brain has languished from disuse; the "causal faculty" or ability to analyze and explain has had no exercise. Thus "under the power of this comparatively modern male selection woman may become whatever man shall desire her to be, and the ideal woman . . . will become more and more the real woman."[18]

Gilman echoed Ward's warning that male domination seriously limited the physical and social progress of the whole human race. Undeveloped woman passed her disabilities along in the genes she gave her offspring, and poorly educated children mirrored maternal ignorance. He allowed that the female mind probably differed from the male "in many important and fortunate respects," but he insisted that "intellect is one and the same everywhere." Ward concluded, therefore, that

> Accepting evolution as we must, recognizing heredity as the distinctive attribute of the female sex, it becomes clear that it must be from the steady advance of woman rather than from the uncertain fluctuations of man that the sure and solid progress of the future is to come. . . . The way to civilize the race is to civilize woman. And now, thanks to science, we see why this is so. Woman is the unchanging trunk of the great genealogic tree, while man, with all his vaunted superiority, is but a branch, a grafted scion, as it were, whose acquired qualities die with the individual, while those of woman are handed on to futurity. Woman *is* the race, and the race can be raised up only as she is raised up.[19]

Here was the "gynaecocentric" theory that Gilman considered "the greatest single contribution to the world's thought since Evolution"; "nothing so important to women," she added in the dedication of one of her later books to Ward, "has ever been given to the world."[20]

Mrs. Gilman had succumbed to one of her periods of mental depression in early July 1897, when she fell "to work in sheer despair" drafting her accumulating thoughts about the woman question into a book-length manuscript. She did little special reading for her book—only an essay by Ward and a volume on the evolution of sex, both of which stressed differences between the sexes. Most of her themes, however, came from the ideas she had been discussing with reform-minded thinkers and developing with audiences across the nation for the previous five or more years. "Full of the passion for world improvement and seeing the position of women as responsible for much, very much, of our evil condition, I had been studying it for years as a problem of instant importance." She completed the original draft of *Women and Economics* within seventeen days and revised and completed the text in less than two months.[21]

Mrs. Gilman supported the swelling suffragist movement of the early twentieth century, but her association with it remained an uneasy one. She preferred to consider herself a "sociologist" rather than a "feminist," a social scientist more than a political activist. Over the years suffragists played down differences between the sexes and stressed those ways in which women were innately identical to men. Most suffragists believed that woman's participation in the political process would remove the main remaining block to equality and establish each sex in its most appropriate sphere. But Mrs. Gilman, citing Ward and her authorities on evolutionary biology, acknowledged important differences between the sexes and argued that male domination had created significant feminine inferiority. The centuries of oppression which, she argued, had reduced woman's capacity for equality could not be tossed off easily. Once the social environment encouraged rather than discouraged feminine development, she believed it would take woman approximately three generations to regain her former capacities. The argument that environment affected physical inheritance from one generation to the next brought the rationalist who stressed the importance of social conditioning perilously close to challenging Mendelian genetic theory. Accepting Mendel's ideas without question, the suffragists denied that social inferiority had weakened woman's physical or mental inheritance or thus seriously hampered the current generation's search for equality.

Because she thought the roots of contemporary inequality were much deeper than the suffragists realized or would admit, Mrs. Gilman believed that the cure required much broader and deeper social change than they wanted. Her own desperate and persistent struggle for economic autonomy dominated both her life and thought, and her socialist friends and reading constantly emphasized the overwhelming importance of society's mode of production. Believing that nothing was a more fundamental part of the social environment than the means of acquiring food, shelter, and clothing, Mrs. Gilman did not see how woman could ever gain equality without economic independence. "The political equality demanded by the suffragists was not enough to give real freedom. Women whose industrial position is that of a house-servant, or who do no work at all, who are fed, clothed, and given pocket-money by men, do not reach freedom and equality by the use of the ballot."[22]

The suffragists and Mrs. Gilman argued most specifically over whether the political status of men and women reflected their economic condition in the home. Suffragist argument concerning the particular nature of the home paralleled that of the nature of women in general: As woman was essentially equal to man, so the wife contributed as much as the husband to support the family. Since the wife converted the money which her husband earned into the final products which the family required—food, clothing, and shelter—the husband and wife were economically interdependent; hence neither supported the other. Suffragists thought that if men once recognized this existing economic equality, they would more readily accord women the political equality they obviously deserved. Most suffragists did not perceive a need for any essential change in relationships within the home.

Charlotte Gilman, on the other hand, demanded the vote, far-reaching changes in the home, and many other reforms because she believed that women were economic dependents. Suffrage, she agreed, would provide one small step toward economic independence, but meaningful autonomy required extensive changes in the domestic duties of women as well. In *Women and Economics* she outlined her proposal for large housing units which would provide professional nurseries, central kitchens, and cleaning services. She extended her attack on the conventional domestic routine in *The Home: Its Work and Influence* (1903). Her disagreement with the suffragists led to a formal debate in 1909 with Dr. Anna Howard Shaw at a convention of the Women's Trade Union League. The delegates heard both arguments and then voted overwhelming support for Dr. Shaw's familiar suffragist position. Mrs. Gilman, who recognized that "the suffragists thought me a doubtful if not dangerous ally on account of my theory of the need of economic independence of women," accepted such defeats philosophically. One suffrage leader reportedly told her that "you will do our cause more good than harm because what you ask is so much worse than what we ask that they will grant our demands in order to escape yours."[23]

Having achieved full economic independence and financial solvency by 1900, Charlotte married her cousin, G. Houghton Gilman. The couple, joined by Mrs. Gilman's daughter, initially practiced the domestic routines preached in *Women and Economics*. For a period they resided in a flat in New York City and boarded out: "We had 'a home without a kitchen,' all the privacy and comfort, none of the work and care—except for beds and a little cleaning."[24]

Mrs. Gilman continued her extensive writing and lecturing. A wide range of periodicals, from the most popular magazines to the *American Journal of Sociology*, published her articles and discussed her thought. But the breadth of her attacks upon woman's traditional roles closed a large number of publications to her. In 1909 she circumvented the problem of unfriendly editors by starting her own magazine, *The Forerunner*, which she filled almost entirely with her own work. Every issue included an installment of a novel, a book published serially, a short story, essays of various length, poems, humor and nonsense, book reviews, and comment on current events:

> Consider the theses this one woman was advancing against the previous convictions of the world: in religion a practical, impersonal Deism, seeing God as a working power which asks no worship, only fulfillment: . . . with no concern for immortality or salvation, merely a carrying out of the divine will. In ethics its presentation as a wholly social science, applicable to every act in life, the measure of merit being the effect on social advancement. In economics, a change in the basis of that science, as with ethics, from the individual to the group, involving a complete reversal of most of our previous economic theories; and in what is of far more interest to most of us, our domestic and sex relationships, the claim that we as a race of animals are oversexed—abnormally developed in that function from long centuries of excessive indulgence, and that it is disadvantageous to social progress to have the feeding of humanity and the care of young children carried on by amateurs.

She continued the *Forerunner* for seven years, ending publication when "I had said all I had to say."[25]

The careful distance suffragists, editors, and others kept from Mrs. Gilman's feminism has tended to obscure the limits she placed upon action by rejecting Marxist analysis, remaining aloof from political activism, and denouncing revolutionary tactics. Yet her evolutionary socialism was in some ways closer to Marx's than to the communitarians of Brook Farm,

New Harmony, or Oneida. Like Marx and Bellamy, she saw utopia as the end of an inexorable historical process that human beings could affect but not prevent. In contrast, the earlier communitarians were voluntarists who believed socialism could be established only by specific acts of human will. Mrs. Gilman carried her feminism from the realm of theory to the field of action just about as far as the Nationalists had pushed their socialism. Having concluded that a certain course of events was inevitable, she felt little of the revolutionary's or communitarian's urgency to strike the chains from women and establish equality between the sexes. She considered the operations of natural and social forces as a socialistic "hidden hand" at work which mankind could facilitate and for which it should prepare.

Her faith in the inevitability of sexual equality owed much to the scientific socialist's and evolutionist's belief in the Enlightenment doctrine of progress. As the only constant in the natural order, change needed no explanation: The causative element was immanent within the changing condition. Permanence or stagnation, on the other hand, required elucidation: Human prejudice and superstition, the rationalist explained, hindered change and caused social stagnation. Believing firmly in the power of reason and experience to liberate humanity from wrongheadedness and bring mankind into harmony with the natural order, Charlotte Gilman chose to be a publicist.

Progressive thinking denied the validity of revolutionary acts and obviated the need to reform by instructive example. The communitarians had set out to create a little corner of heaven on earth to advertise to humanity the advantages of their good society. Mrs. Gilman, however, never attempted to establish an example of associational living nor practiced very many of her other proposed domestic reforms. The communitarians had also explored and then experimented with a wider range of institutional reform than Gilman anticipated. Shakers, Harmonists, and Perfectionists had believed that for utopian socialism to succeed, the institutions of conventional marriage and the family needed to be revised as much as the traditional home. Thus utopians experimented with celibacy, complex marriage, and communal living. While an occasional feminist explored the virtues of pre- or extra-marital intercourse, considered trial marriage, or proposed the abolition of marriage as a legal institution, Mrs. Gilman preferred more conventional marital and familial patterns.[26]

Charlotte Gilman's feminist impulse was to diminish, if not ultimately to eradicate, sexual differences. She extolled the maternal functions of woman but defined them so narrowly as to allow a wide range for her other activities or interests. She had no interest in exploring or emphasizing the sexual drive or sex energy beyond its reproductive uses. Emotionally starved in youth and disabled in her first marriage, she was likewise intellectually committed to the rationalist's preference for reason over emotion. Thus she rejected the emotional element within sexual intercourse and denied the value of sexual self-expression.

The irrational, psychological, and particularly the Freudian currents of the early twentieth century naturally met her thorough disapproval. She termed popular Freudianism and the new sex ethic a "highly masculine philosophy" which preyed upon woman's emergence "from long repression . . . overcharged with sex-energy" by proclaiming "the theory that the purpose of sex is recreation." The "most salient change" she noted in the twenties and early thirties was the resulting "lowering of standards in sexual relations, approaching some of the worst periods in ancient history." She considered the newer and freer sexual mores as "a preliminary promiscuity of approach," a degree of sexual indulgence "utterly without parallel in nature." Those who questioned conventional marriage, she concluded, demonstrated their ignorance of biology, for "monogamy is a 'natural' form of sex relationship, practiced widely among birds and beasts, who are neither 'Puritan' nor 'Mid-Victorian.' " But Mrs. Gilman always reaffirmed the "immanent possibilities of swift improvement" for woman and man through reason and science:

> If our so ostentatiously revolted youth would outgrow their infantile delight in 'self-expression,' playing with their new freedom as a baby does with its fingers and toes, and see their real power, their real duty, things would move. This is the woman's century, the first chance for the mother of the world to rise to her full place, her transcendent power to remake humanity, to rebuild the suffering world—and the world waits while she powders her nose.[27]

NOTES

1. For a complete and accessible edition, see Charlotte Perkins Gilman, *Women and Economics: A Study of the Economic Relation between Men and Women as a Factor in Social Evolution* (New York: Harper and Row Publishers, Inc., 1966). Professor Carl Degler's introduction is quite useful, especially for giving detailed examples of times when Gilman anticipated the ideas of post–World War II feminists. For a general summary of Gilman's thought, see Carl Degler, "Charlotte Perkins Gilman on the Theory and Practice of Feminism," *American Quarterly* VIII, Spring 1956, 21–39.

2. Mrs. Gilman's contributions to social Darwinist thought have gone largely unrecognized. She received only one cursory footnote reference in Richard

Hofstadter, *Social Darwinism in American Thought, 1860–1915* (Philadelphia: University of Pennsylvania Press, 1944), 100n–101n.

3. Charlotte Perkins Gilman, *The Living of Charlotte Perkins Gilman: An Autobiography* (New York: D. Appleton-Century Company, Inc., 1935), 260; Degler, *American Quarterly* VIII, 21; Aileen S. Kraditor, *The Ideas of the Woman Suffrage Movement, 1890–1920* (New York: Columbia University Press, 1965), 97n; Charles A. and Mary R. Beard, *The Rise of American Civilization,* revised edition (2 volumes, New York: The Macmillan Company, 1935), II, 431.

4. The quotations in this paragraph and much of the biographical information in this introduction have been taken from Gilman, *Living,* 5–6, 51.

5. Gilman, *Living,* 19, 29.

6. Gilman, *Living,* 26–27, 49, 61.

7. Gilman, *Living,* 67.

8. Gilman, *Living,* 42.

9. Gilman, *Living,* 111.

10. For a brief interpretation of William Dean Howells' social philosophy, see Daniel Aaron, *Men of Good Hope: A Story of American Progressives* (New York: Oxford University Press, 1962 reprinting of 1951 edition), 172–207.

11. For a convenient analysis of Edward Bellamy's ideas, see Aaron, *Men of Good Hope,* 92–132.

12. Gilman, *Living,* 131, 198, 320.

13. Gilman, *Living,* 316; Kraditor, *Woman Suffrage,* 136–137; Elizabeth Cady Stanton, Susan B. Anthony, Matilda J. Gage, and Ida H. Harper (eds.), *History of Woman Suffrage* (6 volumes, Rochester, New York, and New York, 1881–1922), V, 78.

14. Quoted in Stanton et al., *Woman Suffrage,* IV, 256.

15. Gilman, *Living,* 240.

16. Gilman, *Living,* 137, 182, 187. Samuel Chugerman, *Lester F. Ward: The American Aristotle* (Durham: Duke University Press, 1939), offers the fullest statement and interpretation of Ward's ideas. For a briefer summary, see Henry Steele Commager, *The American Mind: An Interpretation of American Thought and Character since the 1880's* (New Haven: Yale University Press, 1950), 199–226.

17. Quoted in Commager, *American Mind,* 206. For a succinct analysis of the conservative and reform strains of social Darwinism, see Eric F. Goldman, *Rendezvous with Destiny: A History of Modern American Reform,* revised edition (New York: Vintage Books, Inc., 1959), 66–81.

18. Lester Frank Ward, *Dynamic Sociology, or Applied Social Science, as Based upon Statistical Sociology and the Less Complex Sciences* (2 volumes, New York: D. Appleton and Company, 1883), II, 614–619. See also Lester Frank Ward, "Our Better Halves," *Forum* VI, 1888, 266–275.

19. Ward, *Dynamic Sociology,* II, 619; Ward, *Forum* VI, 275.

20. Gilman, *Living,* 187; Charlotte Perkins Gilman, *The Man-Made World or, Our Androcentric Culture* (New York: Charlton Company, 1911), dedication.

21. Gilman, *Living,* 228–238, 259. Immediately before writing *Women and Economics,* Gilman read Ward's 1888 *Forum* article (VI, 266–275) and Patrick Geddes and J. Arthur Thomson, *The Evolution of Sex* (London: The Walter Scott Publishing Co., Ltd., 1889).

22. Gilman, *Living,* 235. For a more extended discussion of Gilman's association with the suffragists, see Kraditor, *Woman Suffrage,* 96–122, and William L. O'Neill, *Everyone Was Brave: The Rise and Fall of Feminism in America* (Chicago: Quadrangle Books, Inc., 1969), 38–48.

23. Gilman, *Living,* 198; O'Neill, *Everyone Was Brave,* 38–44.

24. Gilman, *Living,* 283.

25. Gilman, *Living,* 308–310.

26. For further discussion of Gilman's reaction to the new sexual ethic, see O'Neill, *Everyone Was Brave,* 46–48, 132–133, 275, 319.

27. Quoted in O'Neill, *Everyone Was Brave,* 319; Gilman, *Living,* 323–324, 330–331.

WOMEN AND ECONOMICS: A STUDY OF THE ECONOMIC RELATION BETWEEN MEN AND WOMEN AS A FACTOR IN SOCIAL EVOLUTION (1898)

I.

Since we have learned to study the development of human life as we study the evolution of species throughout the animal kingdom, some peculiar phenomena which have puzzled the philosopher and moralist for so long begin to show themselves in a new light. We begin to see that, so far from being inscrutable problems requiring another life to explain, these sorrows and perplexities of our lives are but the natural results of natural causes and that as soon as we ascertain the causes, we can do much to remove them.

In spite of the power of the individual will to struggle against conditions, to resist them for a while, and sometimes to overcome them, it remains true that the human creature is affected by his environment, as is every other living thing. . . . We are affected by climate and locality, by physical, chemical, electrical forces, as are all animals and plants. With the animals we farther share the effect of our own activity, the reactionary force of exercise. What we do, as well as what is done to us, makes us what we are. But beyond these forces we come under the effect of a third set of conditions peculiar to our human status, namely, social conditions. In the organic interchanges which constitute social life, we are affected by each other to a degree beyond what is found even among the most gregarious of animals. This third factor, the social environment, is of enormous force as a modifier of human life. Throughout all these environing conditions, those which affect us through our economic necessities are most marked in their influence.

Without touching yet upon the influence of the social factors, treating the human being merely as an individual animal, we see that he is modified most by his economic conditions, as is every other animal. Differ as they may in color and size, in strength and speed, in minor adaptation to minor conditions, all animals that live on grass have distinctive traits in common, and all animals that eat flesh have distinctive traits in common—so distinctive and so common that it is by teeth, by nutritive apparatus in general, that they are classified rather than by means of defense or locomotion. The food supply of the animal is the largest passive factor in his development; the processes by which he obtains his food supply, the largest active factor in his development. It is these activities, the incessant repetition of the exertions by which he is fed, which most modify his structure and develop his functions. . . .

. . . We are the only animal species in which the female depends on the male for food, the only animal species in which the sex-relation is also an economic relation. With us an entire sex lives in a relation of economic dependence upon the other sex, and the economic relation is combined with the sex-relation. The economic status of the human female is relative to the sex-relation.

It is commonly assumed that this condition also obtains among other animals, but such is not the case. There are many birds among which, during the nesting season, the male helps the female feed the young and partially feeds her; and, with certain of the higher carnivora, the male helps the female feed the young and partially feeds her. . . . In no case is the female throughout her life supported by the male.

In the human species the condition is permanent and general, though there are exceptions and though the present century is witnessing the beginnings of a great change in this respect. We have not been accustomed to face this fact beyond our loose generalization that it was "natural" and that other animals did so too.

To many this view will not seem clear at first; and the case of working peasant women or females of savage tribes and the general household industry of women will be instanced against it. Some careful and honest discrimination is needed to make plain to ourselves the essential facts of the relation, even in these cases. The horse in his free natural condition is economically independent. He gets his living by his own exertions, irrespective of any other creature. The horse in his present condition of slavery is economically dependent. He gets his living at the hands of his master; and his exertions, though strenuous, bear no direct relation to his living. In fact, the horses who are the best fed and cared for and the horses who are the hardest worked are quite different animals. The horse works, it is true; but what he gets to eat depends on the power and will of his master. His living comes through another. He is economically dependent. So with the hard-worked savage or peasant women. Their labor is the property of another: They work under another will, and what they receive depends not on their labor but on the power and will of another. They are economically dependent. This is true of the human female both individually and collectively.

In studying the economic position of the sexes collectively, the difference is most marked. As a social animal, the economic status of man rests on the combined and exchanged services of vast numbers of progressively specialized individuals. The economic progress of the race, its maintenance at any period, its continued advance, involve the collective activities of all the trades, crafts, arts, manufactures, inventions, discoveries, and all the civil and military institutions that go to maintain them. The economic status of any race at any time, with its involved effect on all the constituent individuals, depends on their world-wide labors and their free exchange. Economic progress, however, is almost exclusively masculine. Such economic processes as women have been allowed to exercise are of the earliest and most primitive kind. Were men to perform no economic services save such as are still performed by women, our racial status in economics would be reduced to most painful limitations.

To take from any community its male workers would paralyze it economically to a far greater degree than to remove its female workers. The labor now performed by the women could be performed by the men, requiring only the setting back of many advanced workers into earlier forms of industry; but the labor now performed by the men could not be performed by the women without generations of effort and adaptation. Men can cook, clean, and sew as well as women;

but the making and managing of the great engines of modern industry, the threading of earth and sea in our vast systems of transportation, the handling of our elaborate machinery of trade, commerce, government—these things could not be done so well by women in their present degree of economic development.

This is not owing to lack of the essential human faculties necessary to such achievements, nor to any inherent disability of sex, but to the present condition of woman, forbidding the development of this degree of economic ability. The male human being is thousands of years in advance of the female in economic status. Speaking collectively, men produce and distribute wealth, and women receive it at their hands. . . .

Studied individually, the facts are even more plainly visible, more open and familiar. From the day laborer to the millionaire, the wife's worn dress or flashing jewels, her low roof or her lordly one, her weary feet or her rich equipage—these speak of the economic ability of the husband. The comfort, the luxury, the necessities of life itself which the woman receives are obtained by the husband and given her by him. . . . But we are instantly confronted by the commonly received opinion that, although it must be admitted that men make and distribute the wealth of the world, yet women earn their share of it as wives. This assumes either that the husband is in the position of employer and the wife as employee or that marriage is a "partnership" and the wife an equal factor with the husband in producing wealth.

Economic independence is a relative condition at best. In the broadest sense, all living things are economically dependent upon others—the animals upon the vegetables, and man upon both. In a narrower sense, all social life is economically interdependent, man producing collectively what he could by no possibility produce separately. But in the closest interpretation, individual economic independence among human beings means that the individual pays for what he gets, works for what he gets, gives to the other an equivalent for what the other gives him. I depend on the shoemaker for shoes and the tailor for coats; but if I give the shoemaker and the tailor enough of my own labor as a house-builder to pay for the shoes and coats they give me, I retain my personal independence. I have not taken of their product and given nothing of mine. As long as what I get is obtained by what I give, I am economically independent. . . .

Grateful return for happiness conferred is not the method of exchange in a partnership. The comfort a man takes with his wife is not in the nature of a business partnership, nor are her frugality and industry. A housekeeper, in her place, might be as frugal, as industrious, but would not therefore be a partner. Man and wife are partners truly in their mutual obligation to their children—their common love, duty, and service. But a manufacturer who marries, or a doctor, or a lawyer, does not take a partner in his business when he takes a partner in parenthood, unless his wife is also a manufacturer, a doctor, or a lawyer. . . .

If the wife is not, then, truly a business partner, in what way does she earn from her husband the food, clothing, and shelter she receives at his hands? By house service, it will be instantly replied. This is the general misty idea upon the subject—that women earn all they get and more by house service. Here we come to a very practical and definite economic ground. Although not producers of wealth, women serve in the final processes of preparation and distribution. Their labor in the household has a genuine economic value. . . .

To take this ground and hold it honestly, wives, as earners through domestic service, are entitled to the wages of cooks, housemaids, nursemaids, seamstresses, or housekeepers, and to no more. This would of course reduce the spending money of the wives of the rich and put it out of the power of the poor man to "support" a wife at all, unless, indeed, the poor man faced the situation fully, paid his wife her wages as house servant, and then she and he combined their funds in the support of their children. He would be keeping a servant: She would be helping keep the family. But nowhere on earth would there be "a rich woman" by these means. . . .

But the salient fact in this discussion is that whatever the economic value of the domestic industry of women is, they do not get it. The women who do the most work get the least money, and the women who have the most money do the least work. Their labor is neither given nor taken as a factor in economic exchange. It is held to be their duty as women to do this work; and their economic status bears no relation to their domestic labors, unless an inverse one. Moreover, if they were thus fairly paid—given what they earned and no more—all women working in this way would be reduced to the economic status of the house servant. Few women—or men either—care to face this condition. The ground that women earn their living by domestic labor is instantly forsaken, and we are told that they obtain their livelihood as mothers. . . .

If this is so, if motherhood is an exchangeable commodity given by women in payment for clothes and food, then we must of course find some relation between the quantity or quality of the motherhood and the quantity and quality of the pay. This being true, then the women who are not mothers have no economic status at all; and the economic status of those who are must be shown to be relative to their motherhood. This is obviously absurd. The childless wife has as much money as the mother of many—more, for the children of the latter consume what would otherwise be hers; and the inefficient mother is no less provided for than the efficient one. Visibly and upon the face of it, women are not maintained in economic prosperity proportioned to their motherhood. . . .

. . . Driven off these alleged grounds of women's economic independence; shown that women, as a class, neither produce nor distribute wealth; that women, as individuals, labor mainly as house servants, are not paid as such, and would not be satisfied with such an economic status if they were so paid; that wives are not business partners or co-producers of wealth with their husbands unless they actually practice the same profession; that they are not salaried as mothers . . . —what remains to those who deny that women are supported by men? This (and a most amusing position it is)—that the function of maternity unfits a woman for economic production and, therefore, it is right that she should be supported by her husband. . . .

. . . As the maternal duties of other females do not unfit them for getting their own living and also the livings of their young, it would seem that the human maternal duties require the segregation of the entire energies of the mother to the service of the child during her entire adult life, or so large a proportion of them that not enough remains to devote to the individual interests of the mother. Such a condition, did it exist, would of course excuse and justify the pitiful dependence of the human female and her support by the male. . . . Do we see before us the human race, with all its females segregated entirely to the uses of motherhood, consecrated, set apart, specially developed, spending every power of their nature on the service of their children?

We do not. We see the human mother worked far harder than a mare, laboring her life long in the service, not of her children only, but of men: husbands, brothers, fathers, whatever male relatives she has; for mother and sister also; for the church a little, if she is allowed; for society, if she is able; for charity and education and reform —working in many ways that are not the ways of motherhood.

It is not motherhood that keeps the housewife on her feet from dawn till dark: it is house service, not child service. Women work longer and harder than most men and not solely in maternal duties. The savage mother carries the burdens and does all menial service for the tribe. The peasant mother toils in the fields and the workingman's wife in the home. Many mothers, even now, are wage-earners for the family, as well as bearers and rearers of it. . . . Women of ease and wealth provide for their children better care than the poor woman can, but they do not spend more time upon it themselves, nor more care and effort. . . .

The working power of the mother has always been a prominent factor in human life. She is the worker *par excellence,* but her work is not such as to affect her economic status. Her living, all that she gets—food, clothing, ornaments, amusements, luxuries—these bear no relation to her power to produce wealth, to her services in the house, or to her motherhood. These things bear relation only to the man she marries, the man she depends on—to how much he has and how much he is willing to give her. The women whose splendid extravagance dazzles the world, whose economic goods are the greatest, are often neither houseworkers nor mothers but simply the women who hold most power over the men who have the most money. The female of genus homo is economically dependent on the male. He is her food supply.

II.

. . . Rudely classifying the principal fields of human difficulty, we find one large proportion lies in the sex-relation and another in the economic relation between the individual constituents of society. To speak broadly, the troubles of life as we find them are mainly traceable to the heart or the purse. The other horror of our lives—disease—comes back often to these causes, to something wrong either in economic relation or in sex-relation. To be ill-fed or ill-bred, or both, is largely what makes us the sickly race we are. In this wrong breeding, this maladjustment of the sex-relation in humanity, what are the principal features? We see in social evolution two main lines of action in this department of life. One is a gradual, orderly development of monogamous marriage as the form of sex-union best calculated to advance the interests of the individual and of society. It should be clearly understood that this is a natural development, inevitable in the course of social progress, not an artificial condition, enforced by laws of our making. Monogamy is found among birds and mammals: It is just as natural a condition as polygamy or promiscuity or any other form of sex-union; and its permanence and integrity are introduced and increased by the needs of the young and the advantage to the race, just as any other form of reproduction was introduced. . . .

But with the natural process of social advancement has gone an unnatural process, an erratic and morbid action making the sex-relation of humanity a frightful source of evil. So prominent have been these morbid actions and evil results that hasty thinkers of all ages have assumed that the whole thing was wrong and that celibacy was the highest virtue. Without the power of complete analysis, without knowledge of the sociological data essential to such analysis, we have sweepingly condemned as a whole what we could easily see was so allied with pain and loss. But like all natural phenomena, the phenomena of sex may be studied, both the normal and the abnormal, the physiological and the pathological; and we are quite capable of understanding why we are in such evil case and how we may attain more healthful conditions. . . .

Very early in the development of species it was ascertained by nature's slow but sure experiments that the establishment of two sexes in separate organisms, and their differentiation, was to the advantage of the species. Therefore, out of the mere protoplasmic masses, the floating cells, the amorphous early forms of life, grew into use the distinction of the sexes—the gradual development of masculine and feminine organs and functions in two distinct organisms. Developed and increased by use, the distinction of sex increased in the evolution of species. As the distinction increased, the attraction increased, until we have in all the higher races two markedly different sexes, strongly drawn together by the attraction of sex and fulfilling their use in the reproduction of species. These are the natural features of sex-distinction and sex-union, and they are found in the human species as in others. The unnatural feature by which our race holds an unenviable distinction consists mainly in this —a morbid excess in the exercise of this function.

It is this excess, whether in marriage or out, which makes the health and happiness of humanity in this relation so precarious. It is this excess, always easily seen, which law and religion have mainly striven to check. Excessive sex-indulgence is the distinctive feature of humanity in this relation.

To define "excess" in this connection is not difficult. All natural functions that require our conscious co-operation for their fulfillment are urged upon our notice by an imperative desire. We do not have to desire to breathe or to digest or to circulate the blood because that is done without our volition; but we do have to desire to eat and drink because the stomach cannot obtain its supplies without in some way spurring the whole organism to secure them. So hunger is given us as an essential factor in our process of nutrition. In the same manner sex-attraction is an essential factor in the fulfillment of our processes of reproduction. In a normal condition the amount of hunger we feel is exactly proportioned to the amount of food we need. It tells us when to eat and when to stop. In some diseased conditions "an unnatural appetite" sets in, and we are impelled to eat far beyond the capacity of the stomach to digest, of the body to assimilate. This is an excessive hunger. . . .

. . . The immediately acting cause of sex-attraction is sex-distinction. The more widely the sexes are differentiated, the more forcibly they are attracted to each other. The more highly developed becomes the distinction of sex in either organism, the more intense is its attraction for the other. . . . Normal sex-distinction manifests itself in all species in what are called primary and secondary sex-characteristics. The primary are those organs and functions essential to reproduction; the secondary, those modifications of structure and function which subserve the uses of reproduction ultimately but are not directly essential—such as the horns of the stag, of use in sex-combat; the plumage of the peacock, of use in sex-competition. All the minor characteristics of beard or mane, comb, wattles, spurs, gorgeous color or superior size which distinguish the male from the female—these are distinctions of sex. These distinctions are of use to the species through reproduction only, the processes of race-preservation. They are not of use in self-preservation. The creature is not profited personally by his mane or crest or tail-feathers: They do not help him get his dinner or kill his enemies.

On the contrary, they react unfavorably upon his personal gains if, through too great development, they interfere with his activity or render him a conspicuous mark for enemies. Such development would constitute excessive sex-distinction, and this is precisely the condition of the human race. Our distinctions of sex are carried to such a degree as to be disadvantageous to our progress as individuals and as a race. The sexes in our species are differentiated not only enough to perform their primal functions, not only enough to manifest all sufficient secondary sexual characteristics and fulfill their use in giving rise to sufficient sex-attraction, but so much as seriously to interfere with the processes of self-preservation on the one hand and, more conspicuous still, so much as to react unfavorably upon the very processes of race-preservation which they are meant to serve. Our excessive sex-distinction, manifesting the characteristics of sex to an abnormal degree, has given rise to a degree of attraction which demands a degree of indulgence that directly injures motherhood and fatherhood. We are not better as parents, nor better as people, for our existing degree of sex-distinction, but visibly worse. To what conditions are we to look for the developing cause of these phenomena?

Let us first examine the balance of forces by which these two great processes, self-preservation and race-preservation, are conducted in the world. Self-preservation involves the expenditure of energy in those acts, and their ensuing modifications of structure and function, which tend to the maintenance of the individual life. Race-preservation involves the expenditure of energy in those acts, and their ensuing modifications of structure and function, which tend to the maintenance of the racial life, even to the complete sacrifice of the individual. This primal distinction should be clearly held in mind. Self-preservation and race-preservation are in no way identical processes and are often directly opposed. In the line of self-preservation, natural selection, acting on the individual, develops those characteristics which enable it to succeed in "the struggle for existence," increasing by use those organs and functions by which it directly profits. In the line of race-preservation, sexual selection, acting on the individual, develops those characteristics . . . by which its young are to profit, directly or indirectly. The individual has been not only modified to its environment under natural selection but modified to its mate under sexual selection, each sex developing the qualities desired by the other by the simple process of choice, those best sexed being first chosen and transmitting their sex-development as well as their racial development.

The order mammalia is the resultant of a primary sex-distinction developed by natural selection, but the gorgeous plumage of the peacock's tail is a secondary sex-distinction developed by sexual selection. If the peacock's tail were to increase in size and splendor till it shone like the sun and covered an acre, . . . such excessive sex-distinction would be so inimical to the personal prosperity of that peacock that he would die and his tail-tendency would perish with him. . . . In herds of deer and cattle the male is larger and stronger, the female smaller and weaker; but unless the latter is large and strong enough to keep up with the male in the search for food or the flight from foes, one is taken and the other left, and there is no more of that kind of animal. Differ as they may in sex, they must remain alike in species, equal in race-development, else destruction overtakes them. The force of natural selection, demanding and producing identical race-qualities, acts as a check on sexual selection with its production of different sex-qualities. . . .

When, then, it can be shown that sex-distinction in the human race is so excessive as . . . to check and pervert the progress of the race, it becomes a matter for most serious consideration. Nothing could be more inevitable, however, under our sexuo-economic relation. By the economic dependence of the human female upon the male, the balance of forces is altered. Natural selection no longer checks the action of sexual selection but co-operates with it. Where both sexes obtain their food through the same exertions, from the same sources, under the same conditions, both sexes are acted upon alike and developed alike by their environment. Where the two sexes obtain their food under different conditions and where that difference consists in one of them being fed by the other, then the feeding sex becomes the environment of the fed. Man, in supporting woman, has become her economic environment. Under natural selection every creature is modified to its environment, developing perforce the qualities needed to obtain its livelihood under that environment. . . . Under sexual selection the human creature is of course modified to its mate, as with all creatures. When the mate becomes also the master, when economic necessity is added to sex-attraction, we have the two great evolutionary forces acting together to the same end, namely, to develop sex-distinction in the human female. For in her position of economic dependence in the sex-relation, sex-distinction is with her not only a means of attracting a mate, as with all creatures, but a means of getting her livelihood, as is the case with no other creature under heaven. Because of the economic dependence of the human female on her mate, she is modified to sex to an excessive degree. This excessive modification she transmits to her children; and so is steadily implanted in the human constitution the morbid tendency to excess in this relation which has acted so universally upon us in all ages, in spite of our best efforts to restrain it. It is not the normal sex-tendency, common to all creatures, but an abnormal sex-tendency, produced and maintained by the abnormal economic relation which makes one sex get its living from the other by the exercise of sex-functions. This is the immediate effect upon individuals of the peculiar sexuo-economic relation which obtains among us.

III.

In establishing the claim of excessive sex-distinction in the human race, much needs to be said to make clear to the general reader what is meant by the term. To the popular mind, both the coarsely familiar and the over-refined, "sexual" is thought to mean "sensual"; and the charge of excessive sex-distinction seems to be a reproach. This should be at once dismissed as merely showing ignorance of the terms used. A man does not object to being called "masculine," nor a woman to being called "feminine." Yet whatever is masculine or feminine is sexual. To be distinguished by femininity is to be distinguished by sex. To be over-feminine is to be over-sexed. To manifest in excess any of the distinctions of sex, primary or secondary, is to be over-sexed. Our hypothetical peacock with his too large and splendid tail would be over-sexed, and no offense to his moral character! . . .

. . . Sex-energy in its primal manifestation is exhibited in the male of the human species to a degree far greater than is necessary for the processes of reproduction—enough, indeed, to subvert and injure those processes. . . . In a certain over-coarseness and hardness, a too great belligerence and pride, a too great subservience to the power of sex-attraction, we find the main marks of excessive sex-distinction in men. It has been always checked and offset in them by the healthful activities of racial life. Their energies have been called out and their faculties developed along all the lines of human progress. In the growth of industry, commerce, science, manufacture, government, art, religion, the male of our species has become human far more than male. Strong as this passion is in him, inordinate as is his indulgence, he is a far more normal animal than the female of his species—far less over-sexed. To him this field of special activity is but part of life, an incident. The whole world remains besides. To her it is the world. . . .

Physically, woman belongs to a tall, vigorous, beautiful animal species, capable of great and varied exertion. In every race and time when she has opportunity for racial activity, she develops accordingly and is no less a woman for being a healthy human creature. In every race and time where she is denied this opportunity—and few, indeed, have been her years of freedom—she has developed in the lines of action to which she was confined; and those were always lines of sex-activity. In consequence the body of woman, speaking in the largest generalization, manifests sex-distinction predominantly.

Woman's femininity . . . is more apparent in proportion to her humanity than the femininity of other animals in proportion to their caninity or felinity or equinity. "A feminine hand" or "a feminine foot" is distinguishable anywhere. We do not hear of "a feminine paw" or "a feminine hoof." A hand is an organ of prehension, a foot an organ of locomotion; they are not secondary sexual characteristics. The comparative smallness and feebleness of woman is a sex-distinction. We have carried it to such an excess that women are commonly known as "the weaker sex." . . .

The degree of feebleness and clumsiness common to women, the comparative inability to stand, walk, run, jump, climb, and perform other race-functions common to both sexes, is an excessive sex-distinction; and the ensuing transmission of this relative feebleness to their children, boys and girls alike, retards human development. Strong, free, active women, the sturdy, field-working peasant, the burden-bearing savage, are no less good mothers for their human strength. But our civilized "feminine delicacy," which appears somewhat less delicate when recognized as an expression of sexuality in excess, makes us no better mothers, but worse. The relative weakness of women is . . . apparent in her to a degree that injures motherhood, that injures wifehood, that injures the individual. . . .

In its psychic manifestation this intense sex-distinction is equally apparent. The primal instinct of sex-attraction has developed under social forces into a conscious passion of enormous power, a deep and lifelong devotion, overwhelming in its force. This is excessive in both sexes, but more so in women than in men—not so commonly in its simple physical form but in the unreasoning intensity of emotion that refuses all guidance and drives those possessed by it to risk every other good for this one end. . . .

. . . In our steady insistence on proclaiming sex-distinction, we have grown to consider most human attributes as masculine attributes for the simple reason that they were allowed to men and forbidden to women. . . . But while with the male the things he fondly imagined to be "masculine" were merely human and very good for him, with the female the few things marked "feminine" were feminine indeed; and her ceaseless reiteration of one short song, however sweet, has given it a conspicuous monotony. In garments whose main purpose is unmistakably to announce her sex, with a tendency to ornament which marks exuberance of sex-energy, with a body so modified to sex as to be grievously deprived of its natural activities, with a manner and behavior wholly attuned to sex-advantage and frequently most disadvantageous to any human gain, with a field of action most rigidly confined to sex-relations, with her overcharged sensibility, her prominent modesty, her "eternal femininity"—the female of genus homo is undeniably over-sexed.

This excessive distinction shows itself again in a marked precocity of development. Our little children, our very babies, show signs of it when the young of other creatures are serenely asexual in general appearance and habit. We eagerly note this precocity. We are proud of it. We carefully encourage it by precept and example, taking pains to develop the sex-instinct in little children, and think no harm. One of the first things we force upon the child's dawning consciousness is the fact that he is a boy or that she is a girl and that, therefore, each must regard everything from a different point of view. They must be dressed differently, not on account of their personal needs, which are exactly similar at this period, but so that neither they nor any one beholding them may for a moment forget the distinction of sex. . . . Boys and girls are expected, also, to behave differently to each other and to people in general, a behavior to be briefly described in two words. To the boy we say, "Do"; to the girl, "Don't." The little boy must "take care" of the little girl, even if she is larger than he is. . . . Boys are encouraged from the beginning to show the feelings supposed to be proper to their sex. When our infant son bangs about, roars, and smashes things, we say proudly that he is "a regular boy!" When our infant daughter coquettes with visitors or wails in maternal agony because her brother has broken her doll, whose sawdust remains she nurses with piteous care, we say proudly that "she is a perfect little mother already!" What business has a little girl with the instincts of maternity? No more than the little boy should have with the instincts of paternity. They are sex-instincts and should not appear till the period of adolescence. The most normal girl is the "tom-boy"—whose numbers increase among us in these wiser days—a healthy young creature who is human through and through, not feminine till it is time to be. The most normal boy has calmness and gentleness as well as vigor and courage. He is a human creature as well as a male creature and not aggressively masculine till it is time to be. Childhood is not the period for these marked manifestations of sex. That we exhibit them, that we admire and encourage them, shows our over-sexed condition.

VI.

. . . In the original constituents of society, the human animal in its primitive state, economic processes were purely individual. The amount of food obtained by a given man bore direct relation to his own personal exertions. . . . Given a certain supply of needed food, as the edible beasts or fruits in a forest, and a certain number of individuals to get this food, each by his own exertions, it follows that the more numerous the individuals, the less food to be obtained by each and, conversely, the fewer the individuals, the more food to be obtained by each. Wherefore, the primitive savage slew his fellowman at sight on good economic grounds. This is the extreme of individual competition, perfectly logical and in its time economically right. That time is forever past. The basic condition of human life is union: the organic social relation, the interchange of functional service, wherein the individual is most advantaged not by his own exertions for his own goods but by the exchange of his exertions with the exertions of others for goods produced by them together. We are not treating here of any communistic theory as to the equitable division of the wealth produced but of a clear truth in social economics—that wealth is a social product. Whatever one may believe as to what should be done with the wealth of the world, no one can deny that the production of this wealth requires the combined action of many individuals. From the simplest combination of strength that enables many men to overcome the mammoth or to lift the stone—an achievement impossible to one alone—to the subtle and complex interchange of highly specialized skilled labor which makes possible our modern house, the progress of society rests upon the increasing collectivity of human labor. . . .

But as we study this process, . . . we are struck by the visible presence of some counter-force, acting against the normal development and producing most disadvantageous effects. . . . We have our hand upon this hidden spring in the sexuo-economic relation. If we had remained on an individual economic basis, the evil influence would have had far less ill effect; but as we grow into the social economic relation, it increases with our civilization. The sex-relation is primarily and finally individual. It is a physical relation between individual bodies, and while it may also extend to a psychical relation between individual souls, it does not become a social relation, though it does change its personal development to suit social needs.

In all its processes, to all its results, the sex-relation is personal, working through individuals upon individuals and developing individual traits and characteristics to the great advantage of society. The qualities developed by social relation are built into the race through the sex-relation, but the sex-relation itself is wholly personal. Our economic relation, on the contrary, though originally individual, becomes through social evolution increasingly collective. By combining the human sex-relation with the human economic relation, we have combined a permanently individual process with a progressively collective one. . . .

We are so used to considering it the first duty of a man to support his family that it takes a very glaring instance of bribery and corruption in their interests to shake our conviction; but as a sociological law, every phase of the prostitution of public service to private gain, from the degradation of the artist to the exploitation of the helpless unskilled laborer, marks a diseased social action. Our social status rests upon our common consent, common action, common submission to the common will. No individual interests can stand for a moment against the interests of the common weal, either when war demands the last sacrifice of individual property and life or when peace requires the absolute submission of individual property and life to common law—the fixed expression of the people's will. The maintenance of "law and order" involves the very spirit of socialism, the sinking of personal interest in common interest. All this rests upon the evolution of the social spirit, the keen sense of social duty, the conscientious fulfillment of social service; and it is here that the excessive individualism maintained by our sexuo-economic relation enters as a strong and increasingly disadvantageous social factor. . . .

The highest human attributes are perfectly

compatible with the sex-relation but not with the sexuo-economic relation. We see this opposition again in the tendency to collectivity in bodies of single men—their comradeship, equality, and mutual helpfulness as compared with the attitude of the same men toward one another when married. This is why the quality of "organizability" is stronger in men than in women; their common economic interests force them into relation, while the isolated and even antagonistic economic interests of women keep them from it. The condition of individual economic dependence in which women live resembles that of the savage in the forest. They obtain their economic goods by securing a male through their individual exertions, all competing freely to this end. No combination is possible. . . .

On the woman's side we are steadily maintaining the force of primitive individual competition in the world as against the tendency of social progress to develop co-operation in its place, and this tendency of course is inherited by their sons. On the man's side the same effect is produced through another feature of the relation. The tendency to individualism with sex-advantage is developed in man by an opposite process to that operating on the woman. She gets her living by getting a husband. He gets his wife by getting a living. It is to her individual economic advantage to secure a mate. It is to his individual sex-advantage to secure economic gain. The sex-functions to her have become economic functions. . . .

. . . Legitimate sex-competition brings out all that is best in man. To please her, to win her, he strives to do his best. But the economic dependence of the female upon the male, with its ensuing purchasability, does not so affect a man: It puts upon him the necessity for getting things, not for doing them. In the lowest grades of labor, where there is no getting without doing and where the laborer always does more than he gets, this works less palpable evil than in the higher grades, the professions and arts, where the most valuable work is always ahead of the market and where to work for the market involves a lowering of standards. The young artist or poet or scientific student works for his work's sake, for art, for science, and so for the best good of society. But the artist or student married must get gain, must work for those who will pay; and those who will pay are not those who lift and bear forward the standard of progress. Community of interest is quite possible with those who are working most disinterestedly for the social good; but bring in the sex-relation and all such solidarity disintegrates—resolves itself into the tiny groups of individuals united on a basis of sex-union and briskly acting in their own immediate interests at anybody's or everybody's expense. . . .

Besides this maintenance of primeval individualism in the growing collectivity of social economic process and the introduction of the element of sex-combat into the narrowing field of industrial competition, there is another side to the evil influence of the sexuo-economic relation upon social development. This is in the attitude of woman as a non-productive consumer.

In the industrial evolution of the human race, . . . we find that production and consumption go hand in hand; and production comes first. One cannot consume what has not been produced. Economic production is the natural expression of human energy—not sex-energy at all, but race-energy—the unconscious functioning of the social organism. Socially organized human beings tend to produce, as a gland to secrete: It is the essential nature of the relation. The creative impulse, the desire to make, to express the inner thought in outer form, . . . is the distinguishing character of humanity. . . . This is the natural process of production and is followed by the natural process of consumption, where practicable. But consumption is not the main end, the governing force. Under this organic social law working naturally, we have the evolution of those arts and crafts in the exercise of which consists our human living and on the product of which we live. So does society evolve within itself—secrete as it were—the social structure with all its complex machinery; and we function therein as naturally as so many glands, other things being equal.

But other things are not equal. Half the human race is denied free productive expression, is forced to confine its productive human energies to the same channels as its reproductive sex-energies. Its creative skill is confined to the level of immediate personal bodily service, to the making of clothes and preparing of food for individuals. No social service is possible. For the woman there is . . . no relation maintained between what she does produce and what she consumes. She is forbidden to make but encouraged to take. Her industry is not the natural output of creative energy, not the work she does because she has the inner power and strength to do it; nor is her industry even the measure of her gain. She has, of course, the natural desire to consume; and to that is set no bar save the capacity or the will of her husband.

Thus we have painfully and laboriously evolved and carefully maintain among us an enormous class of non-productive consumers—a class which is half the world and mother of the other half. We have built into the constitution of the human race the habit and desire of taking, as divorced from its natural precursor and concomitant of making. . . . To consume food, to consume clothes, to consume houses and furniture and decorations and ornaments and amusements, to take and take and take forever—from one man if they are virtuous, from many if they are vicious, but always to take and never to think of giving anything in return except their womanhood—this is the enforced condition of the mothers of the race. . . .

Between the brutal ferocity of excessive male energy struggling in the market-place as in a battlefield and the unnatural greed generated by the perverted condition of female energy, it is not remarkable that the industrial evolution of humanity has shown peculiar symptoms. One of the minor effects of this last condition—this limiting of female industry to close personal necessities and this tendency of her over-developed sex-nature to overestimate the so-called "duties of her position"—has been to produce an elaborate devotion to individuals and their personal needs—not to the understanding and developing of their higher natures but to the intensification of their bodily tastes and pleasure. The wife and mother, pouring the rising tide of racial power into the same old channels that were allowed her primitive ancestors, constantly ministers to the physicial needs of her family with a ceaseless and concentrated intensity.

. . . The consuming female—debarred from any free production, unable to estimate the labor involved in the making of what she so lightly destroys, and her consumption limited mainly to those things which minister to physical pleasure—creates a market for sensuous decoration and personal ornament, for all that is luxurious and enervating, and for a false and capricious variety in such supplies, which operates as a most deadly check to true industry and true art. As the priestess of the temple of consumption, as the limitless demander of things to use up, her economic influence is reactionary and injurious. Much, very much, of the current of useless production in which our economic energies run waste—man's strength poured out like water on the sand—depends on the creation and careful maintenance of this false market, this sink into which human labor vanishes with no return. Woman, in her false economic position, reacts injuriously upon industry, upon art, upon science, discovery, and progress. The sexuo-economic relation in its effect on the constitution of the individual keeps alive in us the instincts of savage individualism which we should otherwise have well outgrown. It sexualizes our industrial relation and commercializes our sex-relation. And in the external effect upon the market, the over-sexed woman in her unintelligent and ceaseless demands hinders and perverts the economic development of the world.

VII.

. . . When the human animal was still but an animal, but an individual, came the imperative demand for the establishment of a common consciousness between . . . hitherto irreconcilable individuals. The first step in nature toward this end is found in the relation between mother and child. Where the young after birth are still dependent on the mother, the functions of the one separate living body needing the service of another separate living body, we have the overlapping of personality, the mutual need, which brings with it the essential instinct that holds together these interacting personalities. . . . Between mother and child was born love, long before fatherhood was anything more than a momentary incident. But the common consciousness, the mutual attraction between mother and child, stopped there absolutely. It was limited in range to this closest relation; in duration, to the period of infancy.

The common interest of human beings must be served by racial faculties, not merely by the sex-functions of the female or the duties of mother to child. As the male, acting through his natural instincts, steadily encroached upon the freedom of the female until she was reduced to the state of economic dependence, he thereby assumed the position of provider for this creature no longer able to provide for herself. . . . He became, and has remained, a sort of man-mother, alone in creation in his remarkable position. By this common interest, existing now not only between mother and child but between father, mother, and child, grew up a wider common consciousness. And as the father served the child not through sex-function but through race-function, this service was open to far wider development and longer duration than the mother's alone could ever have reached.

Maternal energy is the force through which have come into the world both love and industry. It is through the tireless activity of this desire, the mother's wish to serve the young, that she began the first of the arts and crafts whereby we live. While the male savage was still a mere hunter and fighter, expressing masculine energy, . . . expanding, scattering, the female savage worked out in equally natural ways the conserving force of female energy. She gathered together and saved nutrition for the child. . . . She wrapped it in garments and built a shelter for its head as naturally as the same maternal function had loved, clothed, and sheltered the unborn. Maternal energy, working externally through our elaborate organism, is the source of productive industry, the main current of social life.

But not until this giant force could ally itself with others and work co-operatively, overcoming the destructive action of male energy in its blind competition, could our human life enter upon its full course of racial evolution. This is what was accomplished through the suppression of the free action of maternal energy in the female and its irresistible expression through the male. . . . The subjection of woman has involved to an enormous degree the maternalizing of man. Under its bonds he has been forced into new functions, impossible to male energy alone. He has had to learn to love and care for someone besides himself. He has had to learn to work, to serve, to be human. Through the sex-passion, mightily overgrown, the human race has been led and driven up the long, steep path of progress, over all obstacles, through all dangers, carrying its accompanying conditions of disease and sin (and surmounting them), up and up in spite of all, until at last a degree of evolution is reached in which the extension of human service and human love makes possible a better way.

. . . Sexual equality has been slowly evolved, not only by increasing the importance of the male element in reproduction but by developing race-qualities in the male, so long merely a reproductive agent. The last step of this process has been the elevation of the male of genus homo to full racial equality with the female. . . . If the female had remained in full personal freedom and activity, she would have remained superior to him, and both would have remained stationary. Since the female had not the tendency to vary which distinguished the male, it was essential that the expansive forces of masculine energy be combined with the preservative and constructive forces of feminine energy. The expansive and variable male energy, struggling under its new necessity for constructive labor, has caused that labor to vary and progress more than it would have done in feminine hands alone. Out of her wealth of power and patience, liking to work, to give, she toils on forever in the same primitive industries. He, impatient of obstacles, not liking to work, desirous to get rather than to give, splits his task into a thousand specialties and invents countless ways to lighten his labors. . . .

Human development thus far has proceeded in the male line, under the force of male energy, spurred by sex-stimulus and by the vast storage battery of female energy suppressed. Women can well afford their period of subjection for the sake of a conquered world, a civilized man. In spite of the agony of the process—the black, long ages of shame and pain and horror—women should remember that they are still here; and thanks to the blessed power of heredity, they are not so far aborted that a few generations of freedom will not set them abreast of the age. When the centuries of slavery and dishonor, of torture and death, of biting injustice and slow, suffocating repression, seem long to women, let them remember the geologic ages, the millions and millions of years when puny, pygmy, parasitic males struggled for existence and were used or not, as it happened, like a half-tried patent medicine. What train of wives and concubines was ever so ignominiously placed as the extra husbands carried among the scales of the careful female cirriped, lest she lose one or two! What neglect of faded wives can compare with the scorned, unnoticed death of the drone bee, starved, stung, shut out, walled up in wax, kept only for his momentary sex-function, and not absolutely necessary for that! What Bluebeard tragedy or cruelty of bride-murdering Eastern king can emulate the ruthless slaughter of the hapless little male spider used by his ferocious mate "to coldly furnish forth a marriage breakfast"! Never once in the history of humanity has any outrage upon women compared with these sweeping sacrifices of helpless males in earlier species. The female has been dominant for the main duration of life on earth. She has been easily equal always up to our own race; and in our race she has been subjugated to the male during the earlier period of development for such enormous racial gain, such beautiful and nobles uses, that the sacrifice should never be mentioned nor thought of by a womanhood that knows its power. . . .

And now that the long strain is over, now that the time has come when neither he nor the world is any longer benefited by her subordination, now that she is coming steadily out into direct personal expression, into the joy of racial action in full freedom, of power upon the throne instead of behind it, it is unworthy of this supreme new birth to waste one regret upon the pain that had to be. . . .

The increasing specialization of the modern woman, acquired by inheritance from the ceaselessly specializing male, makes her growing racial faculties strain against the primitive restrictions of a purely sexual relation. The desire to produce—the distinctive human quality—is no longer satisfied with a status that allows only reproduction. In our present stage of social evolution it is increasingly difficult and painful for women to endure their condition of economic dependence, and therefore they are leaving it. . . .

A relation that inevitably produces abnormal development cannot be permanently maintained. The intensification of sex-energy as a social force results in such limitless exaggeration of sex-instinct as finds expression sexually in the unnatural vices of advanced civilization and socially in the strained economic relation between producer and consumer which breaks society in two. The sexuo-economic relation serves to bring social development to a certain level. After that level is reached, a higher relation must be adopted or the lifting process comes to an end, and either the race succumbs to the morbid action of its own forces, or some fresher race comes in and begins the course of social evolution anew.

Under the stimulus of the sexuo-economic relation, one civilization after another has climbed up and fallen down in weary succession. It remains for us to develop a newer, better form of sex-relation and of economic relation therewith and so to grasp the fruits of all previous civilizations and grow on to the beautiful results of higher ones. The true and lasting social progress, beyond that which we have yet made, is based on a spirit of inter-human love, not merely the inter-sexual; and it requires an economic machinery organized and functioned for human needs, not sexual ones.

. . . Social consciousness is at last so vital a force in both men and women that we feel clearly that our human life cannot be fully lived on sex-lines only. We are so far individualized, so far socialized, that men can work without the tearing spur of exaggerated sex-stimulus, work for someone besides mate and young; and women can love and serve without the slavery of economic dependence—love better and serve more. Sex-stimulus begins and ends in individuals. The social spirit is a larger thing, a better thing, and brings with it a larger, nobler life than we could ever know on a sex-basis solely.

Moreover, it should be distinctly understood, as it is already widely and vaguely felt, that the higher development of social life following the economic independence of women makes possible a higher sex-life than has ever yet been known. As fast as the human individual rises in social progress to a certain degree of development, so fast this primitive form of sex-union chafes and drags: It is felt to be unsatisfying and injurious. This is a marked feature in modern life. The long, sure, upward trend of the human race toward monogamous marriage is no longer helped but hindered by the economic side of the relation. The best marriage is between the best individuals; and the best individuals of both sexes today are increasingly injured by the economic basis of our marriage, which produces and maintains those qualities in men and women, and their resultant industrial conditions, which make marriage more difficult and precarious every day.

The woman's movement, then, should be hailed by every right-thinking, far-seeing man and woman as the best birth of our century. The banner advanced proclaims "equality before the law," woman's share in political freedom; but the main line of progress is and has been toward economic equality and freedom. While life exists on earth, the economic conditions must underlie and dominate each existing form and its activities, and social life is no exception. A society whose economic unit is a sex-union can no more develop beyond a certain point industrially than a society like the patriarchal, whose political unit was a sex-union, could develop beyond a certain point politically.

The last freeing of the individual makes possible the last combination of individuals. While sons must bend to the will of a patriarchal father, no democracy is possible. Democracy means, requires, is individual liberty. While the sexuo-economic relation makes the family the center of industrial activity, no higher collectivity than we have today is possible. But, as women become free economic, social factors, so becomes possible the full social combination of individuals in collective industry. With such freedom, such independence, such wider union becomes possible also a union between man and woman such as the world has long dreamed of in vain.

XI.

As a natural consequence of our division of labor on sex-lines, giving to woman the home and to man the world in which to work, we have come to have a dense prejudice in favor of the essential womanliness of the home duties as opposed to the essential manliness of every other kind of work. We have assumed that the preparation and serving of food and the removal of dirt, the nutritive and excretive processes of the family, are feminine functions; and we have also assumed that these processes must go on in what we call the home, which is the external expression of the family. . . .

. . . Food is produced by the human race collectively—not by individuals for their own consumption but by interrelated groups of individuals all over the world for the world's consumption. This collectively produced food circulates over the earth's surface through elaborate processes of transportation, exchange, and preparation before it reaches the mouths of the consumers; and the final processes of selection and preparation are in the hands of woman. . . .

. . . If the private housekeeper had the technical intelligence as purchaser which is needed to discriminate in the selection of foods, if she were prepared to test her milk, to detect the foreign substance in her coffee and spices, rightly to estimate the quality of her meat and the age of her fruit and vegetables, she would then be able at least to protest against her supply and to seek, as far as time, distance, and funds allowed, a better market. This technical intelligence, however, is only to be obtained by special study and experience; and its attainment only involves added misery and difficulty to the private purchaser, unless accompanied by the power to enforce what the intelligence demands.

As it is, woman brings to her selection from the world's food only the empirical experience gained by practising upon her helpless family, . . . and each daughter begins again as ignorant as her mother was before her. This "rule of thumb" is not transmissible. It is not a genuine education, such as all important work demands, but a slow animal process of soaking up experience—hopelessly ineffectual in protecting the health of society. As the ultimate selecting agent in feeding humanity, the private housewife fails, and this not by reason of any lack of effort on her part but by the essential defect of her position as individual purchaser. Only organization can oppose such evils as the wholesale adulteration of food; and woman, the house-servant, belongs to the lowest grade of unorganized labor.

Leaving the selection of food and examining its preparation, one would naturally suppose that the segregation of an entire sex to the fulfillment of this function would insure most remarkable results. It has, but they are not so favorable as might be expected. The art and science of cooking involve a large and thorough knowledge of nutritive value and of the laws of physiology and hygiene. As a science, it verges on preventive medicine. As an art, it is capable of noble expression within its natural bounds. . . .

On the side of knowledge it is permanently impossible that half the world, acting as amateur cooks for the other half, can attain any high degree of scientific accuracy or technical skill. The development of any human labor requires specialization, and specialization is forbidden to our cook-by-nature system. What progress we have made in the science of cooking has been made through the study and experience of professional men cooks and chemists, not through the Sisyphean labors of our endless generations of isolated women, each beginning again where her mother began before her. . . .

But low as is the status of cooking as a science, as an art it is lower. Since the wife-cook's main industry is to please—that being her chief means of getting what she wants or of expressing affection—she early learned to cater to the palate instead of faithfully studying and meeting the needs of the stomach. For uncounted generations the grown man and the growing child have been subject to the constant efforts of her who cooked from affection, not from knowledge. . . .

. . . The art of cooking can never be lifted to its true place as a human need and a social function by private service. Such an arrangement of our lives and of our houses as will allow cooking to become a profession is the only way in which to free this great art from its present limitations. It should be a reputable, well-paid profession, wherein those women or those men who were adapted to this form of labor could become cooks, as they would become composers or carpenters. Natural distinctions would be developed between the mere craftsman and the artist, and we should have large, new avenues of lucrative and honorable industry and a new basis for human health and happiness.

This does not involve what is known as "co-operation." Co-operation, in the usual sense, is the union of families for the better performance of their supposed functions. The process fails because the principle is wrong. Cooking and cleaning are not family functions. . . . Co-operation is not what is required for this, but trained professional service and such arrangement of our methods of living as shall allow us to benefit by such service. When numbers of people patronize the same tailor or baker or confectioner, they do not co-operate. Neither would they co-operate in patronizing the same cook. The change must come from the side of the cook, not from the side of the family. It must come through natural functional development in society, and it is so coming. Woman, recognizing that her duty as feeder and cleaner is a social duty, not a sexual one, must face the requirements of the situation, and prepare herself to meet them. A hundred years ago this could not have been done. Now it is being done, because the time is ripe for it.

If there should be built and opened in any of our large cities today a commodious and well-served apartment house for professional women with families, it would be filled at once. The apartments would be without kitchens; but there would be a kitchen belonging to the house from which meals could be served to the families in their rooms or in a common dining-room, as preferred. It would be a home where the cleaning was done by efficient workers, not hired separately by the families but engaged by the manager of the establishment; and a roof-garden, day nursery, and kindergarten, under well-trained professional nurses and teachers, would insure proper care of the children. The demand for such provision is increasing daily and must soon be met, not by a boarding-house or a lodging-house, a hotel, a restaurant, or any makeshift patching together of these, but by a permanent provision for the needs of women and children, of family privacy with collective advantage. This must be offered on a business basis to prove a substantial business success; and it will so prove, for it is a growing social need. . . .

Meals could of course be served in the house as long as desired; but when people become accustomed to pure, clean homes where no steaming industry is carried on, they will gradually prefer to go to their food instead of having it brought to them. It is a perfectly natural process and a healthful one to go to one's food. And, after all, the changes between living in one room, and so having the cooking most absolutely convenient, going as far as the limits of a large house permit to one's own dining-room, and going a little further to a dining-room not in one's own house, but near by—these differ but in degree. Families could go to eat together, just as they can go to bathe together or to listen to music together; but, if it fell out that different individuals presumed to develop an appetite at different hours, they could meet it without interfering with other people's comfort or sacrificing their own. Any housewife knows the difficulty of always getting a family together at meals. Why try? Then arises sentiment and asserts that family affection, family unity, the very existence of the family depend on their being together at meals. A family unity which is only bound together with a table-cloth is of questionable value.

There are several professions involved in our clumsy method of housekeeping. A good cook is not necessarily a good manager, nor a good manager an accurate and thorough cleaner, nor a good cleaner a wise purchaser. Under the free development of these branches a woman could choose her position, train for it, and become a most valuable functionary in her special branch, all the while living in her own home; that is, she would live in it as a man lives in his home, spending certain hours of the day at work and others at home.

This division of the labor of housekeeping would require the service of fewer women for fewer hours a day. Where now twenty women in twenty homes work all the time and insufficiently accomplish their varied duties, the same work in the hands of specialists could be done in less time by fewer people; and the others would be left free to do other work for which they were better fitted, thus increasing the productive power of the world. Attempts at co-operation so far have endeavored to lessen the existing labors of women without recognizing their need for other occupation, and this is one reason for their repeated failure.

It seems almost unnecessary to suggest that women as economic producers will naturally choose those professions which are compatible with motherhood, and there are many professions much more in harmony with that function than the household service. Motherhood is not a remote contingency but the common duty and the common glory of womanhood. If women did choose professions unsuitable to maternity, Nature would quietly extinguish them by her unvarying process. Those mothers who persisted in being acrobats, horse-breakers, or sailors before the mast would probably not produce vigorous and numerous children. If they did, it would simply prove that such work did not hurt them. There is no fear to be wasted on the danger of women's choosing wrong professions when they are free to choose. Many women would continue to prefer the very kinds of work which they are doing now, in the new and higher methods of execution. Even cleaning, rightly understood and practised, is a useful, and therefore honorable, profession. It has been amusing heretofore to see how this least desirable of labors has been so innocently held to be woman's natural duty. It is woman, the dainty, the beautiful, the beloved wife and revered mother, who has by common consent been expected to do the chamber-work and scullery work of the world. All that is basest and foulest she in the last instance must handle and remove. Grease, ashes, dust, foul linen, and sooty ironware—among these her days must pass. As we socialize our functions, this passes from her hands into those of man. The city's cleaning is his work. And even in our houses the professional cleaner is more and more frequently a man.

The organization of household industries will simplify and centralize its cleaning processes, allowing of many mechanical conveniences and the application of scientific skill and thoroughness. We shall be cleaner than we ever were before. There will be less work to do and far better means of doing it. The daily needs of a well-plumbed house could be met easily by each individual in his or her own room or by one who liked to do such work; and the labor less frequently required would be furnished by an expert, who would clean one home after another with the swift skill of training and experience. The home would cease to be to us a workshop or a museum, and would become far more the personal expression of its occupants—the place of peace and rest, of love and privacy—than it can be in its present condition of arrested industrial development. And woman will fill her place in those industries with far better results than are now provided by her ceaseless struggles, her conscientious devotion, her pathetic ignorance and inefficiency.

XIII.

In reconstructing in our minds the position of woman under conditions of economic independence, it is most difficult to think of her as a mother.

We are so unbrokenly accustomed to the old methods of motherhood, so convinced that all its processes are inter-relative and indispensable and that to alter one of them is to endanger the whole relation, that we cannot conceive of any desirable change.

When definite plans for such change are suggested—ways in which babies might be better cared for than at present—we either deny the advantages of the change proposed or insist that these advantages can be reached under our present system.

. . . In the training of children . . . the private home has ceased to be sufficient, or the isolated, primitive, dependent woman capable. Not that the mother does not have an intense and overpowering sense of loyalty and of duty; but it is duty to individuals, just as it was in the year one. What she is unable to follow, in her enforced industrial restriction, is the higher specialization of labor and the honorable devotion of human lives to the development of their work. She is most slavishly bound to her daily duty, it is true; but it does not occur to her as a duty to raise the grade of her own labor for the sake of humanity, nor as a sin so to keep back the progress of the world by her contented immobility.

She cannot teach what she does not know. She cannot in any sincerity uphold as a duty what she does not practise. The child learns more of the virtues needed in modern life—of fairness, of justice, of comradeship, of collective interest and action—in a common school than can be taught in the most perfect family circle. We may preach to our children as we will of the great duty of loving and serving one's neighbor; but what the baby is born into, what the child grows up to see and feel, is the concentration of one entire life—his mother's—upon the personal aggrandizement of one family, and the human service of another entire life—his father's—so warped and strained by the necessity of "supporting his family" that treason to society is the common price of comfort in the home. For a man to do any base, false work for which he is hired, work that injures producer and consumer alike, to prostitute what power and talent he possesses to whatever purchaser may use them—this is justified among men by what they call duty to the family and is unblamed by the moral sense of dependent women. . . .

It is not the home as a place of family life and love that injures the child but as the center of a tangled heap of industries, low in their ungraded condition and lower still because they are wholly personal. Work the object of which is merely to serve one's self is the lowest. Work the object of which is merely to serve one's family is the next lowest. Work the object of which is to serve more and more people in widening range till it approximates the divine spirit that cares for all the world is social service in the fullest sense and the highest form of service that we can reach.

It is this personality in home industry that keeps it hopelessly down. The short range between effort and attainment, the constant attention given to personal needs, is bad for the man, worse for the woman, and worst for the child. It belittles his impressions of life at the start. It accustoms him to magnify the personal duties and minify the social ones, and it greatly retards his adjustment to larger life. This servant-motherhood, with all its unavoidable limitation and ill results, is the concomitant of the economic dependence of woman upon man, the direct and inevitable effect of the sexuo-economic relation.

. . . We demand measureless personal attention and devotion because we have been born and reared in a very hotbed of these qualities. A baby who spent certain hours of every day among other babies, being cared for because he was a baby and not because he was "my baby," would grow to have a very different opinion of himself from that which is forced upon each new soul that comes among us by the ceaseless adoration of his own immediate family. . . . The earlier and more easily a child can learn that human life means many people and their behavior to one another, the happier and stronger and more useful his life will be.

. . . Education, which is our human motherhood, has crept nearer and nearer to its true place, its best work, the care and training of the little child. Some women there are, and some men, whose highest service to humanity is the care of children. Such should not concentrate their powers upon their own children alone—a most questionable advantage—but should be so placed that their talent and skill, their knowledge and experience would benefit the largest number of children. Many women there are, and many men, who, though able to bring forth fine children, are unable to educate them properly. Simply to bear children is a personal matter, an animal function. Education is collective, human, a social function.

As we now arrange life, our children must take their chances while babies and live or die, improve or deteriorate, according to the mother to whom they chance to be born. An inefficient mother does not prevent a child from having a good school education or a good college education, but the education of babyhood, the most important of all, is wholly in her hands. It is futile to say that mothers should be taught how to fulfill their duties. You cannot teach every mother to be a good school educator or a good college educator. Why should you expect every mother to be a good nursery educator? Whatever our expectations, she is not; and our mistrained babies, such of them as survive the maternal handling, grow to be such people as we see about us.

The growth and change in home and family life goes steadily on under and over and through our prejudices and convictions; and the education of the child has changed and become a social function while we still imagine the mother to be doing it all.

. . . The beautiful development of the kindergarten has brought education to the nursery door. Even our purblind motherhood is beginning to open that door; and we have at last entered upon the study of babyhood, its needs and powers, and are seeing that education begins with life itself. It is no new and daring heresy to suggest that babies need better education than the individual mother now gives them. It is simply a little further extension of the steadily expanding system of human education which is coming upon us as civilization grows. And it no more infringes upon the mother's rights, the mother's duties, the mother's pleasures than does the college or the school. . . .

Better surroundings and care for babies [and] better education do not mean, as some mothers may imagine, that the tiny monthling is to be taught to read or even that it is to be exposed to cabalistical arrangements of color and form and sound which shall mysteriously force the young intelligence to flower. It would mean, mainly, a far quieter and more peaceful life than is possible for the heavily loved and violently cared for baby in the busy household; and the impressions which it did meet would be planned and maintained with an intelligent appreciation of its mental powers. The mother would not be excluded but supplemented, as she is now by the teacher and the school. . . .

In this larger grouping, in full companionship, the child would unconsciously absorb the knowledge that "we" were humanity, that "we" were creatures to be so fed, so watched, so laid to sleep, so kissed and cuddled and set free to roll and play. The mother-hours would be sweetest of all, perhaps. Here would be something wholly one's own and the better appreciated for the contrast. But the long, steady days would bring their peaceful lessons of equality and common interest instead of the feverish personality of the isolated one-baby household or the innumerable tyrannies and exactions, the forced submissions and exclusions of the nursery full of brothers and sisters of widely differing ages and powers. Mothers accustomed to consider many babies besides their own would begin, on the one hand, to learn something of mere general babyness, and so understand that stage of life far better, and, on the other, . . . to recognize a difference in babies and so to learn a new ideal in their great work of motherhood. . . .

After all is said of loving gratitude to our unfailing mother-nurse, we must have a most exalted sense of our own personal importance so to canonize the service of ourselves. The mother as a social servant instead of a home servant will not lack in true mother duty. She will love her child as well, perhaps better, when she is not in hourly contact with it, when she goes from its life to her own life and back from her own life to its life with ever new delight and power. She can keep the deep, thrilling joy of motherhood far fresher in her heart, far more vivid and open in voice and eyes and tender hands, when the hours of individual work give her mind another channel for her own part of the day. From her work, loved and honored though it is, she will return to the home life, the child life, with an eager, ceaseless pleasure, cleansed of all the fret and friction and weariness that so mar it now. . . .

There are three reasons why the individual mother can never be fit to take all the care of her children. . . . First, not every woman is born with the special qualities and powers needed to take right care of children: She has not the talent for it. Second, not every woman can have the instruction and training needed to fit her for the right care of children: She has not the education for it. Third, while each woman takes all the care of her own children herself, no woman can ever have the requisite experience for it. That is the final bar. That is what keeps back our human motherhood. No mother knows more than her mother knew: No mother has ever learned her business; and our children pass under the well-meaning experiments of an endless succession of amateurs.

We try to get "an experienced nurse." We insist on "an experienced physician." But our idea of an experienced mother is simply one who has borne many children, as if parturition was an educative process! . . .

The economically independent mother, widened and freed, strengthened and developed by her social service, will do better service as mother than it has been possible to her before. No one thing could do more to advance the interests of humanity than the wiser care and wider love of organized human motherhood around our babies. This nobler mother, bearing nobler children and rearing them in nobler ways, would go far toward making possible the world which we want to see. And this change is coming upon us overpoweringly in spite of our foolish fears.

XIV.

The changes in our conception and expression of home life, so rapidly and steadily going on about us, involve many far-reaching effects, all helpful to human advancement. Not the least of these is the improvement in our machinery of social intercourse.

This necessity of civilization was unknown in those primitive ages when family intercourse was sufficient for all and when any further contact between individuals meant war. Trade and its travel, the specialization of labor and the distribution of its products, with their ensuing development have produced a wider, freer, and more frequent movement and interchange among the innumerable individuals whose interaction makes society. Only recently, and as yet but partially, have women as individuals come to their share of this fluent social intercourse which is the essential condition of civilization. . . .

. . . Every human being needs a home—bachelor, husband, or widower, girl, wife, or widow, young or old. They need it from the cradle to the grave, and without regard to sex-connections. We should so build and arrange for the shelter and comfort of humanity as not to interfere with marriage and yet not to make that comfort dependent upon marriage. With the industries of home life managed professionally, with rooms and suites of rooms and houses obtainable by any person or persons desiring them, we could live singly without losing home comfort and general companionship, we could meet bereavement without being robbed of the common conveniences of living as well as of the heart's love, and we could marry in ease and freedom without involving any change in the economic base of either party concerned. . . .

Take the kitchens out of the houses, and you leave rooms which are open to any form of arrangement and extension; and the occupancy of them does not mean "housekeeping." In such living, personal character and taste would flower as never before; the home of each individual would be at last a true personal expression, and the union of individuals in marriage would not compel the jumbling together of all the external machinery of their lives. . . . The sense of lifelong freedom and self-respect and of the peace and permanence of one's own home will do much to purify and uplift the personal relations of life, and more to strengthen and extend the social relations. The individual will learn to feel himself an integral part of the social structure, in close, direct, permanent connection with the needs and uses of society.

This is especially needed for women, who are generally considered, and who consider themselves, mere fractions of families, and incapable of any wholesome life of their own. The knowledge that peace and comfort may be theirs for life, even if they do not marry—and may be still theirs for life, even if they do—will develop a serenity and strength in women most beneficial to them and to the world. It is a glaring proof of the insufficient and irritating character of our existing form of marriage that women must be forced to it by the need of food and clothes, and men by the need of cooks and housekeepers. We are absurdly afraid that, if men or women can meet these needs of life by other means, they will cheerfully renounce the marriage relation. And yet we sing adoringly of the power of love! . . .

. . . This is a world of persons as well as of families. We are persons as soon as we are born, though born into families. We are persons when we step out of families, and persons still, even when we step into new families of our own. As persons we need more and more in each generation to associate with other persons. . . . When our sex-relation is made pure and orderly by the economic independence of women, when sex-attraction is no longer a consuming fever forever convulsing the social surface under all its bars and chains, we shall not be content to sit down forever with half a dozen blood relations for our whole social arena. We shall need each other more, not less, and shall recognize that social need of one another as the highest faculty of this the highest race on earth. . . .

Acting always under the heated misconceptions of our over-sexed minds, we have pictured mankind as a race of beasts whose only desire to be together was based on one great, overworked passion and who were only kept from universal orgies of promiscuity by being confined in homes. This is not true. It is not true even now in our over-sexed condition. It will be still less true when we are released from the artificial pressure of the sexuo-economic relation and grow natural again.

Men, women, and children need freedom to mingle on a human basis, and that means to mingle in their daily lives and occupations, not to go laboriously to see each other with no common purpose. We all know the pleasant acquaintance and deep friendship that springs up when people are thrown together naturally, at school, at college, on shipboard, in the cars, in a camping trip, in business. The social need of one another rests at bottom on a common, functional development; and the common, functional service is its natural opportunity. . . .

The assembling-room is as deep a need of human life as the retiring-room—not some ballroom or theater to which one must be invited of set purpose, but great common libraries and parlors, baths and gymnasia, workrooms and playrooms to which both sexes have the same access for the same needs and where they may mingle freely in common human expression. The kind of buildings essential to the carrying out of the organization of home industry will provide such places. There will be the separate rooms for individuals and the separate houses for families; but there will be, also, the common rooms for all. These must include a place for the children, planned and built for the happy occupancy of many children for many years, a home such as no children have ever had. This, as well as rooms everywhere for young people and old people, in which they can be together as naturally as they can be alone, without effort, question, or remark. . . .

. . . To free an entire half of humanity from an artificial position; to release vast natural forces from a strained and clumsy combination and set them free to work smoothly and easily as they were intended to work; to introduce conditions that will change humanity from within, making for better motherhood and fatherhood, better babyhood and childhood, better food, better homes, better society—this is to work for human improvement along natural lines. It means enormous racial advance, and that with great swiftness; for this change does not wait to create new forces but sets free those already potentially strong so that humanity will fly up like a released spring. And it is already happening. All we need do is to understand and help.

XV.

. . . Not woman, but the condition of woman, has always been a doorway of evil. The sexuo-economic relation has debarred her from the social activities in which . . . are developed the social virtues. She was not allowed to acquire the qualities needed in our racial advance; and, in her position of arrested development, she has maintained the virtues and the vices of the period of human evolution at which she was imprisoned. At a period of isolated economic activity—mere animal individualism—at a period when social ties ceased with the ties of blood, woman was cut off from personal activity in social economics and confined to the functional activities of her sex. . . .

We have trained in men the large qualities of social usefulness which the pressure of their economic conditions was also developing; and we have done this by means of conscious praise and blame, reward and punishment, and with the aid of law and custom. We have trained in women, by the same means, the small qualities of personal usefulness which the pressure of their economic conditions was also developing. . . .

The largest and most radical effect of restoring women to economic independence will be in its result in clarifying and harmonizing the human soul. With a homogeneous nature bred of two parents in the same degree of social development, we shall be able to feel simply, to see clearly, to agree with ourselves, to be one person and master of our own lives, instead of wrestling in such hopeless perplexity with what we have called "man's dual nature." Marry a civilized man to a primitive savage, and their child will naturally have a dual nature. Marry an Anglo-Saxon to an African or Oriental, and their child has a dual nature. Marry any man of a highly developed nation, full of the specialized activities of his race and their accompanying moral qualities, to the carefully preserved, rudimentary female creature he has so religiously maintained by his side, and you have as result what we all know so well —the human soul in its pitiful, well-meaning efforts, its cross-eyed, purblind errors, its baby fits of passion, and its beautiful and ceaseless upward impulse through all this wavering.

We are quite familiar with this result, but we have not so far accurately located the cause. We have had our glimmering perception that woman had something to do with it; and she has been treated accordingly, by many simple races, to her further injury and to that of the whole people. What we need to see is that it is not woman as a sex who is responsible for this mis-mothered world but the economic position of woman which makes her what she is. If men were so placed, it would have the same effect. Not the sex-relation but the economic relation of the sexes has so tangled the skein of human life.

Besides the essential evils of an unbalanced nature, many harmful qualities have been developed in human characters by these conditions. For countless centuries we have sought to develop, by selection and education, a timid submission in woman. When there did appear "a curst shrew," she was left unmarried; and her temper perished with her, or she was "tamed" by some Petruchio. The dependence of women on the personal favor of men has produced an exceeding cleverness in the adaptation of the dependent one to the source of her supplies. Under the necessity of pleasing, whether she wished or no, of interceding for a child's pardon or of suing for new pleasures for herself, "the vices of the slave" have been forever maintained in this housemaid of the world.

Another discord introduced by the condition of servitude is that between will and action. A servant places his time and strength at the disposal of another will. He must hold himself in readiness to do what he is told; and the mere physical law of conservation of energy, to say nothing of his own conscious judgment, forbids wasting nerve-force in planning and undertaking what he may not be able to accomplish. This produces a condition of inactivity save under compulsion and, on the other side, a perverse, capricious wilfulness in little things—the reaction from a forced submission.

A more insidious, disintegrating force to offset the evolution of human character could hardly be imagined than this steady training of the habits of servitude into half the human race—the mother of all of it. These results have been modified, of course, by the different education and environment of men, developing in them opposite qualities and transmitting the contradictory traits to the children indiscriminately.

Heredity has no Salic law. The boy inherits from his mother as well as from his father; the girl from her father as well as from her mother. This has prevented the full evil of the results that might have ensued but has also added to the personal difficulties of each of us and retarded the general progress of the race.

Worse than the check set upon the physical activities of women has been the restriction of their power to think and judge for themselves. The extended use of the human will and its decisions is conditioned upon free, voluntary action. In her rudimentary position, woman was denied the physical freedom which underlies all knowledge, she was denied the mental freedom which is the path to further wisdom, she was denied the moral freedom of being mistress of her own action and of learning by the merciful law of consequences what was right and what was wrong; and she has remained, perforce, undeveloped in the larger judgment of ethics.

Her moral sense is large enough, morbidly large, because in this tutelage she is always being praised or blamed for her conduct. She lives in a forcing-bed of sensitiveness to moral distinctions, but the broad judgment that alone can guide and govern this sensitiveness she has not. Her contribution to moral progress has added to the anguish of the world the fierce sense of sin and shame, the desperate desire to do right, the fear of wrong, without giving it the essential help of a practical wisdom and a regulated will. . . .

Recognizing her intense feeling on moral lines and seeing in her the rigidly preserved virtues of faith, submission, and self-sacrifice—qualities which in the Dark Ages were held to be the first of virtues—we have agreed of late years to call woman the moral superior of man. But the ceaseless growth of human life, social life, has developed in him new virtues, later, higher, more needful; and the moral nature of woman, as maintained in this rudimentary stage by her economic dependence, is a continual check to the progress of the human soul. The main feature of her life—the restriction of her range of duty to the love and service of her own immediate family—acts upon us continually as a retarding influence, hindering the expansion of the spirit of social love and service on which our very lives depend. It keeps the moral standard of the patriarchal era still before us and blinds our eyes to the full duty of man.

An intense self-consciousness, born of the ceaseless contact of close personal relation; an inordinate self-interest, bred by the constant personal attention and service of this relation; a feverish, torturing, moral sensitiveness, without the width and clarity of vision of a full-grown moral sense; a thwarted will, used to meek surrender, cunning evasion, or futile rebellion; a childish, wavering, short-range judgment, handicapped by emotion; a measureless devotion to one's own sex relatives; and a maternal passion swollen with the full strength of the great social heart but denied social expression—such psychic qualities as these, born in us all, are the inevitable result of the sexuo-economic relation.

It is not alone upon woman and, through her, upon the race that the ill-effects may be observed. Man, as master, has suffered from his position also. The lust for power and conquest, natural to the male of any species, has been fostered in him to an enormous degree by this cheap and easy lordship. His dominance is not that of one chosen as best fitted to rule or of one ruling by successful competition with "foemen worthy of his steel"; but it is a sovereignty based on the accident of sex and holding over such helpless and inferior dependents as could not question or oppose. The easy superiority that needs no striving to maintain it, the temptation to cruelty always begotten by irresponsible power, the pride and self-will which surely accompany it—these qualities have been bred into the souls of men by their side of the relation. When man's place was maintained by brute force, it made him more brutal; when his place was maintained by purchase, by the power of economic necessity, then he grew into the merciless use of such power as distinguishes him today.

Another giant evil engendered by this relation is what we call selfishness. Social life tends to reduce this feeling, which is but a belated individualism; but the sexuo-economic relation fosters and develops it. To have a whole human creature consecrated to his direct personal service, to pleasing and satisfying him in every way possible—this has kept man selfish beyond the degree incidental to our stage of social growth. Even in our artificial society life, men are more forbearing and considerate, more polite and kind, than they are at home. Pride, cruelty, and selfishness are the vices of the master; and these have been kept strong in the bosom of the family through the false position of woman. And every human soul is born, an impressionable child, into the close presence of these conditions. Our men must live in the ethics of a civilized, free, industrial, democratic age; but they are born and trained in the moral atmosphere of a primitive patriarchate. No wonder that we are all somewhat slow to rise to the full powers and privileges of democracy, to feel full social honor and social duty, while every soul of us is reared in this stronghold of ancient and outgrown emotions—the economically related family.

So we may trace from the sexuo-economic relation of our species not only definite evils in psychic development, bred severally in men and women and transmitted indifferently to their offspring, but the innate perversion of character resultant from the moral miscegenation of two so diverse souls—the unfailing shadow and distortion which has darkened and twisted the spirit of man from its beginnings. We have been injured in body and in mind by the too dissimilar traits inherited from our widely separated parents, but nowhere is the injury more apparent than in its ill effects upon the moral nature of the race.

Yet here, as in the other evil results of the sexuo-economic relation, we can see the accompanying good that made the condition necessary in its time, and we can follow the beautiful results of our present changes with comforting assurance. A healthy, normal moral sense will be ours, freed from its exaggerations and contradictions; and with that clear perception, we shall no longer conceive of the ethical process as something outside of and against nature but as the most natural thing in the world.

Where now we strive and agonize after impossible virtues, we shall then grow naturally and easily into those very qualities; and we shall not even think of them as especially commendable. Where our progress hitherto has been warped and hindered by the retarding influence of surviving rudimentary forces, it will flow on smoothly and rapidly when both men and women stand equal in economic relation. When the mother of the race is free, we shall have a better world by the easy right of birth and by the calm, slow, friendly forces of social evolution.

PART VI

Margaret Sanger:

Romantic Irrationalist

Margaret Higgins Sanger (1883–1966) represented much that Charlotte Gilman had questioned, and yet both were deeply committed feminists. Immigrant pressure on the native born, the challenge of European anarchism to American socialism, the re-emerging Romantic emphasis upon intuition and the individual as opposed to scientific rationalism and the group, the sexual revolution which lauded self-expression irrespective of marriage—all of these issues marked the range of differences between the two women. Each sought the liberation of woman, although they defined it differently, proposed separate paths to freedom, and emphasized the special needs of different social classes.

Margaret Sanger was the sixth of eleven children born to Irish parents in upstate New York. Like the Perkinses, the Higginses suffered economic insecurity and hardship without descending into the spiritually destructive culture of poverty. The Chemung River divided Corning, New York, into the quarters of the poor workers who huddled by the factories in the valley and those of the wealthy owners who lived atop the surrounding hills. Daughter of an artisan who belonged to neither class, Margaret looked at the Corning social structure from a certain distance. She early associated the poverty, toil, drunkenness, quarrelling, and debt of "the people down below" with large families. Those on the hilltops, whom the young girl occasionally visited, owned their own homes, had few children, and kept their property and progeny clean and well ordered.[1]

Margaret Sanger's father, whom she credited with having "done most in shaping my growth," was "a philosopher, a rebel, and an artist" without much interest in mundane economic matters. Through excessive begetting —"in part responsible for my mother's premature death"—and a failure to serve as "guardian of his home," he also failed to conserve the limited physical resources of a tubercular wife.[2] But his intellectual fearlessness built character in his children. A socialist of Henry George's persuasion and follower of the religious freethinker Colonel Robert Ingersoll, Michael Higgins once spent the family savings for the next winter's coal on a banquet for Henry George and later sacrificed his Roman Catholic customers when he sponsored an Ingersoll lecture. Her father's fight for "free libraries, free education, free books in the public schools, and freedom of the mind from dogma and cant" taught Margaret "the value of freedom of speech and personal liberty." Soon isolated "as children of the Devil, atheists and heretics," the hitherto Catholic Higginses had "the juvenile stamp of disapproval . . . set upon us." Patronage was withdrawn, "and while father's income was diminishing, the family was increasing." For while Mr. Higgins advocated many reforms, including the equality of the sexes, woman suffrage, and the Bloomer costume, few manifestations of his professed feminism ever appeared in the household's routines.[3]

"As children of poorer parents," the Higgins youth found that everything they "desired most was forbidden. Our childhood was one of longing for things that were always denied. We were made to feel inferior to teachers, to elders, to all." When ridiculed by her eighth-grade teacher for coming to school late, Margaret left and refused to return. Her older sisters, fearing she was doomed to poverty, donated their earnings to send the proud, stubborn Margaret to a Methodist boarding school, where she carried the family's heretical banners high. She argued vigorously for female suffrage, "for anything which would 'emancipate' women and humanity." "Father was still the spring from which I drank, and I sent long letters home, getting in reply still longer ones, filled with ammunition about the historical background of the importance of women." She even espoused the cause of free silver as preached by William Jennings Bryan. "I, also, in an obscure and unformed way, wanted to help grasp utopia from the skies and plant it on earth."[4]

Before Margaret could turn her education toward utopia, her father called her home to nurse her dying mother and care for the younger children. Reading medical books in a futile effort to forestall her mother's death, she linked medicine with her "latent desire to be of service in the world" and rejected all "thought of marriage" as "akin to suicide."[5] Thus she went into nurse's training near New York City in 1899. At the completion of her work, however, she married William Sanger. Apparently the road to utopia had numerous detours.

Sanger, who often reminded Margaret of her father, aroused a continuing ambivalence in his wife. A would-be artist, an armchair socialist, and a financially carefree Romantic, he also had capital, established social position, and cosmopolitan tastes. The couple lived for nearly a decade in suburban comfort. Although Charlotte Gilman and Margaret Sanger each found conventional housewifery stultifying, the latter tolerated it for a full decade. By 1912, however, the Sangers felt a certain "world hunger, the pull and haul towards wider horizons." A "tame domesticity . . . bordering on stagnation" left Margaret adrift in "a swamp." She was "glad to leave when, in one of our financial doldrums, we plunged back into the rushing stream of New York life."[6] There, at least, she could resume her nursing career and the search for humanitarian service.

The Sangers embarked upon city life just as youthful adherents of what Henry F. May called the Rebellion collected on New York's East Side.[7] Sanger's association with the artistic and literary avant-garde brought his wife into contact with a form of radicalism distant from her father's village idols. The young couple met and absorbed some of the doctrines of the leading rebels of the day, who were deeply influenced by European irrationalists. With the thought of Friedrich Nietzsche, Sigmund Freud, and Henri Bergson as scripture, the new radicals attacked a host of prevailing ideas, including rationalism, scientism, capitalism, progressivism, and puritanism.

In the lyrical poet and German philosopher, Nietzsche, the rebels found confirmation of their diagnosis that the excessive development of the rational faculty at the expense of the spontaneous creativity of human instinct or will was spawning Western decadence. Since the days of Socrates, Nietzsche reported, the rationality of the scientific mind had hobbled the human spirit. Christ had supplanted Dionysus, who, worshipped through ecstatic and orgiastic ritual dances, symbolized the creative life force; Christianity had thereby crucified the love of life. The great irrationalist probed the submerged, unconscious, "Dionysian" springs of human creativity that lay so much deeper than reason. Anticipating Freud, Nietzsche recognized the life force as partly sexual, and he suggested that Christianity and conventional morality had grievously damaged mankind by surrounding sex with taboos.

Absorbing Nietzschean thought from other rebels and through the words and paintings of European artists, Margaret did not begin to read Nietzsche directly until her British exile in late 1914. She admired the message of the lyrical German iconoclast—the renunciation of materialism, the portrayal of conventional morality as mere conformity, the affirmation of physical joy, the call to develop the God within oneself.

Indeed she closed her autobiography with Nietzsche's words: "Build thou beyond thyself."[8]

The rebels also absorbed much of Freud's thought through the works of others. Like Nietzsche, Freud built on a dualism of reason and emotion, the conscious and unconscious. But Freud paid attention almost exclusively to the unconscious, which he explored in greater depth and presented in more scientific language. The strongest human impulse, Freud argued, was the sexual drive. Sublimated in or expressed through creative activity, the sex drive fulfilled the human being. But repressed, as was frequently the case in Western society, the thwarted primary drive reduced people to emotional cripples, neurotics.

The French irrationalist philosopher, Henri Bergson, was more accessible than either Freud or Nietzsche to New York's East Side rebels. Also a Romantic idealist, Bergson considered the rational, conceptualizing intellect as a useful tool for acquiring a limited practical knowledge about the typical and the repetitive. He saw evolution, however, as a continuing, creative, unpredictable process which an organism operating on intuition could significantly direct. If, as he believed, only intuitive understanding could grasp reality—if reality is a life force that runs through immediate experience—then the scientific function which breaks the flow of time into separate instants for purposes of analysis distorts whatever is alive and developing. Self-conscious or reflective instinct touched the essentials of life in a manner that logic-chopping intellect could never approach.

Margaret Sanger listened carefully to some of America's most learned young men explain and extoll the thought of the great European irrationalists. Walter Lippmann, a few years out of Harvard, admired Bergson and employed Freudian insights with unusual subtlety. The "soft-voiced, lethargic poet," Max Eastman, discussed the Rebellion's irreverence for reason, conventional morality, traditional art, and progressive politics through the pages of the *Masses,* which he edited and which Margaret read avidly.[9] Will Durant, who had recently abandoned a Jesuit seminary, expounded the sexual freedom preached by Havelock Ellis and others. Margaret Sanger listened in respectful silence as the passionate spoke with authority about liberation and rebellion.

Any plan for social improvement, the rebels thought, had to include a program for spiritual and artistic liberation. The good society must be varied, spontaneous, and interesting as well as just and free. They therefore regarded nineteenth-century socialism—whether Marxist, Fabian, or utopian—as admirable but dated. Most of the rebels enlisted in the common war against bourgeois society under the socialist banner raised by the British radical, H. G. Wells. He respected differences in human capabilities and advocated sexual and artistic, as well as economic, freedom. Wells rejected logic, remained skeptical of categories and classes, and asserted that all movements were intrinsically more important than their goals. Belief, which he considered a human necessity, should be constructed by living, not merely by thinking. He wanted to give women economic independence, for example, so they might be free for sexual self-expression and for the fulfillment of other fundamental emotional drives. Wells, who rejected conventional marriage in favor of transitory relationships between the sexes, proposed education through what would conventionally be labelled promiscuity. Impressed and awed by Wells' reputation, Margaret Sanger welcomed the opportunity to meet him on her 1920 visit to Britain, and the two became close friends.[10]

Some American rebels combined the new British radicalism with Continental anarchism or proletarian syndicalism, that is, the idea of using a general strike or other direct action by organized workers to gain control of production. The International Workers of the World (I.W.W.) transplanted the doctrines of Bergson's disciple, Georges Sorel, to American soil. Sorel rejected the rationalism and materialism of orthodox socialism in favor of political irrationalism and idealism. Marxism, he argued, must be understood as a great spiritual movement, a religion, committed to direct action and the propaganda of the deed rather than to words, reason, and elections. The goal of anarcho-syndicalism, he concluded, must be to abolish church and state, as well as economic oppression, and thereby free each individual to develop and fulfill his essentially nonrational being.

"Our living room," Margaret Sanger recorded, "became a gathering place where liberals, anarchists, socialists, and I.W.W.'s could meet." Because she was "not at all sure my opinions would be accepted by this very superior group," Sanger generally only listened. Her unspoken "personal feelings" drew her "towards the individualist, anarchist philosophy." She, like many of the other rebels, considered it necessary to approach the anarchist's ideal "by way of socialism; as long as the earning of food, clothing, and shelter was on a competitive basis, man could never develop any true independence." And so, although an "anarchist," she joined the Socialist party.[11]

Her city life had stimulated Margaret's will to change society and provided ideological underpinnings for far-reaching programs; once again she took charge of her own future. Since her humanitarian passion remained tied to nursing, she often refused to take an active part in I.W.W. labor struggles except when her nurse's training could be useful. On one occasion she took charge of children of striking Lowell, Massachusetts, textile workers, and on others she spoke to socialist women's groups on health topics. Most of her nursing activities, however, centered on home-bound maternity cases in the economically depressed areas of the city. The poorer the family, the more children there seemed to be, much as it had appeared in Corning years before. For many financially pressed women, another baby meant little joy; for those who successfully inflicted abortion upon themselves, there was a temporary reprieve or the permanent relief of death. Witness to the degradation inflicted upon the poor by large families, dunned by involuntary mothers for the secrets of contraception, and exposed to the influence of anarchists, Margaret Sanger soon developed her own special interest, the cause of birth control.

No East Side radical overlooked the signal importance which the European irrationalists and their American interpreters assigned to the sexual drive. Margaret Sanger, however, considered it a more fundamental cause of individual and social malaise than economics. Delivering babies in squalid bedrooms and walking the picket line, she became obsessed with the idea "that something more was needed to assuage the condition of the very poor. It was both absurd and futile to struggle over pennies when fast-coming babies required dollars to feed them." Male labor leaders overlooked the connection she saw between reproduction and the worker's standard of living. And orthodox Marxists opposed contraception because they feared that population control might ameliorate conditions for the proletariat and thus blunt the class struggle against the major enemy, capitalism.[12]

Attuned to irrationalism, anarchism, and syndicalism, Sanger rejected the "purely masculine reasoning" of labor leaders and Marxists. The labor leaders' concentration upon "strikes for higher wages was based on man's economic need of supporting his family, and that was a shallow principle upon which to found a new civilization." "To blame everything upon the capitalist and the environment produced by capitalism," as Marxists did, focused attention upon "merely one of the elements of the problem." Unlimited reproduction, she argued, preceded and indeed caused capitalism, not the reverse. She was, furthermore, "enough of a feminist to resent the fact that woman and her requirements were not being taken into account in reconstructing this new world about which all were talking." Men would seek solutions to social ills in vain "as long as the mother remains the passive victim of blind instinct, instead of the conscious, responsible instrument of the life-force." The key to American social problems, she concluded, rested more in controlling the production of babies than in altering the distribution of goods.[13]

Mrs. Sanger was not the first of the New York rebels to find social significance in contraception. Indeed, Emma Goldman's belief in the right of women to control their own motherhood predated the twentieth century. Nearly two decades before Sanger nursed in East Side immigrant slums, Goldman had served those same districts as nurse and midwife. She also had turned down the many insistent requests of pregnant women to perform abortions, for she understood the serious risks of illicit operations, and she knew no preventive methods. Then in 1900 she attended a Neo-Malthusian conference in Paris, where she heard lengthy arguments for family limitation and witnessed demonstrations of contraceptive methods. Returning to America with contraceptives and printed instructions, Miss Goldman lectured on voluntary motherhood. Still she regarded family limitation as only one aspect of her work.[14] A "friend of Emma Goldman and other anarchists from whom she got her first ideas of birth control," Sanger kept a certain distance from the sharp-tongued Goldman: "Though I disliked both her ideas and her methods I admired her; she was really like a spring house-cleaning to the sloppy thinking of the average American."[15] Sanger was a woman in search of a mission who found it in part through anarchism; Goldman's mission was anarchism.

Although Sanger had forsaken nursing to proclaim the panacea of birth control, her knowledge of the physiology and psychology of sex, the movements for family limitation, and the techniques of contraception was discouragingly vague and partial. She set about reading Havelock Ellis' multi-volume *Studies in the Psychology of Sex* and foraged through various New York City libraries without uncovering the technical information she sought. Gradually she warmed to the advice of city rebels that she ought to make the same pilgrimage to Paris and the French syndicalists that Emma Goldman had undertaken more than a decade earlier. William Sanger, who wished to pursue painting in Paris, also welcomed the 1913 trip. In Paris he set up a studio on Montparnasse while Margaret met Sorel's disciples, who passed along their theories and practices concerning family limitation. Soon anxious to return to America to put her knowledge to social use, Margaret sailed for home at the end of the year with the children in tow and her husband cut adrift. Once defined, her humanitarian mission led beyond the bounds of marriage—"the interests of each had widened beyond those of the other."[16]

Margaret Sanger opened her planned two-part campaign for anarchistic feminism with the *Woman Rebel,* first issued in March 1914 and directed to the working-class woman. Taking its slogan of "No Gods, No Masters" from an I.W.W. handbill circulated at the Lawrence strike of 1912, *Rebel* was distributed by I.W.W. locals and at Emma Goldman's lectures. The first issue featured a tribute to Mary Wollstonecraft, Goldman's address on "free motherhood," the I.W.W. preamble, and an article urging contraception as a weapon in the struggle against the "capitalist class." Having condemned conventional marriage as a form of property regulation which reduced women to sex chattels, Mrs. Sanger looked forward to its ultimate transformation into a "voluntary association." Only then would there be a "new character, a new essence of personality, a new individuality." Sanger and her *Rebel* friends coined the term "birth control" to designate the "new movement" which they launched, a cause somewhat distinct from socialism and labor unionism and yet carrying social implications that extended well beyond contraception. The *Rebel* produced immediate and "extraordinary results, striking vibrations that brought contacts, messages, inquiries, pamphlets, books, and even some money."[17]

However, few of these "striking vibrations" emanated from the cadres or leadership of the organized feminist movement in America, not even from its more militant contingent. She "struck no responsive chord" in Charlotte Gilman. Sanger charged that feminists like Gilman were trying to free woman "from the new economic ideology but were doing nothing to free her from her biological subservience to man, which was the true cause of her enslavement":

> It seemed unbelievable that they could be serious in occupying themselves with what I regarded as trivialities when mothers within a stone's throw of their meetings were dying shocking deaths. Who cared whether a woman kept her Christian name—Mary Smith instead of Mrs. John Jones? Who cared whether she wore her wedding ring? Who cared about her demand for the right to work? Hundreds of thousands of laundresses, cloakmakers, scrub women, servants, telephone girls, shop workers would gladly have changed places with the Feminists in return for the right to have leisure, to be lazy a little now and then. When I suggested that the basis of feminism might be the right to be a mother regardless of church or state, their inherited prejudices were instantly aroused. They were still subject to the age-old, masculine atmosphere compounded of protection and dominance.[18]

Since, like Gilman, Sanger challenged the contention that suffrage would cure the major feminine disabilities, she also received little sympathy from suffragists. Sanger's rejection of suffragists, mainstream progressives, "idealists and reformers who think that by the ballot society may be led to an earthly paradise" was even more emphatic than Gilman's. Mrs. Sanger recalled the time when a group of striking women laundry workers told her "that we women might be dead and buried if we waited for politicians and lawmakers to right our wrongs." She joined the laundresses in questioning "how much any male politician could understand of the wrongs inflicted upon poor working women."[19]

The second part of Sanger's campaign attacked the so-called Comstock Law of 1873, which prohibited the mailing, transporting, or importing of "obscene, lewd, or lascivious" articles, including all contraceptive devices and information. That the national government, seconded by the states and supported by the churches, would attempt to prevent working-class women from learning how to control their reproductive functions seemed altogether logical to this anarchistic feminist. Refusal to honor a law of capitalistic subjection was equally in keeping with her ideological position. Thus she had a fellow anarchist secretly print *Family Limitation,* which Sanger wrote for women with a limited vocabulary to explain the contraceptive methods of the French syndicalists. First printed in a surreptitious edition of 100,000, *Family Limitation* was ultimately translated into thirteen languages and reprinted in more than ten million copies. The federal authorities, however, chose to bring a nine-count indictment against her for violating the Comstock Law with the *Rebel.*

Not prepared to defend herself when called to trial in October 1914, Mrs. Sanger fled to England. The next ten months abroad deeply influenced her developing mission by narrowing her attention to birth and population control and broadening her knowledge of the movement's history and rationale. She increased her understanding of birth control as an important medical matter and received a substantial and systematic exposure to sexual psychology. The First World War would eventually destroy the progressive era, sour the American rebellion, and eliminate radical influence. But thanks to her brief European exile, Margaret Sanger learned how to adapt her mission to changed conditions.

She drew important nourishment for her movement from the leaders of the English Neo-Malthusian League. They sketched the history of the movement for their rather uninformed American guest: Starting with Thomas Malthus' predictions that the number of people would inevitably outstrip food production, they continued her education by describing the support that the utilitarian liberal John Stuart Mill and the utopian socialist Robert Owen had given to efforts for population control and by outlining the spectacular Charles Bradlaugh-Annie Besant trial, which had established the legal right to circulate contraceptive information throughout Great Britain. Instead of giving the advice of Malthus to marry late, his later followers proposed early marriage, the use of contraceptives, and family size determined by the father's earning capacity. Margaret lamented only that "the emphasis was still placed on the social and economic aspects rather than the personal tragedies of women."[20]

Of still greater importance was her introduction to Dr. Havelock Ellis. "I have never felt about any other person as I do about Havelock Ellis," she later confided. She "developed a reverence, an affection, and a love which have strengthened with the years." Ellis designed a systematic reading program for her, answered her questions in detail, and explained his own ideas on sex and population control at length. "He, beyond any other person, had been able to clarify the question of sex and free it from the smudginess connected with it from the beginning of Christianity, raise it from the dark cellar, set it on a higher plane."[21]

She accepted Ellis' rejection of both "that superstition of the inferiority of women" central to male supremacist thought and feminist denials of fundamental differences between the sexes. Ellis believed that the "banner of Equality" under which feminists often fought, "while a wholesome and necessary assertion in the social and political realms," lacked biological foundation. His was not "the abstract demand of a mere class for equality, but the affirmation that the two halves of the race are compensatory in their unlikeness, and that so long as each fails to carry its due weight in life humanity has not attained complete development."[22]

After granting the wisdom of equal social and political rights for women, Ellis and Sanger nevertheless insisted that woman's "special sphere" remained in maternity, child rearing, and domestic activity, while man's lay in industry, invention, and the arts outside the home. "Woman breeds and tends; man provides; it remains so even when the spheres tend to overlap. This is demonstrated over and over again from all parts of the world, among all kinds of races, in every period, under any civilization." But woman's greatest association "with Nature's main concern," reproduction, cultivates the deepest and most important human experiences. It increases her sensitivity to the great, interior sexual drives at the same time that it exposes her to subjugation by the omnipotent and less sensitive male.[23]

Ellis shared much of the Romantic philosophy preached by the New York rebels and accepted by Margaret Sanger concerning the liberation of human emotions. Orthodox socialists emphasized the impact of active social or external factors upon the relatively passive interior life, whereas Ellis and Sanger thought primarily of freeing the active internal being from the restraints of exterior forms. They considered the sexual drive an important part of the deepest and most volatile human feelings and a catalyst for enormous creative potential. Human creativity and fulfillment, however, were possible only when disciplined self-expression was permitted for both sexes without interference from such external controls as conventional marriage. Woman, whose erotic needs and potential had been depressed or dismissed by the male-dominated world, suffered a special loss, since her natural sexual sensitivity was alleged to be superior to man's.[24]

Unlike an overwhelming number of earlier feminists, Margaret Sanger romanticized sex and consistently included sexual fulfillment as a significant element in her thought. Marital happiness, she argued, must be achieved by conscious effort and rested in important measure upon sexual fulfillment. Employing one of Ellis' similes, Sanger compared the sex act to a dance or symphony in which each part held its own delight and followed without break to the harmonic consummation "in which two humans are no longer separate and distinct persons, but in which their beings are co-mingled in a new and higher unity."[25] But there could be little harmonic consummation where the woman's sexual drives were inhibited or where she lived in constant fear of conception.

By learning about and practicing birth control, woman "denies that the sole purpose of sexual activity is procreation, . . . that sex should be reduced to the level of sensual lust, or that woman should permit herself to be the instrument of its satisfaction." By "increasing and differentiating her love demands," she elevated sex "into another sphere, whereby it may subserve and enhance the possibility of individual and human expression." Sanger believed, therefore, that man would profit from woman's emancipation, for "in the liberation of womankind, all of humanity will experience the joys of a new and fuller freedom."[26]

In early 1915 Margaret Sanger visited Dr. Johannes Rutgers' pioneer birth-control clinic, established at The Hague under the spreading influence of Neo-Malthusianism several decades earlier. She found social conditions admirable in those Dutch provinces where clinics operated—labor conditions were better, more children went to school for more years, fewer professional prostitutes solicited, and better public health and physical fitness existed.

Mrs. Sanger began to reflect upon the implications for the American birth-control movement of what she was learning during her exile. Most of her conclusions led away from anarchistic rebellion and towards sustained reform from a narrower and more popular ideological base. Her English friends contended that she should concentrate her energies exclusively on the issue of birth control and shelve stock anarchist targets. Ellis warned against "being too reckless and smashing your head against a blank wall, for not one rebel, or even many rebels, can crush law by force." To modify the law "needs *skill* even more than it needs strength."[27] Uninterrupted and systematic reading had broadened and deepened her understanding of contraception and grounded her rationale for birth control more firmly in the Neo-Malthusian tradition. "We beyond the Atlantic were still uncertain of our ethics, and even of our morals," she stated. "We needed the sanction of British public opinion and the approval of their great philosophers, so that we could be strong in our beliefs."[28]

The trip to Holland also "revolutionized" her thinking. Now fully convinced that contraception was fundamentally a medical matter and that clinics were a feasible means of accomplishing the medical objective, she no longer looked at birth control as primarily "a struggle for free speech," for free public access to contraceptive information. Irrevocably parting company with Emma Goldman's birth-control efforts on ideological and technical grounds, Mrs. Sanger concluded that "only doctors had the requisite knowledge of anatomy and physiology and training in gynecology to examine properly and prescribe accurately."[29] If birth control as panacea for the liberation of women, children, and the poor required the good offices of doctors to succeed, then the movement would have to take care that its ideology and strategies were not altogether uncongenial to those middle-class professionals.

Events in the United States overtook Margaret Sanger's exile. The movement she now felt confident to direct was booming under the diverse leadership of anarchists and suffragist-feminists. Neither group pursued the kind of program that she understood to be necessary, and either might give the movement a permanent tone unless she acted quickly. Anxious to draw the exiled Margaret out of hiding, Anthony Comstock set a trap in late 1914 for William Sanger, newly returned to New York from Paris. A decoy came to the Sanger residence and begged the unsuspecting and estranged husband for a copy of Margaret's pamphlet, *Family Limitation,* "to distribute amongst the poor people he worked with."[30] William fell for the ploy, and Comstock himself arrested his prey for violating the state law against distribution of obscene, lewd literature. Sanger's trial, which aroused considerable public support for birth control as a free speech issue, mobilized the radicals. Emma Goldman began a coast-to-coast tour in 1915 to speak explicitly on contraception. The great Socialist party leader, Eugene V. Debs, and the famous I.W.W. organizer, Elizabeth Gurley Flynn, were only two of the many radicals who pressed for the formation of birth-control groups across the country. Still more ominous from Margaret's new perspective was the March 1915 reorganization of the National Birth Control League (N.B.C.L.) under the leadership of upper middle-class liberals exclusively dedicated to the repeal of all laws that made the dissemination of contraceptive information and devices illegal.

Immediately upon her return to New York in October 1915, Mrs. Sanger declared her readiness to stand trial on the *Rebel* indictment. Ignoring the advice of powerful liberal lawyers and radicals, she refused to plead guilty, make a deal with the government, or argue the case on other than constitutional grounds. Her prominent British friends, including H. G. Wells, addressed a public letter to President Woodrow Wilson asking the government to stop prosecution of the case. With public outcry growing, the government lawyers determined not to make a martyr of Mrs. Sanger by prosecuting her.

She capitalized on the public interest generated by the threatened trial with a three-month cross-country lecture tour in early 1916. At first speaking mostly to radical and working-class audiences, she described her nursing experiences on New York's East Side, urged unhampered dissemination of sexual and contraceptual knowledge, warned of the dangers of abortion and the birth of defectives, dismissed charity as a solution to social ills, and demanded the emancipation of women. Birth control, she argued along Neo-Malthusian lines, should be practiced when parents have transmissible disease, when a wife's disease would be aggravated by pregnancy, when parents were adolescents or had subnormal children, when the husband's earning capacity was inadequate, and when a couple had been married less than two years or had had a child in the previous two or three years.

Speaking to social workers in Indianapolis and to middle-class women in Denver especially pleased her, for such audiences "had the power to change public opinion." The poor, who she thought knew the importance of contraception all too well, did not need her lecture; they needed clinics where birth-control information and devices could be distributed. To establish clinics without legal harrassment required the support of "reflective hearers who not only themselves used contraceptives, but who advanced thought through literature, discussions, and papers." "Stimulating them offered the best possibility of getting something done."[31]

The next move in the Sanger campaign came in October 1916, when Margaret and her sister, Ethel Byrne, opened a clinic in Brownsville, an immigrant section of Brooklyn. Although without a doctor, the clinic emulated those she had visited in Holland. It dramatized the desire of many working-class women for contraception: Over 150 lined up before the clinic opened its doors on the first day. It demonstrated the efficacy of the anarchist tactic of direct action as opposed to legislative lobbying. Instead of the N.B.C.L.'s "slow and tortuous" attempts to revise the law through the legislature, Sanger set the stage for a challenge of the constitutionality of the prohibitive New York statute in the courts.[32] And, finally, in the event of her expected arrest, the clinic offered even greater opportunities for publicity and support.

The ploy succeeded beyond expectation. Following the arrest of the clinic's personnel, a "Committee of 100" prominent New York ladies gathered to support them and to work for revision of the obnoxious state law. "Formerly, a few women of wealth but of liberal tendencies had been actively concerned in the movement," Mrs. Sanger recorded. Now "women who were prominent socially were coming to believe on principle that birth control should not be denied to the masses. The subject was in the process of ceasing to be tagged as radical and revolutionary, and becoming admittedly humanitarian."[33] Her friends quickly gathered the new converts into the fold of the New York Birth Control League (N.Y.B.C.L.), organized in December 1916 to provide an institutional base to the Sanger program.

In spite of the support of fifty socially prominent women who sat through the trial of Margaret's sister, the judge sentenced her to thirty days in jail. Following the example of the English suffragettes, Mrs. Byrne declared her intention to go on a hunger strike as a protest against imprisonment. The daily accounts of her unwavering resolve and failing health won so much additional public sympathy that the governor finally ordered her release. "It will be hard," noted the *New York Tribune,* "to make the youth of 1967 believe that in 1917 a woman was imprisoned for doing what Mrs. Byrne did."[34] Mrs. Sanger was also convicted and sentenced to thirty days in jail. On her release a crowd singing the "Marseillaise" greeted her at the prison gates. Although the superior courts upheld her conviction, they redefined the law to legalize birth-control clinics conducted by licensed physicians. The Brownsville clinic had accomplished its major tactical purposes.

During the years of the First World War, Margaret Sanger devoted much of her time to broadening her base of nonradical, middle-class supporters. She needed the endorsement of "writers, teachers, ministers, editors, who form a class dictating, if not creating, public opinion" to establish public acceptance of contraception. She knew from her clinical experiences that she needed the help of scientists and technicians to create cheaper and simpler contraceptive devices in order to make the practice of birth control feasible for most of the poor. She required the aid of the medical profession to dispense contraceptive information and devices. She wanted, finally, the help of social workers, public health officials, and other welfare professionals to carry the birth-control message directly to the poverty stricken and the mentally or physically defective.[35] Mrs. Sanger made innumerable personal appearances, encouraged the establishment of local birth-control groups, and published the *Birth Control Review* as part of the wide-ranging educational campaign for professional support. Unlike the *Woman Rebel's* raucous and irreverent radicalism, the *Review* focused with genteel decorum upon scientific and quasi-scientific matters relating to contraception.

As a part of her effort to woo the middle classes across the nation, she also wrote two books—her "heart book," *Woman and the New Race* (1920), and her "head book," *The Pivot of Civilization* (1922). She let loose her "pent-up feelings" on feminism and birth control in the draft of *Woman,* which she wrote rapidly and sent to William E. Williams, former managing editor of the Kansas City *Star,* to edit. *Woman,* at the stiff price of two dollars each, sold 250,000 copies largely to middle-class women, a fact which pleased Mrs. Sanger. But her "heart ache[d] to know that poor women who could ill afford it were buying the book" hoping to find detailed information on contraceptive methods.[36]

During the twenties and thirties Margaret Sanger's pursuit of middle-class support for the liberation of women and the poor through birth control succeeded only in part. Her middle-class backers, who often lacked her wider social vision, reduced the reform impulse which she brought to the movement. As she reviewed the growing momentum for birth control in the late 1930's, Margaret Sanger knew that the movement had not abolished any given social injustice, although research towards the development of cheaper and more easily applied contraceptives was well under way and public acceptance of birth control had advanced markedly. Yet "the fact remains that . . . progress has been painfully slow. Countless women still die before their time because the bit of knowledge essential to very life is still not theirs. Birth control must seep down until it reaches the strata where the need is greatest; until it has been democratized there can be no rest."[37]

But the new biological control and sexual freedom which the prewar rebels, Romantic English sex psychologists, and Margaret Sanger herself had welcomed did not even lead the contraceptive-using middle-class women of the twenties and later to modify social or domestic patterns in substantial ways. "With God, Freud, Marx, Nature, and a host of lesser authorities apparently agreed that woman's unique character was sexual and her destiny maternal," concluded the feminist historian William L. O'Neill, "ambitious women eager to play out the old drama of emancipation had little working for them."[38] Charlotte Gilman, who had continually charged that Western civilization was oversexed, sensed the dangers in the renewed emphasis upon sexual differences. Separateness, she warned, is inherently inegalitarian. Contraception could readily coexist with the sexual objectification of women, and emphasis upon the special inner feminine development and unique sexual nature could blunt the drive to social, economic, and political equality by minimizing the ways in which the sexes are alike.

Margaret Sanger saw sexual differentiation and liberation in another light. To her they offered an opportunity to complement the goal of social, economic, and political equality for a greater number. Without a similar mission or comparable needs, the new middle-class woman more often treated sexual liberation as a substitute for equality and thus fell victim to "the feminine mystique."

NOTES

1. Margaret Sanger, *My Fight for Birth Control* (New York: Farrar & Rinehart, Incorporated, 1931), 5. Both Sanger's *Birth Control* and Margaret Sanger, *An Autobiography* (New York: W. W. Norton & Company, Inc., 1938), provide the best printed source material for her biography. Two current biographies are also especially useful: David M. Kennedy, *Birth Control in America: The Career of Margaret Sanger* (New Haven: Yale University Press, 1970), and Emily Taft Douglas, *Margaret Sanger: Pioneer of the Future* (New York: Holt, Rinehart and Winston, 1970).

2. Sanger, *Autobiography,* 13, 493, 494; Sanger, *Birth Control,* 5.

3. Sanger, *Birth Control,* 6, 7; Sanger, *Autobiography,* 17, 21.

4. Sanger, *Birth Control,* 9; Sanger, *Autobiography,* 38–39.

5. Sanger, *Birth Control,* 31; Sanger, *Autobiography,* 45.

6. Sanger, *Autobiography,* 66–67.

7. For a description and analysis of the cultural and intellectual rebellion, see Henry F. May, *The End of American Innocence: A Study of the First Years of Our Own Time, 1912–1917* (Chicago: Quadrangle Books, Inc., 1964 paperback reissue of 1959 edition), 219–329.

8. Douglas, *Sanger,* 58–59; Sanger, *Autobiography,* 496.

9. Sanger, *Autobiography,* 182.

10. Douglas, *Sanger,* 140–141.

11. Sanger, *Autobiography,* 70, 75; Kennedy, *Birth Control,* 28.

12. Sanger, *Autobiography,* 85.

13. Margaret Sanger, *The Pivot of Civilization* (New York: Brentano's Publishers, 1922), 8, 51–52, 163–164; Sanger, *Autobiography,* 85.

14. Richard Drinnon, *Rebel in Paradise: A Biography of Emma Goldman* (Chicago: University of Chicago Press, 1961), 165–172.

15. Hutchins Hapgood, as quoted in Kennedy, *Birth Control,* 20; Sanger, *Autobiography,* 72.

16. Sanger, *Autobiography,* 136.

17. Quoted in Kennedy, *Birth Control,* 22–23; Sanger, *Autobiography,* 107–108, 111–112.

18. Sanger, *Autobiography,* 107–109.

19. Sanger, *Pivot,* 4–5.

20. Sanger, *Autobiography,* 128.

21. Sanger, *Autobiography,* 135, 141; Sanger, *Birth Control,* 102.

22. Havelock Ellis, *Man and Woman: A Study of Secondary and Tertiary Sexual Characters* (Boston: Houghton Mifflin Company, 1929 revised edition of 1894 work), iv-v.

23. Ellis, *Man and Woman,* 468–469, 479.

24. Douglas, *Sanger,* 70–79. For a more extended discussion of the new

sexual ethic, see William L. O'Neill, *Divorce in the Progressive Era* (New Haven: Yale University Press, 1967), 89–167.

25. Margaret Sanger, *Happiness in Marriage* (Elmsford, New York: Maxwell Reprint Company, 1969 reissue of 1926 edition), 132. Sanger's *Happiness* is a decidedly Romantic and quite general early version of a contemporary marriage manual.

26. Sanger, *Pivot,* 211–213, 218–219.

27. Quoted in Kennedy, *Birth Control,* 30.

28. Sanger, *Autobiography,* 131.

29. Sanger, *Autobiography,* 152, 414.

30. Quoted in Kennedy, *Birth Control,* 72.

31. Sanger, *Autobiography,* 202.

32. Sanger, *Autobiography,* 211.

33. Sanger, *Autobiography,* 229.

34. Quoted in Kennedy, *Birth Control,* 86.

35. Sanger, *Pivot,* 15, 221.

36. Sanger, *Autobiography,* 266, 299, 362; Douglas, *Sanger,* 138–139. Margaret Sanger, *Woman and the New Race* (New York: Brentano's Publishers, 1920), was reprinted in a limited edition by Pergamon Press, Maxwell Reprint Co., Elmsford, New York, in 1969.

37. Sanger, *Autobiography,* 494.

38. William L. O'Neill, *Everyone Was Brave: The Rise and Fall of Feminism in America* (Chicago: Quadrangle Books, Inc., 1969), 316.

WOMAN AND THE NEW RACE*
(1920)

I. WOMAN'S ERROR AND HER DEBT

The most far-reaching social development of modern times is the revolt of woman against sex servitude. The most important force in the remaking of the world is a free motherhood. Beside this force, the elaborate international programmes of modern statesmen are weak and superficial. Diplomats may formulate leagues of nations and nations may pledge their utmost strength to maintain them, statesmen may dream of reconstructing the world out of alliances, hegemonies and spheres of influence, but woman, continuing to produce explosive populations, will convert these pledges into the proverbial scraps of paper; or she may, by controlling birth, lift motherhood to the plane of a voluntary, intelligent function, and remake the world. When the world is thus remade, it will exceed the dream of statesman, reformer and revolutionist.

Only in recent years has woman's position as the gentler and weaker half of the human family been emphatically and generally questioned. Men assumed that this was woman's place; woman herself accepted it. It seldom occurred to anyone to ask whether she would go on occupying it forever.

Upon the mere surface of woman's organized protests there were no indications that she was desirous of achieving a fundamental change in her position. She claimed the right of suffrage and legislative regulation of her working hours, and asked that her property rights be equal to those of the man. None of these demands, however, affected directly the most vital factors of her existence. Whether she won her point or failed to win it, she remained a dominated weakling in a society controlled by men.

Woman's acceptance of her inferior status was the more real because it was unconscious. She had chained herself to her place in society and

* Reprinted by permission from Margaret Sanger, *Woman and the New Race* (New York: Brentano's, 1920). We gratefully acknowledge the generous consent of Grant Sanger, M.D.

the family through the maternal functions of her nature, and only chains thus strong could have bound her to her lot as a brood animal for the masculine civilizations of the world. In accepting her role as the "weaker and gentler half," she accepted that function. In turn, the acceptance of that function fixed the more firmly her rank as an inferior.

Caught in this "vicious circle," woman has, through her reproductive ability, founded and perpetuated the tyrannies of the Earth. Whether it was the tyranny of a monarchy, an oligarchy or a republic, the one indispensable factor of its existence was, as it is now, hordes of human beings—human beings so plentiful as to be cheap, and so cheap that ignorance was their natural lot. Upon the rock of an unenlightened, submissive maternity have these been founded; upon the product of such a maternity have they flourished.

No despot ever flung forth his legions to die in foreign conquest, no privilege-ruled nation ever erupted across its borders, to lock in death embrace with another, but behind them loomed the driving power of a population too large for its boundaries and its natural resources.

No period of low wages or of idleness with their want among the workers, no peonage or sweatshop, no child-labor factory, ever came into being, save from the same source. Nor have famine and plague been as much "acts of God" as acts of too prolific mothers. They, also, as all students know, have their basic causes in over-population.

The creators of over-population are the women, who, while wringing their hands over each fresh horror, submit anew to their task of producing the multitudes who will bring about the *next* tragedy of civilization.

While unknowingly laying the foundations of tyrannies and providing the human tinder for racial conflagrations, woman was also unknowingly creating slums, filling asylums with insane, and institutions with other defectives. She was replenishing the ranks of the prostitutes, furnishing grist for the criminal courts and inmates for prisons. Had she planned deliberately to achieve this tragic total of human waste and misery, she could hardly have done it more effectively.

Woman's passivity under the burden of her disastrous task was almost altogether that of ignorant resignation. She knew virtually nothing about her reproductive nature and less about the consequences of her excessive child-bearing. It is true that, obeying the inner urge of their natures, *some* women revolted. They went even to the extreme of infanticide and abortion. Usually their revolts were not general enough. They fought as individuals, not as a mass. In the mass they sank back into blind and hopeless subjection. They went on breeding with staggering rapidity those numberless, undesired children who become the clogs and the destroyers of civilizations.

Today, however, woman is rising in fundamental revolt. Even her efforts at mere reform are . . . steps in that direction. Underneath each of them is the feminine urge to complete freedom. Millions of women are asserting their right to voluntary motherhood. They are determined to decide for themselves whether they shall become mothers, under what conditions and when. This is the fundamental revolt referred to. It is for woman the key to the temple of liberty.

Even as birth control is the means by which woman attains basic freedom, so it is the means by which she must and will uproot the evil she has wrought through her submission. As she has unconsciously and ignorantly brought about social disaster, so must and will she consciously and intelligently *undo* that disaster and create a new and a better order.

The task is hers. It cannot be avoided by excuses, nor can it be delegated. It is not enough for woman to point to the self-evident domination of man. Nor does it avail to plead the guilt of rulers and the exploiters of labor. It makes no difference that she does not formulate industrial systems nor that she is an instinctive believer in social justice. In her submission lies her error and her guilt. By her failure to withhold the multitudes of children who have made inevitable the most flagrant of our social evils, she incurred a debt to society. Regardless of her own wrongs, regardless of her lack of opportunity and regardless of all other considerations, *she* must pay that debt.

She must not think to pay this debt in any superficial way. She cannot pay it with palliatives —with child-labor laws, prohibition, regulation of prostitution and agitation against war. Political nostrums and social panaceas are but incidentally and superficially useful. They do not touch the source of the social disease.

War, famine, poverty and oppression of the workers will continue while woman makes life cheap. They will cease only when she limits her reproductivity and human life is no longer a thing to be wasted.

Two chief obstacles hinder the discharge of this tremendous obligation. The first and the lesser is the legal barrier. Dark-Age laws would still deny to her the knowledge of her reproductive nature. Such knowledge is indispensable to intelligent motherhood and she must achieve it, despite absurd statutes and equally absurd moral canons.

The second and more serious barrier is her own ignorance of the extent and effect of her submission. Until she knows the evil her subjection has wrought to herself, to her progeny and to the world at large, she cannot wipe out that evil.

To get rid of these obstacles is to invite attack from the forces of reaction which are so strongly entrenched in our present-day society. It means warfare in every phase of her life. Nevertheless, at whatever cost, she must emerge from her ignorance and assume her responsibility.

She can do this only when she has awakened to a knowledge of herself and of the consequences of her ignorance. The first step is birth control. Through birth control she will attain to voluntary motherhood. Having attained this, the basic freedom of her sex, she will cease to enslave herself and the mass of humanity. Then, through the understanding of the intuitive forward urge within her, she will not stop at patching up the world; she will remake it.

II. WOMAN'S STRUGGLE FOR FREEDOM

Behind all customs of whatever nature; behind all social unrest, behind all movements, behind all revolutions, are great driving forces, which in their action and reaction upon conditions, give character to civilization. If, in seeking to discover the source of a custom, of a movement or of a revolution, we stop at surface conditions, we shall never discern more than a superficial aspect of the underlying truth.

This is the error into which the historian has almost universally fallen. It is also a common error among sociologists. It is the fashion nowadays, for instance, to explain all social unrest in terms of economic conditions. This is a valuable working theory and has done much to awaken men to their injustice toward one another, but it ignores the forces *within* humanity which drive it to revolt. It is these forces, rather than the conditions upon which they react, that are the important factors. Conditions change, but the animating force goes on forever.

So, too, with woman's struggle for emancipation. Women in all lands and all ages have instinctively desired family limitation. Usually this desire has been laid to economic pressure. Frequently the pressure has existed, but the driving force behind woman's aspiration *toward freedom* has lain deeper. It has asserted itself among the rich and among the poor, among the intelligent and the unintelligent. It has been manifested in such horrors as infanticide, child abandonment and abortion.

The only term sufficiently comprehensive to define this motive power of woman's nature is the *feminine spirit*. That spirit manifests itself most frequently in motherhood, but it is greater than maternity. Woman herself, all that she is, all that she has ever been, all that she may be, is but the outworking of this inner spiritual urge. Given free play, this supreme law of her nature asserts itself in beneficent ways; interfered with, it becomes destructive. Only when we understand this can we comprehend the efforts of the feminine spirit to liberate itself.

When the outworking of this force within her is hampered by the bearing and the care of too many children, woman rebels. Hence it is that, from time immemorial, she has sought some form of family limitation. When she has not employed such measures consciously, she has done so instinctively. Where laws, customs and religious restrictions do not prevent, she has recourse to contraceptives. Otherwise, she resorts to child abandonment, abortion and infanticide, or resigns herself hopelessly to enforced maternity.

These violent means of freeing herself from the chains of her own reproductivity have been most in evidence where economic conditions have made the care of children even more of a burden than it would otherwise have been. But, whether in the luxurious home of the Athenian, the poverty-ridden dwelling of the Chinese, or the crude hut of the primitive Australian savage, the woman whose development has been interfered with by the bearing and rearing of children has tried desperately, frantically, too often in vain, to take and hold her freedom.

Individual men have sometimes acquiesced in these violent measures, but in the mass they have opposed. By law, by religious canons, by public opinion, by penalties ranging all the way from ostracism to beheading, they have sought to crush this effort. Neither threat of hell nor the infliction of physical punishment has availed. Women have deceived and dared, resisted and defied the power of church and state. Quietly, desperately, consciously, they have marched to the gates of death to gain the liberty which the feminine spirit has desired. . . .

Society, in dealing with the feminine spirit, has its choice of clearly defined alternatives. It can continue to resort to violence in an effort to enslave the elemental urge of womanhood, making of woman a mere instrument of reproduction and punishing her when she revolts. Or, it can permit her to choose whether she shall become a mother and how many children she will have. It can go on trying to crush that which is uncrushable, or it can recognize woman's claim to freedom, and cease to impose diverting and destructive barriers. If we choose the latter course, we must not only remove all restrictions upon the use of scientific contraceptives, but we must legalize and encourage their use.

This problem comes home with peculiar force to the people of America. Do we want the millions of abortions performed annually to be multiplied? Do we want the precious, tender qualities of womanhood, so much needed for our racial development, to perish in these sordid, abnormal experiences? Or, do we wish to permit woman to find her way to fundamental freedom through safe, unobjectionable, scientific means? We have our choice. Upon our answer to these questions depends in a tremendous degree the character and the capabilities of the future American race.

IV. TWO CLASSES OF WOMEN

. . . Most women who belong to the workers' families have no accurate or reliable knowledge of contraceptives, and are, therefore, bringing children into the world so rapidly that they, their families and their class are overwhelmed with numbers. Out of these numbers . . . have grown many of the burdens with which society in general is weighted; out of them have come, also, the want, disease, hard living conditions and general misery of the workers.

The women of this class are the greatest sufferers of all. Not only do they bear the material hardships and deprivations in common with the rest of the family, but in the case of the mother, these are intensified. It is the man and the child who have first call upon the insufficient amount of food. It is the man and the child who get the recreation, if there is any to be had, for the man's hours of labor are usually limited by law or by his labor union.

It is the woman who suffers first from hunger, the woman whose clothing is least adequate, the woman who must work all hours, even though she is not compelled, as in the case of millions, to go into a factory to add to her husband's scanty income. It is she, too, whose health breaks first and most hopelessly, under the long hours of work, the drain of frequent childbearing, and often almost constant nursing of babies. There are no eight-hour laws to protect the mother against overwork and toil in the home; no laws to protect her against ill health and the diseases of pregnancy and reproduction. In fact there has been almost no thought or consideration given for the protection of the mother in the home of the workingman.

There are no general health statistics to tell the full story of the physical ills suffered by women as a result of too great reproductivity. But we get some light upon conditions through the statistics on maternal mortality, compiled by Dr. Grace L. Meigs for the Children's Bureau of the United States Department of Labor. These figures do not include the deaths of women suffering from diseases complicated by pregnancy.

"In 1913, in this country at least 15,000 women, it is estimated, died from conditions caused by childbirth; about 7,000 of these died from childbed fever and the remaining 8,000 from diseases now known to be to a great extent preventable or curable," says Dr. Meigs in her summary. "Physicians and statisticians agree that these figures are a *great underestimate.*"

Think of it—the needless deaths of 15,000 women a "great underestimate"! Yet even this number means that virtually every hour of the day and night two women die as the result of childbirth in the healthiest and supposedly the most progressive country in the world. . . .

Still, leaving out all the hundreds of thousands of women who die because pregnancy has complicated serious diseases, Dr. Meigs finds that "in 1913, the death rate per 100,000 of the population from all conditions caused by childbirth was little lower than that from typhoid fever. This rate would be almost quadrupled if only the group of the population which can be affected, women of child-bearing ages, were considered. In 1913, childbirth caused more deaths among women 15 to 44 years old than any disease except tuberculosis."

From what sort of homes come these deaths from childbirth? Most of them occur in overcrowded dwellings, where food, care, sanitation, nursing and medical attention are inadequate. Where do we find most of the tuberculosis and much of the other disease which is aggravated by pregnancy? In the same sort of home.

The deadly chain of misery is all too plain to anyone who takes the trouble to observe it. A woman of the working class marries and with her husband lives in a degree of comfort upon his earnings. Her household duties are not beyond her strength. Then the children begin to come—one, two, three, four, possibly five or more. The earnings of the husband do not increase as rapidly as the family does. Food, clothing and general comfort in the home grow less as the numbers of the family increase. The woman's work grows heavier, and her strength is less with each child. Possibly—probably—she has to go into a factory to add to her husband's earnings. There she toils, doing her housework at night. Her health goes, and the crowded conditions and lack of necessities in the home help to bring about disease—especially tuberculosis. Under the circumstances, the woman's chances of recovering from each succeeding childbirth grow less. Less too are the chances of the child's surviving. . . .

Nor is the full story of the woman's sufferings yet told. Grievous as is her material condition, her spiritual deprivations are still greater. By the very fact of its existence, mother love demands its expression toward the child. By that same fact, it becomes a necessary factor in the child's development. The mother of too many children, in a crowded home where want, ill health and antagonism are perpetually created, is deprived of this simplest personal expression. She can give nothing to her child of herself, of her personality. Training is impossible and sympathetic guidance equally so. Instead, such a mother is tired, nervous, irritated and ill-tempered; a determent, often, instead of a help to her children. Motherhood becomes a disaster and childhood a tragedy.

It goes without saying that this woman loses also all opportunity of personal expression outside her home. She has neither a chance to develop social qualities nor to indulge in social pleasures. The feminine element in her—that spirit which blossoms forth now and then in women free from such burdens—cannot assert itself. She can contribute nothing to the well-being of the community. She is a breeding machine and a drudge—she is not an asset but a liability to her neighborhood, to her class, to society. She can be nothing as long as she is denied means of limiting her family.

In sharp contrast with these women who ignorantly bring forth large families and who thereby enslave themselves, we find a few women who have one, two or three children or no children at all. These women, with the exception of the childless ones, live full-rounded lives. They are found not only in the ranks of the rich and the well-to-do, but in the ranks of labor as well. They have but one point of basic difference from their enslaved sisters—they are not burdened with the rearing of large families.

We have no need to call upon the historian, the sociologist nor the statistician for our knowledge of this situation. We meet it every day in the ordinary routine of our lives. The women who are the great teachers, the great writers, the artists, musicians, physicians, the leaders of public movements, the great suffragists, reformers, labor leaders and revolutionaries are those who are not compelled to give lavishly of their physical and spiritual strength in bearing and rearing large families. The situation is too familiar for discussion. Where a woman with a large family is contributing directly to the progress of her times or the betterment of social conditions, it is usually because she has sufficient wealth to employ trained nurses, governesses, and others who perform the duties necessary to child rearing. She is a rarity and is universally recognized as such.

The women with small families, however, are free to make their choice of those social pleasures which are the right of every human being and necessary to each one's full development. They can be and are, each according to her individual capacity, comrades and companions to their husbands—a privilege denied to the mother of many children. Theirs is the opportunity to keep abreast of the times, to make and cultivate a varied circle of friends, to seek amusements as suits their taste and means, to know the meaning of real recreation. All these things remain unrealized desires to the prolific mother.

Women who have a knowledge of contraceptives are not compelled to make the choice between a maternal experience and a marred love life; they are not forced to balance motherhood against social and spiritual activities. Motherhood is for them to choose, as it should be for every woman to choose. Choosing to become mothers, they do not thereby shut themselves away from thorough companionship with their husbands, from friends, from culture, from all those manifold experiences which are necessary to the completeness and the joy of life.

Fit mothers of the race are these, the courted comrades of the men they choose, rather than the "slaves of slaves." For theirs is the magic power—the power of limiting their families to such numbers as will permit them to live full-rounded lives. Such lives are the expression of the feminine spirit which is woman *and all of her*—not merely art, nor professional skill, nor intellect—but all that woman is, or may achieve.

VI. CRIES OF DESPAIR AND SOCIETY'S PROBLEMS

Before we pass to a further consideration of our subject, shall we not pause to take a still closer look at the human misery wrought by the enslavement of women through unwilling motherhood? . . . Learn at first hand what it means to make a broken drudge of a woman who might have been the happy mother of a few strong children. Learn from the words of the victims of involuntary motherhood what it means to them, to their children and to society to force the physically unfit or the unwilling to bear children. When you have learned, stop to ask yourself what is the worth of the law, the moral code, the tradition, the religion, that for the sake of an outworn dogma of submission would wreck the lives of these women, condemn their progeny to pain, want, disease and helplessness. Ask yourself if these letters, these cries of despair, born of the anguish of woman's sex slavery are not in themselves enough to stop the mouths of the demagogues, the imperialists and the ecclesiastics who clamor for more and yet more children? And if the pain of others has no power to move your heart and stir your hands and brain to action, ask yourself the more selfish question: Can the children of these unfortunate mothers be other than a burden to society—a burden which reflects itself in innumerable phases of cost, crime and general social detriment? . . .

Each and every unwanted child is likely to be in some way a social liability. It is only the wanted child who is likely to be a social asset. If we have faith in this intuitive demand of the unfortunate mothers, if we understand both its dire and its hopeful significance, we shall dispose of those social problems which so insistently and menacingly confront us today. For the instinct of maternity to protect its own fruits, the instinct of womanhood to be free to give something besides surplus of children to the world, cannot go astray. The rising generation is always the material of progress, and motherhood is the agency for the improvement and the strengthening and guiding of that generation.

The excerpts contained in this chapter are typical of the letters which come to me by the thousands. They tell their own story, simply—sometimes ungrammatically and illiterately, but nevertheless irresistibly. It is the story of slow murder of the helpless by a society that shields itself behind ancient, inhuman moral creeds—which dares to weigh those dead creeds against the agony of the living who pray for the "mercy of death."

Can a mother who would "rather die" than bear more children serve society by bearing still others? Can children carried through nine months of dread and unspeakable mental anguish and born into an atmosphere of fear and anger, to grow up uneducated and in want, be a benefit to the world? Here is what the mother says:

> I have read in the paper about you and am very interested in Birth Control. I am a mother of four living children and one dead the oldest 10 and baby 22 months old. I am very nervous and sickly after my children. I would like you to advise me what to do to prevent from having any more as I would rather die than have another. I am keeping away from my husband as much as I can, but it causes quarrels and almost separation. All my babies have had marasmus in the first year of their lives and I almost lost my baby last summer. I always worry about my children so much. My husband works in a brass foundry it is not a very good job and living is so high that we have to live as cheap as possible. I've only got 2 rooms and kitchen and I do all my work and sewing which is very hard for me.

Shall this woman continue to be forced into a life of unnatural continence which further aggravates her ill health and produces constant discord? Shall she go on having children who come into being with a heritage of ill health and poverty, and who are bound to become public burdens? Or would it be the better policy to let motherhood follow its instinct to save itself, its offspring and society from these ills?

Or shall women be forced into abortion, as is testified by the mother whose daughters are mothers, and who, in the hope of saving them from both slavery and the destruction of their unborn children, wrote the letter which follows:

> I have born and raised 6 children and I know all the hardships of raising a large family. I am now

53 years old and past having children but I have 3 daughers that have 2 children each and they say they will die before they will have any more and every now and again they go to a doctor and get rid of one and some day I think it will kill them but they say they don't care for they will be better dead than live in hell with a big family and nothing to raise them on. It is for there sakes I wish you to give me that information.

What could the three women mentioned in this letter contribute to the well-being of the future American race? Nothing, except by doing exactly what they wish to do—refusing to bear children that they do not want and cannot care for. Their instinct is sound—but what is to be said of the position of society at large, which forces women who are in the grip of a sound instinct to seek repeated abortions in order to follow that instinct? Are we not compelling women to choose between inflicting injury upon themselves, their children and the community, and undergoing an abhorrent operation which kills the tenderness and delicacy of womanhood, even as it may injure or kill the body?

Will the offspring of a paralytic, who must perforce neglect the physical care and training of her children, enhance the common good by their coming? Here is a letter from a paralytic mother, whose days and nights are tortured by the thought of another child, and whose reason is tottering at the prospect of leaving her children without her care:

I sent for a copy of your magazine and now feel I must write you to see if you can help me.

I was a high school girl who married a day laborer seven years ago. In a few months I will again be a mother, the fourth child in less than six years. While carrying my babies am always partly paralyzed on one side. Do not know the cause but the doctor said at last birth we must be 'more careful,' as I could not stand having so many children. Am always very sick for a long time and have to have chloroform.

We can afford help only about 3 weeks, until I am on my feet again, after confinement. I work as hard as I can but my work and my children are always neglected. I wonder if my body does survive this next birth if my reason will.

It is terrible to think of bringing these little bodies and souls into the world without means or strength to care for them. And I can see no relief unless you give it to me or tell me where to get it. I am weaker each time and I know that this must be the last one, for it would be better for me to go, than to bring more neglected babies into the world. I can hardly sleep at night for worrying. Is there an answer for women like me? . . .

The very word "syphilis" brings a shudder to anyone who is familiar with the horrors of the malady. Not only in the suffering brought to the victim himself and in the danger of infecting others, but in the dire legacy of helplessness and disease which is left to the offspring of the syphilitic, is this the most destructive socially of all "plagues." Here is a letter which, as a criticism of our present public policy in regard to national waste and to contraceptives, defies comment:

I was left without a father when a girl of fourteen years old. I was the oldest child of five. My mother had no means of support except her two hands, so we worked at anything we could, my job being nurse girl at home while mother worked most of the time, as she could earn more money than I could, for she could do harder work. . . .

. . . At the age of seventeen I married a man, a brakeman on the ——— Railroad, who was eleven years older than I. He drank some and was a very frail-looking man, but I was very ignorant of the world and did not think of anything but making a home for myself and husband. After eleven months I had a little girl born to me. I did not want more children, but my mother-in-law told me it was a terrible sin to do anything to keep from having children and that the Lord only sent just what I could take care of and if I heard of anything to do I was told it was injurious, so I did not try.

In eleven months again, October 25, I had another little puny girl. In twenty-three months, Sept. 25th, I had a seven-lb. boy. In ten months, July 15, I had a seven-months baby that lived five hours. In eleven months, June 20, I had another little girl. In seventeen months, Nov. 30, another boy.

In nine months a four months' miscarriage. In twelve months another girl, and in three and a half years another girl.

All of these children were born into poverty; the father's health was always poor, and when the third girl was born he was discharged from the road because of his disability, yet he was still able to put children into the world. . . .

Now, Mrs. Sanger, I did not want those children, because even in my ignorance I had sense enough to know that I had no right to bring those children into such a world where they could not have decent care, for I was not able to do it myself nor hire it done. I prayed and I prayed that they would die when they were born. Praying did no good and today I have read and studied enough to know that I am the mother of seven living children and that I committed a crime by bringing them into the world, their father was syphilitic (I did not know about such things when I was a girl). . . .

I raised my family in a little college town in ——— and am well known there, for I made my living washing and working for the college people while I raised my little brood. I often wondered why those educated well-to-do people never had so many children. I have one married daughter who is tubercular, and she also has two little girls, only a year apart. I feel so bad about it, and write to ask you to send me information for her. Don't stop your good work; don't think it's not appreciated; for there are hundreds of women like myself who are not afraid to risk their lives to help you to get this information to poor women who need it.

There is no need to go on repeating these cries. These letters have come to me by the thousands. . . . Every ill that we are trying to cure today is reflected in them. The wife who through an unwilling continence drives her husband to prostitution; habitual drunkenness, which prohibition may or may not have disposed of as a social problem; mothers who toil in mills and whose children must follow them to that toil, adding to the long train of evils involved in child labor; mothers who have brought eight, ten, twelve or fifteen undernourished, weakly children into the world to become public burdens of one sort or another—all these and more, with the ever-present economic problem, and women who are remaining unmarried because they fear a large family which must exist in want; men who are living abnormal lives for the same reason. All the social handicaps and evils of the day are woven into these letters—and out of each of them rises these challenging facts: First, oppressed motherhood knows that the cure for these evils lies in birth control; second, society has not yet learned to permit motherhood to stand guard for itself, its children, the common good and the coming race. . . .

VIII. BIRTH CONTROL—A PARENT'S PROBLEM OR WOMAN'S?

The problem of birth control has arisen directly from the effort of the feminine spirit to free itself from bondage. Woman herself has wrought that bondage through her reproductive powers and while enslaving herself has enslaved the world. The physical suffering to be relieved is chiefly woman's. Hers, too, is the love life that dies first under the blight of too prolific breeding. Within her is wrapped up the future of the race —it is hers to make or mar. All of these considerations point unmistakably to one fact—it is woman's duty as well as her privilege to lay hold of the means of freedom. . . .

The basic freedom of the world is woman's freedom. A free race cannot be born of slave mothers. A woman enchained cannot choose but give a measure of that bondage to her sons and daughters. No woman can call herself free who does not own and control her body. No woman can call herself free until she can choose consciously whether she will or will not be a mother.

It does not greatly alter the case that some women call themselves free because they earn their own livings, while others profess freedom because they defy the conventions of sex relationship. She who earns her own living gains a sort of freedom that is not to be undervalued, but in quality and in quantity it is of little account beside the untrammeled choice of mating or not mating, of being a mother or not being a mother. She gains food and clothing and shelter, at least, without submitting to the charity of her companion, but the earning of her own living does not give her the development of her inner sex urge, far deeper and more powerful in its outworkings than any of these externals. In order to have that development, she must still meet and solve the problem of motherhood.

With the so-called "free" woman, who chooses a mate in defiance of convention, freedom is largely a question of character and audacity. If she does attain to an unrestricted choice of a mate, she is still in a position to be enslaved through her reproductive powers. Indeed, the pressure of law and custom upon the woman not legally married is likely to make her more of a slave than the woman fortunate enough to marry the man of her choice.

Look at it from any standpoint you will, suggest any solution you will, conventional or unconventional, sanctioned by law or in defiance of law, woman is in the same position, fundamentally, until she is able to determine for herself whether she will be a mother and to fix the number of her offspring. This unavoidable situation is alone enough to make birth control, first of all, a woman's problem. . . .

It is persistently urged, however, that since sex expression is the act of two, the responsibility of controlling the results should not be placed upon woman alone. Is it fair, it is asked, to give her, instead of the man, the task of protecting herself when she is, perhaps, less rugged in physique than her mate, and has, at all events, the normal, periodic inconveniences of her sex?

We must examine this phase of her problem in two lights—that of the ideal, and of the conditions working toward the ideal. In an ideal society, no doubt, birth control would become the concern of the man as well as the woman. The hard, inescapable fact which we encounter today is that man has not only refused any such responsibility, but has individually and collectively sought to prevent woman from obtaining knowledge by which she could assume this responsibility for herself. She is still in the position of a dependent today because her mate has refused to consider her as an individual apart from his needs. She is still bound because she has in the past left the solution of the problem to him. Having left it to him, she finds that instead of rights, she has only such privileges as she has gained by petitioning, coaxing and cozening. Having left it to him, she is exploited, driven and enslaved to his desires.

While it is true that he suffers many evils as the consequence of this situation, she suffers vastly more. While it is true that he should be awakened to the cause of these evils, we know that they come home to her with crushing force every day. It is she who has the long burden of carrying, bearing and rearing the unwanted children. It is she who must watch beside the beds of pain where lie the babies who suffer because they have come into overcrowded homes. It is her heart that the sight of the deformed, the subnormal, the undernourished, the overworked child smites first and oftenest and hardest. It is *her* love life that dies first in the fear of undesired pregnancy. It is her opportunity for self-expression that perishes first and most hopelessly because of it.

Conditions, rather than theories, facts, rather than dreams, govern the problem. They place it squarely upon the shoulders of woman. She has learned that whatever the moral responsibility of the man in this direction may be, he does not discharge it. She has learned that, lovable and considerate as the individual husband may be, she has nothing to expect from men in the mass, when they make laws and decree customs. She knows that regardless of what ought to be, the brutal, unavoidable fact is that she will never receive her freedom until she takes it for herself.

Having learned this much, she has yet something more to learn. Women are too much inclined to follow in the footsteps of men, to try to think as men think, to try to solve the general problems of life as men solve them. If after attaining their freedom, women accept conditions in the spheres of government, industry, art, morals and religion as they find them, they will be but taking a leaf out of man's book. The woman is not needed to do man's work. She is not needed to think man's thoughts. She need not fear that the masculine mind, almost universally dominant, will fail to take care of its own. Her mission is not to enhance the masculine spirit, but to express the feminine; hers is not to preserve a man-made world, but to create a human world by the infusion of the feminine element into all of its activities.

Woman must not accept; she must challenge. She must not be awed by that which has been built up around her; she must reverence that within her which struggles for expression. Her eyes must be less upon what is and more clearly upon what should be. She must listen only with a frankly questioning attitude to the dogmatized opinions of man-made society. When she chooses her new, free course of action, it must be in the light of her own opinion—of her own intuition. Only so can she give play to the feminine spirit. Only thus can she free her mate from the bondage which he wrought for himself when he wrought hers. Only thus can she restore to him that of which he robbed himself in restricting her. Only thus can she remake the world.

The world is, indeed, hers to remake, it is hers to build and to recreate. Even as she has permitted the suppression of her own feminine element and the consequent impoverishment of industry, art, letters, science, morals, religions and social intercourse, so it is hers to enrich all these.

Woman must have her freedom—the fundamental freedom of choosing whether or not she shall be a mother and how many children she will have. Regardless of what man's attitude may be, that problem is hers—and before it can be his, it is hers alone.

She goes through the vale of death alone, each time a babe is born. As it is the right neither of man nor the state to coerce her into this ordeal, so it is her right to decide whether she will endure it. That right to decide imposes upon her the duty of clearing the way to knowledge by which she may make and carry out the decision.

Birth control is woman's problem. The quicker she accepts it as hers and hers alone, the quicker will society respect motherhood. The quicker, too, will the world be made a fit place for her children to live.

IX. CONTINENCE—IS IT PRACTICABLE OR DESIRABLE?

Thousands of well-intentioned people who agree that there are times and conditions under which it is woman's highest duty to avoid having children advocate continence as the one permissible means of birth control.

The majority of physicians and sex psychologists hold that the practice of absolute continence is, for the greater part of the human race, an absurdity. Were such continence to be practiced, there is no doubt that it would be a most effective check upon the birth rate. It is seldom practiced, however, and when adhered to under compulsion the usual result is injury to the nervous system and to the general health. Among healthy persons, this method is practicable only with those who have a degree of mentally controlled development as yet neither often experienced nor even imagined by the mass of humanity.

Absolute continence was the ideal of the early Christian church for all of its communicants. . . . The church abandoned this standard and now confines the doctrine of celibacy to the unmarried, to the priesthood and the nuns.

Celibacy has been practiced in all ages by a few artists, propagandists and revolutionists in order that their minds may be single to the work which has claimed their lives and all the forces of their beings may be bent in one direction. Sometimes, too, such persons have remained celibate to avoid the burden of caring for a family.

The Rev. Dr. Thomas Robert Malthus, who in 1798 issued the first of those works which exemplified what is called the Malthusian doctrine, also advocated celibacy or absolute continence until middle age. Malthus propounded the now widely recognized principle that population tends to increase faster than the food supply and that unlimited reproduction brings poverty and many other evils upon a nation. His theological training naturally inclined him to favor continence—not so much from its practicability, perhaps, as because he believed that it was the only possible method.

We would be ignoring a vital truth if we failed to recognize the fact that there are individuals who through absorption in religious zeal, consecration to a cause, or devotion to creative work are able to live for years or for a lifetime a celibate existence. It is doubtless true that the number of those who are thus able to transmute their sex forces into other creative forms is increasing. It is not with these, however, that we are concerned. Rather it is with the mass of humanity, who practice continence under some sort of compulsion.

What is the result of forcing continence upon those who are not fitted or do not desire to practice it? The majority opinion of medical science and the evidence of statistics are united on this point. Enforced continence is injurious—often highly so.

"Physiology," writes Dr. J. Rutgers . . . "teaches that every function gains in power and efficiency through a certain degree of control, but that the too extended suppression of a desire gives rise to pathological disturbances and in time cripples the function. Especially in the case of women may the damage entailed by too long continued sexual abstinence bring about deep disturbances." . . .

Virtually all of the dangers to health involved in absolute continence are involved also in the practice of continence broken only when it is desired to bring a child into the world. In the opinion of some medical authorities, it is even worse, because of the almost constant excitation of unsatisfied sex desire by the presence of the mate. People who think that they believe in this sort of family limitation have much to say about "self-control." Usually they will admit that to abstain from all but a single act of sexual intercourse each year is an indication of high powers of self-restraint. Yet that one act, performed only once a year, might be sufficient to "keep a woman with one child in her womb and another at her breast" during her entire childbearing period. . . .

Loathing, disgust or indifference to the sex relationship nearly always lies behind the advocacy to continence except for the conscious purpose of creating children. In other words, while one in ten thousand persons may find full play for a diverted and transmuted sex force in other creative functions, the rest avoid the sex union from repression. These are two widely different situations—one may make for racial progress and the happiness of the few individuals capable of it; the other poisons the race at its fountain and brings nothing but the discontent, unhappiness and misery which follow enforced continence. For all that, an increasing number of persons, mostly women, are advocating continence within marriage.

Sexual union is nearly always spoken of by such persons as something in itself repugnant, disgusting, low and lustful. Consciously or unconsciously, they look upon it as a hardship, to be endured only, to bring "God's image and likeness" into the world. Their very attitude precludes any great probability that their progeny will possess an abundance of such qualities.

Much of the responsibility for this feeling upon the part of many thousands of women must be laid to two thousand years of Christian teaching that all sex expression is unclean. Part of it, too, must be laid to the dominant male's habit of violating the love rights of his mate.

The habit referred to grows out of the assumed and legalized right of the husband to have sexual satisfaction at any time he desires, regardless of the woman's repugnance for it. The law of the state upholds him in this regard. A husband need not support his wife if she refuses to comply with his sexual demands.

Of the two groups of women who regard physical union either with disgust and loathing, or with indifference, the former are the less numerous. Nevertheless, there are many thousands of them. I have listened to their stories often, both as a nurse in obstetrical cases and as a propagandist for birth control. An almost universal cause of their attitude is a sad lack of understanding of the great beauties of the normal, idealistic love act. Neither do they understand the uplifting power of such unions for both men and women. Ignorance of life, ignorance of all but the sheer reproductive function of mating, and especially a wrong training, are most largely responsible for this tragic state of affairs. When this ignorance extends to the man in such a degree as to permit him to have the all too frequent coarse and brutal attitude toward sex matters, the tragedy is only deepened.

Truly the church and those "moralists" who have been insisting upon keeping sex matters in the dark have a huge list of concealed crimes to answer for. The right kind of a book, a series of clear, scientific lectures, or a common-sense talk with either the man or woman will often do away with most of the repugnance to physical union. When the repugnance is gone, the way is open to that upliftment through sex idealism which is the birthright of all women and men.

When I have had the confidence of women indifferent to physical union, I have found the fault usually lay with the husband. His idea of marriage is too often that of providing a home for a female who would in turn provide for his physical needs, including sexual satisfaction. Such a husband usually excludes such satisfaction from the category of the wife's needs, physical or spiritual.

This man is not concerned with his wife's sex urge, save as it responds to his own at times of his choosing. Man's code has taught woman to be quite ashamed of such desires. Usually she speaks of indifference without regret; often proudly. She seems to regard herself as more chaste and highly endowed in purity than other women who confess to feeling physical attraction toward their husbands. She also secretly considers herself far superior to the husband who makes no concealment of his desire toward her. Nevertheless, because of this desire upon the husband's part, she goes on "pretending" to mutual interest in the relationship.

Only the truth, plainly spoken, can help these people. The woman is condemned to physical, mental and spiritual misery by the ignorance which society has fixed upon her. She has her choice between an enforced continence, with its health-wrecking consequences and its constant aggravation of domestic discord, and the sort of prostitution legalized by the marriage ceremony. The man may choose between enforced continence and its effects, or he may resort to an unmarried relationship or to prostitution. Neither of these people—the one schooled directly or indirectly by the church and the other trained in the sex ethics of the gutter—can hope to lift the other to the regenerating influences of a pure, clean, happy love life. As long as we leave sex education to the gutter and houses of prostitution, we shall have millions of just such miserable marriage failures. . . .

Summing it all up, then, continence may meet the needs of a few natures, but it does not meet the needs of the masses. To enforce continence upon those whose natures do not demand it is an injustice, the cruelty and the danger of which has been underestimated rather than exaggerated. It matters not whether this wrong is committed by the church, through some outworn dogma; by the state, through the laws prohibiting contraceptives, or by society, through the conditions which prevent marriage when young men and women reach the age at which they have need of marriage.

The world has been governed too long by repression. The more fundamental the force that is repressed the more destructive its action. The disastrous effects of repressing the sex force are written plainly in the health rates, the mortality statistics, the records of crime and the entry books of the hospitals for the insane. Yet this is not all the tale, for there are still the little understood hosts of sexually abnormal people and the monotonous misery of millions who do not die early nor end violently, but who are, nevertheless, devoid of the joys of a natural love life.

As a means of birth control, continence is as impracticable for most people as it is undesirable. Celibate women doubtless have their place in the regeneration of the world, but it is not they, after all, who will through experience and understanding recreate it. It is mainly through fullness of expression and experience in life that the mass of women, having attained freedom, will accomplish this unparalleled task.

The need of women's lives is not repression, but the greatest possible expression and fulfillment of their desires upon the highest possible plane. They cannot reach higher planes through ignorance and compulsion. They can attain them only through knowledge and the cultivation of a higher, happier attitude toward sex. Sex life must be stripped of its fear. This is one of the great functions of contraceptives. That which is enshrouded in fear becomes morbid. That which is morbid cannot be really beautiful.

A true understanding of every phase of the love life, and such an understanding alone, can reveal it in its purity—in its power of upliftment. Force and fear have failed from the beginning of time. Their fruits are wrecks and wretchedness. Knowledge and freedom to choose or reject the sexual embrace, according as it is lovely or unlovely, and these alone, can solve the problem. These alone make possible between man and woman that indissoluble tie and mutual passion, and common understanding, in which lies the hope of a higher race.

XII. WILL BIRTH CONTROL HELP THE CAUSE OF LABOR?

Labor seems instinctively to have recognized the fact that its servitude springs from numbers. Seldom, however, has it applied its knowledge logically and thoroughly. The basic principle of craft unionism is limitation of the number of workers in a given trade. This has been labor's most frequent expedient for righting its wrongs. Every unionist knows, as a matter of course, that if that number is kept small enough, his organization can compel increases of wages, steady employment and decent working conditions. Craft unionism has succeeded in attaining these insofar as it has been able to apply this principle. It has failed insofar as it has been unable to apply it.

The weakness of craft unionism is that it does not carry its principle far enough. It applies its policy of limitation of numbers only to the trade. In his home, the worker, whether he is a unionist or non-unionist, goes on producing large numbers of children to compete with him eventually in the labor market. . . .

The great mass of the workers—including children and women—are unskilled and unorganized. Not only that, they are for some considerable part of the time seeking employment. They are, of course, poorly paid. Thus, through their low wages and their seeking of employment, they always come into direct competition with one another and with the skilled and organized workmen. As their families live in want and are often diseased, they create the chief social problems of the day. They bring children into the world as fast as women can bear them. With each child they increase their own misery. . . . The children thus carelessly produced undermine the health of the mother, deepen the family's poverty, destroy the happiness of the home, and dishearten the father; all this in addition to being future competitors in the labor market. Too often their increasing number drives the mother herself into industry, where her beggarly wages tend to lower the level of those of her husband.

The first sickening feature of this general situation is the high infant mortality among the children of the workers. Many children come merely to sap the strength of the mother, suffer and die, leaving to show for their coming and going only an increased burden of sorrow and debt. The lower the family income, the more of these babies die before they are a year old. . . .

When all is said and done, the workers who produce large families have themselves to blame for the hundreds of thousands of unemployed grasping for jobs, for the strike breakers, for the policemen who beat up and arrest strikers and for the soldiers who shoot strikers down. All these come from the families of workingmen. Their fathers and mothers are workers for wages. Out of the loins of labor they come into the world and compel surplus labor to betray labor that is employed.

Nor is this all. When a workman of superior strength and skill, protected by his union, manages to maintain a large or moderate sized family in a degree of comfort, there always comes a time when he must strike to preserve what he has won. If he is not beaten by unorganized workers who seek his job, he still has to face the possibility of listening to the cries of several hungry children. If the strike is a long one, these cries often down the promptings of loyalty and class interest—often they defeat him when nothing else could.

Is it any wonder that under handicaps like these labor becomes confused and flounders? It has been offered a multitude of remedies—political reforms, wage legislation, statutory regulation of hours, and so on. It has been invited to embrace craft and industrial unionism, syndicalism, anarchism, socialism as panaceas for its liberation. Except in a few countries, it has not attained to aggressive power, but has been a tool for unscrupulous politicians.

Even with the temporary advantages gained by the wiping out of millions of workers in the Great War, labor's problem remains unsolved. It has now, as always, to contend with the crop of young laborers coming into the market, and with the ever-present "labor-saving" machine which, instead of relieving the worker's situation, makes it all the harder for him to escape. Fewer laborers are needed today for a given amount of production and distribution than before the invention of these machines. Yet, owing to the increase in the number of the workers, labor finds itself enslaved instead of liberated by the machine. . . .

. . . We blame capitalism and its wasteful, brutal industrial system for all our social problems, but our numbers were vast and our bondage grievous before modern industry came into existence. We may curse the trusts, but our subjection was accomplished before the trusts had emerged from the brain of evolution. We may blame public officials and individual employers, but our burdens were crushing before these were born. We look now here, now there, for the cause of our condition—everywhere but at the one to blame. We fight again and again for our rights, only to be conquered by our own kind, our own children, our brother's, our neighbor's.

Let us carry to its logical conclusion the principle of limitation which has been partially applied by labor unions. The way to get rid of labor problems, unemployment, low wages, the surplus, unwanted population, is to stop breeding. They come from our own ranks—from our own families. The way to get better wages, shorter hours, a new system for the advancement of labor, is to make labor's numbers fewer. Let us not wait for war, famine and plague to do it. Let us cease bringing unwanted children into the world to suffer awhile, add to our burdens and die. Let us cease bringing others into the world to compete with us for a living. Let the women workers practice birth control.

What are the concrete things which the worker can gain at once through birth control? First, a small family can live much better than a large one upon the wages now received. Workers could be better fed, clothed and educated. Again, fewer children in the families of the workers would tend to check the rise in the prices of food, which are forced up as the demand increases. Within a few years it would reduce the number of workers competing for jobs. The worker could the more easily force society to give him more of the product of his labor—or all of it. And while these things are taking place, the slums, with their disease, their moral degradation and all their sordid accompaniments, would automatically disappear. No worker would need to live in such tenements—hence they would be modernized or torn down. At the same time, the few children that were being born to the workers would be stronger, healthier, more courageous. They would be fit human beings—not miserable victims of murderous conditions.

Birth control does not propose to replace any of the idealistic movements and philosophies of the workers. It is not a substitute, it precedes. It is of itself a principle that lifts the heaviest of the burdens that afflict labor. It can and it must be the foundation upon which any permanently successful improvement in conditions is attained. It is, therefore, a necessary prelude in all effective propaganda.

A few years of systematic agitation for birth control would put labor in a position to solve all its problems. Labor, organized or unorganized, must take heed of this fact. Groups and parties working for a new social order must include it in their programmes. No social system, no workers' democracy, no Socialist republic can operate successfully and maintain its ideals unless the practice of birth control is encouraged to a marked and efficient degree. . . .

XIII. BATTALIONS OF UNWANTED BABIES THE CAUSE OF WAR

In every nation of militaristic tendencies we find the reactionaries demanding a higher and still higher birth rate. Their plea is, first, that great armies are needed to *defend* the country from its possible enemies; second, that a huge population is required to assure the country its proper place among the powers of the world. At bottom the two pleas are the same.

As soon as the country becomes overpopulated, these reactionaries proclaim loudly its moral right to expand. They point to the huge population, which in the name of patriotism they have previously demanded should be brought into being. Again pleading patriotism, they declare that it is the moral right of the nation to take by force such room as it needs. Then comes war—usually against some nation supposed to be less well prepared than the aggressor.

Diplomats make it their business to conceal the facts, and politicians violently denounce the politicians of other countries. There is a long beating of tom-toms by the press and all other agencies for influencing public opinion. Facts are distorted and lies invented until the common people cannot get at the truth. Yet, when the war is over, if not before, we always find that "a place in the sun," "a path to the sea," "a route to India" or something of the sort is at the bottom of the trouble. These are merely other names for expansion.

The "need of expansion" is only another name for overpopulation. One supreme example is sufficient to drive home this truth. That the Great War, from the horror of which we are just beginning to emerge, had its source in overpopulation is too evident to be denied by any serious student of current history.

For the past one hundred years most of the nations of Europe have been piling up terrific debts to humanity by the encouragement of unlimited numbers. The rulers of these nations and their militarists have constantly called upon the people to breed, breed, breed! Large populations meant more people to produce wealth, more people to pay taxes, more trade for the merchants, more soldiers to protect the wealth. But more people also meant need of greater food supplies, an urgent and natural need for expansion. . . .

Robert Thomas Malthus, formulator of the doctrine which bears his name, pointed out, in the closing years of the eighteenth century, the relation of overpopulation to war. He showed that mankind tends to increase faster than the food supply. He demonstrated that were it not for the more common diseases, for plague, famine, floods and wars, human beings would crowd each other to such an extent that the misery would be even greater than it now is. These he described as "natural checks," pointing out that as long as no other checks are employed, such disasters are unavoidable. If we do not exercise sufficient judgment to regulate the birth rate, we encounter disease, starvation and war.

Both Darwin and John Stuart Mill recognized, by inference at least, the fact that so-called "natural checks"—and among them war—will operate if some sort of limitation is not employed. In his *Origin of Species,* Darwin says: "There is no exception to the rule that every organic being naturally increases at so high a rate, if not destroyed, that the earth would soon be covered by the progeny of a single pair." Elsewhere he observes that we do not permit helpless human beings to die off, but we create philanthropies and charities, build asylums and hospitals and keep the medical profession busy preserving those who could not otherwise survive. John Stuart Mill, supporting the views of Malthus, speaks to exactly the same effect in regard to the multiplying power of organic beings, among them humanity. In other words, let countries become overpopulated and war is inevitable. It follows as daylight follows the sunrise.

When Charles Bradlaugh and Mrs. Annie Besant were on trial in England in 1877 for publishing information concerning contraceptives, Mrs. Besant put the case bluntly to the court and the jury:

"I have no doubt that if natural checks were allowed to operate right through the human as they do in the animal world, a better result would follow. Among the brutes, the weaker are driven to the wall, the diseased fall out in the race of life. The old brutes, when feeble or sickly, are killed. If men insisted that those who were sickly should be allowed to die without help of medicine or science, if those who are weak were put upon one side and crushed, if those who were old and useless were killed, if those who were not capable of providing food for themselves were allowed to starve, if all this were done, the struggle for existence among men would be as real as it is among brutes and would doubtless result in the production of a higher race of men.

"But are you willing to do that or to allow it to be done?"

We are not willing to let it be done. Mother hearts cling to children, no matter how diseased, misshapen and miserable. Sons and daughters hold fast to parents, no matter how helpless. We do not allow the weak to depart; neither do we cease to bring more weak and helpless beings into the world. Among the dire results is war, which kills off, not the weak and the helpless, but the strong and the fit.

What shall be done? We have our choice of one of three policies. We may abandon our science and leave the weak and diseased to die, or kill them, as the brutes do. Or we may go on overpopulating the earth and have our famines and our wars while the earth exists. Or we can accept the third, sane, sensible, moral and practicable plan of birth control. . . . This remedy can be applied only by woman and she will apply it. She must and will see past the call of pretended patriotism and of glory of empire and perceive what is true and what is false in these things. She will discover what base uses the militarist and the exploiter make of the idealism of peoples. Under the clamor of the press, permeating the ravings of the jingoes, she will hear the voice of Napoleon, the archtype of the militarists of all nations, calling for "fodder for cannon."

"Woman is given to us that she may bear children," said he. "Woman is our property, we are not hers, because she produces children for us—we do not yield any to her. She is, therefore, our possession as the fruit tree is that of the gardener."

That is what the imperialist is *thinking* when he speaks of the glory of the empire and the prestige of the nation. Every country has its appeal—its shibboleth—ready for the lips of the imperialist. German rulers pointed to the comfort of the workers, to old-age pensions, maternal benefits and minimum wage regulations, and other material benefits, when they wished to inspire soldiers for the Fatherland. England's strongest argument, perhaps, was a certain phase of liberty which she guarantees her subjects, and the protection afforded them wherever they may go. France and the United States, too, have their appeals to the idealism of democracy—appeals which the politicians of both countries know well how to use, though the peoples of both lands are beginning to awake to the fact that their countries have been living on the glories of their revolutions and traditions, rather than the substance of freedom. Behind the boast of old-age pensions, material benefits and wage regulations, behind the bombast concerning liberty in this country and tyranny in that, behind all the slogans and shibboleths coined out of the ideals of the peoples for the uses of imperialism, woman must and will see the iron hand of that same imperialism, condemning women to breed and men to die for the will of the rulers.

Upon woman the burden and the horrors of war are heaviest. Her heart is the hardest wrung when the husband or the son comes home to be buried or to live a shattered wreck. Upon her devolve the extra tasks of filling out the ranks of workers in the war industries, in addition to caring for the children and replenishing the war-diminished population. Hers is the crushing weight and the sickening of soul. And it is out of her womb that those things proceed. When she sees what lies behind the glory and the horror, the boasting and the burden, and gets the vision, the human perspective, she will end war. She will kill war by the simple process of starving it to death. For she will refuse longer to produce the human food upon which the monster feeds.

XIV. WOMAN AND THE NEW MORALITY

Upon the shoulders of the woman conscious of her freedom rests the responsibility of creating a new sex morality. The vital difference between a morality thus created by women and the so-called morality of today, is that the new standard will be based upon knowledge and freedom while the old is founded upon ignorance and submission.

What part will birth control play in bringing forth this new standard? What effect will its practice have upon woman's moral development? Will it lift her to heights that she has not yet achieved, and if so, how? Why is the question of morality always raised by the objector to birth control? All these questions must be answered if we are to get a true picture of the relation of the feminine spirit to morals. They can best be answered by considering, first, the source of our present standard of sex morals and the reasons why those standards are what they are; and, second, the source and probable nature of the new morality.

We get most of our notions of sex morality from the Christian church—more particularly from the oldest existing Christian church, known as the Roman Catholic. The church has generally defined the "immoral woman" as one who mates out of wedlock. Virtually, it lets it go at that. In its practical workings, there is nothing in the church code of morals to protect the woman, either from unwilling submission to the wishes of her husband, from undesired pregnancy, nor from any other of the outrages only too familiar to many married women. Nothing is said about the crime of bringing an unwanted child into the world, where often it cannot be adequately cared for and is, therefore, condemned to a life of misery. The church's one point of insistence is upon the right of itself to legalize marriage and to compel the woman to submit to whatever such marriage may bring. It is true that there are remedies of divorce in the case of the state, but the church has adhered strictly to the principle that marriage, once consummated, is indissoluble. Thus, in its operation, the church's code of sex morals has nothing to do with the basic sex rights of the woman, but enforces, rather, the assumed property rights of the man to the body and the services of his wife. They are man-made codes; their vital factor, as they apply to woman, is submission to the man.

Closely associated with and underlying the principle of submission, has been the doctrine that the sex life is in itself unclean. It follows, therefore, that all knowledge of the sex physiology or sex functions is also unclean and taboo. Upon this teaching has been founded woman's subjection by the church and, largely through the influence of the church, her subjection by the state to the needs of the man. . . .

The church has sought to keep women ignorant upon the plea of keeping them "pure." To this end it has used the state as its moral policeman. Men have largely broken the grip of the ecclesiastics upon masculine education. The ban upon geology and astronomy, because they refute the biblical version of the creation of the world, are no longer effective. Medicine, biology and the doctrine of evolution have won their way to recognition in spite of the united opposition of the clerics. So, too, has the right of woman to go unveiled, to be educated, and to speak from public platforms been asserted in spite of the condemnations of the church, which denounced them as destructive of feminine purity. Only in sex matters has it succeeded in keeping the bugaboo alive.

It clings to this last stronghold of ignorance, knowing that woman free from sexual domination would produce a race spiritually free and strong enough to break the last of the bonds of intellectual darkness.

It is within the marriage bonds, rather than outside them, that the greatest immorality of men has been perpetrated. Church and state, through their canons and their laws, have encouraged this immorality. It is here that the woman who is to win her way to the new morality will meet the most difficult part of her task of moral house cleaning. . . .

If Christianity turned the clock of general progress back a thousand years, it turned back the clock two thousand years for woman. Its greatest outrage upon her was to forbid her to control the function of motherhood under any circumstances, thus limiting her life's work to bringing forth and rearing children. Coincident with this, the churchmen deprived her of her place in and before the courts, in the schools, in literature, art and society. They shut from her heart and her mind the knowledge of her love life and her reproductive functions. They chained her to the position into which they had thrust her, so that it is only after centuries of effort that she is even beginning to regain what was wrested from her. . . .

Thus the position attained by women of Greece and Rome through the exercise of family limitation, and in a considerable degree of voluntary motherhood, was swept away by the rising tide of Christianity. It would seem that this pernicious result was premeditated, and that from the very early days of Christianity, there were among the hierarchy those who recognized the creative power of the feminine spirit, the force of which they sought to turn to their own uses. Certain it is that the hierarchy created about the whole love life of woman an atmosphere of degradation.

Fear and shame have stood as grim guardians against the gate of knowledge and constructive idealism. The sex life of women has been clouded in darkness, restrictive, repressive and morbid. Women have not had the opportunity to know themselves, nor have they been permitted to give play to their inner natures, that they might create a morality practical, idealistic and high for their own needs.

On the other hand, church and state have forbidden women to leave their legal mates, or to refuse to submit to the marital embrace, no matter how filthy, drunken, diseased or otherwise repulsive the man might be—no matter how much of a crime it might be to bring to birth a child by him.

Woman was and is condemned to a system under which the lawful rapes exceed the unlawful ones a million to one. She has had nothing to say as to whether she shall have strength sufficient to give a child a fair physical and mental start in life; she has had as little to do with determining whether her own body shall be wrecked by excessive child-bearing. She has been adjured not to complain of the burden of caring for children she has not wanted. Only the married woman who has been constantly loved by the most understanding and considerate of husbands has escaped these horrors. Besides the wrongs done to women in marriage, those involved in promiscuity, infidelities and rapes become inconsequential in nature and in number.

Out of woman's inner nature, in rebellion against these conditions, is rising the new morality. Let it be realized that this creation of new sex ideals is a challenge to the church. Being a challenge to the church, it is also, in less degree, a challenge to the state. The woman who takes a fearless stand for the incoming sex ideals must expect to be assailed by reactionaries of every kind. Imperialists and exploiters will fight hardest in the open, but the ecclesiastic will fight longest in the dark. He understands the situation best of all; he best knows what reaction he has to fear from the morals of women who have attained liberty. For, be it repeated, the church has always known and feared the spiritual potentialities of woman's freedom.

And in this lies the answer to the question why the opponent of birth control raises the moral issue. Sex morals for women have been one-sided; they have been purely negative, inhibitory and repressive. They have been fixed by agencies which have sought to keep women enslaved; which have been determined, even as they are now, to use woman solely as an asset to the church, the state and the man. Any means of freedom which will enable women to live and think for themselves first will be attacked as immoral by these selfish agencies.

What effect will the practice of birth control have upon woman's moral development? As we have seen in other chapters, it will break her bonds. It will free her to understand the cravings and soul needs of herself and other women. It will enable her to develop her love nature separate from and independent of her maternal nature.

It goes without saying that the woman whose children are desired and are of such number that she can not only give them adequate care but keep herself mentally and spiritually alive, as well as physically fit, can discharge her duties to her children much better than the overworked, broken and querulous mother of a large, unwanted family.

Thus the way is open to her for a twofold development; first, through her own full-rounded life, and next, through her loving, unstrained, full-hearted relationship with her offspring. The bloom of mother love will have an opportunity to infuse itself into her soul and make her, indeed, the fond, affectionate guardian of her offspring that sentiment now pictures her but hard facts deny her the privilege of being. She will preserve also her love life with her mate in its ripening perfection. She will want children with a deeper passion, and will love them with a far greater love.

In spite of the age-long teaching that sex life in itself is unclean, the world has been moving to a realization that a great love between a man and woman is a holy thing, freighted with great possibilities for spiritual growth. The fear of unwanted children removed, the assurance that she will have a sufficient amount of time in which to develop her love life to its greatest beauty, with its comradeship in many fields—these will lift woman by the very soaring quality of her innermost self to spiritual heights that few have attained. Then the coming of eagerly desired children will but enrich life in all its avenues, rather than enslave and impoverish it as do unwanted ones today.

What healthier grounds for the growth of sound morals could possibly exist than the ample spiritual life of the woman just depicted? Free to follow the feminine spirit, which dwells in the sanctuary of her nature, she will, in her daily life, give expression to that high idealism which is the fruit of that spirit when it is unhampered and unviolated. The love for her mate will flower in beauty of deeds that are pure because they are the natural expression of her physical, mental and spiritual being. The love for desired children will come to blossom in a spirituality that is high because it is free to reach the heights.

The moral force of woman's nature will be unchained—and of its own dynamic power will uplift her to a plane unimagined by those holding fast to the old standards of church morality. Love is the greatest force of the universe; freed of its bonds of submission and unwanted progeny, it will formulate and compel of its own nature observance to standards of purity far beyond the highest conception of the average moralist. The feminine spirit, animated by joyous, triumphant love, will make its own high tenets of morality. Free womanhood, out of the depths of its rich experiences, will observe and comply with the inner demands of its being. The manner in which it learns to do this best may be said to be the moral law of woman's being. So, in whatever words the new morality may ultimately be expressed, we can at least be sure that it will meet certain needs.

First of all, it will meet the physical and psychic requirements of the woman herself, for she cannot adequately perform the feminine functions until these are met. Second, it will meet the needs of the child to be conceived in a love which is eager to bring forth a new life, to be brought into a home where love and harmony prevail, a home in which proper preparation has been made for its coming.

This situation implies in turn a number of conditions. Foremost among them is woman's knowledge of her sexual nature, both in its physiology and its spiritual significance. She must not only know her own body, its care and its needs, but she must know the power of the sex force, its use, its abuse, as well as how to direct it for the benefit of the race. Thus she can transmit to her children an equipment that will enable them to break the bonds that have held humanity enslaved for ages.

To achieve this she must have a knowledge of birth control. She must also assert and maintain her right to refuse the marital embrace except when urged by her inner nature.

The truth makes free. Viewed in its true aspect, the very beauty and wonder of the creative impulse will make evident its essential purity. We will then instinctively idealize and keep holy that physical-spiritual expression which is the foundation of all human life, and in that conception of sex will the race be exalted.

What can we expect of offspring that are the result of "accidents"—who are brought into being undesired and in fear? What can we hope for from a morality that surrounds each physical union, for the woman, with an atmosphere of submission and shame? What can we say for a morality that leaves the husband at liberty to communicate to his wife a venereal disease?

Subversion of the sex urge to ulterior purposes has dragged it to the level of the gutter. Recognition of its true nature and purpose must lift the race to spiritual freedom. Out of our growing knowledge we are evolving new and saner ideas of life in general. Out of our increasing sex knowledge we shall evolve new ideals of sex. These ideals will spring from the innermost needs of women. They will serve these needs and express them. They will be the foundation of a moral code that will tend to make fruitful the impulse which is the source, the soul and the crowning glory of our sexual natures. . . .

XVIII. THE GOAL

What is the goal of woman's upward struggle? Is it voluntary motherhood? Is it general freedom? Or is it the birth of a new race? For freedom is not fruitless, but prolific of higher things. Being the most sacred aspect of woman's freedom, voluntary motherhood is motherhood in its highest and holiest form. It is motherhood unchained—motherhood ready to obey its own urge to remake the world.

Voluntary motherhood implies a new morality —a vigorous, constructive, liberated morality. That morality will, first of all, prevent the submergence of womanhood into motherhood. It will set its face against the conversion of women into mechanical maternity and toward the creation of a new race.

Woman's role has been that of an incubator and little more. She has given birth to an incubated race. She has given to her children what little she was permitted to give, but of herself, of her personality, almost nothing. In the mass, she has brought forth quantity, not quality. The requirement of a male dominated civilization has been numbers. She has met that requirement.

It is the essential function of voluntary motherhood to choose its own mate, to determine the time of childbearing and to regulate strictly the number of offspring. Natural affection upon her part, instead of selection dictated by social or economic advantage, will give her a better fatherhood for her children. The exercise of her right to decide how many children she will have and when she shall have them will procure for her the time necessary to the development of other faculties than that of reproduction. She will give play to her tastes, her talents and her ambitions. She will become a full-rounded human being.

Thus and only thus will woman be able to transmit to her offspring those qualities which make for a greater race.

The importance of developing these qualities in the mothers for transmission to the children is apparent when we recall certain well-established principles of biology. In all of the animal species below the human, motherhood has a clearly discernible superiority over fatherhood. It is the first pulse of organic life. Fatherhood is the fertilizing element. Its development, compared to that of the mother cell, is comparatively new. Likewise, its influence upon the progeny is comparatively small. There are weighty authorities who assert that through the female alone comes those modifications of form, capacity and ability which constitute evolutionary progress. It was the mothers who first developed cunning in chase, ingenuity in escaping enemies, skill in obtaining food, and adaptability. It was they also who attained unfailing discretion in leadership, adaptation to environment and boldness in attack. When the animal kingdom as a whole is surveyed, these stand out as distinctly feminine traits. They stand out also as the characteristics by which the progress of species is measured.

Why is all this true of the lower species yet not true of human beings? The secret is revealed by one significant fact—the female's functions in these animal species are not limited to motherhood alone. Every organ and faculty is fully employed and perfected. Through the development of the individual mother, better and higher types of animals are produced and carried forward. In a word, natural law makes the female the expression and the conveyor of racial efficiency.

Birth control itself, often denounced as a violation of natural law, is nothing more or less than the facilitation of the process of weeding out the unfit, of preventing the birth of defectives or of those who will become defectives. So, in compliance with nature's working plan, we must permit womanhood its full development before we can expect of it efficient motherhood. If we are to make racial progress, this development of womanhood must precede motherhood in every individual woman. Then and then only can the mother cease to be an incubator and be a mother indeed. Then only can she transmit to her sons and daughters the qualities which make strong individuals and, collectively, a strong race.

Voluntary motherhood also implies the right of marriage without maternity. Two utterly different functions are developed in the two relationships. In order to give the mate relationship its full and free play, it is necessary that no woman should be a mother against her will. There are other reasons, of course—reasons more frequently emphasized—but the reason just mentioned should never be overlooked. It is as important to the race as to the woman, for through it is developed that high love impulse which, conveyed to the child, attunes and perfects its being.

Marriage, quite aside from parentage, also gives two people invaluable experience. When parentage follows in its proper time, it is a better parentage because of the mutual adjustment and development—because of the knowledge thus gained. Few couples are fitted to understand the sacred mystery of child life until they have solved some of the problems arising out of their own love lives.

Maternal love, which usually follows upon a happy, satisfying mate love, becomes a strong and urgent craving. It then exists for two powerful, creative functions. First, for its own sake, and then for the sake of further enriching the conjugal relationship. It is from such soil that the new life should spring. It is the inherent right of the new life to have its inception in such physical ground, in such spiritual atmosphere. The child thus born is indeed a flower of love and tremendous joy. It has within it the seeds of courage and of power. This child will have the greatest strength to surmount hardships, to withstand tyrannies, to set still higher the mark of human achievement.

. . . A free womanhood turns of its own desire to a free and happy motherhood, a motherhood which does not submerge the woman, but which is enriched because she is unsubmerged. When we voice, then, the necessity of setting the feminine spirit utterly and absolutely free, thought turns naturally not to rights of the woman, nor indeed of the mother, but to the rights of the child—of all children in the world. For this is the miracle of free womanhood, that in its freedom it becomes the race mother and opens its heart in fruitful affection for humanity. . . .

When motherhood becomes the fruit of a deep yearning, not the result of ignorance or accident, its children will become the foundation of a new race. There will be no killing of babies in the womb by abortion, nor through neglect in foundling homes, nor will there be infanticide. Neither will children die by inches in mills and factories. No man will dare to break a child's life upon the wheel of toil.

Voluntary motherhood will not be passive, resigned, or weak. Out of its craving will come forth a fierceness of love for its fruits that will make such men as remain unawakened stand aghast at its fury when offended. The tigress is less terrible in defense of her offspring than will be the human mother. The daughters of such women will not be given over to injustice and to prostitution; the sons will not perish in industry nor upon the battlefield. Nor could they meet these all too common fates if an undaunted motherhood were there to defend. Childhood and youth will be too valuable in the eyes of society to waste them in the murderous mills of blind greed and hate.

This is the dawn. Womanhood shakes off its bondage. It asserts its right to be free. In its freedom, its thoughts turn to the race. Like begets like. We gather perfect fruit from perfect trees. The race is but the amplification of its mother body, the multiplication of flesh habitations—beautified and perfected for souls akin to the mother soul.

The relentless efforts of reactionary authority to suppress the message of birth control and of voluntary motherhood are futile. The powers of reaction cannot now prevent the feminine spirit from breaking its bonds. When the last fetter falls the evils that have resulted from the suppression of woman's will to freedom will pass. Child slavery, prostitution, feeblemindedness, physical deterioration, hunger, oppression and war will disappear from the earth.

In their subjection women have not been brave enough, strong enough, pure enough to bring forth great sons and daughters. Abused soil brings forth stunted growths. An abused motherhood has brought forth a low order of humanity. Great beings come forth at the call of high desire. Fearless motherhood goes out in love and passion for justice to all mankind. It brings forth fruits after its own kind. When the womb becomes fruitful through the desire of an aspiring love, another Newton will come forth to unlock further the secrets of the earth and the stars. There will come a Plato who will be understood, a Socrates who will drink no hemlock, and a Jesus who will not die upon the cross. These and the race that is to be in America await upon a motherhood that is to be sacred because it is free.

PART VII

Suzanne LaFollette:

Radical Libertarian

When Suzanne LaFollette ran unsuccessfully for Congress in 1964, a puzzled reporter asked how one previously open to radical causes could now serve the Conservative party and endorse the conservative Republican presidential nominee, Senator Barry Goldwater. "The only progressive political thinking today is conservative thinking," she replied. "I haven't moved. The world has moved to the left of me."[1] Although Miss LaFollette's response minimized certain shifts of emphasis, it called attention to a persistent ideological nucleus which has anchored her thought increasingly outside the mainstream of twentieth-century America.

She disciplined the reform impulses of Henry George and the progressives with libertarian ideals derived from the physiocrats, Jeffersonians, and liberals. The result was an anarchistic liberalism or radical libertarianism—an uncompromising commitment to the freedom of the individual to think and do as he pleases without interference from social and political institutions as long as his actions do not infringe upon the liberties of others. While she absorbed the progressive political faith of her relatives, she also expanded her social and intellectual horizons through intimate contact with legislative leaders and political analysts in the national capital and sharpened her analysis with the help of New York intellectuals and journalists. Wielding an ideological sword with a well-honed edge, she cut cleanly through the corporate and conformist tendencies in modern America to demand full and equal freedom for each individual. The same radical libertarian thrust infused her feminist treatise, *Concerning Women* (1926), and earned her an accolade as "the most original feminist writer of the 1920's."[2]

Because the woman suffrage movement and related feminist organizations were declining in the mid-twenties, her book received little public attention. The occasional reviewer recognized, however, that she called for a "new era of feminism" transcending the prevailing suffragist mentality. Young women who enjoyed "sensible clothing, sensible employment and sensible freedom in pleasure" during the twenties did not find the "old battle cries" of suffragist feminism very relevant, even though political and economic equality still eluded them. Yet "the forces which made feminism are still at work, though their task has been merged into far wider ones; men and women are no longer opposed to one another, but stand together comrades, though half-slaves, facing the forces which exploit them equally."[3]

Born in the state of Washington in 1893, Suzanne LaFollette grew up in a sparsely settled agrarian region where Jeffersonian values and life-styles persisted. Her father, William, managed several large ranches which produced wheat, cattle, and fruit for East Coast markets. Mother and father "had little time and not too much patience" to offer their seven children. The LaFollette boys and girls grew up on horseback, roamed the unfenced ranges at will, and relied on Grandpa, a forty-niner, Indian fighter, and former stock man for the love and attention which never failed to provide them with a "sense of security."[4]

While she was in her teens, Suzanne's father sold his orchards, rented his wheat ranches, moved to Pullman, where he "prepared to see his family through college," and soon became deeply involved in partisan politics. Elected in 1911 as a progressive Republican to the United States House of Representatives, he served until his pronounced opposition to American entry into World War I brought about his defeat in 1918.

During the family's eight-year residence in Washington, D. C., Suzanne completed her undergraduate work at Trinity College, participated in national progressive politics, and joined the woman suffrage movement. For the first four years, Senator Robert M. LaFollette of Wisconsin, the great progressive leader and first cousin of her father, lived nearby; for the next four years, the two families shared a large house. In such a milieu Suzanne and her siblings easily learned "a good deal about the workings of politics." When not in college, she frequently helped in the congressional office of her father and the senatorial office of his cousin. The senator, who "had a great love for young people, . . . always had time to discuss any question one brought him. And he took us in on everything, so that we had a feeling of participation in the political process."[5]

Suzanne absorbed the reforming Jeffersonian anti-imperialism of the LaFollette progressives. These Western progressives followed the trail worn by middle-class farm folk for at least half a century. Theirs was a reform program of rural and agrarian values for industrial, corporate, and urban America. They wished to take the advantages of political privilege away from industry and subject it to the competitive economic forces that controlled agriculture and small business. Interference in the economy through such political means as subsidy, tariff, imperialism, and other special-privilege governmental acts had created, from the progressive's point of view, oppressive social and economic power. On the other hand, competitive economic forces would discipline all persons and businesses justly in a laissez-faire world and prevent the establishment of monopolistic and oligopolistic power. Once government was reduced to the appropriate role of general social umpire and policeman and returned to the control of the people, it would no longer provide a haven for the corrupt, the privilege seeker, and the machine boss.

Progressive political reformers stressed the repeal of special-interest legislation and the enactment of institutional safeguards to keep the people from losing control of government. The progressive emphasis upon political democratization opened the LaFollettes to the woman suffrage movement. The senator, the congressman, and their wives were "of course good feminists." Suzanne—who grew up free from many conventional feminine restrictions, received a college education, and lived in the eye of national reform efforts—embraced feminism. Joining a suffrage parade that turned into "an obscene spectacle," she learned "something of what women were up against in the struggle for their rights." Without police enforcement of a division between the parade and the Washington, D. C., crowd, "a seething mob of men . . . surged around the struggling marchers, shouting obscenities" for hours. No later parade in which she participated created as vivid an impression of the forceful opposition that even modest steps towards feminine equality aroused.

The decision to pursue a career upon college graduation seemed quite natural to Suzanne; indeed it appeared as "the usual thing" for girls in her situation to do. Cousin Fola LaFollette had warned Suzanne against taking a secretarial job, and her presence in the national capital made entreé into the magazine field quite easy. When her family left Washington following her father's defeat, she accepted a position in New York City with the *Nation,* where she served as temporary editor of the journal's International Relations Section under the superintendence of Albert Jay Nock. Fully dedicated to her work, she lived the committed, independent life that Charlotte Gilman had advocated and never complicated it with marriage or motherhood. Nock once claimed that she was one of those rare persons who would not break her work routine even "to eat lunch with the King."[6]

Miss LaFollette soon became Nock's "special pride and able disciple." He served on the staffs of at least three periodicals with her, and when over the years they were not working on the same journal, they kept in touch by letter and through visits. He provided her with "a wonderful schooling in libertarianism." An "exacting taskmaster," he disciplined her thought and shaped her style of writing. She found him "a true intellectual aristocrat" who was less interested in people than in ideas. He sought out ability, "not as a conscious service to society or his country or even to the beneficiary" but rather as an "instinct to serve truth." He "was a libertarian not only in theory but in practice," a man who encouraged and supported the intellectual development of others without commanding them, even when he was their superior. He "wanted liberty for others as much as for himself" realizing, "indeed, that without liberty man is a slave no matter how many subsidies and services officious overlords may impose upon him."[7]

Nock's influence upon her was so great that his reading, social analysis, and style deeply informed her work, especially *Concerning Women.*[8] LaFollette found few white Americans deprived of as much liberty as were women. She knew of no one as acutely knowledgeable and actively committed to libertarianism nor as facile with the pen as Albert Nock. Under his influence she came to view the question of woman's status as primarily a matter of restricted liberty, an example of a larger problem in modern society. And in *Concerning Women* she developed explicitly feminist corollaries to the libertarian theorems that he explicated. She was a feminist before becoming a thoroughgoing libertarian, but thanks to Nock, her feminist analysis was immensely enriched because of her further immersion in that important tradition of Western thought.

Nock's refusal to compromise with land and industrial monopoly and his disapproval of expanding governmental activity harmonized with the Jeffersonian strains of LaFollette progressivism. Both opposed state meddling "with the individual's pursuit of happiness—'Can any individual be happy when he is continually conscious of not being his own man?' " Both limited and ordered legitimate state functions: " 'first, freedom; second, justice.' In other words, the state's business is to *let people alone,* and to coerce them only in the measure necessary to ensure their letting one another alone."[9]

Both Nock and LaFollette viewed Wilsonian idealism as a perversion of libertarian principles, a liberalism that failed. Instead of freeing people from government, Wilson increasingly used government to effect his particular goals. Instead of ending American intervention abroad, he plunged the nation into an ever greater coercive internationalism. Instead of promoting civil liberties, he allowed his administrators to restrict them. When Wilson promised to keep the nation out of the Great War in 1916, Nock abandoned his aloofness from politics to campaign for Wilson's re-election, only to be deeply disillusioned by the president's war policies of 1917. Nock's opposition to American involvement in World War I and to the resulting growth of state power and restriction of civil liberties was as profound as the LaFollette family's and for many of the same reasons.

Like the LaFollettes, Nock opposed socialism. He deplored the *Nation*'s drift from liberal reform to socialism and objected as much to putting industry under government ownership as to having government under the control of business. Neither case, he contended, led to freedom for the individual. "Socializing industry means nothing but increasing the number of your shareholders. It does not change the economic basis of industry a single iota."[10] He found no social cure, only more disease, in Wilsonianism and socialism.

By citing various of its leaders as authorities and supporting a variety of its principles and policies, Suzanne LaFollette and Albert Nock paid homage to the rationalist tradition. She invoked Enlightenment thinkers from physiocrats and Founding Fathers to feminists. Deeply interested in the French physiocrats of the eighteenth century who had influenced the Anglo-American heirs of the Enlightenment, she endorsed their thought in her feminist treatise. The physiocrats worshipped the self-reliant, independent individual who, free from the domination of government, promoted the general welfare by developing his own interests. They insisted upon full liberty of economic activity, based on individual property rights in a freely competitive economy. This system entailed the elimination of government regulation, removal of tariffs, and drastic simplification of the tax system. Holding pronounced agrarian and free-trade biases, the physiocrats argued that only land should be taxed, for it alone created value beyond human labor. Physiocracy meant an equality of economic rights, although by no means an equality in wealth or status, since human beings have unequal abilities. When Suzanne LaFollette chose to open *Concerning Women* with a quotation from Mary Wollstonecraft calling for an end to social coercion so that with "the common law of gravity prevailing, the sexes will fall into their proper places," she accented her commitment to the laissez-faire tradition that Enlightenment thinkers had developed. Her appeals to justice over expediency and to liberty over order further affirmed her grounding in eighteenth-century rationalism.

Nock and LaFollette pursued the libertarian path from Enlightenment rationalism and physiocracy through nineteenth-century liberalism. John Stuart Mill, whom she was especially fond of quoting, and other important utilitarians adapted Enlightenment thought to advancing industrialism, sharpened the argument that individualism was at the root of the general welfare, and used the resulting liberal ideology as a basis for reform efforts. Laissez-faire and social reform need not, after all, be incompatible, for the liberals found considerable challenge in eliminating special privileges and governmentally created inequalities. Liberal reformers hoped to establish a uniform set of laws which treated all people exactly alike and left each individual maximum liberty. Such formal equality of opportunity, when combined with the different talents of each person, would inevitably allow for the development of a certain amount of economic inequality. But the liberals rejected any system which compelled individuals to share the product of their labor—whether through special privilege or socialism—as both unjust and ultimately unworkable. Like Alexis de Tocqueville, they also distrusted an uncontrolled majority and rejected the divine right of any form of government. The invasion of individual liberty by either a single ruler or a tyrannous majority undermined the general welfare by meddling in processes that otherwise encouraged each person to seek his own fullest development. Inspiration from John Stuart Mill, commitment to individualism, opposition to monopoly, and a predisposition to an economic interpretation of politics seasoned LaFollette's thought with a strong dose of British liberalism.

Suzanne LaFollette also followed Nock in combining the Enlightenment–liberal libertarian tradition with the thought of the American reformer, Henry George. Although she made few specific references to George in *Concerning Women,* she adopted his agrarian bias, definition of terms, and general statement of the social problem. In *Progress and Poverty* (1879) George lectured the middle classes on how to struggle against monopoly without resort to socialism or revolution. His patron saint was Thomas Jefferson, and his rhetoric overflowed with references to "Liberty, Justice, Truth, Natural Law, and other strange eighteenth century superstitions." Like the physiocrats and many of the moral philosophers of the Enlightenment, Henry George and his followers thought the roots of most social questions lay in political economy, that is, in the relationships between the political and economic patterns of society.[11]

George defined his terms along classical nineteenth-century liberal lines. The "value" of any object depended upon the labor involved in its creation; "wealth" consisted of natural resources worked by labor into goods; and "capital" amounted to accumulated wealth. "Land," however, was neither the product of labor, reproducible like wealth, nor of unlimited supply. George asserted that God had created mankind with a natural right to the use of the earth. Yet one person's ownership of land that another used to survive left the latter a servant of the former. Indeed the only reason for holding land that one did not use was to charge others for access to God-made resources.

Much as LaFollette and Nock admired Enlightenment thinkers, liberals, and Georgians, the America of Wilson, Harding, and Coolidge left little hope that the principles and stratagems of libertarian forbears would finally achieve prominence in the modern world. Enlightenment leaders had elegantly proclaimed important principles of life, liberty, and the pursuit of happiness, and some had engaged in revolutionary action to reach these goals. But none had established a libertarian society. Nineteenth-century liberals had raised the banner of laissez-faire capitalism without abolishing monopoly. And the Georgians had failed in their attempts to regulate politically generated economic privilege. The early twentieth-century Western world engaged in a mammoth imperialist slaughter; fundamental civil liberties were betrayed; Americans increasingly chose between only oligopolistic or bureaucratic paternalism and socialism; and the prewar hopefulness of New York rebels soured into pessimism, cynicism, and complete alienation. Noble principles had been proclaimed, ignoble deeds performed.

LaFollette and Nock offered a radical proposal to avoid the failures of their intellectual predecessors. Rationalists from the eighteenth century to the present had diagnosed the social disease without prescribing what now seemed to be the only sure cure—the destruction of the engine of privilege or the abolition of the state. With the state intact, libertarian principles were inevitably eroded and monopoly gradually reestablished. Their analysis of the state as the primary source of privilege and their advocacy of anarchism as the surest way to reform were strongly influenced by the work of the twentieth-century German sociologist, Franz Oppenheimer.

Oppenheimer stressed the fundamental importance of the human quest for adequate food, clothing, and housing which, he argued, could be obtained either by economic means (labor) or by political means (robbery). Organized according to economic means, mankind lives in "society"—"the totality . . . of all purely natural relations and institutions between man and man." Human beings organized under political means live in a "state"—"that summation of privileges and dominating positions which are brought into being by extra economic power." Oppenheimer believed that "world history, from primitive times up to our own civilization, presents a single phase, a contest namely between the economic and the political means; and it can present only this phase until we have achieved free citizenship."[12]

Oppenheimer traced the evolution of the state through feudalism and absolutism to its modern constitutional mold, noting that the state's "*form* still continues to be domination, its content still remains the exploitation of the economic means." Only the class, the type, and the instruments of exploitation have changed over time. As long as feudal nobles ruled the state, "they exploited it as they would have managed an estate"; when the bourgeoisie came to power in the modern constitutional state, they managed society "as though it were a factory." Oppenheimer wanted to bypass both capitalism and communism and to synthesize individualism and collectivism in his quest for the good society. He proposed the replacement of the state with an international federation of rural-producer cooperatives that would discipline and finally dissolve monopoly through competition. With the political means destroyed, each citizen, free from class domination and exploitation, would then be able to develop his own talents and receive the full fruits of his own labor. Oppenheimer sought his utopia through evolution, for a revolution pressed by any class, he warned Marxists in particular, would only establish another state, not secure freedom by abolishing statism altogether.[13]

For Nock and LaFollette, Oppenheimer's theories rescued libertarianism from its despoilers by establishing the abolition of the state as an ultimate social goal. They needed, however, a far more sympathetic outlet to publicize their new radical libertarianism than that offered by the *Nation.* Nock developed one through his friendship with Francis J. Neilson, a British Liberal M. P. and Georgian who was disillusioned with the parliamentary system, and then insisted that LaFollette be included in the new venture. Neilson, who considered himself heir to John Stuart Mill's philosophic radicals, had moved to the United States. From 1920 through 1924 with his wife's wealth, Neilson and his new associates edited and published a weekly which cut beneath the allegedly superficial "liberalism" of the *Nation* and the *New Republic* to the root of social problems. They declared their weekly a "radical" exponent of anarchistic or nonstatist libertarianism and entitled it "Freeman," that is, one who enjoyed Oppenheimer's utopia of "freeman citizenship" or civil and political liberty.[14] Mrs. Neilson shared the editors' antipathy for making the journal commercial and therefore a part of the levelling, bourgeois culture they all disliked, so the *Freeman* never accepted advertising nor modified an editorial policy in order to court public support or secure financial self-sufficiency. During the *Freeman*'s four years, Suzanne LaFollette generally served as an informal managing editor under Nock's immediate direction and often wrote on the arts. On two occasions when he was otherwise engaged, she assumed the overall directing editorship.

As radical libertarians or anarchistic liberals who looked forward to the state's withering away, the editors kept an open mind about the Bolshevik revolution in Russia, although they never advocated the violent overthrow of government. They wanted a peaceful revolution in which reason overcame injustice and common sense overwhelmed statism. Governments, however, seemed bent on producing a social cataclysm that the editors did not welcome. By acting to maintain the rights of monopoly, governments had produced so many worldwide labor crises and so much economic disintegration that they pushed "the masses" toward violent revolution. "A peaceful revolution is still possible and practicable," LaFollette asserted in the first issue, "and such is the eager hope of enlightened minds. The aristocratic state has passed; the middle-class state is fast passing, after a much shorter lease of life. The next step, logically, is the proletarian state, whose tenure may be even shorter before the idea of the state is wholly and finally superseded by the idea of Society."[15]

After the *Freeman* ceased publication in 1924, Suzanne LaFollette was never again so closely or protractedly associated with Alfred Nock. She was by this time, however, fully enough schooled in and deeply committed to libertarianism to pursue its implications for her particular interests—the artist and the woman—with Nock's encouragement but only occasional presence. A 1925 article explored the place of the creative individual in modern America in terms that echoed through her later books. She pointed to the artist's crucial function in society, deplored contemporary artistic performance as inadequate, and demanded extended freedom for the creative spirit. The nation's great need for improvement in the "quality and depth of spiritual life" depended largely for its fulfillment upon "the generation and development of ideas" that, she argued, "must necessarily" come from "profound and original individual intelligence." Every artist worked for the liberation of "those spiritual powers which are latent within us all" in order to "contribute their fruits to the increase of human wisdom and human joy."[16]

She saw little chance for unleashing creative individualism in the twenties without first lessening the pervasive influence of institutions. "American culture is in need of sustenance," she argued, but its leaders "are feeding it machinery." The unfortunate individual caught in the corporate machinery of the twenties had importance "only as a part of that machinery, and not at all for what he may be in himself." "Organizing entails rules, observances and institutional habits of a progressive and deleterious formalism. The adjustment of the human parts of the machine entails friction and waste motion; each placeholder is impelled to perform his function with one eye on his work and the other on his relation to the organization." Hence "the demands of organization are directly opposed to those of civilization; for whereas organization demands the suppression of individuality, civilization is best promoted by its free development."

She went on to develop many of the same themes and apply them directly to women the following year in her feminist treatise, *Concerning Women,* which Nock encouraged and got subsidized by certain of his Philadelphia patrons. Suzanne's upbringing on the frontier, her education, her exposure to progressive politics, her participation in the woman suffrage movement, her career activities, and her feminist relatives and associates all predisposed her to become interested in the search for sexual equality. The LaFollettes, Henry George, and Alfred Nock were all feminists. Writing in the prewar years about the famous muckraker, Ida M. Tarbell, Nock premised "that women are not a sex by themselves, any more than men are, but are human folks." If woman is human, "what am I that I should pretend to control, regulate, or dictate another human being's conduct?" The "long and short" of the sex question, he realized, "is proprietary—the man pays the bills." Hopeful that in fifty years "men and women will be walking along in relations of full justice and freedom," he anticipated a "happier and better" world "when the services people render each other are a free gift of good will and devotion." Nock and the other *Freeman* editors had made their firm commitment to woman's rights clear in numerous issues of their journal.[17]

LaFollette grounded her feminism squarely in the rationalist tradition, citing Enlightenment, liberal, and Georgian thinkers as authorities and building from their definitions and upon their principles. Her rationalist commitment was also evidenced by her disagreement with nonrationalist thinkers and principles. This dissent separated her from the feminism of Sarah Grimké, Margaret Fuller, and Margaret Sanger, although her admiration for the creative individual, especially the artist, was not altogether free of Romantic overtones. Though clearly Christian, she was uninterested in the religiously intuitive preoccupation of Sarah Grimké. Suzanne LaFollette carefully limited flights of emotional self-expression and ignored the idealist's world so congenial to Fuller. Her disapproval of the irrationalism of Friedrich Nietzsche, the sexual psychology of Havelock Ellis, and the new sexual morality of Ellen Key separated LaFollette from the intellectual roots of Sanger's feminism.

Through explicit denial or more often by treating the issue as one of secondary importance, LaFollette dismissed most of the nonrationalist feminists' assumptions of significant sexual differences. Her feminism was built squarely upon the Enlightenment-liberal demand for exactly equal political, legal, and economic rights for all persons, regardless of the manifold differences between individuals. Women might be wives and mothers, but in LaFollette's mind such functions were always secondary to their position as individual human beings. The question of woman's position in society was in essence as simple for LaFollette as it had been for Nock—if women were people, they deserved full civil equality. The ways in which they differed from men were of distinctly secondary importance.

LaFollette shared much of Gilman's rationalist feminism. Each believed that feminine subordination was primarily the result of imposed economic dependence, doubted that suffrage would be a panacea for woman, generally questioned the value of traditional political activism, and rejected Marxist analysis and revolution. Neither approved of the new sexual morality associated with irrationalist thought. But the differences between LaFollette and Gilman were almost as important as their similarities. LaFollette's emphasis upon individualism was closer to John Stuart Mill's liberalism than Gilman's evolutionary socialism. The two women each envisioned a rather different good society—Gilman favored the use of the state to remove all artificial barriers to equality; LaFollette sought a society where individuals, free from institutional control, could explore the limits of their infinitely different abilities. Gilman looked forward to social, political, and economic equality; Lafollette, who granted equal rights and opportunities to all, allowed for the development of social and economic differences limited by competitive forces.

The thrust of LaFollette's questioning reached beyond economic and political institutions and the structure of the home to include marriage and family patterns as well. Although Mill had also critically examined conventional marital and familial patterns, Suzanne LaFollette extended attacks on those institutions much further than Gilman or Mill. Gilman's proposals that certain maternal functions and domestic routines should be socialized struck LaFollette as attempts to cure serious social cancers with first aid and small doses of institutional poison. Acutely sensitive to institutional control, LaFollette linked feminine subordination more closely to marriage than any previous feminist thinker with the possible exception of John Mill. She proposed to de-institutionalize all aspects of life, including marriage and the family, and to permit individuals to choose whatever social patterns they preferred. She would allow variety to replace uniform state regulation. Mill had also favored governmental nonintervention in social arrangements; but without abolition of the state, LaFollette believed, relapses into statism were possible and indeed likely. Her anarchism generally defined an individualism that was consistently more radical than Mill's. Where Mill had worked within the parliamentary system and accepted industrialization, LaFollette denied the value of the state and questioned corporate capitalism.

Applying her anarchistic liberalism to the question of woman's status, LaFollette offered a novel feminist analysis. She acknowledged the value of female suffrage, recently won at great effort, and the need to achieve legal equality as well. But she dissented vigorously from the common suffragist belief that political or legal equality would cure feminine subordination. Altogether distrustful of governmental measures, she explored the inadequacies of protective welfare legislation which had only adjusted subjugated women to industrial conditions. LaFollette argued that meaningful freedom for women would occur only when both sexes secured economic justice through a wholesale reconstruction of society. Political and legal reforms could secure equality between the sexes in semifreedom; but woman's liberation awaited human liberation from privilege, monopoly, and the state. The question of woman's place in society, she concluded, could not be analyzed or resolved alone; it must be understood as an essential part of a larger social problem.

LaFollette only vaguely outlined a strategy to achieve the good society. Land monopoly, the political party system, and corporate capitalism, she argued, contained the seeds of their own destruction. Reliance on statism ultimately leads the exploited to revolutionary action. But, like Nock, Oppenheimer, George, and Mill, she did not welcome revolution. Any outbreak of violence left women, the physically weaker sex, at a disadvantage. Women had always paid a greater price than men in periods of violent turmoil, and they would suffer most again. Feminists who since the days of Mary Wollstonecraft had been preoccupied with removing woman's inequalities did not recognize how fragile their gains were. Unless they integrated the fight for sexual equality with the struggle for full freedom for humanity, they would find all they had built at such great cost left in ruins. Among the most oppressed groups in society, women should be especially sensitive to social injustice and their own vulnerability. They should be well prepared to help to avoid the predicted social catastrophe. Marshalling their numbers, they could call the people to a peaceful revolution against statism at the ballot box. Otherwise, twentieth-century rationalists would fail to liberate mankind as completely as had eighteenth-century philosophes.

With her feminist treatise completed, she left for Paris, where she spent a year studying history and economics before Nock suggested that she write a history of American art. She returned home "reluctantly" to draft *Art in America,* published in 1929, which, although well reviewed, became swamped in the social crisis she had long predicted. The Great Depression brought increasing government intervention in society through the New Deal at home and fascism and nazism abroad. Throughout the thirties in numerous articles for *Scribner's Magazine,* the *Nation,* and the

New Republic, she both expressed her distrust of welfare-state measures and New Dealers' motives and exposed the totalitarian implications of nazism.[18] Aided by Nock, she revived the old faith briefly in the *New Freeman,* published from March 1930 through May 1931 with the patronage of a wealthy chemist. The *New Freeman* recalled the old distrust of imperialism, defended civil liberties, and sympathized with the Soviets.

LaFollette's concern about totalitarian advances deepened when the Russian communists purged their remaining nonstatist, Trotskyite idealists. In April 1937 she indicated her final disillusionment with the Soviet experiment by joining the famous progressive philosopher-educator John Dewey and others in an international commission which exonerated Trotsky of the Soviet charges against him. She played a leading role in the commission's activities by serving as its secretary and writing its final report, *Not Guilty.*[19]

Her pronounced dislike of the welfare state and communism became still more strident during and after World War II, her associates were increasingly more conservative, and her libertarian concerns tended more to defend existing freedoms than to strike out for newer or larger ones. From 1943 to 1945 she directed the foreign relief programs of an American Federation of Labor obsessed with ensuring a noncommunist reconstruction of war-torn areas. As President Truman prepared to embark for the Potsdam Conference in mid-1945, she joined John Dewey, Herbert Hoover, Alfred Landon, a number of conservative Roman Catholic prelates, and others in a public letter that bristled with cold war thought and rhetoric. Unless the president abandoned his "foreign policy of weakness, hesitation, and immoral compromise" with the Soviet Union, the writers feared "for the future peace of the world and for democracy at home."[20]

When LaFollette joined Henry Hazlitt and John Chamberlain in 1950 to start publication of yet another *Freeman,* the editors declared their intention "to revive the John Stuart Mill concept of liberalism. We feel we're rescuing an old word from misuse." But in 1953 after managing editor LaFollette and John Chamberlain disagreed with Hazlitt and the board of directors, LaFollette and Chamberlain resolved to start a new publication. Two years later, William F. Buckley, Jr., announced the birth of the *National Review,* which LaFollette would help to edit. He promised that this new magazine would strike out boldly against the nation's welfare-state proclivities and President Eisenhower's "appeasement" of Russian communism.[21]

From one era to another, from one periodical to the next, from feminism to cold war anticommunism, Suzanne LaFollette has espoused the doctrines of radical libertarianism. She has watched "the disintegration of the Western World—above all our own country—and the steady growth of totalitarian influence and power" with "growing concern" and wielded her pen in the cause of individualism. As industrial societies have nevertheless moved further away from her libertarian ideal, she wonders whether her biography might not be most appropriately entitled, "Chasing Wild Geese."

Her feminism—an outgrowth of her social thought at large—at once fuses a radical analysis with certain anachronistic elements. Having cut herself loose from the suffragist outlook, she was prepared for the disappointments that disillusioned so many feminists in the twenties and thirties. She then sought a far wider equality for woman and focused more fully on the institutional basis of inequality than most feminists of those decades. Alienated from the developing mass society, she stepped far enough outside modern America to offer a radical diagnosis of woman's inequality. But she offered a reactionary prescription for its cure by proposing an individualism never reconciled with the need for specialization and organization in any modern industrial society.

She has greeted the contemporary woman's movement with "a great deal of sympathy." Indeed she anticipated some of the current feminists' dismissal of political rights as cure-all, their heightened interest in personal autonomy, and their emphasis upon the institutional basis of sexism. But she also feels "some disagreement." Sisterhood may be powerful enough to raise woman's consciousness of oppression and to permit a few to practice alternative life-styles. For Suzanne LaFollette, however, only a nonsexist brotherhood in a nonstatist society can in the long run establish the social conditions that will permit each human being to reach and sustain his full potential without regard to class, race, or sex.

NOTES

1. *New York Times,* 28 October 1964, 39.

2. Suzanne LaFollette, *Concerning Women* (New York: Albert & Charles Boni, Inc., 1926), has not been reprinted. William L. O'Neill, *Everyone Was Brave: The Rise and Fall of Feminism in America* (Chicago: Quadrangle Books, Inc., 1969), 325.

3. Quotations from John Langdon-Davies' review in *New York Herald Tribune Books* III, No. 19, 23 January 1927, 1, 6. For other reviews, see *New Republic* XLIX, 12 January 1927, 228; *New York Times,* 26 June 1927, 6; *Booklist* XXIII, May 1927, 329; *Bookman* LXIV, 27 January 1927, 640.

4. Miss Suzanne LaFollette graciously provided the editors with an autobiographical statement and answered a number of specific questions in writing

during the fall of 1971. Quotations from Miss LaFollette in this and ensuing paragraphs which are not otherwise cited were taken from that correspondence. The editors wish to express their gratitude to Miss LaFollette for her kind and generous assistance.

5. In addition to the LaFollette autobiographical statement, see Belle Case LaFollette and Fola LaFollette, *Robert M. LaFollette* (2 volumes, New York: The Macmillan Co., 1953), I, 604; II, 893, 1083, 1085.

6. Francis J. Nock (ed.), *Selected Letters of Albert Jay Nock* (Caldwell, Idaho: The Caxton Printers, Ltd., 1962), 100.

7. In addition to the LaFollette autobiographical statement, see Susan J. Turner, *A History of the Freeman: Literary Landmark of the Early Twenties* (New York: Columbia University Press, 1963), 170, and Suzanne LaFollette's introduction to Albert Jay Nock, *Snoring as a Fine Art and Twelve Other Essays* (Rindge, New Hampshire: R. R. Smith, 1958), vii-xi.

8. Miss Suzanne LaFollette offered the following summary assessment of Nock's influence on *Concerning Women* in a letter to the editors of 13 October 1971: "What impressed and amused me when I re-read *Concerning Women* a few months ago after forty years was the similarity of the style to his. That is not surprising, really, for he not only influenced my thought; he took on my education in English style, and he was an exacting taskmaster."

9. For Nock's social philosophy, see Albert Jay Nock, *On Doing the Right Thing and Other Essays* (New York: Harper & Brothers Publishers, 1928), and Albert Jay Nock, *Our Enemy, the State* (Caldwell, Idaho: The Caxton Printers, Ltd., 1950 reissue of 1935 edition). Quotations from Nock, *Snoring as a Fine Art,* x.

10. Nock, *Selected Letters,* 42–44, 95.

11. For succinct interpretations of George's social ideas, see Daniel Aaron, *Men of Good Hope: A Story of American Progressives* (New York: Oxford University Press, 1962 reprinting of 1951 edition), 55–91, and Ralph Henry Gabriel, *The Course of American Democratic Thought,* revised edition (New York: The Ronald Press, 1956), 208–215. George Bernard Shaw, as quoted in Aaron, *Men of Good Hope,* 78.

12. Franz Oppenheimer, *The State: Its History and Development Viewed Sociologically,* translated by John M. Gitterman (Indianapolis: The Bobbs-Merrill Company, 1914), 27. For a more detailed analysis of Oppenheimer's ideas, see especially Raymond Aron, *German Sociology* (Glencoe, Illinois: The Free Press, 1957), 37–43, and Harry Elmer Barnes (ed.), *An Introduction to the History of Sociology* (Chicago: The University of Chicago Press, 1948), 332–352.

13. Oppenheimer, *State,* 257–258, 264, 276.

14. Nock, *Selected Letters,* 95, 97. For a fuller discussion of the *Freeman* and its editors, see Turner, *Freeman,* especially 1–55.

15. Quoted in Turner, *Freeman,* 39.

16. Materials for this and the following paragraph were drawn from Suzanne

LaFollette, "The Modern Maecenas," *American Mercury* V, June 1925, 188–193.

17. Nock, *Selected Letters,* 23–24.

18. The articles most closely associated with the subject at hand include: "Götterdammerung," *Scribner's Magazine* XCIV, July 1933, 13–16; "The Government Recognizes Art," *Scribner's Magazine* XCV, February 1934, 131–132; "A Message to Uncle Tom," *Nation* CXXIX, 5 September 1934, 265–266; "New Jersey's Army of Unoccupation," *Nation* CXLII, 13 May 1936, 608–610.

19. *New York Times,* 13 April 1937, 3; 18 April 1937, IV, 10; 16 May 1943, IV, 12.

20. *New York Times,* 19 July 1945, 13.

21. *Time* LVI, 16 October 1950, 46–48; LXI, 26 January 1953, 74–75, *New York Times,* 21 January 1953, 29; 22 January 1953, 21; 14 October 1955, 24.

CONCERNING WOMEN (1926)

I. THE BEGINNINGS OF EMANCIPATION

It will be foolish to assume that women are free until books about them shall have ceased to have more than an antiquarian interest. All such books, including this one, imply by their existence that women may be regarded as a class in society, that they have in common certain characteristics, conditions or disabilities which, predominating over their individual variations, warrant grouping them on the basis of sex. No such assumption about men would be thinkable. Certain masculine qualities, so-called, may be singled out by amateur psychologists and opposed to certain feminine qualities, so-called; but from books about the sphere of man, the rights of man, the intelligence of man, the psychology of man, the soul of man, our shelves are mercifully free. Such books may one day appear, but when they do it will mean that society has passed from its present state through a state of sex-equality and into a state of female domination. In that day, in place of the edifying spectacle of men proclaiming that woman is useful only as a bearer of children, society may behold the equally edifying spectacle of women proclaiming that man is useful only as a begetter of children, since it seems to be characteristic of the dominant sex to regard the other sex chiefly as a source of pleasure and as a means of reproduction. It seems also to be characteristic of the dominant sex—I judge from the world's experience during the domination of men—to regard itself as humanity and the other sex as a class of somewhat lower beings created by Providence for its convenience and enjoyment, just as it is characteristic of a dominant class, such as an aristocracy, to regard the lower classes as being created solely for the purpose of supporting its power and doing its will. When once a social order is well established, no matter what injustice it involves, those who occupy a position of advantage are not long in coming to believe that it is the only possible and reasonable order and imposing their belief, by force if necessary, on those whom circumstances have placed in their power. There is nothing more innately human than the tendency to transmute what has become customary into what has been divinely ordained.

. . . Men themselves have stood for a good deal of subjection during the world's known history. Chattel slavery and serfdom were abolished from the civilized world only at about the time that the subjection of women began to be modified; and men still endure, not only with resignation but with positive cheerfulness, a high degree of industrial and political slavery. The man who is entirely dependent for his livelihood upon the will of an employer is an industrial slave, and the man who may be drafted into an army and made to fight and perhaps die for a cause in which he can have no possible interest is the slave of the State; yet one cannot see that this proves Aristotle's assumption that there are free natures and slave natures, any more than the subjection of women proves that they want to be subjected. . . .

. . . Those anxious critics who protest that women have got more freedom than is good for Society make the mistake of supposing that Society can exist only if its organization remains unchanged. . . . Certainly the present tendency of woman to assume a position of equality with man involves, and will continue even more to involve, profound psychic and material readjustments. But to assume that such readjustments will injure or destroy Society is . . . to attribute to it a personality, to suppose that it is equally capable of destruction with the individual, and that it may in some mystical way derive benefit from the sacrifice of the individual's best interests. But what is Society save an aggregation of individuals, half male, half female? . . . To assume that its "interests" may be promoted by the enslavement of one-half its members is unreasonable. One may be permitted the doubtful assumption that this enslavement promotes the welfare of the other half of Society, but it is obvious that it cannot promote the welfare of the whole, unless we assume that slavery is beneficial to the slave (the classic assumption, indeed, where the slaves have been women). When we consider the political organization known as the State, we have a different matter. The State always represents the organized interest of a dominant class; therefore the subjection of other classes may be said to benefit the State, and their emancipation may be opposed as a danger to the State.

It is evident from the very nature of the State that its interests are opposed to those of Society; and while the complete emancipation of women . . . would undoubtedly imply the destruction of the State, since it must accrue from the emancipation of other subject classes, their emancipation, far from destroying Society, must be of inestimable benefit to it. Those critics, and there are many, who argue that women must submit to restrictions upon their freedom for the good of the State, as well as those advocates of woman's rights who argue that women must be emancipated for the good of the State, simply fail to make this vital distinction between the State and Society; and their failure to do so is one of the potent reasons why the nonsense that has been written about women is limited only by the literature of the subject.

Feminist and anti-feminist arguments from this standpoint center in the function of childbearing; therefore it should be noted that the emphasis which is placed on this function by the interest of the State is quite different from the emphasis that would be placed upon it by the interest of Society; for the interest of the State is numerical, while the interest of Society is qualitative. The State requires as many subjects as possible, both as labor-motors and as fighters. The interest of Society, on the other hand, is the interest of civilization: If a community is to be wholesome and intelligent, it is necessary not that the individuals who compose it shall be as numerous as possible but that they shall be as wholesome and intelligent as possible. . . .

The interest of the State in this respect has

been most concisely expressed by Nietzsche. "Man," said he, "shall be trained for war, and woman for the re-creation of the warrior: all else is folly"; and if one accept his premises, he is exactly right. But there have been many writers on women who have not accepted his premises—not at least without qualification—and who have yet failed to observe the antithesis between the interest which the State has and the interest which Society has in the question of population. Hence, mingled with the voices of those critics who have demanded the subjection of woman for the sake of children, have been the voices of other critics demanding her emancipation for the sake of children; and both these schools of critics have overlooked her claim to freedom on her own behalf. It is for the sake of humanity, and not for the sake of children, that women ought to have equal status with men. That children will gain enormously by the change is true; but this is beside the issue, which is justice.

The argument that woman must be free for the sake of the race is an argument of expediency, as nine-tenths of the arguments against her legal subjection have been and indeed had to be. Unfortunately, humanity is likely to turn a deaf ear to the claims of justice, especially when they conflict with established abuses, unless these claims are backed by the claims of expediency plus a good measure of necessity. Adventitious circumstances have made the social recognition of woman's claims a necessity and their political recognition a matter of expediency. Otherwise she would have to wait much longer for the establishment of her rights as man's equal than now appears likely. In the Western world her battle is very largely won; full equality, social, industrial and legal, seems to be only a matter of time and tactics. This she owes to the great political and industrial revolutions of the eighteenth century.

The conscious movement towards freedom for women may be said to have originated in the great emancipatory movement which found expression in the American and French revolutions. The revolutionists did not succeed in establishing human freedom; they poured the new wine of belief in equal rights for all men into the old bottle of privilege for some, and it soured. But they did succeed in creating political forms which admitted, in theory at least, the principle of equality. Their chief contribution to progress was that they dramatically and powerfully impressed the idea of liberty upon the minds of men and thus altered the whole course of human thought. Mary Wollstonecraft's book, *A Vindication of the Rights of Women,* revolutionary though it seemed in its day, was a perfectly natural and logical application of this idea of liberty to the situation of her sex. This remarkable book may be said to have marked the beginning of the conscious movement towards the emancipation of women.

The unconscious movement was the outgrowth of the revolution in industry, brought about by the introduction of the machine. Women had always been industrial workers, but their work, after the break-up of the guilds, was for the most part carried on at home. When the factory supplanted the family as the producing unit in society, the environment of women was altered. And the change affected not only those women who followed industry to the factories but also those who remained housewives; for where these had before been required to perform, or at least to superintend, a large amount of productive work, they now found their function, as the family became a consuming unit, reduced to the superintendence of expenditures and the operation of the household machinery—a labor which was increasingly lightened by the progress of invention. With domestic conditions so changed, what was more natural than that the daughters should go into the factory; or, if the family were well-to-do, into the schools, which were forced reluctantly to open their doors to women? And what was more natural than that women, as their minds were developed through education, should perceive the injustice and humiliation of their position and organize to defend their right to recognition as human beings? . . .

Women in the factories and shops, women in the schools—from this it was only a moment to their invasion of the professions and not a very long time until they would be invading every field that had been held the special province of men. This is the great unconscious and unorganized woman's movement which has aroused such fear and resentment among people who saw it without understanding it.

The organized movement may be regarded simply as an attempt to get this changing relation of women to their environment translated into the kind of law that the eighteenth century had taught the world to regard as just: law based on the theory of equal rights for all human beings. The opposition that the movement encountered offers ample testimony to the fact that "acceptance in principle" is more than a mere subterfuge of diplomats and politicians. The eighteenth and nineteenth centuries resolutely clung to the theory of equality, and as resolutely opposed its logical application. This is not surprising; most people, no doubt, when they espouse human rights, make their own mental reservations about the proper application of the word "human." Women had hardly been regarded as human in mediaeval Europe; they were considered something a little more from the chivalrous point of view and something a little less from the more common, workaday standpoint. The shadow of this old superstition still clouded the minds of men: Therefore it is hardly surprising that the egalitarians of the French Revolution excluded women from equal political and legal rights with men and that the young American republic, which had adopted the Declaration of Independence, continued to sanction the slavery of Negroes and the subjection of women. . . . Nor does superstition die easily. The masculine assumption, usually quite unconscious, that women are unfit for freedom bids fair to persevere as stubbornly as the feminine assumption that marriage offers a legitimate and established mode of extortion. . . .

IV. WOMAN AND MARRIAGE

I.

Perhaps the most pronounced conventional distinction between the sexes is made in their relation to marriage. For man, marriage is regarded as a state; for woman, as a vocation. For man, it is a means of ordering his life and perpetuating his name; for woman, it is considered a proper and fitting aim of existence. . . . This assumption, I may remark, has been justified expressly or by implication by all those advocates of freedom for women who have assured the world that woman's "mission" of wifehood and motherhood would be better fulfilled rather than worse through an extension of her rights. If we imagine the signers of the Declaration of Independence, in place of proclaiming the natural right of all men to life, liberty, and the pursuit of happiness, arguing with King George that a little more freedom would make them better husbands and fathers, we shall imagine a pretty exact parallel for this kind of argument on behalf of the emancipation of women. . . .

The view of woman as a biological function might be strongly defended on the ground of racial strength if that function were respected and she were free in discharging it. But it is not respected and she is not free. The same restrictions that have kept her in the status of a function have denied her freedom and proper respect even in the exercise of that function. Motherhood, to be sure, receives a great deal of sentimental adulation, but only if it is committed in accordance with rules which have been prescribed by a predominantly masculine society. *Per se* it is accorded no respect whatever. When it results from a sexual relationship which has been duly sanctioned by organized society, it is holy, no matter how much it may transgress the rules of decency, health, or common sense. Otherwise it is a sin meriting social ostracism for the mother and obloquy for the child—an ostracism and an obloquy, significantly enough, in which the father does not share.

The motives behind the universal condemnation of extra-legal motherhood are various and complex; but I believe it is safe to say that the strongest is masculine jealousy. Motherhood out of wedlock constitutes a defiance of that theory of male proprietorship on which most societies are based; it implies on the part of woman a seizure of sexual freedom which, if it were countenanced, would threaten the long-established dominance of the male in sexual matters, a dominance which has been enforced by imposing all manner of unnatural social and legal disabilities upon women, such, for example, as the demand for virginity before marriage and chastity after it. The woman who bears an illegitimate child violates one of these two restrictions. On the other hand, the man who begets an illegitimate child violates no such restriction, for society demands of him neither virginity nor chastity. . . .

. . . There is likely to be a grim consistency in legal injustices. . . . The denial to women of economic opportunity has made expedient denial of freedom in performing the function of motherhood. Men, having enjoyed a virtual monopoly of earning power, have been regarded as the natural providers for women and children; therefore a woman has been required to get a legal provider before she could legally get a child; and if one accepted her legal disabilities without questioning their justice, this restraint might appear quite justifiable. . . . In a society where economic opportunity is pretty well monopolized by men, the task of the mother with children to support is . . . extremely difficult; and it may even be rendered impossible where the disgrace of unmarried motherhood decreases such comparatively slight opportunity as industry, even now, offers a woman. . . .

Instead of joining in the universal condemnation of illegitimacy, it seems more reasonable to question the ethics of a society which permits it to exist. Certainly no social usage could be more degrading to women as mothers of the race than that which makes it a sin to bear a child; and nothing could be more grotesquely unjust than a code of morals, reinforced by laws, which relieves men from responsibility for irregular sexual acts and for the same acts drives women to abortion, infanticide, prostitution and self-destruction. I know of no word that may be said in justification of such a code or of a society that tolerates it. As marriage ceases to be a vested interest with women and as their growing freedom enables them to perceive the insult to their humanity that this kind of morality involves, they will refuse to stand for it. Those who prefer to regard woman as a function will devote their energy to securing conditions under which she may bear and bring up children with a greater degree of freedom and self-respect than conventional morality allows her. As for those who prefer to regard her as a human being, they will naturally demand the abolition of all discriminations based on sex, while all women must certainly repudiate the barbarous injustice of organized society to the illegitimate child. . . .

The importance of abolishing illegitimacy is not to be underrated, for it means the removal of the legal sanctions which have enforced a barbarous custom. But the abolition of illegitimacy cannot be expected entirely to remove the stigma attaching to unmarried motherhood and birth out of wedlock. That will disappear only when the economic independence of women shall have resulted in a spiritual independence which will lead them to examine critically the social dogmas that have been forced upon them and to repudiate those which conflict with justice. In other words, it will involve an adaptation to more humane ethical standards, an adaptation which has begun but may be long in reaching completion, for superstition and taboo are not easily eradicated.

II.

. . . The subjection of women, like all slavery, has been enforced by legally established economic disadvantages; and upon the married woman these disadvantages, or some of them, are still binding in most communities. The law deprived her of the right to her own property and her own labor and in return gave her a claim upon her husband for bare subsistence, which is the claim of a serf. Since woman's partial emergence from her subjection and the consequent modification of the discriminations against her, laws which were logical and effective when her status was that of a chattel have been allowed to survive other laws which made them necessary. The result is a grotesque hodge-podge of illogical and contradictory provisions which involve injustice to both sexes and should be abolished by the simple expedient of making men and women equal in all respects before the law and sweeping away all legal claims which they now exercise against one another by virtue of the marriage-bond.

This would mean, of course, that a woman might no longer legally claim support from her husband by virtue of her wifehood; nor should she in fairness be able to do so when all his claims to her property and services had been abolished. There is . . . a better way of dealing with their economic handicaps than the way of penalizing husbands and demoralizing a large number of women by degrading marriage for them to the level of a means of livelihood, gained sometimes through virtual blackmail. Given complete equality of the sexes, so that prejudice may no longer avail itself of legal sanction for excluding women from the occupations in which they may elect to engage, the economic handicaps from which they may still suffer will be those resulting from the overcrowded condition of the general labor-market. The ultimate emancipation of woman, then, will depend not upon the abolition of the restrictions which have subjected her to man—that is but a step, though a necessary one—but upon *the abolition of all those restrictions of natural human rights that subject the mass of humanity to a privileged class.*

This phase of woman's problem is the main thesis of my book, and since it will come in for detailed consideration in subsequent chapters, I leave it for the present and proceed to discuss some probable results of sex-equality and the removal of legal claims which marriage now gives husband and wife against one another.

The wife would no longer be humiliated by the assumption that as a married woman she is the natural inferior of her husband and entitled to society's protection against the extreme results of the disabilities that her status involves. If she became his housekeeper, she would do so by free choice and not because her services were his legal property; and her resultant claim on his purse would be fixed by mutual arrangement rather than by laws allowing her the claims of a serf. The marriage, if it became an economic partnership, would be so by mutual consent and arrangement and would thus no longer be a one-sided contract, legally defined, in which all the rights were on the side of the husband but compensated in too many cases by unjust privileges on that of the wife. At the same time, the temptation to marry for economic security or ease would be lessened. This temptation besets both men and women, though not in the same degree, because men, through the economic advantage enjoyed by their sex, are oftener in a position of ease than women are. It is the temptation, arising out of man's natural desire to gratify his needs with the least possible exertion, to live by the means of others rather than by one's own labor. Its gratification through marriage would not be rendered impossible by the mere abolition of coercive laws governing the marriage relation; but at least its cruder manifestations, such as the frequent attempts of unscrupulous or demoralized women to use marriage for purposes of extortion, would no longer assail the nostrils of the public. Its reduction to a minimum must await the establishment of an economic order under which self-support will be easy and certain.

More general and binding, even, than the economic obligations that marriage entails are the personal claims that it creates. In so far as these claims are psychological—those of affection and habit or attachment to children—their regulation and abrogation will always afford a problem which must be solved by the two persons concerned. There is at present a strong tendency to equalize the incidence of the laws whereby the State defines these relations and imposes them on married people. The old assumption of feminine inferiority in sexual rights is gradually yielding to a single standard for both sexes. So, also, the requirement that the wife shall in all matters subordinate her will and judgment to the will and judgment of her husband tends to be modified by the new view of woman as a free agent rather than a mere adjunct to man. Qualifications for marriage and grounds for divorce tend to become the same for both sexes as the State is forced to relinquish its right to regard as offences in one sex actions which it does not recognize as offences in the other. It would appear, indeed, that the time is not far distant when the marriage-law, however humiliating its provisions may be, will bear equally on men and women.

But mere equalization of the law's incidence leaves untouched the previous question whether any third person—and the State assumes the role of a third person—has a legitimate right to define and regulate the personal relations of adult and presumably mature people. So long as the basic assumption goes unchallenged that the State may grant to man and woman lifelong monopoly-rights in one another or monopoly-rights which shall endure, despite the inclination of the persons concerned, during the State's pleasure, so long will complaints of harsh or unjust marriage or divorce laws prove the truth of Mill's dictum that "no enslaved class ever asked for complete liberty at once . . . those who are under any power of ancient origin never begin by complaining of the power itself but only of its oppressive exercise." Marriage under conditions arbitrarily fixed by an external agency is slavery; and if we allow the right of an external agency—be it State, family, or community—to place marriage in so degrading a position, we necessarily deny the freedom of the individual in this most intimate of relationships and put ourselves in the position of petitioners for privilege when we sue for an improvement in the rules to which we have subjected ourselves.

When this fundamental fact is borne in mind, it becomes at once apparent that marriage will gain in dignity through the abolition of all legal sanction upon the personal claims that it involves. In a community which had renounced all claim to prescribe legally the nature of the marriage-bond, its duration, and the manner of its observance, there would be no washing of soiled domestic linen in the squalid publicity of courtrooms and newspaper columns. . . . Its regulation would be left to the people whom it concerned, as it properly should be and safely could be; for as Mill remarked, "the modern conviction, the fruit of a thousand years experience, is that things in which the individual is the person directly interested never go right but as they are left to his own discretion and that any regulation of them by authority, save to protect the rights of others, is sure to be mischievous." The only way to protect married people against the bad faith which one may show toward the other is to leave the door wide open for either of them to be quit of the union the minute it ceases to be satisfactory. If society for any reason sees fit to close the door to freedom, it sets union by law above the union by affection on which alone true marriage is based; and in so doing it is responsible for an amount of injustice, spiritual conflict, and suffering which no attempt at equitable regulation can ever compensate. Such attempts are in reality mere efforts to adjust the marriage-relation to the fundamental injustice of the marriage-law.

Perhaps the most serious objection to the union by law is that it is so often an effective barrier against the union by affection; for the union by law complicates marriage with a great many uses that are not properly germane to it, such as the custom of taking on one another's family and friends and the setting up of a common menage where this most intimate and delicate of relationships is maintained in a trying semi-publicity under the critical and unwavering scrutiny of relatives and friends. . . .

I have not forgotten the children. One could hardly do so in an age when sentimentalism offers them as the final and unanswerable reason for continuing to tolerate the injustice involved in institutionalized marriage. . . . Children are really as helpless as women have always been held to be, and in their case the reason is not merely supposition. Woman was supposed to be undeveloped man. The child *is* undeveloped man or woman, and because of its lack of development it needs protection. To place it in the absolute power of its parents as its natural protectors and assume that its interests will invariably be well guarded would be as cruel as was the assumption that a woman rendered legally and economically helpless and delivered over to a husband or other male guardian was sure of humane treatment. . . . Here, then, is a legitimate office for the community: to arbitrate in the interest of justice between children and their guardians.

But the community has a more direct and less disinterested concern in the welfare of children: Every child is a potential power for good or ill; what its children become, that will the community become. It is knowledge of this that prompts the establishment of public schools and colleges and all the manifold associational activities intended to promote the physical and spiritual welfare of children. . . . From all this activity it is only a step to the assumption by the community of entire responsibility for the upbringing and education of every child. This idea has some advocates; it is a perfectly logical corollary of the modern conception of the child's relation to the community. . . . But . . . the substitution of institutionalized care for parental care is more than a little doubtful; for to institutionalize means in great degree to mechanize. To establish such a system and make it obligatory would be to remove many children from the custody of parents entirely unfitted to bring them up; but it would likewise involve the removal of many children from the custody of parents eminently well fitted for such a responsibility. It would imply an assumption that the people who might be engaged to substitute for parents would be better qualified for their task than the parents themselves; and such an assumption would be dangerous so long as the work of educators continues to be as little respected and as poorly paid as it now is. Moreover, so long as society remains organized in the exploiting State, the opportunity to corrupt young minds and turn out rubber-stamp patriots would be much greater than that which is now afforded by the public school system, whose influence intelligent parents are sometimes able to neutralize.

Perhaps the best argument against such a system is that it would not work. If experience teaches anything, it is that what the community undertakes to do is usually done badly. This is due in part to the temptation to corruption that such enterprises involve but even more, perhaps, to the lack of personal interest on the part of those engaged in them. . . .

These same considerations apply to the argument that the rearing of children should be institutionalized in order to emancipate women from the immemorial burden of "woman's work." There is a simpler way of dealing with this problem, a way which eliminates an element that dooms to failure any scheme of human affairs in which it is involved, namely, the element of coercion. To contend that all mothers should be forced to devote themselves exclusively to the rearing of children or that they should be forcibly relieved of this responsibility is to ignore the right of the individual to free choice in personal matters. There is no relation more intimately personal than that of parents to the child they have brought into the world; and there is therefore no relationship in which the community should be slower to interfere.

. . . When society had renounced all claim to regulate the affairs of married people, it would content itself with holding all parents, married or unmarried, jointly liable for the support and care of their children. If the parents were married, then the apportioning of this burden between them would be arranged by mutual agreement, and the community's only interest in the contract would be that of arbiter in case of a dispute between the parties, precisely as in case of other contracts. To assume that the community's interest in children justifies its claim to "preserve the home" by making marriage indissoluble or dissoluble only under humiliating conditions is to confuse issues. The practice of perpetuating marriage merely for the sake of children defeats its own end; for it is, far from being good for children, likely to be injurious to them. It condemns them to be brought up in what Mr. [George Bernard] Shaw has well called a little private hell. For the home, as other critics than Mr. Shaw have pointed out, is a proper place for children only when it provides harmonious conditions for their development; and harmony is not characteristic of homes where mutual love and confidence no longer exist between the parents. The demand that the freedom and happiness of parents shall be sacrificed to the so-called interest of the child is in reality a demand that injustice shall be done one person for the sake of another; and where this demand is effective, it serves no end but that of frustration and discord, as might be expected. . . .

III.

The sanctions of monogamic marriage have been enforced on women only. The Christian Church after some indecision finally decided that indissoluble monogamy was the only allowable form of marriage; and in theory it exacted from man and woman the same faithfulness to the marriage-vows. Practically, of course, it did no such thing. Being dominated by men, it eventually came to condone the sexual irregularities of men, if it did not sanction them; but sexual irregularity in the subject sex continued to be both theoretically and practically intolerable. Woman became the repository of morality in a society which regarded morality as chiefly a matter of sex. But since she was at the same time the means of satisfying those sexual needs which Christianity disparaged, she also bore the brunt of social displeasure at violation of the ascetic creed. Womankind . . . was divided into two classes: the virtuous wives and cloistered virgins who embodied Christian morals and those unfortunate social outcasts who sold their bodies to gratify un-Christian desires. . . . Nothing reflects more discredit upon the dominance of the male under Christianity than the fact that he took advantage of the economic helplessness which forced millions of women to sell their sex for a living and then persecuted them outrageously because he had outrageously mistreated them. For prostitution, however much it may reflect upon the morality and, more especially, upon the taste of men, has nothing whatever to do with the morality of women. It is with women a question of economics, purely and simply. The man who buys gratification of his sexual desire has at least an option in the matter; he will not starve if he abstains; but the woman who sells her body indiscriminately to any man who will buy does so because her need to earn a living for herself or her family forces her to do violence to her natural selective sexual disposition. . . .

. . . So long as human beings may starve in the midst of plenty, so long will woman be under temptation to sell the use of her body. She may prostitute herself because she has literally no other way to get a living; she may do so in order to eke out an insufficient wage; she may do so because prostitution seems to offer a relief from hopeless drudgery; she may do so because she has made what the world calls a misstep and is cut off thereby from respectability and the chance to earn a decent living; or she may prostitute herself legally, in marriage, as women have been forced to do from time immemorial. In every case there is one motive force, and that motive force is economic pressure, which bears hardest upon women because of the social, educational, and economic disadvantages from which they are forced to suffer in a world dominated by men. No amount of masculine chivalry has ever mitigated this evil, and no amount ever will; for chivalry is not compulsory, while prostitution is. No amount of exhortation, no amount of devoted labor on the part of reformers will touch it; for it is not a question of morality. No amount of persecution—of arrests, of manhandling, of night-courts, public insult, fine and imprisonment—will check it, for the necessity which prompts it is too imperious to be balked by the uncomprehending guardians of public decency. . . . The parent who, in a world where celibacy and prostitution are on the increase, fails to give a girl child education or training which will enable her to get her living by her own efforts forces her to take a dangerous risk; for the woman who is brought up in the expectation of getting her living by her sex may ultimately be driven to accept prostitution if she fails to find a husband or, having found one, loses him.

There is only one remedy for prostitution, and that remedy is economic freedom—freedom to labor and to enjoy what one produces. When women have this freedom there will be no more prostitution; for no woman will get a living by doing violence to her deep-rooted selective instinct when opportunities are plentiful and a little labor will yield an ample living. There may still be women who are sexually promiscuous; but there is a vast gulf between promiscuity and prostitution: the sexually promiscuous woman may choose her men; the prostitute may not. It is the abysmal gulf between choice and necessity.

IV.

Marriage, illegitimacy and prostitution are so closely related as social problems that it is impossible to draw firm lines of demarcation between them. The unlegalized union—which is betrayed by illegitimate birth—may be a marriage in all but law; the legalized marriage may be merely a respectable form of prostitution; prostitution may take the form of a more or less permanent union which may even assume the dignity of a true marriage. Illegitimacy, marriage, and prostitution do not exist independently; they exist in relation to one another and are often confused in people's minds—as when it is assumed that all mistresses are essentially harlots. They are the three faces of mankind's disastrous attempt to impose arbitrary regulation upon the unruly and terrifying force of sex; they form a triptych of which the central panel is institutionalized marriage and the other panels the two chief aspects of its failure. The title might appropriately be "The Martyrdom of Woman."

Experience has amply proved that as individualism progresses, it becomes increasingly difficult to impose upon people more than an appearance of conformity in sexual matters. Society cannot really regulate anything so essentially personal and private in its nature as the sexual relation: It can only take revenge upon its natural result—and thereby encourage the prevention of that result by artificial means. For every unmarried mother who is persecuted by society, there are ten unmarried women who escape the social consequences of an unauthorized sexual relation. For every faithful husband there is another who deceives his wife with other women, nor are wedded wives by any means always faithful to their marriage vows. There are people who live together in the sexual uncleanness of loveless marriages; and there are those who live purely in extra-legal union. The sexual impulse is too variable and too imperious to be compressed into a formula. . . .

Any people which wishes to attain dignity and seriousness in its collective life must . . . look at all questions—even the vexed one of sex—squarely and honestly. The person who would do this has first some prepossessions to overcome: He must forget tradition long enough to appraise institutionalized marriage by its value to the human spirit; he must resolve for the time to regard men and women as equally human beings, entitled to be judged by the same standards and not by different sets of traditional criteria; and he must put away fear of sex and fear of autonomy. If he can do these things, he may be able to look clear-eyed down the long vista of the centuries and realize the havoc that has been wrought in the souls of men and women by a sexual code and a system of marriage based on a double standard of spiritual values and of conduct. He may perceive how constant tutelage degrades the human spirit and how much greater would be the sum of human joy if freedom were substituted for coercion and regulation—if men and women were without legal power to harass and bedevil one another simply because the State, through the marriage-bond, allows them humiliating rights in one another; if virginity and chastity were matters of self-respect and taste, instead of being matters of worldly self-interest to women and unconcern to men; if the relations between the sexes were based on equality and regulated only by affection and the desire to serve and give happiness.

The modification which institutionalized marriage has been undergoing since the partial emergence of woman, its chief victim, has been in the direction of equality and freedom. The relative ease with which divorce may now be had marks a long step towards recognition of marriage as a personal rather than a social concern; and so does the tendency to abolish the legal disabilities resulting from the marriage-bond. Nothing augurs better for the elevation of marriage to a higher plane than the growing economic independence of women and the consequent improvement in the social position of the unmarried woman; for only when marriage is placed above all considerations of economic or social advantage will it be in a way to satisfy the highest demands of the human spirit.

But the emergence of women has had another significant effect, namely, an increase in frankness concerning extra-legal sexual relations, if not in their number. Of late there has been much public discussion of the wantonness of our modern youth, which, being interpreted, means the disposition of our girls to take the same liberty of indulgence in pre-nuptial sexual affairs that has always been countenanced in boys. This tendency is an entirely natural result of woman's increased freedom. The conditions of economic and social life have undergone revolutionary change in the past half-century; and codes of morals always yield before economic and social exigency, for this is imperious. . . .

If there is about this attitude an element of bravado, akin to that of the youth who thinks it clever and smart to carry a hip-pocket flask, it bears testimony not to the dangers of freedom but to the bankruptcy of conventional morality. The worst effect of tutelage is that it negates self-discipline, and therefore people suddenly released from it are almost bound to make fools of themselves. The women who are emerging from it, if they have not learned to substitute an enlightened self-interest for the morality of repression, are certainly in danger of carrying sexual freedom to dishevelling extremes, simply to demonstrate to themselves their emancipation from unjust conventions. . . .

The real sins of sex are identical for men and women; and they differ from infractions of the conventional moral code in this respect among others: that they do not have to be found out in order to be punished. They carry their punishment in themselves, and that punishment is their deteriorative effect upon the human spirit. They are infractions of spiritual law; and there is this significant distinction to be observed between spiritual laws and the laws of men: that regulation plays no part in their administration. The law of freedom is the law of God, who does not attempt to regulate the human soul but sets instinct there as a guide and leaves man free to choose whether he will follow the instinct which prompts obedience to spiritual law or the desire which urges disregard of it. The extreme sophistication of the conventional attitude towards sex has dulled the voice of instinct for countless generations, with the inevitable result of much unnecessary suffering and irreparable spiritual loss.

A healthy instinct warns against lightness in sexual relationships, and with reason, for the impulse of sex is one of the strongest motive forces in human development and human action. It touches the obscurest depths of the soul; it affects profoundly the functions of the mind and the imagination—cannot, indeed, be dissociated from them. The fact that it is also strongly physical leads to misunderstanding and disregard of its relation to the mind and spirit: a misunderstanding and disregard which are immensely aggravated in a society where woman, because of her inferior position, may be used for the gratification of physical desire with no consideration of her own desires or her spiritual claims. . . . But degradation of the sex-impulse is inevitably punished. . . . It produces a cleavage between passion and affection which renders impossible the highest and most beautiful form of the sexual relation, the relation in which passion and affection are fused in a love which offers complete understanding and fulfillment. It is to this fusion . . . that we owe "the many and keen pleasures derived from music, poetry, fiction, the drama, etc., all of them having for their predominant theme the passion of love." True monogamy, the product of this highest love, is not a regulation to be observed; it is an ideal to be attained, and it will not be attained by the person who fails to recognize and to respect the spiritual aspects of the sexual relation.

Nor will it be attained by the person who mistakes excitement for love and who flits from one temporary attachment to another, thinking always to find the beautiful in the new. Such promiscuous philandering not only precludes depth of affection and thus renders constancy impossible; it also blunts perception. . . .

Certain women of independent spirit are at present rather conspicuously engaged in proving themselves not merely polygamous but promiscuous; and a great many men have always proved themselves to be monogamous. Probably human beings vary in respect of these tendencies as of others. All people, perhaps, cannot attain the highest plane in love, either for want of capacity or of opportunity; nor can all people conform to a single mode of conduct. But all people can attain sincerity in sexual relations and at least a certain degree of self-knowledge. Sincerity, self-knowledge, respect for oneself and for other people—these are essential to a genuine ethic of sex, and they are uncontemplated by the sanctions of conventional morality. . . .

An increase in extra-legal relationships does not of itself imply spiritual retrogression. It might imply instead one of two things, or both: namely, an increase in the economic obstacles to legal marriage or a growing disinclination to admit an affair so personal as the sex-relation to sanction and regulation by people whom it did not concern. If men and women were economically equal and independent, the number of marriages might increase enormously; on the other hand, institutionalized marriage might be superseded by marriage without legal sanction, which before the birth of children might not be even known or recognized as marriage. Free people would probably want less of official interference in their personal affairs rather than more. But for those who wanted to avoid the terrors of autonomy, there would still be marriage; and for those who wanted to walk in the strait and ennobling way of freedom, there would be the right to love without official permission and to bring forth children unashamed. Those who wished to sell themselves would be free to do so if they could find buyers, but no one would be forced to live by violating the law of love which is the law of life. Freedom implies the right to live badly, but it also implies the right to live nobly and beautifully; and for one who has faith in the essential goodness of the human spirit, in the natural aspiration towards perfection which flowers with touching beauty even in the bleak soil of that hardship, degradation and crime to which injustice condemns the mass of humanity—for one who has this faith in the human spirit, there can be no question what its ultimate choice would be.

V. THE ECONOMIC POSITION OF WOMEN

I.

It is to the industrial revolution more than anything else, perhaps, that women owe such freedom as they now enjoy; yet if proof were wanting of the distance they have still to cover in order to attain, not freedom, but mere equality with men, their position in the industrial world would amply supply it. Men in industry suffer from injustices and hardships due to the overcrowding of the labor-market. Women suffer from these same injustices and hardships, and they have an additional handicap in their sex. The world of work, embracing industry, business, the professions, is primarily a man's world. Women are admitted, but not yet on an equal footing. Their opportunities for employment are restricted, sometimes by law, but more often by lack of training; and their remuneration as wage-earners and salaried workers is generally less than that of men. They have to contend with traditional notions of what occupations are fitting for their sex, with the jealousy of male workers, with the prejudices of employers, and finally with their own inertia and their own addiction to traditional concepts. All these difficulties are immensely aggravated by the keenness of the competition for work. If the opportunity to work were, as it should be, an unimpeded right instead of a privilege doled out by an employer, these handicaps of women would be easily overridden by the demand for their labor. . . . When the [First World] War created a temporary shortage of labor, women were not only employed in but were urged in the name of patriotism to enter occupations in which until then only men had been employed. . . .

. . . If women can make a permanent place for themselves in their new occupations, public officials will eventually come to associate them with these occupations and follow the lead of the semi-public schools in fitting girls to engage in them on an equal footing with boys. But it will take time, and meanwhile women will continue to be at a disadvantage in entering these occupations. So will they be at a disadvantage in entering any occupation where they have not before been employed or where they are employed only in insignificant numbers, so long as prejudice or conservatism continues to debar them and the necessary training is not as freely available to them as it is to men.

Above all, so long as their industrial status continues to be, as the Women's Bureau expresses it, "subsidiary to their home status," they can never be on a really secure footing in the industrial world. While employers assume that all male workers have families to support and that all female workers are in industry rather through choice than necessity and may, in periods when work is slack, fall back on the support of male relatives, so long will women be the first workers to suffer from any slowing down of industry. . . .

In connection with so-called welfare-legislation, it is interesting to observe that women and children are customarily grouped together as classes requiring protection and that various laws affecting their position in industry have been sanctioned by the courts as being for the good of the race and therefore not to be regarded as class-legislation. Such decisions certainly would appear to be reasonable in so far as they apply to children, who are the rising generation of men and women and should be protected during their immaturity. But they can be held valid as they affect women only if woman is regarded as primarily a reproductive function. This view, apparently, is held by most legislators, courts, and uplifters; and they have an unquestionable right to hold it. Whether, however, they are just in attempting to add to the burdens of the working woman by imposing it upon her in the form of rules that restrict her opportunities is another question. One thing is certain: If discriminative laws and customs are to continue to restrict the opportunities of women and hamper them in their undertakings, it makes little difference for whose benefit those laws and customs are supposed to operate, whether for the benefit of men, of the home, of the race, or of women themselves; their effect on the mind of woman and her opportunities will be the same. While society discriminates against her sex for whatever reason, she cannot be free as an individual.

Should nothing, then, be done to protect women from the disabilities and hazards to which they are subject in the industrial world? Better nothing, perhaps, than protection which creates new disabilities. Laws which fix fewer hours of work for women than for men may result in shortening men's hours also in factories where many women are employed; but they may result in the substitution of men—or children—for women in factories where but few have been employed. Laws prohibiting night-work may reduce the chances of women to get much-needed employment. . . . Moreover, it is hard to see on what ground night-work could be held to be more harmful for women than for men. . . . As for those laws which undertake to protect women against the hazards of industry, they have usually, as the Women's Bureau has shown, very little relation to the hazards to which women are actually exposed; but they constitute a real barrier to industrial opportunity. On the whole, the vast and unwieldy array of laws and rules designed either to protect the woman worker or to safeguard the future of the race at her expense are a pretty lame result of a great deal of humanitarian sound and fury. . . .

It is quite natural that the result should be lame, for these protections and safeguards represent so many attempts to mind someone else's business; and the great difficulty about minding someone else's business is that however good one's intentions may be, one can never really know just where that someone's real interests lie or perfectly understand the circumstances under which he may be most advantageously placed in the way to advance them, for the circumstances are too intimately bound up with his peculiar temperament and situation. As Mill has remarked . . . , the world has learned by long experience that affairs in which the individual is the person directly interested go right only when they are left to his own discretion and that any interference by authority, save to protect the rights of others, is mischievous. The tendency of modern welfare-legislation is to make a complete sacrifice of individual rights not to the rights but to the hypothetical interests of others; and for every individual who happens to benefit by the sacrifice, there is another who suffers by it. If it is hard to regulate one human being for his own good, it is impossible to regulate people *en masse* for their own good; for there is no way of making a general rule affect all individuals in the same way, since no two individuals are to be found who are of precisely the same temperament and in precisely the same situation.

There is in all this bungling effort to ameliorate the ills of working women and to safeguard through them the future of the race a tacit recognition of economic injustice and a strange incuriousness about its causes. One would naturally expect that the conditions which move people to seek protective legislation would move them to question the nature of an economic system which permits such rapacity that any class of employees requires to be protected from it. Surely the forces of righteousness must know that there are reasons for the existence of the conditions which move them to pity and alarm; yet they seem quite willing to go on indefinitely battling against the conditions and winning with great effort legislative victories which are constantly being rendered ineffectual through lax administration of laws, through the reluctance of employees to jeopardize their positions by testifying against employers, or through unforeseen changes in economic conditions. During all this waste of time and effort, this building and crumbling and rebuilding of protective walls around the laborer, the causes of economic injustice continue their incessant operation, producing continuously a new crop of effects which are like so many windmills inviting attack by the Don Quixotes of reform.

Let us consider the effects of economic injustice on women, side by side with the reformer's work upon those effects. Women in industry suffer . . . the injustice of inequality with men as regards wages, opportunities, training, and tenure of employment. The reformer attacks the problem of wages and secures minimum-wage laws based on someone's theory of what constitutes a living wage. No allowance is made for dependents because women, theoretically, have none. The amount allowed may from the first be inadequate, even for one person, or it may be rendered inadequate by a rise in the cost of living. . . . The reformer is less zealous in his attempt to provide women with opportunities; his showing in this field is less impressive than in that of wages. Still, he has done something. If he has not been entirely responsible for the opening to women of many positions in government service, he has at least greatly assisted in securing them these opportunities. Farther than this, it must be admitted, it is difficult for him to go. He might, indeed, exert himself to see that women are provided by one means or another with equal opportunities to get training, but he can do little to affect the policies of private employers of labor, who can hardly be dictated to concerning whom they shall hire and whom they shall retain. Nor can he prevent employers from laying off women workers first when there is a slowing down in production. In three, then, out of four of the disadvantages which bear more heavily on women in industry than on men, the reformer, with all his excellent intentions, is unable to be very helpful; . . . in his zeal to safeguard the race, whose future appears to him to depend entirely on the health of the female sex, he has multiplied their disadvantages . . . without, however, having made any noteworthy advance toward the accomplishment of his purpose. . . .

II.

It is in business and in professional pursuits that the occupational progress of women and their emancipation from traditional prejudices are most marked. Although in the lower ranks of labor in these pursuits there is a mass of women who, impelled by necessity, work for low wages at mechanical tasks which offer no chance of advancement, there is nearer the top a large group of women who have been more fortunate in worldly position and education and who are spurred as much either by interest in their work or a desire to be self-supporting as by actual need to earn, who share, in other words, the attitude that leads young men to strike out for themselves even though their fathers may be able to support them. It is the woman animated by these motives who is doing most for the advancement of her sex; for it is she, and not the woman who works through necessity, who really challenges the traditional prejudices concerning the proper place of women. The woman laborer proves the *need* of women to earn; the business woman or professional woman who works because she wants to work is establishing the *right* of women to earn. More than this, as she makes her way into one after another of the occupations that have been held to belong to men by prescriptive right, she is establishing her claim as a human being to choose her work from the whole wide field of human activity. It is owing to the attitude towards life adopted by such women, to their preference of independence and action over the dependence and passivity in vogue not so many years ago, that it is coming to be quite the expected thing that young women of the well-to-do classes shall set out to earn their living, as young men do, instead of stopping under the parental roof with a watchful eye out for men who will marry and support them. . . .

There is still a goodly number of prejudices and discriminations to be overcome before women in business and the professions shall stand on an equal footing with men as regards opportunity and remuneration. Except where she is in business for herself, the woman in these pursuits must generally be content with a lower rate of pay than men; and if observation may be taken to count for anything, she is expected to work somewhat harder for what she gets—less loafing on the job is tolerated in her than in the male employee. She is also more likely to find herself pocketed, that is to say, in a position from which because of her sex there is no possibility of further advance because the higher positions are reserved for men. . . .

. . . The man who does not object to his wife's having a career is considered generous and long-suffering. His insistence on her abandoning it and contenting herself with looking out for his domestic comfort is thought to be quite natural. On the other hand, the woman who interferes in any way with a husband's career is regarded as an extremely selfish person, while any sacrifice of herself and her ambitions to her husband and his is thought of merely as a matter of wifely duty. How often does one hear that such and such a woman has given up her position because "her husband didn't want her to work." There is, too, a very general assumption that every married woman has children and should stay at home and take care of them. Now, perhaps every married woman should have children; perhaps in a future state of society men and women will marry only when they wish to bring up a family. But at present it is not so. . . . It may be contended that these women should stay at home and take care of their husbands, but even if we assume that the unremitting personal attention of his wife is essential to the comfort and happiness of a married man, there would still remain the question of his title to this attention at the cost of her own interests.

We are dealing here with an attitude which, general though it be, has been outmoded by the conditions of modern life. . . . Our social ideology, like our political ideology, is of the eighteenth century; and its especial effectiveness at present is by way of obscuring our vision of the changed world that has emerged from the great economic revolution of the last century. A division of interests and labor which was convenient if not just under the conditions of economic and social life which preceded the industrial revolution is neither convenient nor just under the conditions which prevail today. The care of young children and the management of a household may result in an unequal division of labor in families where the husband's inability to provide for the needs of his family forces the wife to assume the burdens of a breadwinner. When one reads through the literature on the question of hours of labor for women in industry, one is struck by the persistent stressing of the married woman's double burden of breadwinning and housekeeping. These women, it seems, must not only earn money to contribute to their families' support, but they must, before setting out for work and after returning from it, prepare the family meals, get the children ready for school or the day-nursery, take them there and call for them, wash, sew, and perform a hundred other household tasks. This double burden is often made an argument for establishing shorter hours of work for women in industry but never for expecting the husband to share the wife's traditional burden as she has been forced to share his. I have no doubt that innumerable husbands are doing this; but there is no expectation put upon them to do it. . . .

It is possible, of course, that the institution of economic freedom might check the present tendency of women to engage in gainful occupations outside the home. It most certainly would if the vast increase of opportunity which it offered were reserved exclusively for men; but to bring about this result it would be necessary for traditional anti-feminist prejudices to survive much more strongly than they do today. The position of women has too radically changed to admit of their exclusion from direct participation in the benefits of economic freedom; therefore, if they resigned the increased economic opportunities that it offered them and withdrew to the sphere of domesticity, they would do so as a matter of choice. Why should we not expect them to choose the exclusive domesticity which might be rendered possible through the increased earning power of men? They probably would, where it suited their taste to do so; but one of the most powerful incentives to do so would no longer exist, namely, the desire for economic security. Women, to be sure, are not exempt from the characteristic willingness of humankind to live by the exertions of others; but I would remark that there is this difference between the person who does this indirectly, through legalized privilege, and the person who depends directly on the bounty of another: that the former is independent and the latter is dependent. Women are not strangers to the human desire for freedom; and when the fear of want is allayed, they are quite likely to prefer an easy and secure self-support to the alternative of economic dependence. Moreover, economic freedom would set domesticity in competition with the interests of women rather than their needs; for it would set all people free to engage in occupations that interested them, whereas at present the vast majority do whatever offers them a living. Under these circumstances it might reasonably be expected that the number of women who would continue in business and in industrial and professional pursuits, even after marriage and the birth of children, would greatly increase.

Indeed, if we postulate an economic system under which every human being would be free to choose his occupation in accordance with his interests, I see no more reason to suppose that women would invariably choose domesticity than to suppose that all men would choose blacksmithing. Under such a régime I doubt that even the power of the expected which affects them so strongly at present would long continue in an effectiveness which it has already begun to lose. Women, I think, might be expected to choose their occupations with the same freedom as men and to look for no serious interruption from marriage and the birth of children. There are a good many women at present who very ably reconcile motherhood with a chosen career. I think we might expect to find more of them rather than fewer in a free society. One thing is certain, and it is the important thing: They would be free to choose. If it be woman's nature, as some people still believe, to wish to live at second hand, then in a free society they will freely make that choice, and no one can complain of it—unless it be the men on whom they elect to depend. However, to assume from past experience that they do want to live at second hand is to assume that all the social and legal injustices which have been employed to force them to do so were unnecessary; and when have governments and communities wasted their power in exercising compulsion where no compulsion was needed?

VI. WHAT IS TO BE DONE

I.

. . . If it is freedom that women want, they cannot be content to be legally equal with men; but having gained this equality, they must carry on their struggle against the oppressions which privilege exercises upon humanity at large by virtue of an usurped economic power. . . . It can be advanced only through the establishment of an order of society in which every human being shall enjoy the natural right to labor and to enjoy all that his labor produces. It is upon mankind's security in this right that human freedom in whatever mode or aspect—social, philosophical, political, religious—primarily depends.

The right to labor and to enjoy the fruits of one's labor means only the right of free access to the source of subsistence, which is land. [Land . . . does not mean the solid part of the earth's surface—earth as distinguished from water. It means the sum-total of natural resources.] If access to that source may be arbitrarily denied, the right to labor is denied, and the opportunity to get one's living becomes a privilege which may be withheld or granted as suits the need or convenience of the person who bestows it and wholly on his own terms. If access may be had only on the payment of tribute, the condition abrogates the right to enjoy the fruit of one's labor, for the tribute consumes a share of it. . . .

. . . Under the republicanism which succeeded the American and French revolutions, the expropriated classes have gained freedom of movement, a limited freedom of opinion, and a nominal share in the exercise of government. The peasant is no longer bound to the soil he tills; he may leave it at will to seek his fortune elsewhere —on the terms of another landlord. The owning classes no longer directly exercise government or directly enjoy honors and titles by virtue of ownership. The peoples of the Western world, at least where parliamentarism has not broken down, have a nominal freedom with little of the reality. Nominal freedom of movement is worth little to the man who faces the alternative of being exploited where he is or being exploited elsewhere. Nominal freedom of opinion is not extremely valuable when expression of opinion may cost one the opportunity to earn one's living, and the right to vote offers little satisfaction when it means merely a right of choice between rival parties and candidates representing exactly the same system of economic exploitation.

The political revolution which followed the breakdown of feudalism did the world its greatest service in launching the *idea* of freedom; it did nothing—or relatively very little—for its substance. Through its agency the equal right of all human beings to "life, liberty, and the pursuit of happiness" has come to be granted in theory though not in fact; it remained for the Russian Revolution to proclaim the further idea that the basis of this right is not political but economic. The political revolution did more; by establishing political democracy, it put into the hands of the people the power to achieve economic democracy by peaceful means. But by that very act it obscured the essential function of the State and the source of its power, which remained clear as long as those who owned ruled directly by virtue of ownership; and thus it hindered a clear perception of the causal relation between privilege and slavery. By abolishing hereditary power, it effected a redistribution of privilege and at the same time forced privilege to exercise its control of government by indirect means. Privilege was no longer seated on the throne, but it remained, through its control of economic opportunity, the power behind the throne, a power all the more difficult to dislodge now that it exercised control without assuming responsibility. Republicanism has proved the futility of dislodging a privileged class without abolishing privilege; for this simply prepares the way for the rise of a new privileged class which will use government to enforce its exploitation of the propertyless class, in a different way perhaps, but quite as effectively as its predecessors.

The psychological effect of the political equality established under republicanism is extremely demoralizing. . . . The subject classes have never desired freedom so much as a chance at the privileges that they see other people enjoy. Political equality with its breaking-down of class distinctions creates an impression of equality of opportunity—and indeed to the extent that government maintains no disabling legal discriminations among members of the enfranchised class, it actually establishes equality. No member of that class is excluded from the benefits of privilege by anything save his inability to get possession of it; and this fact, especially in a country where opportunity is comparatively plentiful, is more likely to confirm people in their loyalty to a system under which they stand even a dog's chance to become beneficiaries of privilege than it is to stimulate an endeavor to abolish privilege altogether. In this country the incalculable richness of natural resources and the enormous wealth to be gained by speculative enterprise under a government which gives full rein to monopoly contributed immensely to the corruption of the citizenry. Speculation became the normal course of enterprise, the most approved method of money-getting; and the more ruinously did the monopolist exploit the country's resources, as Mr. [Thorstein] Veblen has pointed out, the greater the regard in which he was held by his fellow citizens. Never before in the world's history had so many people a chance at the enjoyment of privilege as in the pioneer period of American development. The country's resources were gutted for profit, not developed for use. . . . Not only was the public mind corrupted by the apparently limitless opportunity to enjoy privilege —not only was speculation confused with production—but all this opportunity was blindly attributed to the blessings of republicanism. "The greatest government on earth" came to be regarded as the guardian of free opportunity for all citizens, in spite of the very evident fact that no government which protects land-monopoly can possibly maintain freedom of opportunity, for in the course of monopoly all available natural resources are shortly pre-empted and those people who are born after occupation is complete will find nothing left to pre-empt. Thus American patriotism took on a religious fervor, and the corruption of the populace was complete.

The rise of industrialism has done as much as anything else to engender misapprehension of the

State's essential nature, its chief function, and the source of its power. It is significant that the physiocrats lived and observed the workings of the State before the industrial era, in an agricultural country where the relation between land-monopoly and government was direct and inescapable, and that Karl Marx lived and wrote after the rise of the factory-system, in a highly industrialized country. The physiocrats, for whom the basic economic problem was unobscured, therefore attributed involuntary poverty to its actual cause, while Marx, confusing capital's fortuitous advantage from monopoly with monopoly itself, laid the responsibility at the door of capitalism. To be sure, Marx recognized and stated the fact that expropriation must precede exploitation, but he did not draw the obvious conclusion that the way to break capital's power to exploit the worker is by simple reimpropriation. At present there is a general impression that the factory-system lured the population into the cities and thus caused the overcrowding that results in scarcity of jobs and inadequacy of wage. As a matter of fact, the factory-system found the cities already overcrowded with exploitable labor. . . . The industrial revolution, then, did not produce the overcrowding of the labor-market; but the capitalist of the revolution profited by an overcrowding that already existed. He reaped indirectly the fruits of monopoly. He profited likewise, and profits still, by every labor-saving device, for it enabled him at once to dispense with some laborers and, because of the increase of unemployment thus caused, to pay his remaining workers less. Capital was thus enabled to appropriate much more than its rightful share of production and hence to amass enormous wealth, by means of which it influenced government on behalf of its own further enrichment. . . . As the exactions of monopoly increase and the exploitation of labor nears the point of diminishing return, the capitalist-monopolist embarks with the protection of government on a policy of economic imperialism. He monopolizes the markets of weak nations at the point of his government's bayonets. He invests in foreign enterprises which offer high returns for himself and risk of war for the government which backs him—that is to say, for the exploited masses at home who must support the government and furnish its soldiers. In short, he constitutes himself a menace to peace and prosperity both at home and abroad, so that it is not to be wondered at if people observing his sinister activities take capital to be the cause of the economic injustice from which it derives its power. . . .

In order to abolish privilege it is not necessary in a political democracy to wait for the economic breakdown which its exactions inevitably bring about—that is to say, it is not necessary to wait until the number of wasteful idlers that production must support shall become so numerous and so wasteful that it can no longer meet their exactions. The ballot has been a pretty ineffectual weapon in the hands of the rank and file, but—so much must be said for republicanism—it could be made effective. First, however, the rank and file would have to learn what it is that this weapon should be used against—it would have to become aware of the nature of real freedom and to wish real freedom to prevail. . . .

The essential nature of freedom . . . comes out in the abolition of monopoly, primarily monopoly of natural resources, resulting in complete freedom of the individual to apply his productive labor where he will. It is freedom to produce, and its corollary, freedom to exchange—the *laissez-faire, laissez-passer* of the physiocrats. How this freedom is to be obtained is not for me to say. I am not a propagandist, nor do I regard the question as at present so important as that of establishing a clear understanding of the nature of freedom. When enough people come to see that the root of all bondage, economic, political, social—even the bondage of superstition and taboo—is expropriation, reimpropriation will not be long in following, and it may be achieved by a method quite different from all those which theorists have thus far devised. When people know what they need, they are usually pretty resourceful about finding means to get it; and so long as they do not know what they need, all the means of securing it that can be suggested, however excellent, must remain ineffective from the lack of sufficient will to use them. . . .

IV.

. . . Without economic freedom, efforts after political and social freedom are nugatory and illusive, except for what educational value they may have for those concerned with them. The women of the United States, having now got about all that is to be had out of these efforts—enough at any rate, to raise an uneasy suspicion that their ends are lamentably far from final—are in a peculiarly good position to discern the nature of real freedom, to see which way it lies, and to feel an ardent interest in what it can do for them. My purpose, then, is not deliberately to discourage their prosecution of any enfranchising measures that may lie in their way to promote and still less to disparage the successes that they have already attained. It is rather to invite them thoughtfully to take stock of what they have really got by these successes, to consider whether it is all they want, and to settle with themselves whether their collective experience on the way up from the status of a subject sex does not point them to a higher ideal of freedom than any they have hitherto entertained.

In the past century, women have gained a great deal in the way of educational, social and political rights. They have gained a fair degree of economic independence. They are no longer obliged to "keep silence in the churches," as they still were at the beginning of the nineteenth century; indeed, certain sects have even admitted them to the ministry. The women who now enjoy this comparative freedom, and accept it more or less as a matter of course, are indebted to a long line of women who carried on the struggle—sometimes lonely and discouraging—against political, legal, social and industrial discrimination, and to the men, as well, who aided and encouraged them. Thanks to the efforts of these pioneers, the women of today have a new tradition to maintain, a nobler tradition than any of those which women were expected to observe in the past: the tradition of active demand for the establishment of freedom. They will be none the less under obligation to continue this demand when the freedom that shall remain to be secured is of a kind not envisaged by their predecessors. Rather, in the measure that they proceed beyond those ends that seemed ultimate to their predecessors, they will prove that these built well; for the best earnest of advancement is the attainment of an ever new and wider vision of progress.

The organized feminist movement in England and America has concerned itself pretty exclusively with securing political rights for women; that is to say, its conception of freedom has been based on the eighteenth-century misconception of it as a matter of suffrage. Women have won the vote, and now they are proceeding to use their new political power to secure the removal of those legal discriminations which still remain in force against their sex. This is well enough; it is important that the State should be forced to renounce its pretension to discriminate against women in favor of men. But even if we assume that the establishment of legal equality between the sexes would result in complete social and economic equality, we are obliged to face the fact that under such a régime women would enjoy precisely that degree of freedom which men now enjoy—that is to say, very little. . . . The State represents the organized interest of those who control economic opportunity; and while the State continues to exist, it may be forced to renounce all legal discriminations against one sex in favor of the other without in any wise affecting its fundamental discrimination against the propertyless, dependent class—*which is made up of both men and women*—in favor of the owning and exploiting classes. Until this fundamental discrimination is challenged, the State may without danger to itself grant, in principle at least, the claims to political and legal equality of all classes under its power. The emancipation of Negroes within the political State has not notably improved their condition; for they are still subject to an economic exploitation which is enhanced by race-prejudice and the humiliating tradition of slavery. The emancipation of women within the political State will leave them subject, like the Negro, to an exploitation enhanced by surviving prejudices against them. The most that can be expected of the removal of discriminations subjecting one class to another within the exploiting State is that it will free the subject class from dual control—control by the favored class and by the monopolist of economic opportunity.

Even this degree of emancipation is worth a good deal, and therefore one is bound to regret that it has no guarantee of permanence more secure than legal enactment. Rights that depend on the sufferance of the State are of uncertain tenure, for they are in constant danger of abrogation either through the failure of the State to maintain them, through a gradual modification of the laws on which they depend, or through a change in the form of the State. . . . The women who rely upon such guarantees to protect them against prejudice and discrimination are leaning on a broken reed. They will do well to bear this in mind as they proceed with their demands for equality and to remember that however great may be their immediate returns from the removal of their legal disabilities, they can hardly hope for security against prejudice and discrimination until their natural rights, not as women but as human beings, are finally established. This is to say that if they wish to be really free, they must school themselves in "the magnificent tradition of economic freedom, the instinct to know that without economic freedom no other freedom is significant or lasting, and that if economic freedom be attained, no other freedom can be withheld."

VII. SIGNS OF PROMISE

. . . Discontent with the established order must necessarily precede any serious move toward its displacement by a new order; and discontent, while it is by no means dominant at present, is widespread enough to cause governments a good deal of anxiety. The very tightening of the grip of government which is evident in the present tendency to suppress legislative bodies and in ruthless persecution of economic dissenters is . . . a sure indication of the extent and strength of the dissenting forces. When those people who now endure the harassment of governmental waste and industrial exploitation shall perceive that relief is to be gained not through futile political reforms aimed at amelioration of their lot but through a radical readjustment of the whole economic system—when, in other words, they realize "what is to be done"—then, and not before, will come the real test of the tenacity of the old order and the strength of the forces moving towards the new. On its side the old order will have governmental organization and armed forces and the enormous influence of the superstitious tendency to regard as right that which is established, supporting the interest of a compact, wealthy, and highly organized exploiting class. The new order will have on its side the newly realized need of the majority without whose acquiescence a highly organized minority cannot long maintain itself in power. The issue will depend, obviously, not only on the intelligence, ability and determination of the majority's leaders but upon their clear understanding of the issue involved. If they compromise, . . . the cause of justice will be lost, and the most that will be gained will be a shifting of privilege. The Western world is faced at present with the alternative of establishing an enduring civilization on the sure foundation of economic justice or of sinking back into barbarism through a long series of civil and international struggles for possession of the power to exploit. . . .

The task before those who wish to avert this fate, whose passionate desire is to bring about an enduring civilization based on the solid foundation of economic justice, is the task of educating themselves in the nature of freedom, of learning to face freedom without fear, and of communicating to others their understanding and their courage. The women of today, especially in this country, are in a peculiarly good position to undertake this task. They enjoy unprecedented advantages in the way of social and intellectual autonomy and of educational opportunity. They have emerged successful from a long struggle for political equality with men, and they are still engaged in an organized effort to secure legal equality. Thus they have their hand in, as it were, with the work of removing the artificial disabilities which organized society imposes on a subject class in order to keep it subject; and this work should have engendered in those who have been active in it a healthy resentment of social injustice and a sense of the value of freedom to the human spirit. They will still have, moreover, even after legal equality is won, a considerable number of discriminations to combat which should operate against the temptation to regard their fight as won and to relax the vigilance which is always necessary to preserve individual rights against encroachment by organized society. The organizations through which they have worked remain intact; it is for them to determine whether those organizations shall continue as mere agencies for political lobbying or whether they will carry on the demand for freedom to its logical end.

. . . If they fail, they are sure to pay for their failure a higher price than men will pay. As they have more to gain from freedom than men, so they have more to lose than men if the Western world shall fail to establish its civilization on the firm basis of economic justice. In the relapse into barbarism which must attend the ultimate breakdown of economic and social life under the monopolistic system, physical force will be even more strongly ascendant than it is at present; and when physical force dominates, the ideals of justice and liberty are . . . without effective influence—the only right is might. The well-being of women depends in very great measure on the prevalence of those ideals; for when force is dominant, woman's physical disadvantage as the child-bearing sex places her in a position to be more readily subjected and exploited than man. Because of this disadvantage she was the first victim of exploitation; because of it she will be the last to escape; and because of it she will be the greater sufferer from exploitation so long as exploitation shall be the basis of the economic and social order. There is potential tragedy in the fact that the Western world has become civilized enough to perceive the injustice involved in women's subjection only when the economic order which determines its social life has become so corrupt that it threatens the destruction of civilization, with all such gains in humanity as civilization has yielded. Women have equality almost within their grasp; they may lose it if this civilization shall follow the path of its predecessors to ruin and oblivion. There is one way to avert this tragedy and one only—the way of economic justice. If the women who have been active in the struggle to emancipate their sex shall enlarge their conception of freedom and with it the scope of their demand, they can help mightily to preserve civilization through the establishment of justice. If they could win their sex away from the exploded formulas of the eighteenth century and bring them to understand that political and social freedom without economic freedom are utterly illusory, that true freedom proceeds from economic justice, and that justice and freedom offer the only hope for the salvaging of this civilization, they would have won half of humanity, and that would be a contribution of no small value. One thing is certain: The question of freedom for women cannot proceed much farther as an independent issue. It has reached the point where it must necessarily merge in the greater question of human freedom. Upon the fate of the greater cause, that of the lesser will depend. It is for feminists to choose whether they will merge the feminist in the humanist or whether they will play at political and social make-believe while the issue is being decided and either suffer in the event the consequences of a failure which they shall have made no effort to avert or enjoy the benefits of a success which they shall have done nothing to attain.